Transforming the Core

Transforming the Core

Restructuring Industrial Enterprises in Russia and Central Europe

**Maurice Ernst,
Michael Alexeev,
and Paul Marer**

WestviewPress

A Division of HarperCollinsPublishers

We dedicate this book to our spouses,
Nina Alexeev, Nell Ernst, and Erika Marer,
in appreciation of their help to, and patience with,
their husbands during the completion of this book.

Copyright © 1996 by Westview Press, Inc., A Division of HarperCollins Publishers, Inc.

Published in 1996 in the United States of America by Westview Press, Inc., 5500 Central Avenue, Boulder, Colorado 80301-2877, and in the United Kingdom by Westview Press, 12 Hid's Copse Road, Cumnor Hill, Oxford OX2 9JJ

Library of Congress Cataloging-in-Publication Data
Ernst, Maurice.
    Transforming the core : restructuring industrial enterprises in
Russia and Central Europe / by Maurice Ernst, Michael Alexeev, and
Paul Marer.
        p.   cm.
    Includes bibliographical references and index.
    ISBN 0-8133-2704-0 (hc) — ISBN 0-8133-2705-9 (pb)
    1. Government business enterprises—Russia (Federation)
2. Government business enterprises—Europe, Eastern.   3. Russia
(Federation)—Economic policy—1991–   4. Europe, Eastern—Economic
policy—1989–   I. Alexeev, Michael, 1953–   .   II. Marer, Paul.
III. Title.
HD4215.15.E76   1996
338.947—dc20   95-41510
                                                                                      CIP

The paper used in this publication meets the requirements of the American National Standard for Permanence of Paper for Printed Library Materials Z39.48-1984.

10   9   8   7   6   5   4   3   2   1

Contents

v

3   Policies Affecting State Enterprises   31

4   Poland   79

Tables, Charts, and Boxes

Tables

Charts

Boxes

Preface

Participating in a seminar on economic transformation at Indiana University, the three of us discovered that each was working independently on issues related to the transformation of state-owned enterprises: Michael Alexeev focused primarily on Russia, Maurice Ernst mainly on Poland and the Czech Republic, and Paul Marer on Hungary. Each of us also had an interest in both the broad and technical issues of transformation and in the comparative experiences of the transforming economies, including China.

We decided to coordinate our research by establishing a common framework and meeting periodically to discuss what relevant insights could be learned from the experiences of the other countries. Our ultimate aim—and the main purpose of this book—was to arrive at broadly generalizable conclusions and lessons about one of the most difficult common problems of economic transformation: restructuring state-owned industrial enterprises. Our research approach was twofold. We tried to make use of relevant materials published in the West and in each of the target countries, as well as those presented at international conferences. Concurrently, we made several field trips to each of the three Central European countries and Russia and one to China to visit enterprises and discuss preliminary findings with policy makers and other experts.

Many excellent studies have been published on the removal of planned economy controls and the accompanying policies of macroeconomic stabilization. Privatization policies and outcomes have also received much attention. In most transition economies, though, this appears to have done little to transform a core of large state industrial enterprises, whether they have been formally privatized or still remain state-owned. A closer look, however, reveals, that substantial restructuring of large industrial enterprises has been taking place. In real life, the restructuring processes at work are more complex than what would be evident by studying only the formal privatization and other restructuring programs. We identify *strategic, defensive*, and *passive* enterprise restructuring (defined in the text). These are different, but not mutually exclusive, types of enterprise adaptations to the dramatic changes occurring in their domestic and external environments.

This book describes what has happened to state industrial enterprises in three Central European countries—Hungary, Poland, and the Czech Republic—as well as in Russia. Frequent comparative references are made also to China. Although there are many similarities among these countries, each is following a different transformation strategy, which is due as much to the force of circumstances as to *ex ante* designs. Fundamental differences among the countries can be identified by examining what *combination* of the "shock therapy," the "let order emerge spontaneously out of chaos," and the "let's proceed gradually" transformation strategies best describe how each country has been proceeding (terms are, again, defined in the text).

After several years of "transition," there is a need not just for a description of what has taken place, but also for an assessment, for comparative stock-taking, for identifying the lessons to be learned, and for presenting expert views on the countries' most likely prospects. The lessons learned should be useful not only for policy makers and prospective investors in the target countries, but also for the two dozen or so other "historically planned economies," most of which are at even earlier stages of transformation than the five countries here studied.

In taking stock of progress at this relatively early stage of transformation, it would be inappropriate to rely mainly on such standard macroeconomic indicators as growth rates, inflation, and unemployment. We have chosen an alternative criterion: corporate governance arrangements. *Corporate governance* refers to the relationships between different stakeholders in a firm—owners, managers, employees, creditors, society at large—who jointly determine its goals and the effectiveness of its operations. We ask—and answer as best we can—the following question: "Are transformation strategies generally, and industrial restructuring policies specifically, creating corporate governance arrangements that are likely to improve, both near- and long-term, the effectiveness of large industrial firms and their successor business units?"

This book would be an appropriate college text in courses focusing on the economic aspects of transformation or comparative economic systems. It:

- compares the experiences of five countries that had different initial conditions and have pursued different transformation strategies;
- deals with the emergence of new forms of "corporate governance" and considers the relevance of various market-economy models;
- provides a concise sociopolitical context for each of the five countries;
- presents plausible scenarios to the year 2000 and beyond; and
- draws generalizable lessons about what policies are more or less effective and under what specific circumstances.

Michael Alexeev
Maurice Ernst
Paul Marer
Bloomington, Indiana

Acknowledgments

The number of experts on three continents who have assisted our work is too numerous to name. The following individuals have provided essential contacts, research materials, valuable time, as well as judgments during the authors' research trips:

In Russia, we express our appreciation to Andrei Cherniavsky, Tatiana Dolgopiatova, Victor Ivanter, and Jakob Pappe for helpful discussions on aspects of enterprise activities in Russia, and for providing us valuable published and unpublished research materials.

In Poland, we thank Professor Wojciech Maciewski, Warsaw University, who arranged interviews with enterprise managers, government officials, and academics throughout Poland and gave freely of his expertise and judgment.

In the Czech Republic, Ing. Vladislav Cislar of the Center for Foreign Economic Relations in Prague is to be thanked for arranging interviews with government officials, university professors, and enterprise managers during our visit to the Czech Republic.

In Hungary, Dr. Ákos Balassa, Managing Director of the National Bank of Hungary; Lajos Csepi, former CEO of the State Property Agency (1990-1993); István Orbán, CEO of Egis Pharmaceuticals; István Tömpe, Chairman of Daiwa Investment and Securities Company in Hungary; Drs. Éva Ehrlich and Gábor Révész of the Hungarian Academy of Sciences; and Stephen C. Eastham and John Harper, American advisors to the State Property Agency on privatization and restructuring, with years of hands-on experience, who provided valuable comments on the drafts.

In connection with our research on China, special thanks are due to Dr. Nao Muhan, Associate Professor of International Business at Soochow University, in Taipei, Taiwan, for making available his background study on China and for his valuable consultations on particular issues.

None of these individuals, of course, should be held accountable for the authors' views and interpretations, with which they will surely not agree in every instance.

Special thanks are due to Susan L. McEachern, Senior Editor of Westview Press, who has skillfully guided us through the difficult process of transforming rough ideas into a book. Only the authors are to blame for being foolish enough not to follow some of her presentation suggestions.

It is with deep appreciation that we acknowledge the assistance of Matthew McGarrett with the charts, the conscientious and able editorial and production help provided by Elizabeth Marer-Banasik, and the superbly skillful layout and typesetting services of Melanie Hunter. We are truly grateful to them for performing so gracefully under extremely tight deadline pressures.

M.A.
M.E.
P.M.

Abbreviations

BRC	Blue Ribbon Commission
CAR	Capital-Asset Ratio
CBR	Central Bank of Russia
CE-3	The three subject Central European countries
CEE	Central and Eastern Europe
CEO	Chief Executive Officer
CIS	Commonwealth of Independent States
CMEA	Council for Mutual Economic Assistance
CMR	Contract-system of management responsibility
CPI	Consumer Price Index
CSFB	Credit Suisse First Boston
CSO	Central Statistical Office
EC	European Community
EU	European Union
FBA	Federal Bankruptcy Administration
FDI	Foreign Direct Investment
FNP	Fund for National Property
FPF	Federal Property Fund
FSU	Former Soviet Union
GDP	Gross Domestic Product
GKI	State Committee on Property
HID	Hungarian Investment and Development Co.
HPE	Historically Planned Economy
HUF	Hungarian forint (HUF 100 = $1.00, as of 1994)
IDA	Inter-enterprise Debt in Arrears
IMF	International Monetary Fund
IPF	Investment Privatization Fund
IPO	Initial Public Offering (New Stock Issue)
JV	Joint Venture
KRP	Small Investor Share-Ownership Program
MBSP	Management Bureau of State Properties
MFN	Most Favored Nations
MOI	Ministry of Industry

MPP	Mass Privatization Program
NATO	North Atlantic Treaty Organization
NEM	New Economic Mechanism
NIF	National Investment Funds
NIS	Newly Independent States
NPF	National Property Fund
OECD	Organization for Economic Cooperation and Development
PPI	Producer Price Index
PPP	Purchasing Power Parity
RPE	Recently Privatized Enterprises
SC	Share Certificate
SEZ	Special Economic Zone
SOE	State-owned Enterprise
SPA	State Property Agency
SHC	State Holding Company
SPHC	State Privatization and Holding Company
TIC	Trust and Investment Corporations
TRE	Transition (transforming) economy
TVE	Township and Village Enterprises
UC	Urban Collectives
VAT	Value-added Tax
VPF	Voucher Privatization Funds
WSE	Warsaw Stock Exchange

1

Introduction

The Nature of the Problem

Among the many complex problems of the transition from centrally planned to market-oriented economies, the most difficult, and the one on which the least progress has been made, is the transformation of the large state industrial enterprises that constitute the great bulk of heavy industry. Even in transition economies where prices are generally free, most restrictions on foreign trade have been lifted, and "non-state" firms create more than half of the national product, heavy industry remains predominantly state-owned, over-staffed, over-capitalized, obsolete and inefficient. In effect, a market economy has grown up around this surviving nucleus of the planned economy.

In East-Central Europe, notably Poland, Hungary, and the Czech Republic, this industrial nucleus is being eroded by market forces and is beginning to slowly undergo restructuring. But in spite of often drastic declines in the demand for the products of this sector, the more painful restructuring steps, such as widespread plant closings and massive layoffs, have generally been avoided. The main reasons are fear of exacerbating already high unemployment and the sector's political importance, due to critical linkages as well as size. Consequently, subsidization and protection of large, inefficient industries is continuing, variously, through grants; preferential loans and debt relief by state-controlled banks; allowing tax, social security contributions, and customs duty arrears; and import protection. This is a heavy burden on the transition economies, drawing scarce funds away from profitable investments, most notably in the private sector.

In China, large state industry has participated in the rapid economic expansion, but has declined in relative terms. As in Eastern Europe and Russia, many large Chinese state firms are losing money and are receiving massive subsidies.

The problem of transforming large state industrial enterprises is particularly difficult in Russia because so much of its heavy industry was designed to support military programs that have been drastically curtailed. Russian

1

heavy industry, formerly considered the crowning achievement of the Communist regime, will require even more drastic structural change than the heavy industries of East-Central Europe and China. Drastic structural change threatens the careers, even the livelihood, of many of Russia's managerial and technical elite and the economies of many cities and towns, and is bound to face determined political opposition.

Objectives

The objective of this study is to assess the effectiveness of policies designed to transform large state industrial enterprises in Poland, Hungary, the Czech Republic, and Russia, and to draw lessons from this experience that could inform policy makers in these and other transition countries as well as in the West. All the subject countries have undertaken a wide range of transition policies and programs, some of which are designed specifically to transform large state industry. Although it is too soon for these policies to show definitive results, many indications of their likely longer-term effects can be found.

The central objective of transformation policies is to make enterprises as a group more efficient while keeping the factors of production as fully employed as possible. This is a problem of great difficulty in formerly planned economies because of their gross "misdevelopment," which has both structural and institutional dimensions.

To a large extent, these economies were insulated (i.e., protected) from the world market. Heavy industry was overdeveloped, both because of high rates of investment and military expenditures in final demand and because little effort was made to minimize inputs of fuels, raw materials, and intermediate products. They typically used obsolete technologies, relying on imports from the West only in narrow areas and using old equipment until it fell apart. Consumer goods production was of low quality, unable to compete on world markets. To facilitate planning and to pursue often illusory economies of scale, production was concentrated in a small number of large, often monopolistic, firms, while the broad base of small, flexible, entrepreneurial firms generally found in Western countries did not exist. Foreign trade was oriented mainly among the Communist countries themselves, often for the convenience of the planning system, and trade with the West was driven by the need to fill shortages rather than occurring in response to comparative advantage. Prices, as well as production and distribution, were planned, and reflected neither world market valuation nor domestic opportunity costs.

Efficiency improvements in the transition should be reflected in increased international competitiveness, which we define here as the extent to which industrial firms can survive with at least normal profits in an environment where the prices of goods and services are fairly close to those on the world market. Since competitiveness is strongly affected by exchange rates and trade barriers, this concept assumes that a country's exchange rate is reasonably close to purchasing power parity for traded goods and that trade barriers are only moderately distorting. Thus a critical element of the transformation process is a fundamental shift from the extreme levels of protection that characterize planned economies, with the resulting extreme distortions in product and factor prices, to something close to a world market price system.

Whenever economic change occurs, there are winners and losers in the adjustment process—some firms expand, many contract, others disappear, and most adapt their production, inputs, and techniques. In the transition from a planned economy, changes in the structure of demand are so large and, at least in East-Central Europe, so rapid that producers cannot adjust nearly fast enough to maintain aggregate employment. The old stock of fixed capital becomes inappropriate and obsolete; in the extreme case of East Germany, where the change in demand was almost instantaneous and wages moved toward parity with West Germany, a large part of the industrial capital stock had a zero or negative value. Although human capital is much more flexible than physical capital, the structure of demand for skills also changes dramatically—for example, away from mechanical engineering in favor of marketing and financial expertise—thereby creating unemployment or underemployment of skills, as well as of labor generally.[1] Substantial unemployment of capital and labor is inevitable in economies in transition, unless new economic activities are growing so fast that they can absorb those released from existing industries, as has been the case in China.

Approach

The country chapters present most of the results of the research. Though they differ in length and emphasis given to the various elements of the transition process, all address the following common fundamental factors:

- Establishing an appropriate economic environment by decontrolling prices, liberalizing foreign trade and payments, creating laws for a market economy, fostering private entrepreneurship, building financial intermediaries, and promoting competitive market conditions.
- Privatization.
- Managing and restructuring state enterprises remaining temporarily or permanently state-controlled to improve their efficiency.

A common theme in this study is that large state enterprises in transition economies are not simply "economic actors," but are also social institutions whose agenda and behavior are determined by unique combinations of political, economic, social and cultural environments. These influences on enterprise behavior include the legacies of central planning, underdevelopment of market institutions, and sometimes sufficient political clout for the enterprises themselves to significantly influence government policies. Consequently, such enterprises do not respond to macroeconomic policies and economic incentives, as they would be expected to in market economies.

The central concept that ties together all the influences on enterprise behavior is that of corporate governance—the relationship between a firm's management and its owners primarily, but also with employees, creditors, and the authorities. The roles of these key actors are assessed for each country. In the concluding chapter, an effort is made to trace the outlines of the corporate governance systems emerging in the subject countries.

An assessment of policies dealing with the transformation of large, state-owned industrial enterprises can be based on actual outcomes only to a slight extent. First, because of severe "misdevelopment" and large external shocks, transition policies are generally associated with declines in the overall economy as well as in specific types of production, increases in unemployment, and, at least temporarily, high inflation. In this recessionary environment, it is difficult to clearly distinguish microeconomic adjustment from the negative macroeconomic influences. Second, transition policies have been introduced over several years, with the typical sequence proceeding from price and foreign trade liberalization and macroeconomic stabilization, to privatization, and later to measures targeted at the remaining state-owned enterprises. Third, microeconomic information that can reveal the effects of these policies on individual firms most often is available only with a long lag. Such information as is obtained from enterprise surveys, therefore, either tends to reflect only the early phase of enterprise transformation policies, or covers periods in which certain policies were not yet in effect.

In the absence of sufficient direct evidence on policy outcomes, it is necessary to employ an indirect approach, which consists essentially of analyzing transformation policies in order to determine the extent to which their design and implementation satisfy certain conditions or success criteria, and to use whatever evidence exists on the impact of those policies. The differing conditions and constraints in each of the subject countries, however, affect greatly both the choice of policies and the manner in which they were designed and implemented.

While considering the desirability of alternative transformation policies, or assessing their future impact, the likely improvement in efficiency at the enterprise level must be weighed against the economic and social cost of releasing productive resources that may not find alternative employment. Many varied but interactive forces affect the impact of transformation policies. There may be problems with incentives; even with strong incentives, the resources to bring about change may be lacking; or otherwise promising changes may be blocked by groups who fear becoming losers.

At least during the first year or two of the transition, there is generally too much instability in prices and markets, and too much distortion in enterprise accounting, to determine readily what steps would improve long-term profitability, or to identify those firms that are most likely to be profitable in the long run. The distortions in prices and costs are greatest and longest lasting in economies where inflation remains high. Consequently, strong policies that require rapid enterprise adjustment run a high risk that many potentially profitable firms will fail, leading to unnecessarily large unemployment and economic, social and political disruption.

Accordingly, our assessments of the potential impact of policies for the transformation of state industrial enterprises rest on indications of the extent to which each of these policies meet at least some of the following criteria. One criterion was whether incentives were created for enterprise owners to make efficiency-promoting changes. Under central planning, enterprises were managed by a large bureaucracy that responded to a wide variety of incentives, both political and economic—in effect, they had no real owners. For the transition, institutional arrangements under which economic agents can exercise ownership functions effectively are essential to the restructuring of enterprises so that they can compete in a market economy. They must be able to undertake changes designed to increase the market value or net worth of an enterprise in the long run.

Opportunities also had to be created to obtain additional resources to implement such changes. Although some efficiency-promoting changes, involving, for example, management and organization may require little capital and only limited changes in personnel, other changes, such as major restructuring, are possible only if substantial resources become available for investment.

The cooperation of major stakeholders, such as management and labor, had to be facilitated so that desired changes could be undertaken. Otherwise, well-designed transformation policies may be rendered ineffective if they are opposed by workers and managers (who consider themselves the *de facto* owners of an enterprise), fearing the loss of jobs and privileges.

Severe disruption also had to be avoided while bringing about these changes. For example, although a tough bankruptcy law will create strong incentives for efficiency-improving changes, it is also likely to trigger numerous plant closures and contribute to large declines in output. Severe disruptive impacts may be not only economically undesirable, but also may induce political opposition that will make transformation policies impossible to sustain.

A further criterion was the promotion of consistent and credible policy. Well-intentioned, even well-designed, policies, are unlikely to be effective if they are not viewed as being credible. They must be generally consistent with the main lines of policy and the government must be seen as having an established track record for implementation.

The transformation policies of government—or, in some cases, the absence of well-defined and enforced policies and rules—will have an impact on the restructuring of enterprises. We identify *strategic, defensive, and passive* enterprise restructuring. These are different, but not mutually exclusive, types of enterprise adaptations to the dramatic changes occurring in their domestic and external environments. *Strategic restructuring* refers to comprehensive, long-term business responses to fundamental environmental changes. *Defensive restructuring's* primary goal is the firm's immediate survival. *Passive restructuring* takes place when an enterprise's assets erode, whether legally or illegally, by design or by happenstance.

Organization of the Study

This study is organized as follows: Chapters 2 and 3 present the analysis and judgments on a comparative basis. Chapter 2 considers the common and country-specific conditions that have driven transition policies in the subject countries, the broad outlines of these policies and of macroeconomic performance, and the microeconomic evidence on producers' response to changing conditions. Chapter 3 then summarizes and compares those policies dealing with large state enterprises in the subject countries: the creation of an appropriate economic environment, privatization, and transformation of the remaining state enterprises.

The country chapters (4 on Poland, 5 on the Czech Republic, 6 on Hungary, and 7 on Russia) cover each country's preconditions for transition, overall transition policies, the economic, political, and social influences on those policies, the specific policies to deal with large state enterprises and their implementation and impact, and the lessons to be learned from the country's experience. These topics are also addressed with regard to China, but in less depth than for the other subject countries. A separate chapter on China was not prepared.

The main conclusions and lessons from the entire study are presented in Chapter 8.

Notes

1. For an excellent review of the problems of restructuring state enterprises in transition economies, including the former East Germany, see United Nations, Economic Commission for Europe, *Economic Survey of Europe in 1993-1994*, especially the chapter on "Restructuring Policies."

2

Initial Conditions and Performance During Transition

Legacies and Preconditions

Overview

Before attempting to assess transformation policies, both the common conditions and the individual characteristics of the subject countries are examined. The differences among the countries are large: some are rooted in history and culture; others flow from legacies of the Communist era; still others reflect economic and political trends during the transition itself. Both commonalities and differences are extremely important in judging the extent to which a country's policies are relevant to other countries.

This section describes how a variety of factors affected the position of each of the five countries as they began their transition and assesses the manner in which those policies facilitated or complicated the transition. This raises an obvious question—namely, when did the transition begin? The answer is that, except in China, the transition began after political revolutions that destroyed the hegemony of the Communist party. A convenient common reference point for the analysis of transformation policies is January 1990, the date for the launching of the "Big Bang" in Poland. Actions taken after that date can be viewed as transformation policies, while those taken before that date are treated as "pre-conditions." This date also roughly coincides with the wave of political revolutions in Central and Eastern Europe during the early months of 1990, when Communist governments collapsed and new, democratic governments set course for building market economies.

In Hungary, the revolution occurred in several stages during 1989 and the early months of 1990. In the Czech Republic the Communist collapse occurred in December 1989. In the Soviet Union, the Communist system, as well as the "inner empire," underwent a series of convulsions during 1990-1991, with the final collapse and breakup not occurring until after the

7

abortive August 1991 coup. For this reason, Russia could not begin a transition like that in Eastern Europe until the start of 1992.

China is quite different. Its Communist Party firmly holds onto a monopoly of political power, yet its economy has been in transition continuously since the late 1970s. Although continuing to reject capitalism, the Chinese government and the Communist Party have accepted the goal of developing a market-oriented economy that the state guides increasingly by indirect means.

To compare the preconditions of the five subject countries, we use 1989 for Poland, Hungary, the Czech Republic, and Russia. Although the Russian transition did not begin until 1992, there was little structural or institutional change during 1990 and 1991. To compare China with the other countries, we use both 1989 and 1979, the latter being the year when market-oriented reforms were launched. The preconditions are grouped as follows:

- Structural factors, such as the size and structure of the economies, which affect their production possibilities, degree of "misdevelopment," and policy trade-offs.
- Institutional factors, such as the size of the private, or other non-state, sector, entrepreneurial traditions, the prior development of market infrastructure, the degree of autonomy of state enterprises, and the degree of openness to the world market.
- The extent of macroeconomic imbalances with which transition governments had to deal: open and repressed inflation and the burden of servicing the government's domestic and foreign debts.

In very general terms, we can say that an economy will be more constrained and its transition more difficult, the more severe is its misdevelopment, the less developed are its market institutions, and the greater are its macroeconomic imbalances.[1]

A rather impressionistic characterization of how these three groups of factors affected the degree of preparation for and difficulty of the transition can be presented in simple, ordinal diagrams, which show the approximate relative position of the five countries for each group of factors. In Chart 2.1, we plot the estimated relative position of the countries with regard to the structural and the institutional factors. Not surprisingly, we find that these two sets of factors are highly correlated. Russia was the most ill-prepared country for the transition with respect to both structural and institutional factors. Next comes the Czech Republic, while Hungary and Poland were in a much better position. China was structurally better off in 1979 than Russia was in 1989, but its institutional development was at least as weak. By 1989, however, China was in the best relative position with respect to both structure and institutions.

CHART 2.1 Initial Conditions: Country Preparedness to Move to a Market Economy

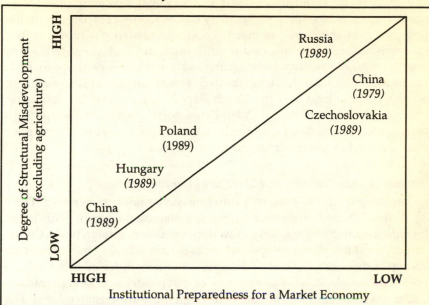

Degree of Structural Misdevelopment (excluding agriculture)

HIGH — LOW (vertical axis)

HIGH — LOW (horizontal axis)

Russia (1989)

China (1979)

Czechoslovakia (1989)

Poland (1989)

Hungary (1989)

China (1989)

Institutional Preparedness for a Market Economy

CHART 2.2 Initial Conditions: Country Preparedness to Move to a Market Economy and Macroeconomic Disequilibrium

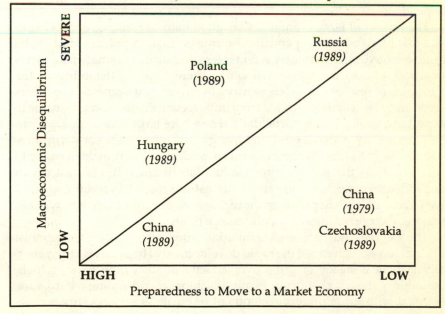

Macroeconomic Disequilibrium

SEVERE — LOW (vertical axis)

HIGH — LOW (horizontal axis)

Russia (1989)

Poland (1989)

Hungary (1989)

China (1979)

Czechoslovakia (1989)

China (1989)

Preparedness to Move to a Market Economy

The fact that structural and institutional preconditions are closely corre-lated (that is, all countries lie near the 45° line) makes it possible to qualitatively combine them so that they can be jointly compared with the third condition, the degree of macroeconomic imbalance (Chart 2.2). The best combination is low macro-disequilibrium and high preparedness to move to a market economy. Here again, Russia is in the worst shape for both of these synthetic variables, whereas China and Hungary in 1989 are in the best shape. In Poland and the Czech Republic, however, the following factors tend to be offsetting: Poland has good preconditions but high macroeconomic imbalances, while the Czech Republic has relatively poor preconditions but low macroeconomic imbalance.

Economic Characteristics and Structural Imbalances

The subject countries have very different economic characteristics (Table 2.1). Two of them, Russia and China, are continental-sized, with large, diversified economies, and have a low dependence on foreign trade. China, however, is still underdeveloped whereas Russia is highly industrialized. Among the three subject Central European countries (referred to as the "CE-3 countries"), Poland is the largest and least dependent on foreign trade.

Economic size and dependence on foreign trade are closely related. The larger the economy, the greater the scope for economic specialization within the domestic market at an acceptable cost. A strong endowment in natural resources, which is generally also found in continental-sized economies such as Russia and China, is another factor tending to reduce foreign trade dependence.

The impact of large economic size, good natural resource endowment, and low foreign trade dependence on transformation policies tends to be double-edged. Such a country is under less pressure than smaller countries to integrate into the world economy. There is more flexibility in the allocation of resources and less sacrifice of efficiency if domestic producers continue to be heavily protected from import competition and are unable to export at a profit. This is particularly true where large economic rents can be obtained by exporting oil, natural gas, or other low-cost natural re-sources, as in Russia. By the same token, such conditions make it easier to sustain policies that fail to improve industrial efficiency. By contrast, a high dependence on foreign trade and weak natural resources mean that Hun-gary and the Czech Republic cannot achieve an effective transition without making their firms internationally competitive.

The degree and nature of industrialization also matter. Communist policies have emphasized the rapid development of heavy industry, gener-ally leaving a legacy of gross overcapacity in such industries as fuels, metallurgy, heavy chemicals, heavy machinery, and military hardware, coupled with gross underdevelopment of business services, finance, so-

TABLE 2.1   Economic Characteristics of the Five Countries in 1992

	Russia	*China*	*Poland*	*Hungary*	*Czech Rep*
Population *(millions)*	149	1,166	38	10	10
GDP *(billion $)*	398	442	75	31	25
GDP per cap. *(dollars)*	2,680	380	1,960	2,750	2,700
Share of Export/GDP (%)	6	26	19	33	58

Note on GDP Estimates: GDP estimates in U.S. dollars are calculated from average exchange rates over several years (usually three). The results of this 1992 calculation understate the purchasing power of U.S. dollars over domestic goods and services in these countries by factors of the following approximate magnitude: 2/1 in Russia, Poland and Hungary; 2.5/1 in the Czech Republic; 3/1 in China. Use of purchasing power parity estimates for GDP would reduce the share of exports in GDP.

Source: The World Bank, *Atlas 1994* (Washington, DC: 1995).

phisticated consumer goods, and modern electronics, as well as a misallocation of resources in agriculture.

Although this structural legacy is common to all transition economies, its scope varies among the countries. Russia has the most serious structural problem, owing to having been longer under central planning and to its massive military programs. Among the CE-3 countries, the Czech Republic's economy was the most distorted by Communist policies because its pre-Communist lead in industrialization led to the assignment of a very important role as a supplier of heavy industrial goods in the Council for Mutual Economic Assistance (CMEA). The economic structures of Poland and Hungary were somewhat less distorted by Communist industrialization. In China, heavy industry developed under the Communists was generally inefficient, but made up a smaller part of a relatively undeveloped and still rural-based economy.

The over-development and obsolescent technology of heavy industry forces so large a reallocation of resources during the transformation that many become unemployed. For the most part, heavy industry is capital-intensive. A large, structural fall in demand results in specialized machinery and equipment becoming superfluous. It is easier for China, with a relatively small heavy industry and a prevalence of labor-intensive production, to shift labor to new uses without losing the use of much capital.

Prior Development of Institutions for a Market Economy

At the start of 1990, China, Poland, and Hungary were much further along in building market-oriented institutions than the Czech Republic and Russia. The many factors in institutional development for a market economy include: the size and role of the private or non-state sector; the strength of entrepreneurial, free market traditions; the past development of a market infrastructure, such as laws and regulations; the degree of autonomy of state enterprises; the decentralization of state authority; and the degree of openness to world markets. The starting position of all the transition economies in these respects was, in turn, influenced by each country's history and by the political strength or weakness of the previous Communist rule.

Size of the Private and Non-State Sectors. Inter-country comparisons of the relative share of economic activity according to the form of ownership must be interpreted with care because of the differing roles of private and other non-state units.

In China, the non-state sector probably constituted half of GDP in 1989. There were three linked elements in earlier Chinese reforms.[2] First, agriculture had been effectively decollectivized from the early 1980s through long-term leases of much of the land to peasant families. This policy began as an experiment during 1978-1980 and became universal in 1981. It stimulated increased effort by farmers, promoted long-term investment, and brought about a more efficient allocation of resources in agriculture—the result being impressive improvements in agricultural output and productivity.

Second, as increased agricultural productivity freed up large amounts of labor for other uses, while raising farm purchasing power, the central government took advantage of this opportunity by permitting local governments to establish Township and Village Enterprises (TVEs) and Urban Collectives (UCs). These firms, typically owned by a combination of local government, workers, managers, and other local firms, were rarely subsidized, were subject to few price controls and, for the most part, have been interested mainly in earning profits. They have been extremely dynamic. Already in 1989, such industries, together with the relatively small private industries and joint ventures, accounted for 44 percent of industrial production (by far the largest non-state share among the transition countries) and for the bulk of domestic and foreign trade. By 1993, the two sectors combined had a larger share in industry than the state sector.[3]

Third, parts of China were opened up to foreign trade and investment by permitting joint ventures in 1979 and creating Special Economic Zones (SEZs) in the coastal regions. The SEZs quickly became enclaves of capitalism, with positive spillover effects—both directly and by demonstrating the benefits of free markets and foreign investment to the rest of China.

In Poland, agriculture had been 80 percent private for many years, although private operations were so constrained that the structure of landholdings and most agricultural techniques were largely frozen at pre-Communist levels. Agriculture largely accounts for Poland's share of the non-state sector in GDP in 1989 being the largest in Eastern Europe (41 percent).

Hungary had the largest non-agricultural private sector, which made up close to 25 percent of GDP. Agriculture was still mainly formally collectivized, but with considerable scope for private incentives.

The Czech and Russian private sectors were tiny, representing less than 5 percent of GDP respectively, to which can be added in Russia the independent cooperatives launched by the Gorbachev government. Russia also possessed a large underground economy, which accounted for a sizeable share of urban household income. Although the other Communist countries also had substantial underground economies, the increasing legalization of market activity may have occurred partly at the expense of illegal activity.

Entrepreneurial Traditions. All the CE-3 countries, and parts of China, had much longer traditions of large-scale private enterprise and entrepreneurship than Russia. As the former industrial center of the Austro-Hungarian Empire, the Czech lands had the strongest such tradition. The CE-3 countries, and especially China, also had the advantage of large diasporas of entrepreneurs with both world market expertise and capital, a major asset that Russia lacks. Russia also suffers from the association in the public mind of entrepreneurship with illegal activity.

Early Start in Building a Market Infrastructure. Hungary was the leader in building a market infrastructure well before 1990, including establishing a modern commercial code, placing private enterprises on the same legal basis as state enterprises, breaking up the "monobank," legalizing foreign investment, and beginning to reform the tax system. Poland was only slightly behind Hungary. The Czech Republic did not even begin this process until after its "velvet revolution." China lagged far behind the other transition countries in the development of a formal legal framework for a market economy: for the most part, China still relied on policy pronouncements and informal arrangements. Russia adopted a patchwork of laws and regulations that neither made up a substantial basis for efficient market development nor were consistently applied.

Increased Autonomy of State Enterprises. Hungary entered the transition with more autonomy in its state enterprise sector than any other former Communist country. Ever since the initial introduction of the New Economic Mechanism in 1968, Hungary had attempted to plan and direct the economy more by setting parameters (or rules) for enterprises than by command. Poland tried to introduce such a system in 1982. Czechoslovakia reverted to tight central planning after the Prague Spring had been repressed in 1968. The Soviet Union under Gorbachev introduced a wide variety of reforms, including the use of state orders ("gosakazy") instead of directive plans.

None of the "parametric" reforms, however, did much to make state enterprises more efficient. Even in Hungary, the priority given to state investment and intra-CMEA trade, the ad hoc interference of the state bureaucracy in enterprise operations, the continued state control over the careers of enterprise managers, and a continued soft budget constraint for many prevented the development of effective market pressures and incentives. To quote Kornai:

> The firm's manager watches the customer and the supplier with one eye and his superiors in the bureaucracy with the other eye. Practice teaches him that it is more important to keep the second eye wide open: managerial career, the firm's life and death, taxes, subsidies and credit, prices and wages—all financial "regulators" affecting the firm's prosperity—depend more on the higher authorities than on market performance.[4]

In Poland and the Soviet Union, state orders, supported by central allocations of critical supplies, still drove the bulk of industrial production.

The economy of China was never as centrally planned as those of the Soviet Union and Central Europe. At the peak of central planning, China's central government was planning and allocating two or three hundred products, compared with thousands in the Soviet Union. As reforms progressed during the 1980s, market forces were permitted to govern an increasing part of enterprise activities and contracts with enterprises were increasingly substituted for directive planning under the "Contract Responsibility System."

At least in the CE-3 countries and the Soviet Union, the attempts to increase enterprise autonomy, in the context of growing political weakness, began to undermine the economic authority of the state and the coherence of the planning process. In Hungary and, to a lesser extent, Poland, firms were developing a dual dependency—on the authorities and on the market. By 1989 the entire structure of economic authority in Poland was falling apart, and this process was beginning in Hungary. In the Soviet Union both the state planning and control mechanisms and the Union itself were breaking down during 1990-1991. Formal economic planning continued but, with the ability of the government to deliver scarce goods rapidly diminishing, enterprises increasingly had to fend for themselves to find supplies and buyers.

Decentralization. Even under Mao, China's economic system was more decentralized than the Soviet and East European systems because of a low level of economic development and different historical traditions. Local and provincial governments had considerable authority over most small and medium-sized firms. Although there was no collapse of central authority in the post-Mao period, an increasing decentralization of authority to provincial and local government occurred. This differentiated economic reforms among localities and provinces, enabling the more market-oriented ones to proceed at a faster pace and demonstrate outstanding results. Decentralization has also resulted in a less monopolized production structure, which provides a basis for competition as markets spread.

Openness to the World Market. Openness is reflected less in the share of hard currency trade in total foreign trade and in GDP, than in the extent to which world market forces are permitted to affect relative domestic prices and exchange rates. The more open an economy, the less distorted its domestic price system is likely to be by world market standards, and consequently, the less wrenching the change in prices and production that will be required to effect the transition.

Hungary had the most open economy. Hard currency trade (exports or imports) accounted for about half of total foreign trade and for some 20 percent of GDP. Although many prices were still controlled in 1989, the structure of producer prices had been linked increasingly with those of hard currency imports. Despite heavy taxes and large subsidies, the Hungarian price-cost structure was probably the least distorted.

Poland comes next with regard to openness, with hard currency trade of more than one half of total foreign trade, but a share in GDP less than half that in Hungary. Price distortions were probably somewhat greater than in Hungary. On the other hand, in order to encourage remittances from the Polish diaspora, the government had legalized dollar deposits and permitted the growth of limited free foreign exchange markets. Czechoslovakia retained tight central control over hard currency trade and payments, which accounted for less than 40 percent of total trade.

China had decentralized more and more import licensing functions to regions and localities. Moreover, by 1989 China had made special provisions for firms in the SEZs to retain much of their hard currency earnings, which provided strong export incentives.

The Soviet Union by 1989 was allowing enterprises to retain some of their foreign exchange earnings, and was permitting some limited foreign exchange markets to develop. By and large, however, the economy was still largely insulated from the world market.

Macroeconomic Imbalances

The extent and type of macroeconomic imbalance prevailing at the time that transition is initiated has an important bearing on the design and potential speed of transition policies. Countries close to macroeconomic equilibrium have greater latitude to implement transition programs than those with severe imbalances. The latter must focus on eliminating, or at least greatly reducing, the imbalances before market reforms can be fully effective.

Eliminating macroeconomic imbalances is important also for microeconomic reasons. In an environment of high open or repressed inflation, prices lose their ability to accurately reflect relative scarcities, and uncertainty in estimating future profits forces enterprises to become excessively oriented toward the short term.

Finally, macroeconomic imbalances greatly increase the political difficulties of the transition. Dealing with large imbalances is politically difficult in market economies; it is even more difficult in formerly planned economies, where governments have fewer policy instruments to work with, those instruments are often less effective, and the pain and disruption associated with stabilization programs is greater.

Though all the transition countries inherited severe economic imbalances of a structural nature, only some of them had to contend with serious macroeconomic imbalances. Russia and Poland had to deal with combinations of severe repressed and open inflation. Such pressures were much less in Hungary, which, however, had to service a large hard currency debt. The Czech Republic and China inherited little inflationary pressure and a low level of debt.

Hungary managed to keep inflation under control, with annual rates peaking at below 40 percent. Shortages were also less severe, but the hard currency debt was even larger than Poland's on a per capita basis. The decision to continue servicing the debt imposed a heavy economic burden.

Inflationary pressures in Russia had built up during Gorbachev's "perestroika" period, as state revenues declined. Inflation surged during 1990-1991 as both the planning system and the Union were breaking up. Escalating budget deficits were financed by printing money, resulting in a rapid acceleration of open as well as repressed inflation.

Poland's inflation and foreign debt were a direct consequence of the Communist government's political weakness. In the early and mid-1970s, the Gierek government undertook a massive industrialization program, financed by Western credits, in an effort to buy increased popular support. The failure of that program, coupled with the Western embargo that followed the imposition of martial law in 1991, led to default on the debt. Once martial law was lifted, the government let wages grow largely unchecked while failing to prevent a rapid increase in consumer price subsidies, creating an unsustainable macroeconomic imbalance. In early 1989, the Communists negotiated a sharing of power with Solidarity and freed food prices. By the second half of 1989, the inflation rate had surpassed 1,000 percent. There were still large budget deficits, due mainly to subsidies, and shortages were still widespread.

The severe macroeconomic imbalances in these two countries have greatly complicated their transition by forcing economic stabilization to become a crucial policy priority. When an economy is being subjected to wrenching structural changes, and when the removal of price controls—at least initially—causes large price increases for goods formerly in short supply to push up the entire price level, it is extremely painful to also have to cut aggregate demand sharply. The Czech Republic had a much easier task. And in China, the periods of fairly rapid inflation have resulted from cyclically rapid economic growth rather than from inherited imbalances.

Policies and Trends During the Transition

Political Trends During the Transition

The political makeup of the subject countries during the transition runs the gamut from complete rejection of Communism in Poland, Hungary, and the Czech Republic, through a revolution in stages in the Soviet Union and Russia, to a continued Communist political system in China. China's rapid economic expansion during the transition was certainly facilitated by gradualist policies that themselves required political stability. In sharp contrast, the political instability in Russia and the former USSR clearly damaged the economy. There is no question that Gorbachev's vacillations and compromises, the collapse of the Soviet Union, and the long gridlock between Yeltsin and the legislature all contributed greatly to a lack of policy coherence, as well as to a more difficult environment for the transition.

In the CE-3 countries, where Communism had been imposed by Soviet power, its rejection was an inevitable part of reasserting national sovereignty. The timing and, in most countries, the suddenness of the revolution, dictated the subsequent economic transition. In the post-Communist era, Poland, Hungary and the Czech Republic share an overriding common objective—to join the European Community (EC) as soon as possible. This goal appears to be supported by a broad consensus of national elites, ranging from right wing parties through the former Communists. Although rarely articulated in public debates, it also appears to have broad implicit popular support. Membership in the EC (or the European Union, as it is now called) is seen not only as the route to long-term economic success, but also as a door into NATO or some European security structure. The existence of such a goal largely explains why there has been a high degree of continuity in economic policy.

Nevertheless, political differences among the CE-3 countries had substantial effects on transition policies. The strength of Polish labor, based mainly on its dominant role in the Solidarity movement, forced successive post-Communist Polish governments to give labor interests a large weight in transition policies, including representation in enterprise management, rights to company shares on preferential terms, and access to leases to gain control of firms. In contrast, the Czech government—once the economic liberal Vaclav Klaus had won a political struggle over a more social-democratic opposition and become Prime Minister—was able to largely ignore labor interests. But initial cuts in real wages were compensated by policies that minimized unemployment, thereby spreading more evenly the costs associated with (but not caused by) the transformation.

The experience of the CE-3 countries shows that popular opposition to transition policies builds over time and is likely to continue increasing even after an economic recovery has begun. Although many people are better off as a result of the changes, many are worse off, and they resent the inequities from which they are suffering. Moreover, rapid change, especially increasing unemployment, make many people feel highly insecure. So it may take a number of years of economic growth to recover some sense of security.

The victory of the left-wing parties in the Polish and Hungarian legislative elections during 1993-1994 was clearly due to an accumulation of such grievances. Nevertheless, the new left-wing governments have refrained from major policy changes. In Poland, the government has held down the budget deficit despite strong internal pressures for increased spending and has successfully negotiated the second stage of foreign debt reduction. In Hungary, the new left-wing government was forced by circumstances in 1995 to introduce severe macro-stabilization policies.

Economic Policies

To varying degrees, all of the subject countries have addressed the major elements of changing to a market economy since the end of 1989.[5] They have:

- Eliminated, or, in the case of China, diminished the role of central planning and of economic directives;
- Made money count by freeing most prices and by allowing most microeconomic decisions to be determined by market forces;
- Made considerable progress in macroeconomic stabilization;
- Greatly reduced quantitative restrictions on foreign trade and established generally low import tariffs;
- Unified the exchange rate, and made the currency freely convertible for most current account transactions;
- Developed the institutional structure for a market economy, such as laws, banks and other financial institutions, and tax systems;
- Permitted or encouraged the formation of private enterprise and, except in China, undertaken privatization of an increasing part of existing state enterprises;
- Devised more flexible and efficient means of governing those enterprises that remain state-owned.

Transition policies are discussed at length in the following comparative policies chapter and in the country chapters. In most respects, the CE-3 countries have arrived at about the same point in all the major elements of the transition, although with differences in timing and, to a lesser extent, in phasing. *China* has achieved a considerable degree of economic liberalization, although not promoting privatization in the state sector. *Russia* lags behind in both economic liberalization and institutional development, but has been a leader in the rate of privatization, at least in a formal sense.

Poland is considered to provide the classic case of "shock therapy," and did indeed decontrol the bulk of prices and nearly all foreign trade transactions and made the zloty convertible for residents on January 1, 1990. At the same time, tight money and a massive reduction in the state budget deficit were pursued, a heavy tax on wage increases in excess of norms was imposed, and a fixed exchange rate "anchor" was maintained for 16 months to achieve macroeconomic stabilization, as well as to contain the inflationary pressures triggered by decontrol.

Although the massive macroeconomic imbalance greatly complicated the transition, it also made drastic stabilization an urgent priority, which could be coupled with decontrol. And the political rout of the Communist Party by a Solidarity-led coalition created a window of opportunity to undertake fundamental change with strong initial popular support. Privatization, however, was a slow process, because of the political strength of labor, the low level of foreign investment (until 1993), and the inability to agree on the details of a voucher privatization program in 1995.

Hungary undertook the decontrol and stabilization of its economy more gradually than Poland—in several steps in the course of 1988-1990—but by mid-1990 had reached about the same point as Poland. It employed the same policy instruments as Poland in its stabilization program, with the exception that the exchange rate was not fixed for a long period. Hungarian gradualism was an outgrowth of a lengthy process of economic reform that began in 1958 with the introduction of the "New Economic Mechanism," and a reform process that had accelerated in the late 1980s. It also reflected the more gradual relinquishment of power by the Communist Party in Hungary than in Poland, which culminated with the national elections in April 1990. The macroeconomic imbalance was also much less than in Poland, and consequently did not dictate drastic, immediate stabilization.

Liberal laws on private enterprise, foreign direct investment, and commercial transactions, and laws reforming the banking and tax systems were on the books by 1987-1988. A head start in institutional reform, as well as a relatively open economy, made Hungary the most attractive place for foreign investment in East-Central Europe during 1990-1992, when it attracted more than half of the total foreign direct investment to the area. During those early years, foreign investment financed the bulk of privatization as well as many "green field" projects. Hungary was the first former Communist country to implement a tough bankruptcy law.

The Czech Republic used the first year after its "velvet revolution" of December 1989 to pass legislation for a market economy and to break up some of the very large state conglomerates. This was necessary because the former Communist government had taken virtually no steps to reform the planned economy or prepare for a market economy. Unlike Poland or Hungary, moreover, there was little macroeconomic imbalance, and consequently no pressing reason for drastic measures. In January 1991, however, one year after Poland, Czechoslovakia liberalized virtually all prices and foreign trade and exchange transactions, a step that was accompanied by tough macroeconomic policies to keep inflation in check.

Privatization also began in 1991, including a massive voucher privatization program. As the economic liberals under Vaclav Klaus gained political ascendancy, a process that was further strengthened in the Czech Republic by the split with Slovakia, the government was able to follow the most coherent set of policies among the former Communist countries. In particular, privatization was pursued in all but a small number of industries in order to remove the government from microeconomic management as quickly as possible. Such policies were feasible because of the complete discrediting of the old economic and political system, the weakness of organized labor, and the broad popularity of the Klaus government.

In *Russia*, fundamental economic reform was delayed, first by the partial nature of and inconsistencies in Gorbachev's reforms of the late 1980s—including an absence of agricultural reforms, the half-hearted promotion of cooperative enterprises, the excessive use of state orders that certainly limited enterprise flexibility, and an unwillingness to allow true legal markets to operate—then by a retreat from reform during 1990-1991, after the Shatalin plan, the first more or less coherent plan for economic transition, was rejected, and finally by the disintegration of the Soviet Union.[6]

The abortive coup of August 1991 gave Yeltsin a political opportunity to launch a thoroughgoing reform program. Lacking a fundamental political consensus for economic transformation, other than a felt need for leadership in the wake of the collapse of both the Soviet Union and the Communist Party, Yeltsin apparently decided to take basic steps toward a market economy that would be difficult to reverse. These steps included the freeing of most prices on January 1, 1992, and, later that year, launching a massive privatization program, mainly using vouchers.

Although some basic legislation had been passed, the Russian reforms had a weaker institutional base than those in the CE-3 countries. They were also less thorough: price controls over most fuels and raw materials were maintained at the national level; local governments controlled certain consumer prices; and a large part of foreign trade continued to be controlled through 1993. Unlike the CE-3 countries, moreover, Russia has been unable to control inflation. After an initial period of very tight credit during the first half of 1992, the central bank has provided enough subsidized credits to keep state enterprises operating, despite drastic declines in demand.

In *China*, fundamental reforms were well under way by the beginning of 1990, as was described above. The reform process slowed during 1990-1991, as a cyclical program of financial stabilization coincided with the political reaction to the Tienamen Square demonstrations. The stabilization measures, including a tightening of bank credit and cuts in budgetary spending, were undertaken to slow inflation, which had been accelerating to double-digit rates as a result of exceptionally rapid economic growth during the late 1980s. The political reaction took the form of attempts by Communist conservatives to restore some central controls over enterprises, but these were successfully opposed by local and provincial governments.[7]

By 1992, the political tide had turned in favor of reform, as the Party leadership proclaimed development of a market economy to be a central objective. The reform process accelerated during 1992-1993, as most remaining price controls were abolished, the exchange rate was unified, private enterprise was encouraged, and steps were taken to make large state enterprises more efficient. In 1994, renewed rapid inflation triggered another attempt at economic stabilization and reimposition of some central controls, but the benefits of rapid economic growth seemed too widely spread to put the fundamental market reforms at risk.

Macroeconomic Trends

Except in China, the early years of the transition were accompanied by a severe economic recession—declines of 20–25 percent in GDP between 1989 and 1992, as shown in Table 2.2. The timing of these declines varies among

TABLE 2.2   Trends in Gross Domestic Product of the Five Countries
(1989=100)

	Russia	China	Poland	Hungary	Czech Rep.
1980	76*	45	93*	91*	89**
1989	100	100	100	100	100
1990	100	104	88	96	99
1991	91	111	81	86	85
1992	76	124	83	82	79
1993	67	141	86	80	79
1994	58	157	90	82	81

*Net Material Product
**Net Material Product for all of Czechoslovakia
Sources: 1980-1992: World Bank, *Historically Planned Economies: A Guide to the Data,* 1993 edition. 1993: United Nations, *Economic Survey of Europe in 1993-1994.* 1994: various official sources, some reported in secondary publications; for China, *Financial Times Survey,* November 7, 1994.

countries, depending mainly on when prices were liberalized and economic stabilization policies introduced. Since 1992, however, there is a sharp contrast in economic performance between the CE-3 countries, where output has begun to recover, and Russia, where it has continued to fall rapidly. The economic recovery in Poland has been under way since the spring of 1992 and Polish output may have reached pre-transition levels if under-reporting of economic activity is considered. The Hungarian and Czech economies leveled off in 1993 and rose slowly in 1994. But in Russia, measured output has fallen more than 40 percent over the past five years and, as yet, shows few signs of imminent recovery.

The economic recession has substantially reduced living standards and, together with the freeing of markets, has brought heavy unemployment in Poland and Hungary (13-16 percent of the labor force), but not in the Czech Republic and not yet in Russia. There is no doubt that a substantial drop in both production and welfare occurred despite considerable under-reporting of economic activity in East European and Russian statistics. And, even where average per capita real incomes have recovered, as in Poland, a majority of the population considers itself worse off than before because of increased uncertainty and greater inequality in income distribution. Investment has declined more than consumption, but also has begun to recover in Poland, Hungary and the Czech Republic.

Market liberalization was accompanied initially by a large jump in official prices in all the transition economies of the CE-3 countries, then by much lower and declining inflation rates in countries with effective stabilization programs, but not in Russia. An important element of the transition was a drastic shift in the direction of foreign trade from the formerly planned and protected CMEA markets to Western markets.

China's economy presents an extraordinary contrast to those of Eastern and Central Europe, with a growth of 57 percent (almost 10 percent annually) from 1989 to 1994 (although statistics probably inflate growth to some extent). Both consumption and investment in China have boomed and the shares of exports and imports in economic activity have tripled.

In *Poland*, output and measured real incomes dropped sharply in the early months of 1990, due to the combined effects of macroeconomic stabilization and price liberalization. There was another substantial output drop in 1991 as a result of the collapse of CMEA trade and renewed tightness in monetary policy. Industrial production has been steadily rising since the spring of 1992, and increased more than 10 percent from 1993 to 1994, although it has not yet returned to pre-transition peaks.

Construction activity is increasing rapidly. The recovery is being driven by an expanding private sector. Unemployment continued to increase during the first year of the economic recovery, but edged off in 1994 from a peak of about 16 percent of the labor force. Prices more than doubled during the first two months of 1990, but since then inflation has slowed to annual rates of 30–40 percent for consumer prices.

Macroeconomic trends in *Hungary* are similar to, but less pronounced than, those in Poland. Production declines in 1990 and 1991 occurred for the same basic reasons as in Poland, but were somewhat milder because Hungary's transition policies were more gradual. By the same token, the decline in production continued into 1993 and a recovery began only near the end of the year. GDP growth was about 2 percent in 1994. As in Poland, unemployment has been increasing, reaching some 14 percent of the labor force. Because of relatively gradual decontrol and the absence of a severe macroeconomic imbalance, Hungary has avoided big leaps in prices and has kept inflation in a range of 20–30 percent a year.

In the *Czech Republic* price liberalization occurred one year later than in Poland, but simultaneously with the collapse of CMEA trade, on which the country was highly dependent. Consequently, although economic stabilization measures did not have to be as severe as in Poland and Hungary, the decline in output was of a similar magnitude. Recovery of output has been hindered by the break with Slovakia, which sharply reduced trade with that former part of Czechoslovakia. Still, increases in all major economic sectors occurred in 1994 and both consumption and investment are rising. Moreover, the Czechs have been able to hold the unemployment rate to below 5 percent, and inflation rates are in the range of 10-20 percent.

Russia's economy began to slide during 1990 and 1991, then took a plunge in 1992, as prices leaped ahead of wages, investment spending fell because of budget constraints and uncertainty, and trade with the countries of the (former) Soviet Union collapsed. The slide continued in 1993 and 1994. Measured Russian GDP has fallen more than 40 percent since 1989, more than double the drop in the three East European countries, although official statistics probably overstate the drop more in Russia than in Eastern Europe. Personal consumption has fallen considerably less than investment and military expenditures. Monthly inflation was reduced after the massive initial jump accompanying price liberalization, but then rose to double-digits because of an extremely accommodating monetary policy in the second half of 1992 and most of 1993. A renewed tightening of credit and cuts in the budget deficit once again brought monthly inflation rates down to single digits in most of 1994, but by the last quarter inflation was accelerating again. Overt unemployment remains moderate because enterprises have not yet been under strong enough pressure to restructure, although there is massive disguised unemployment in enterprises.

China, like Japan in the 1960s and Taiwan and South Korea in the 1970s and 1980s, has achieved an average rate of economic growth of over 10 percent in the past 15 years, with double-digit growth rates in boom periods alternating with "slowdowns" to about 5 percent growth when the government tried periodically to reduce overheating. Growth slowed in 1990 and 1991 in response to government policies designed to slow inflation, but then accelerated to double-digit rates in 1992, 1993, and 1994. Inflation has reached double-digit annual rates during periods of particularly rapid growth because of weak controls over bank credit, continued budget deficits, and supply bottlenecks. Exports have increased from 7 percent of GDP in 1980 to about 25 percent in 1993.

The Problem of Producers' Response

The Nature of the Problem

In the CE-3 countries and the former Soviet Union, the introduction of transition policies brought a larger drop in output and more rapid inflation than governments had expected. This disappointing outcome is blamed partly on the slow response by producers to the changing market environment. In turn, producer resistance forced some governments to at least modify their macroeconomic policies. Sluggish adjustment by producers reflects in good measure the many political and economic uncertainties inherent in the transition, especially during its first year. Faced with great uncertainties about economic conditions, government policies, and their own career prospects, enterprise managers at first tried to protect themselves by continuing to cultivate close relations with their traditional suppliers and customers as well as with the workforce. Yet some adjustments were made early and most state-owned firms made considerable further adjustments as markets developed and economic conditions stabilized.

Adjustment was clearly more rapid among private firms than among state-owned firms. This is partly because nearly all the private firms were relatively small and generally labor-intensive, and had little access to budget subsidies and subsidized credit.

Where privatized firms are large, capital-intensive, and considered important enough by the government to receive special treatment, their responsiveness to changing conditions may be limited. There is also a self-selection bias, in that entrepreneurs who start private firms, or who purchase state-owned firms, tend to be the most market-oriented and have the most market skills. Moreover, the most profitable and efficient state firms are often the first to be privatized.

In this section, the evidence on producers' response available from enterprise surveys is analyzed to aid in the subsequent assessments of transformation policies. While the bulk of the survey data are from Poland (see notes to chapter on Poland), the patterns from the few Russian and Hungarian surveys are similar.

Evidence from Enterprise Surveys

The most basic finding is that state enterprises make all the adjustments they can when their management becomes convinced that the government will not bail them out one way or another—i.e., that they truly face a "hard budget constraint." The degree of stability in the economic rules of the game and in the economic environment are also important determinants of enterprise adjustment. Their ability to make adjustments, however, depends also on such factors as labor-management relations and the availability of funding for restructuring purposes. The nature and extent of adjustments increases over the transition period: as one Polish survey observes, by 1992 (the third year of the Polish transition), all the surveyed state enterprises had made significant adjustments.[8] The surveys did not, however, include any very large enterprises, which tend to make the smallest adjustments.

Especially for the first year or so of the transition, and in Russia into the third year, many firms follow survival strategies with an exclusively short-term focus—using depreciation allowances to raise wages and bonuses, holding on to labor, extending credit to regular suppliers, and raising prices to gain revenue, even at the expense of long-term market share. The many political, legal, economic, and career uncertainties faced by managers during the early transition period all contribute to a short-term focus.[9] Even as such uncertainties are reduced, loss-making firms that have little opportunity for restructuring, or that continue to be subsidized by the government, also tend to follow such a strategy.

Rapid inflation also contributes greatly to a short-term bias by making long-term economic calculations extremely difficult. It creates temporary paper profits (as adjustment of inventory and fixed capital values lags behind sales prices), depreciates enterprise debt and receivables, obscures price signals, and increases the uncertainty of projections. The much more rapid and lasting inflation in Russia than in the CE-3 countries during the transition has been a major factor in the relatively slow adjustment of Russian producers, both state-owned and privatized, in 1992-1994.

The extreme case of weak adjustment occurred in Russia during the first few months of 1992, when prices were first decontrolled and credit was tightened. Enterprises generally maintained production levels in the face of a sharp drop in sales and a curtailment of bank credit. They obtained the necessary financing through a massive growth of inter-enterprise credit. Such a buildup of inventories and inter-enterprise credit could not have been sustained for long unless enterprises expected to be bailed out through a resumption of bank credit. And that is what happened. Faced with an escalating liquidity crunch and an indecipherable inter-enterprise credit mess, the central bank, under pressure from industrial interests, loosened the reins, creating sufficient liquidity but also accelerating inflation. In turn, the reversal of a tight credit policy undermined the government's credibility and caused a lasting weakening of incentives for adjustment by firms.

Enterprises make various adjustments, with varying lags, to the freeing of markets. The most common and quick adjustment is a shift in managerial emphasis from production and procurement to marketing and finance. This takes little money and is essential to survival. Actions range from establishing new sales outlets and contacts to developing promotion and advertising. Russian firms, as well as those in Eastern Europe, are making at least the simpler changes of this type.

A widespread adjustment, representing part of defensive restructuring, is a "passive" adjustment in the product mix. This involves producing as much as possible with existing resources of items in demand, while drastically cutting production of those no longer in demand. Russian producers appear to have been slower than those in the CE-3 countries in making such adjustments. "Active" adjustment, such as developing new products and changing production techniques or substantially increasing the capacity for products that are in demand, is fairly rare in state enterprises, partly because of investment limitations. These kinds of adjustments tend to increase as firms develop market niches, establish a track record of profitability, and consequently, gain more access to long-term bank loans.

Major changes in the structure of firms and the organization of work are rarely undertaken, except where powerful incentives exist, such as the immediate prospect of privatization. Adjustments in employment are sluggish and may take several years to complete. Declines in employment were small in the first year of transition in Poland, Hungary, the Czech Republic and Russia. In the CE-3 countries cuts in employment increased substantially in the second and third transition years. Excess labor in state-owned industry in these countries was estimated as being still in the range of 10-20 percent in 1992, which explains why employment in Poland continued to decline during the first year or two of economic recovery. Russian enterprises clearly are still greatly over-staffed even in the fourth year of the transition.

Employment has been cut mainly through accelerated attrition, including early retirement and some individual firings for cause. Mass layoffs were rarely used, except where an enterprise, or one of its units, was closed. This policy was followed, not so much because of threatened strikes, but rather because managers wanted to maintain smooth relations with the workforce. In the uncertain conditions of the transition, management and labor often believe that they need to cooperate. This means, on the one hand, avoiding mass layoffs and major reorganizations of work on the factory floor, and, on the other hand, not striking without a very strong cause. Another factor is the higher cost of mass layoffs owing to severance pay requirements.

The speed and extent of adjustment varies among types of firms. Adjustment is clearly the most rapid for fully independent private firms, but not for those that receive direct or indirect state subsidies, which is often still the case in Russia. Small and medium-sized state firms are the next quickest to adjust, except those that are captive subcontractors of large firms. Compared with large firms, they are more nimble, less bureaucratic, use more flexible production processes, carry less social infrastructure, have better communication between labor and management, and, especially, are less likely to receive financial support from the government. Among such firms, those that face the most competitive markets tend to make the strongest adjustments. And the firms that sell directly to retail trade or consumer markets tend to adjust more quickly than those that sell mainly to other producers, because they are more aware of changes in demand and are less likely to receive credit from their customers.

Very large state-owned firms (e.g., those with 10,000 workers in the principal location plus thousands more in fully-owned, captive suppliers) are by far the slowest to adjust. The main reason for this is that they often enjoy a soft budget constraint because the government is unwilling to accept the economic and social effects of shutting them down. Such firms either receive subsidized bank credit or are able to accumulate arrears on tax liabilities. They also delay payments to suppliers. Transformation of such "elephants" involves unique problems that require special measures.

Adjustments tend to be greater and more rapid in firms that use labor-intensive methods, such as producers of clothing and furniture, than in capital-intensive firms, like steel mills or basic chemical plants, because labor is generally less specialized than equipment and, consequently, the product mix in the labor-intensive firms can be more readily changed. This is apparent, not only in survey data, but also in the stronger output performance of labor-intensive than of capital-intensive industries in countries which have been in transition for several years. As pointed out earlier, this factor is also important in explaining China's strong economic performance.

Influence of Various Actors on Enterprises

The response of enterprise managers to the introduction of market reforms has been strongly influenced by their interactions with both internal and external actors—labor, government, private owners, and financial institutions. Chart 2.3 shows, for example, the main parties that interact with a firm that is to be privatized. The same chart also shows the main groups whose views a country's privatization authority must take into account as it makes privatization decisions. The strength of these groups of actors varies greatly among transition countries, and these variations explain many differences in policies and instruments, their timing, and their

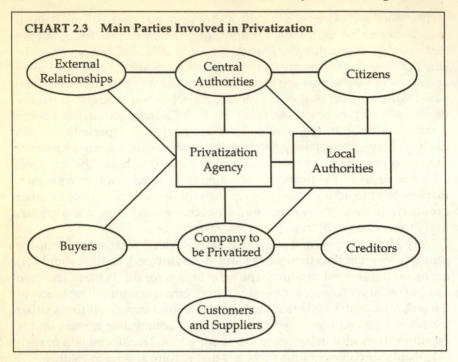

CHART 2.3   Main Parties Involved in Privatization

effectiveness. In the case of government, strength comes less from direct authority over enterprise decisions than from policy credibility and coherence. Where enterprises do not believe a government policy will be sustained, they are likely to work to make it fail. And where the implementation of government policy is hindered by internal bureaucratic and political conflicts, its impact will be greatly weakened.

A strong government has been the essential basis for transition policies in the *Czech Republic*. Clear priorities were established and coherent policies were followed. Consequently, government policies, such as tight money and privatization, have high credibility in enterprises. Insiders, especially labor, have less power and fewer privileges than in any of the other subject countries. There are no workers' councils, and no representation of workers on the supervisory boards of the newly formed corporations. Although existing management has prepared most of the privatization plans that were adopted by the government, new private owners, including especially investment funds owned by banks, are already active in setting policy for individual firms. The main problem has been a tendency for managers to mark time, and sometimes to strip off or allow the depreciation of assets, during the year or more between initiation and completion of privatization of firms, a period in which management is uncertain about its future.

In *Poland*, workers are more powerful than in any other subject country, and their views must be taken into account in any major changes contemplated by both government and management. Workers' councils acquired *de facto* control of many enterprises when the government control system collapsed. They must approve any decision to convert an enterprise into a corporation and to privatize it. To gain such approval, government and management have had to give labor a variety of incentives, such as ownership shares at reduced prices and possibilities for leveraged buyouts by labor/management groups on favorable terms. In most enterprises, management has been the main force in formulating policy, but workers' councils and labor unions have had to be consulted and persuaded. So far, banks and other financial institutions have not been much involved in enterprise decisions, but this is beginning to change.

Industrial ministries still play an important role in the restructuring and privatization of large enterprises. However, ministries have often marched to different drummers, reflecting political fracturing and reliance on coalitions of parties to form governments, which has made decisions difficult and slow. Nevertheless, there has been enough continuity of overall policy to develop considerable credibility, especially in the financial area.

In *Hungary*, management has been the strongest group, owing mainly to the country's decades-long history of economic decentralization, but also to labor's modest clout. Concessions to workers have been similar to, but on a smaller scale, than those in Poland. The government has been fairly strong, and has been able to make such policies as tight money and bankruptcy credible and to implement policy with a single voice. On the other hand, attempts to centralize privatization and enterprise restructuring have so bogged down the process that increased initiatives from enterprise management have had to be permitted, even encouraged.

In *Russia*, the weakness of the central government and the great uncertainties facing enterprises have given enterprise management a dominant position. Although in principle, government can select, promote, and relieve managers of state-owned enterprises, in practice the managers control the enterprise and decide on both operations and policy. As in Poland, managers have to elicit cooperation from the workers on some matters. But, unlike Poland, their position has almost always been secure.

The central government not only has to share authority with local governments, but also suffers from a severe lack of credibility, the result of having had to back down from announced policies, notably the tight credit policies of the first half of 1992. Fundamental policy differences within various parts of the executive branch, and between the government and the central bank, almost ensure a lack of policy continuity and coherence.

In *China*, authority is generally shared among various parties and is often ambiguous. As a rule, only the larger enterprises are under central government control, and even these may encompass a variety of ownership forms, such as joint ventures; this means that their policies may be determined by diverse groups. The smaller firms are mainly under local and provincial control, but management and labor groups also play a major role. Almost everywhere, China's system involves a process of bargaining and working out issues among interested parties. Except in a few industries and very large firms, however, the central objective is profitability because that is the main condition under which the objectives of all parties can be satisfied.

Notes

1. This analytical framework was developed by Paul Marer in "Economic Reform in Hungary: From Central Planning to Regulated Market," *East European Economies: Slow Growth in the 1980s; Vol. 3, Country Studies in Eastern Europe and Yugoslavia* (Washington, DC: U.S. GPO, 1986).

2. See, for example, Michael Bell and Kalpana Kochhar, "China: An Evolving Market Economy—A Review of Reform Experience," *IMF Working Paper* WP/92/89, International Monetary Fund, November 1992.

3. By 1993, the two sectors combined had a larger share in industry than the state sector. See World Bank, *Meeting the Challenge of Chinese Enterprise Reform* (Washington, DC : 1995).

4. János Kornai, "The Hungarian Reform Process: Visions, Hopes, Reality," *Journal of Economic Literature*, December 1986, p. 1703.

5. Two excellent analyses of the sequencing problem in the transition are contained in Paul Marer and Salvatore Zecchini, eds, *The Transition to a Market Economy, Volume 1: The Broad Issues* (Paris: OECD, 1991), Chapter 4. The articles are; Rudi Dornbush, "Strategies and Priorities for Reform," and Stanley Fisher and Alan Gelb, "Issues in Socialist Economy Reforms."

6. See, for example, Robert W. Campbell, "Economic Reform in the USSR and its Successor States," in Shafiqul Islam and Michael Mandelbaum, eds., *Making Markets: Economic Transformation in Eastern Europe and the Post-Soviet States*, (New York: Council on Foreign Relations Press, 1993).

7. See article by Kang Chen, *The Failure of Recentralization in China: Interplays Among Enterprises, Local Governments, and the Center*, The World Bank, Socialist Economic Reform Unit, Research Paper Series, no. 6, October 1990.

8. Brian Pinto, Marek Belka, and Stefan Krajewski, *Transforming State Enterprises in Poland: Microeconomic Evidence on Adjustment*, The World Bank, Policy Research Working Papers, WPS 1101, February 1993.

9. The characteristics and motivations of the "survival-oriented enterprise" are fully developed in an article by Barry W. Ickes and Randi Ryterman, "From Enterprise to Firm: Notes for a Theory of Enterprise in Transition," in Robert Campbell, ed., *The Postcommunist Economic Transformation: Essays in Honor of Gregory Grossman* (Westview Press, 1994).

3

Policies Affecting State Enterprises

Establishing an Appropriate Economic Environment

The subject countries have all taken major steps to establish an appropriate economic environment for the transformation of industrial enterprises. They have:

- Made money count by removing most controls over prices, production, distribution, foreign trade and foreign exchange;
- Promoted, or at least permitted, the development of private entrepreneurs to take advantage of market opportunities and tried to create more competitive conditions;
- Been building a legal and regulatory market framework;
- Begun to transform banks into independent institutions capable of allocating loans according to creditworthiness and of channeling national savings into productive investments;
- Drastically changed tax systems from an ex post collection of nearly the entire difference between market prices and costs to ex ante instruments of revenue collection;
- Developed instruments for a modern monetary policy;
- Proceeded to shift social welfare functions and expenditures from enterprises to local governments;
- Begun to apply bankruptcy laws, and other regulations governing the financial restructuring, reorganization and exit of loss-making firms.

Large differences exist among the subject countries in the nature and speed of progress in these areas, however, owing to differences in initial conditions and post-Communist political, economic, and social situations.

Creating Markets

Making Money Count. No market economy can operate unless money, rather than status or political and military power, determines purchasing power over goods and services, and at least most product and factor prices are freely determined under reasonably competitive conditions. "Making money count" is technically a fairly simple task, involving mainly the removal of government controls and the hardening of the budget constraint. In formerly planned economies this means the removal not only of price controls, but also of the entire network for microeconomic planning and control of production and distribution. At least in the smaller countries, it is also essential to eliminate quantitative restrictions on all but a few imports and exports and to make foreign exchange freely available to residents and the currency convertible on current account. Freedom of capital flows is a long-term goal, not a short-term necessity, in the unstable conditions of the transition.

The main issues in the subject countries, and the main differences among them, have been over the pace of decontrol and the priority given to freeing foreign trade and foreign exchange markets. Not surprisingly, the larger countries, Russia and China, have been much slower to liberalize their foreign trade and payments than the CE-3 countries. With respect to internal market liberalization, China has taken a much more gradual course than any of the other countries, although it has reached nearly the same position after 15 years. In the CE-3 countries, decontrol was very rapid, partly because the Communist control system had largely fallen apart, partly because of the opportunity created by the political revolutions, and, in some countries, partly because of the immediate need for severe macroeconomic stabilization, with which it could be combined.

Decontrol policies have also been greatly affected by the extent of the macroeconomic imbalance. Even where macroeconomic imbalances were small, as in Czechoslovakia, shortages were prevalent, so that decontrol alone was bound to considerably raise the overall official price level. But where inflationary pressures were great, as in Russia and Poland, decontrol had to be coupled with drastic stabilization measures.

Unlike the CE-3 countries, however, Russia maintained quotas on exports of fuels, key raw materials, and some imports; failed to stabilize the exchange rate; and for some time required exporters to turn in a portion of their foreign exchange earnings. The exchange rate was officially unified, but through 1992 nearly half the imports from outside the former Soviet Union, paid for by foreign aid and credits, were controlled by the government in a special account and sold internally at heavily subsidized prices. Moreover, a great deal of the trade with countries of the former Soviet Union continued to be transacted at prices below world market levels. Russia also maintained price controls on fuels and, by default, local governments had authority to impose price controls on selected consumer products.

In the CE-3 countries and Russia, product markets were freed faster than factor markets. Controls over state enterprise wages, generally in the form of high taxes on wage increases above norms, became important instruments of macroeconomic policy in Poland, Hungary, the Czech Republic, and Russia. As of late 1994, capital markets were still at an early stage of development, though improving rapidly in the CE-3 countries. In Russia, however, subsidized bank credit was still used, albeit on a smaller scale than in 1992-1993.

China liberalized its economy in stages over more than a decade. As the communes were broken up in the early 1980s, individual farmers were permitted to sell an increasing part of their products in free markets. As agricultural reform raised farm incomes and released labor, development of Township and Village Enterprises (TVEs) was encouraged. These firms, which by 1992 accounted for some one-third of industrial production, sold their outputs and purchased most of their inputs in the free market. At the same time, centrally owned industrial firms continued to sell planned quantities of products at controlled prices that were generally well below those on the free market, and were allocated planned amounts of specified inputs at controlled prices. "Above plan" production was sold and additional inputs were bought on the free market.

The share of production sold at controlled prices, and thus subject to quantitative planning and quotas, declined over time. In 1992-1993, following a two-year stabilization during which excess consumer demand was largely eliminated, consumer prices and producer prices were almost entirely freed, except for fuels and power, and the powerful State Price Bureau was abolished. In 1994, however, renewed double-digit inflation led to the reimposition of controls over prices of some basic consumer goods.

Although China achieved almost the same degree of internal price liberalization as the other countries, its labor and foreign trade and exchange markets continued to be subject to many controls. By late 1994, most workers in centrally controlled firms still had an "iron rice bowl" of assured basic wages with little differentiation for work or skills. Still, efforts were being made to move to a contract system, under which wages and even employment are tied to productivity and the performance of certain tasks. Outside the centrally controlled firms, wages were much more market-determined, but were also influenced by local government policies.

Controls over foreign trade and payments were highly differentiated by type of firm and region. Import quotas were administered centrally for very large firms and regionally or locally for smaller ones. Foreign exchange was also rationed, although the exchange rate was unified in 1994, legal free markets existed, and firms in the Special Economic Zones (SEZs) and some other firms obtained special retention rights that they could freely exercise. The Chinese foreign exchange system of 1994 seems roughly similar to that of Poland and Hungary in 1988-1989, but with a stronger institutional base. Government policy was to establish currency convertibility on current account in the fairly near future.

In its attempt to develop a market economy that continues to be directed by economic plans, China is beginning to look more like Taiwan and South Korea in the 1970s and Japan in the 1960s than like the CE-3 countries. Central, and especially regional and local, government influence on economic activity remains strong. China, like the Japanese, Koreans, and Taiwanese before them, hopes to use mainly the allocation of bank credit and foreign exchange on preferential terms as instruments of planning and control. In addition, an authoritarian government with a single political party, as well as a culture favoring the use of informal influence over formal legal rules, facilitates the implementation of government policy directives without requiring widespread microeconomic management.

Laws for a Market Economy. Although the simple withdrawal of barriers is sufficient to let markets develop, their efficient operation in a modern economy requires a set of laws that establishes contract procedures and property rights, and provides for the settlement of contract disputes (bankruptcy law is discussed below). All the CE-3 countries have adopted a civil code based on those in Western Europe. Poland was able to simply reinstitute its prewar (1934) code because it was never formally abolished. The rights of private persons to own property has also been established. All three countries are now in similar positions. What is still missing is a trained judiciary and a case record to fill in details of the law and resolve issues.[1]

In Russia, there are still restrictions on private ownership of land, and regulations are used in a number of areas pending the passage of formal legislation. A virtual absence of a commercial real estate market constitutes a serious obstacle to the development of private business. Even more serious are the uncertainties concerning the authority and property rights of the central vs. the local governments. It is often unclear whether central or local regulations and legislation are in operation, and they are sometimes inconsistent. Hopefully the new constitution will help resolve this problem.

In China, there was very little formal legislation on commercial transactions and property rights, at least until 1993-1994. Government policy statements were treated as law, and details were elaborated through bureaucratic regulation. Many issues were left open and there were many areas of uncertainty as to whether central, regional or local regulations were governing. This apparent confusion is not at all foreign to Chinese culture, which puts a premium on informal processes of working out differences, rather than disputing over the interpretation of formal laws and rules. Indeed, one of the features of Confucian culture is an acceptance of political-social hierarchies in the interest of social harmony and of "rule by men" rather than "rule by laws."

The absence of a clear legal framework in China does not yet appear to have seriously hindered foreign direct investment (FDI), which was more than $30 billion during 1986-1992, another $26 billion in 1993, and probably

$30 billion in 1994, for a cumulative total of nearly $90 billion in 8 years.[2] Foreign investors were protected through a joint venture law that took precedence over other regulations in dispute resolution. And the great bulk of foreign investors in China have been overseas Chinese who were both comfortable in this culture and accustomed to operating in countries where contacts matter much more than law. The absence of a sound legal system would be likely, however, to impede the future development of China's economy. As market institutions develop and as the role of non-Chinese investors increases, steps are being taken to build such a framework.

Fostering Private Entrepreneurship. Newly formed markets work best when traders and producers are quick to take advantage of profit opportunities. Although state-owned producers will tend to respond slowly, as shown in the previous chapter, private trade can develop rapidly under the right conditions. In turn, a responsive trading system can force substantial changes by state-owned producers.

In Poland, Hungary, and the Czech Republic, thousands reacted to the freeing of prices and the removal of controls by quickly selling virtually every kind of domestic and imported good. They set up shop on sidewalks, even in front of state-owned department stores, largely ignoring licensing and zoning laws, with at least tacit police approval. Private traders purchased consumer goods both from abroad and from domestic producers and sold them at what the market would bear. State retailers that continued to simply add standard markups to their acquisition costs often found themselves with excess inventories, and so had to cut their purchases from producers. The producers then responded by selling directly to consumers or to private traders. As the sale and leasing of state-owned retail outlets and wholesale firms to private parties progressed, private retail trade left the sidewalks for more permanent locations. This process quickly created a very competitive market, first at the retail level, and before long in wholesale trade as well. Shortages disappeared, the prices of consumer goods quickly approached those in nearby Western countries, and obtaining needed supplies ceased to be anything but a money problem for producers.

As the transition progressed and market institutions developed, private entrepreneurs entered most areas of production on an increasing scale. Beginning with small, family operations, new private firms found niche markets that had been ignored under Communism, then started to compete with state producers. They took advantage of free foreign exchange markets by adding value to imported goods. While in most cases, lack of capital limited new entrepreneurs to labor-intensive and skill-intensive processes, some had accumulated considerable capital before the transition through rent-seeking, arbitrage-type operations.

In China also there was little attempt to impede the rapid development of small-scale private entrepreneurs, although the retention of some price, import, and foreign exchange controls, as well as distance and poor trans-port infrastructure, kept many markets highly segmented. Imported goods became readily available in the SEZs, less so in the inland areas. Domestic goods prices varied greatly around the country. Local trade restrictions and taxes stimulated corruption on a large scale. Consequently, markets were generally dynamic, but much less efficient than in Central Europe.

In Russia, the picture is mixed. Official tolerance of new small private entrepreneurs varied a great deal from city to city and region to region. In some places, local governments imposed time-consuming licensing re-quirements that, in practice, involved numerous payoffs, and applied zoning laws restrictively or selectively. In other places, they made the establishment of new business very easy. Unlike the CE-3 countries, whole-sale markets in many products remained underdeveloped. Given the long distances, poor infrastructure, and high cost of imports, it was often easy for cartels, producer "associations," and sometimes organized crime groups, to control distribution with official connivance, at least on a local level.

Promoting Competition. Building efficient markets requires competi-tive conditions. The methods used to foster competition in transition countries include: facilitating the development of private entrepreneur-ship, as discussed above; deconcentration of production; anti-monopoly, pro-competition legislation; and exchange rate and foreign trade policies.

In the CE-3 countries, a large number of state enterprises were broken up, or parts of these enterprises spun off, even prior to privatization. Further deconcentration has occurred as a result of privatization. Consequently, the number of small enterprises, both private and state-owned, has increased greatly, while the number of large ones has declined. In China, industry was never as concentrated as in Russia or Central Europe. With few exceptions, China's industrial firms were relatively small, and even the larger enter-prises consisted of a group of fairly small plants.[3] Consequently, China considers that sufficient competitive potential exists. Indeed, China has begun to promote mergers of unprofitable state firms with profitable ones. In Russia, the trends are not yet clear but some state firms have been broken up. In all five countries, private entrepreneurship and deconcentration have created a large base of small industrial firms that did not exist under Communism, but most of the very large firms have survived.

All the CE-3 countries and Russia have adopted legislation, patterned after the U.S. and Western Europe, that bans certain kinds on anti-competi-tive behavior, such as agreements to fix prices and restrain entry of potential competitors. The legislation also helps to determine whether or not pro-posed mergers and purchases of other firms, including foreign investments, are likely to overly limit competition. Hungary appears to have applied anti-monopoly laws most diligently. In Poland and the Czech Republic, although the legislation is strong on paper, its implementation has generally been subordinated to other policy objectives. Russia introduced new anti-monopoly regulations in 1994, but implementing them will be difficult.

Exchange rate and import policy have been the principal instruments of competition policy in Eastern Europe since 1990. The move to currency convertibility on current account generally entailed establishing exchange rates that initially undervalued the currency in relation to its internal purchasing power.[4] Most imported goods were thus priced far above domestic substitutes, thereby protecting domestic producers. As real exchange rates appreciated in Poland and Hungary, imports became cheaper, putting growing competitive pressure on domestic firms. In Russia, the market exchange rate grossly undervalued the currency during 1992, making imports extremely expensive and virtually shutting out most foreign competition. Since late 1993, the real exchange rate for the ruble has appreciated considerably, but part of the impact on the prices of imported goods has been offset by increases in tariffs.

Financial Intermediation and Control

General. A central but extremely difficult task in transition is the development of financial institutions that can operate as the principal instruments of both macro- and microeconomic regulation and control. The functions of banks had to be drastically changed from merely auditing the implementation of plan directives to becoming the main decision makers in the allocation of credit. Banks and other financial institutions, such as insurance companies and funds of various kinds, had to be developed from scratch to aid in channeling savings into productive investments. Capital markets for government securities and for private debt and equity had to be established. Reforms to make central banks at least partly independent and a tax system appropriate to a market economy were critical to the effectiveness of macroeconomic policies.

For enterprises, the shift from bureaucratic control to financial regulation was designed to bring about a "hard budget constraint," so their sustenance, expansion, and survival had to be justified in the market from funds available on commercial terms in accordance with expected return and risk criteria. Under the inflationary and rapidly changing conditions of at least the first year or two of the transition, however, it was difficult for financial institutions to judge the creditworthiness of firms, and they continued to give soft credits to at least the large, politically important state firms.

While the credit needs of many loss-making state enterprises continued to be accommodated and private firms were squeezed out of access to credit, taxes strongly discriminated against state firms, both because some taxes applied only to state enterprises and because tax evasion was more widespread among private firms. The heavy tax burden further worsened the financial problems of state firms. Tax reform is beginning to counter this trend by introducing broad value added taxes and individual income taxes.

Banking. Development of a modern banking system is furthest along in Poland, Hungary and the Czech Republic. It is at an early stage in Russia and is just beginning in China. Hungary abolished the "monobank" and established a central bank separate from the commercial banks in 1987, but still has not given these institutions full autonomy. Poland and the Czech Republic made similar institutional reforms.[5] All three countries are in the process of privatizing the commercial banks. The Czech central bank appears to be the most independent of the government, and, even under Communism, carried more weight in top economic policy decisions than other central banks, which partly explains that country's historically low inflation rate.

Banks in the transition economies have been slow to play their designated role as profit-driven allocators of credit and monitors of the debtor's performance. Bankers had been trained mainly as financial accountants and had no knowledge or experience with assessing creditworthiness, except for those few who had been involved in international banking.

Credit markets differ from most markets in that differences in risk among products (i.e., loans) cannot be fully reflected in their prices (i.e., lending terms) because of the severe self-selection by the potential borrowers. Banks set terms for various categories of loans and degrees of risk, and extend credit only to those borrowers who meet the criteria for at least one of these categories. But under the uncertain conditions of the transition economies, clear lending criteria for the banks could not be quickly established, and the banks continued to lend mainly to traditional state enterprise customers, even those who were losing money.

Responses of managers in enterprise surveys in Poland and Hungary generally characterize the banks as having been "unhelpful" and "passive"; only by 1992 did the World Bank find indications of commercial banks in Poland beginning to play a more active role in advising enterprises, assessing their financial plans, and differentiating among those with good from those with bad track records. In the case of private firms, very few were able to obtain any bank credit, because of their generally small size and lack of a track record. During 1993 and 1994, however, major strides were made in the East European countries, especially Poland and the Czech Republic, to develop effective banking.

There are several basic reasons why banks have been generally ineffective in transition economies. Many large banks continued to be state owned. Because they are not putting their own capital at risk and can expect to be bailed out if they become insolvent, they have strong incentives to continue "business as usual" rather than try to resolve the debts of problem enterprises. The Czech Republic has privatized most of the commercial banks, though the state still holds a large minority share in them; Poland only three out of six; Hungary none as yet, though quite a few new foreign banks have been established. Many Russian banks are now privately owned, with the state retaining a share in some and considerable indirect influence.

Banks had too many non-performing assets, the value of which sometimes exceeded bank reserves. If such banks try to accumulate reserves by setting an unusually large spread between interest rates on deposits and those on loans, this reduces the effectiveness of financial intermediation. But if they expect to be bailed out by the state, they will have no incentive to stop the accumulation of bad debt. Many state enterprises were in financial difficulty because important customers during the Communist era (when neither enterprises nor banks had much control over their transactions), could not pay their obligations.

The payments systems have been very slow and inefficient. Under Communism, the payments system was designed mainly to ensure the accuracy of transactions and accounts; processing was fast in a "monobank" system. The breakup of the monobank system led to long delays in the settlement of accounts between independent banks, severely inhibiting the development of financial and capital markets.

In the past, it was particularly difficult for banks to assess creditworthiness in the early years of the transition—that is, to distinguish among debtors those who were simply illiquid from those who were insolvent. Even after most prices had been liberalized, they continued to be distorted for at least two years by continued controls on some products, monopoly practices, and lags in adjusting cost accounting for rapid inflation. Moreover, it takes time—at least a year or two—for firms to adjust their inputs, outputs, and methods to the new market environment. Even then, the many uncertainties about future economic policies make it extremely difficult to assess a firm's potential profitability and account must be taken of the possibility that firms with poor prospects will be kept alive by government subsidies. Finally, the long-term viability of a firm may be obscured by debt obligations that reflect non-market conditions and for which current management was not responsible, or by a large volume of inter-enterprise debt, accumulated in a mutual effort to sustain purchases and output despite difficult access to bank credit.

So far in the transition, commercial banks have provided mainly short-term credit to enterprises. This reflects the uncertain and inflationary conditions that made it very difficult to set terms for long-term credits without government subsidies or guarantees. As inflation diminishes, however, and financial and capital markets develop, commercial banks are expected to play an increasing role as sources of financing for investment.

In Poland, the Czech Republic, Russia, and recently also in Hungary, commercial banks are permitted to own enterprise equity and to engage in investment banking. This means that they must develop a capacity to evaluate an enterprise's long-term potential and to strongly influence its restructuring and expansion—functions that will require even more sophistication than decisions on short-term credit.

In Russia, the central bank has been legally responsible to Parliament and has been highly responsive to the requests of government departments to provide increased liquidity and low interest credits. Such credits have been channeled to enterprises through commercial banks. To protect themselves, many Russian enterprises have become share owners in commercial banks, with which they are considered preferred customers for low real interest credit. In Poland, Hungary and the Czech Republic, it is the banks that are becoming part owners of enterprises, and this is beginning to happen in Russia as well.

In China, the allocation of bank credit, a major instrument of government policy, has become one of the few remaining instruments of central control over the provinces. The Chinese envisage using credit controls in place of direct planning and allocation of products to guide the economy in directions desired by the political leadership. This follows the general approach of Japan in the 1950s and South Korea and Taiwan in the 1960s and 1970s.

Other Financial Institutions and Markets. A network of financial institutions and markets to facilitate the flow of savings into investment has been developing in all the transition economies, but is still very rudimentary. This network includes a rudimentary market for treasury bills in Hungary and Poland that is used by the central banks for open market operations and a developing secondary market for government bonds purchased mainly by banks and other institutions and used to finance increasing shares of budget deficits. A third element is the stock market in which the shares of private and public corporations are traded.

Only about 40 firms are traded in this market in Poland and Hungary, but, with the completion of voucher privatization in the Czech Republic, the shares of some 3,000 firms are being, or will soon be, traded in that country, although most of these over-the-counter. After a slow start, the Polish market boomed in 1993, with share values increasing several-fold, then lost more than half the gains in 1994. The Czech market also took off during October-November 1993 and fell off in the first half of 1994. The Hungarian market has been relatively sluggish, showing a similar, but milder cycle.[6] Company shares are also sold on a large scale in Russia and are marketable, but well organized secondary markets have not yet developed. In China, securities exchanges were opened in Shanghai and Shenzhen. The shares of only a few firms were traded and shares available to foreigners were segregated from those sold to Chinese. Fueled by massive Chinese savings, the narrowness of other opportunities for financial investments, and global interest in sharing in rapid Chinese growth, a speculative binge developed until the bubble burst in 1994.

The final element of the network is the increasing number of insurance companies and investment companies or funds. Strong investment funds have been formed in the Czech Republic to invest in shares offered during the voucher privatization program. Nine of the ten largest funds are owned by banks. Russia has a large number of investment funds, but most of them are small and have little capital. Poland is organizing a few large investment funds to serve as intermediaries in its own "mass privatization" that is likely to be launched in 1995. In China, many Trust and Investment Corporations (TICs) were organized for long-term lending and trust business.

Monetary Policy. The CE-3 countries have been slowly developing the necessary instruments for a modern monetary policy, while Russia and China are still at a primitive stage. To an increasing extent, reserve requirements, rediscount rates, and open market operations have been replacing direct credit rationing as the primary means of monetary control.[7] Even in Central Europe, however, monetary policy can be used only as a blunt weapon, and not yet as a sophisticated method of regulating macroeconomic activity.

In Poland, monetary policy was extremely tight during the "Big Bang" of January-February 1990, and again in early 1991, in response to an acceleration of inflation. At other times during 1990-1992, monetary policy was somewhat accommodating, as most of the credit needs of state-owned firms were met and wages were permitted to keep up with prices. Since early 1993, however, banks have become much more selective in extending credit and real wages have been about flat, despite an economic recovery.

In Hungary, monetary policy was tight during the first three years of transformation (mid-1990 to mid-1992) in order to control inflation and the balance of payments. The primary instruments of monetary policy were high mandatory reserves, tight reins on refinancing credits and a real appreciation of the exchange rate. There followed (from mid-1992 through mid-1994) a period of more erratic monetary policies, in which real interest rates sometimes turned negative.

In the Czech Republic, monetary policy was very tight throughout the transition period. Tight credit and a highly undervalued currency kept wages low, which in turn helped to keep down unemployment.

The much larger increase in the price level in Russia during 1992 than in Poland during 1990, the year of the "Big Bang," was due partly to a more severe initial macroeconomic imbalance, and partly to the lack of a exchange rate peg. Much of the difference, however, can be attributed to less responsive supply behavior, which in turn forced the government to shift to an easy money policy beginning in August 1992.

Initially, enterprises tried to sustain recent production levels in spite of large declines in demand, while passing on increases in input prices. Since bank credit was severely rationed, the only way sufficient liquidity could be maintained was by delaying payments to suppliers. In turn, the suppliers delayed payments to their suppliers, resulting in a lengthy "queuing" process. The increase in inter-enterprise credit during the first few months of 1992 was so large that most enterprises were technically insolvent, since it was impossible to unravel mutual obligations. The clamors from industry for the government to provide more liquidity became irresistible, and the government gave in. Monthly inflation rates, after slowing to the single digits during the summer of 1992, shot back up to large double digits, with the exchange rate depreciating at the same time. Credit was again tightened in late 1993 and most of 1994.

Fiscal Policy. During the transition, there have been conflicts between the microeconomic goals of stimulating enterprise adjustment and the goal of macroeconomic stabilization. During the periods of large-scale price liberalization in Poland, Hungary, the Czech Republic and Russia, fiscal policy was highly deflationary, as subsidies were drastically reduced while other government expenditures, notably those for military purposes, were also cut and tax revenues from the paper profits of enterprises increased. This net fiscal contraction, at a time when investment was curtailed because of increased uncertainty and consumers were holding back because of price shock, contributed to sharp declines in production and real incomes. Later in the transition, the fiscal effect became expansionary (and inflationary) as reduced production in state enterprises cut the tax base, while tax collection from the private sector was weak and expenditures on the social safety net increased. In Russia, moreover, there was a massive increase in subsidized credits to enterprises. The resulting fiscal deficits in turn impeded continued economic stabilization in Poland and Hungary and caused renewed rapid inflation in Russia.

The trend in the CE-3 countries has been to finance state budget deficits increasingly with sales of bonds to commercial banks rather than simply through direct financing by the central bank, with its inflationary impact. In Hungary and Poland, bond sales covered large parts of the growing budget deficits in 1992 and 1993. The 1993 deficits are estimated as about 4 percent of GDP in Poland and 6 percent in Hungary. To make the bonds attractive to the banks, the government had to pay high rates of interest, with the effect of squeezing out many other potential borrowers. In these uncertain times, the banks would rather earn a small, but assured real return than make high risk loans, even at substantially higher rates.

The shrinking size of the public sector and the weak collection of taxes on the private sector have forced major tax reforms. Hungary, Poland, the Czech Republic, and Russia have all introduced a value added tax on the West European model, as a substitute for the turnover tax. Hungary was the first to do so; Poland was the last. The main advantage of the value added tax over the turnover tax or a general sales tax is that it gives producers the responsibility and the incentive to determine that their suppliers have paid the tax, so that they can then deduct it from their own tax base.

The same countries also have been broadening the individual income tax to cover all sources of income, rather than only wages and salaries as in the past. Corporate income tax rates are being cut from the high rates of over 50 percent that private firms generally escaped, joint ventures were exempt from, and many state firms were unable to pay.

While there has been considerable progress in reforming the tax system, the same cannot be said of government expenditures. None of the subject countries have yet tackled the politically sensitive issues of systemic pension, medical insurance, and education reform. Even in Poland, Hungary, and the Czech Republic, which had large declines in expenditures for both military purposes and subsidies, social spending is excessive for the income level, putting a severe strain on budgets. As a result, government employees are often paid too little and, more important, tax rates are set so high (especially on firms) that producers' incentives are weakened and tax evasion becomes rampant. The social insurance tax on employers in Hungary, for example, is 53 percent of direct wages, which is high even for the much wealthier West European countries. Russia also faces these problems, and continues to subsidize enterprises on a significant scale.

State enterprises were subjected to increasing tax discrimination in both the CE-3 countries and China, not only because they could not escape taxes, but also because some special taxes, such as the Polish "dividend tax" on fixed assets formerly funded from the state budget and the tax on wage increases in Poland, Hungary, and the Czech Republic, were levied solely on the state sector. But as the financial condition of state enterprises worsened, they became unable to pay their tax obligations, which led to growing tax arrears. In Poland until 1993, large, loss-making state firms were supported, not through direct subsidies but rather by allowing tax arrears to accumulate.

Transfer of Welfare Responsibilities from Enterprises. In the centrally planned economies, state enterprises—especially large ones—managed and funded a wide range of social welfare functions that in market economies are normally performed by the central and local governments. First, they employed and paid a great many workers they did not need, and who would have been unemployed in market economies. The transition countries have had to expand their social safety net to include unemployment compensation for those workers who were released. Second, they provided a wide variety of specific social services, including schools, hospitals and other medical facilities, nurseries, restaurants, and sports facilities. Large enterprises also financed vacation resorts for their workers and professional sports teams. In many smaller cities and towns, where a single enterprise was the main employer, it often provided the bulk of social services in the town. While enterprise responsibility for many welfare functions was characteristic of all the centrally planned economies, in China it took on the characteristics of a comprehensive cradle-to-grave system. In effect, income security and access to services went with employment, and few services were available outside the place of work.

In all the subject countries, except China, efforts have been made for enterprises to transfer their "social assets" and responsibilities to local governments, or anyone else who might be interested. Unfortunately, local governments have not yet acquired the sources of revenue necessary to pay for such services. In most countries they still rely mainly on specified percentage shares of national taxes for their revenue and have yet to develop substantial independent sources of income. Consequently, many services, such as sports teams and vacation facilities, have been cut out, a few services have been privatized, and some have been picked up by local government free of charge. Local governments have tried to raise revenue by charging high rents for the leasing of their property to private parties, to the point of slowing the privatization process. Eventually, they will have to establish a system of property taxes that brings in more revenue without discouraging business and real estate development.

Financial Restructuring and Bankruptcy

Cutting Bad Debt. Non-performing loans are a very serious problem in Eastern Europe and Russia. In Poland, for example, they amounted to some 24 percent of the total loans of the 14 largest banks in February 1993, much exceeding bank reserves. In Russia, overdue loans are mainly those among enterprises, although the banks also became exposed. Moreover, the bad debt problem is not merely inherited from the Communist era; to a large extent it is an ongoing problem that will not become fully manageable until the entire financial system works properly, which requires both institutional improvements and reasonable macroeconomic stability. In Poland, the great bulk of enterprise debt was accumulated in 1991 and 1992, as enterprise losses about offset profits. The financial position of enterprises improved slowly in 1993 and 1994, but a large fraction are still losing money. This is also true in other countries.

All the CE-3 countries and Russia have taken steps to reduce bad debts, but, as of late 1994, the banks remained greatly under-capitalized by Western standards. There are two major problems with bad debt reduction. One of these is that it constitutes a cost to society and must be paid for somehow: the question is how and by whom? The other problem is "moral hazard"—the perverse incentives that debt concessions can create for debtors if they lead to the expectation that they will be repeated in the future. Debt reduction or elimination is designed to give firms the opportunity to improve their performance, not the expectation of future bailouts.

Debt reduction has been funded and managed in a variety of ways. For the most part, the process involved the issuance of government bonds and their sale to creditor banks, with two major variants. A decentralized approach is for the bonds to be used to increase bank reserves so that the banks will become capable of managing the non-performing loans themselves. A centralized approach is to exchange the bonds for the non-performing assets that are then deposited in a special government fund—what is sometimes called in the U.S. the "Resolution Trust Approach."

The centralized approach was used in Czechoslovakia in 1991, when over one billion dollars of bad debts were transferred to a "Consolidation Fund." Then in 1992, the Czechs used the other approach: The National Property Fund issued some bonds to increase commercial bank reserves, leaving the responsibility to deal with the remaining non-performing loans with the banks. The bonds were secured by income from privatization.

The Poles also are using a decentralized approach. In 1993 they increased bank reserves with a bond issue, and the commercial banks established special departments for managing enterprises with serious debt arrears. The Polish bonds are backed by foreign aid—the billion dollar Exchange Stabilization Fund that was never drawn upon and several hundred million dollars of World Bank loans.

The Hungarians delayed comprehensively addressing a growing bad debt problem until 1992, when the banking system was threatened with insolvency. Between 1992 and the end of 1994, the government implemented a series of sequential programs to recapitalize the banks, but took few steps to address the problems of enterprises whose non-performing loans it assumed. By the end of 1994, a line had been drawn between old and new bad debts and the program of "consolidating" (taking care of) the bad debts of the banking system had essentially been completed, at a future (and unfunded) cost to the state of about 9 percent of GDP. In spite of the huge cost, this is quite an achievement, generally not well recognized in the country, or even by foreign experts. This is because a series of banking problems, many of them quite visible, have remained unsolved. For example, there is no set aside program to cover the bonds when they are redeemed in 20 years; and in return for recapitalizing the banks, the government has increased its control over them and has drawn back from earlier plans to privatize them.

The Polish approach to managing bad debt from special departments of commercial banks has advantages in dealing with a continuing problem. Besides gaining increased reserves, the banks are developing the capability of debt restructuring. In particular, they, as well as the Hungarian banks, are engaging in debt-to-equity swaps, thereby gaining control of, or at least influence over, loss-making enterprises, some of which might be salvageable. There is at least some evidence that special funds do not do a good job of managing such enterprises because they are too distant and bureaucratic. On the other hand, it is a lot to ask of banks, whose personnel are not even trained adequately to assess creditworthiness, to manage the far harder task of financial restructuring and to guide enterprise management.

Other steps taken by the CE-3 governments to prevent the renewed accumulation of bad debts include increased pressure on loss-making enterprises through restructuring programs and the use of bankruptcy procedures. At the same time, the banks are being forced to set aside reserves against loans, classified by degree of risk. In Poland loans have been classified as "Pass," "Watch," "Substandard," "Doubtful," and "Loss," with set-asides of 2, 5, 20, 50, and 100 percent, respectively. Since early 1993, banks have been forbidden to issue new credit to firms with non-performing loans, except under special conditions that generally involve restructuring and government subsidies. Hungary and the Czech Republic have similar classifications and reserve requirements. These systems have been in effect too short a time, however—they were introduced in mid and late 1993—for their effectiveness to be fully evaluated, although there are signs of improvement, especially in Poland.

Closely related to debt reduction and debt management is the problem of reducing inter-enterprise debt. Hungary and the Czech Republic tried to net out as much of this debt as possible, so as to alleviate the problem without making anyone worse off, but the amount of debt canceled in this manner has apparently been fairly small. In Russia, where inter-enterprise debt was much larger, a variety of solutions were tried, including mutual "clearing," establishing pre-payment requirements, and the issuance of transferable obligations called "veksels," issued by banks, that could be used by one firm to pay off the debt of another. By the end of 1992, the bulk of this debt had been eliminated or enormously devalued through inflation, although the problem reappeared in 1994.

Bankruptcy. Bankruptcy is a threat to discipline firms, a mechanism for reorganizing or restructuring loss-making firms, and a procedure for liquidating a firm's assets. In a planned economy, bankruptcy did not exist because enterprises were never closed down and real assets were rarely taken out of use. During the transition, bankruptcy procedures had to be developed, sometimes by reviving prewar laws, as in Poland, but mostly from scratch. Bankruptcy laws were needed to deal with the thousands of new private firms, many of which were failing because of inexperience, low capitalization, and difficulties in adjusting to rapidly changing market conditions. Some form of bankruptcy threat was also needed to force state-owned firms into major, often painful adjustments and to stop the continued accumulation of non-performing loans.

In the economies in transition, as in the West, bankruptcy must provide for either the reorganization or the liquidation of a firm. Typically, reorganization is initiated and managed by the debtors, under court supervision and with the agreement of creditors, while liquidation is managed by a court-appointed party who represents the debtors' interests and is mainly concerned with the disposition of assets. Formal procedures for these two distinct functions differ among countries: in the U.S. they are covered by two bankruptcy laws (Chapters 11 and 7 respectively), whereas in Germany, reorganization is treated as a pre-bankruptcy workout and only liquidation itself falls under the bankruptcy law.

The subject countries all have passed bankruptcy laws, but these apply only to firms subject to commercial law, which means to private firms and state corporations. In Poland, where few state corporations existed until 1994, this largely limited bankruptcy proceedings to the private sector. In Hungary, which "corporatized" nearly all its state firms, the bankruptcy law has had much broader application. In the Czech Republic and Russia, bankruptcy law has a potentially broad, but so far quite limited, application. In all the subject countries, governments have been willing to use bankruptcy proceedings to stimulate restructuring, but have been extremely wary of forcing firms, especially large ones, to close down.

Hungary has pioneered in the use of bankruptcy law. The Hungarian law passed in September 1991 and took effect in January 1992. It was designed largely to stop the accumulation of inter-enterprise debt that had been caused by a tight monetary policy coupled with expectations of government bailouts. The law is one of the toughest in the world. Any business with a debt of even a single forint in arrears for more than 3 months is obliged to submit to a bankruptcy procedure. Management then has 60 days to submit a restructuring/refinancing plan. Only if all the creditors accept this plan can liquidation be avoided. Under liquidation, the firm is taken over by a court-appointed trustee and its assets are sold at auction (normally for very low prices) and distributed to the creditors. Distribution priorities differ from those in the West in that wages and severance payments have first claim in Hungary, followed by secured creditors, and then unsecured creditors and the government.

Implementation of the Hungarian law was premature. Not surprisingly, the courts were swamped. There was an avalanche of bankruptcy cases (about 16,000), which bankruptcy courts were completely unprepared to handle. The Budapest court had only 8 judges, each handling 147 restructuring and 337 liquidation cases, resulting in lengthy delays. The extended delays (a year or more) forced most creditors into agreements in almost two thirds of the concluded cases and often made it impossible for creditors to collect any revenue before the remaining assets were used up or squandered. There was much uncertainty, which contributed to a paralysis of decision making. And several hundred firms, some of which were probably solvent, were liquidated, contributing importantly to the continued decline in Hungarian GDP in 1992. In 1993, several bankruptcy conditions were eased, bringing the law into line with those found in market economies.

The *Czech Republic* also passed a tough bankruptcy law, in 1992, but decided not to put it into effect until June 1993 in order not to interfere with large-scale "voucher privatization" and to first complete debt restructuring programs. The Czech law is somewhat less stringent than the Hungarian, allowing up to 90 days for firms to get a reorganization plan approved before liquidation procedures are initiated. With voucher privatization completed, the bankruptcy law will presumably be used mainly to pressure the newly formed private firms into restructuring. The government has established special programs and procedures to restructure state-owned firms in certain industries, such as coal, and apparently does not intend to apply the bankruptcy law to these firms.

Poland has revived and revised its prewar (1934) bankruptcy law, which is patterned on the German model in that it covers only court-ordered liquidation, with reorganization procedures being covered by a separate law. Neither the bankruptcy nor the reorganization laws have been applied to state enterprises, only to private firms and state corporations, that operate under commercial law. One form of "liquidation" in Poland, described later in this chapter, is a kind of government-managed bankruptcy procedure involving a combination of negotiated debt workouts, distribution of assets, and attempts to salvage a potentially viable firm from the remains.

China has a bankruptcy law that applies to private firms but has not taken any steps to apply it to state enterprises.

Russia's bankruptcy law (which went into effect in March 1993), like that of Hungary, provides for reorganization (either under existing management or under a court-appointed "receiver"), liquidation, or a reconciliation agreement between debtors and creditors. The law applies to both private firms and state corporations, a legal form to which almost all state enterprises have been converted. The government evidently much prefers reorganization to liquidation. Reorganization procedures are not allowed to last more than 18 months. By early 1994, only eight bankruptcy cases had been filed. The filing process accelerated, however, in the course of 1994, with several hundred firms having been declared insolvent by late in the year.

Privatization

Main Issues and Characteristics

Public ownership in Communist countries has meant the absence of "real owners" and the substitution of politicized bureaucratic control (with its varied and often dissonant incentive systems) for owners with a personal stake in preserving and enhancing the value of a firm's net assets. Although in principle state-owned firms could operate efficiently in a market environment, history shows that such firms, both in Communist countries and in the West, can rarely be insulated from political influence, even when governments are able to refrain from micro-management. The results have been excessive, subsidized investment, over-staffing, rigid work rules, and strong resistance to reorganizations and layoffs. In formerly planned economies, where drastic changes in most firms are essential to their survival, the reasons to reject continued state ownership are especially strong. Nearly all the new governments in Eastern Europe and the former USSR adopted privatization of the bulk of state enterprises as a central policy objective.

But privatization has turned out to be a slow and politically difficult task. In Poland and Hungary, the fairly broad initial consensus in favor of privatization among the leadership and economic policy elites was generally not shared by the population. Although most people supported the privatization of small shops and firms, they were generally wary of large-scale capitalism because of job security concerns, residual socialist ideology, and questions about how such privatization could be achieved equitably. Issues of equity and nationalism were quick to engender popular reactions. Evidence of the misuse of power and influence to obtain valuable assets, or of foreign nationals buying up the most profitable local firms at seemingly bargain prices, are excellent grist for the political mill. Because of political resistance and sensitivity, even Poland and Hungary, countries with a head-start in creating markets and otherwise establishing an appropriate environment, have been slow to privatize large state-owned firms.

In addition to raising sensitive issues of equity and nationalism, large-scale privatization is greatly constrained by insufficient private domestic capital and the need to placate inside stakeholders. In transition economies, domestic capital can readily be found to purchase small shops and firms, but not large corporations. All these considerations explain the contrast between privatization in the broad sense—the growing share of the private sector in the economy—with privatization in the narrow sense—the transfer of state assets in large enterprises to private ownership. By the end of 1994, the share of the private sector in recorded GDP was about 55 percent in Poland, Hungary, and Russia, and probably close to 70 percent in the Czech Republic. If under-reporting of private incomes is taken into account, these shares probably increase to over 60 percent and 75 percent respectively (Table 3.1). The share of the private sector in trade, construction, and small manufacturing and handicraft exceeded 80 percent in the subject European countries. In medium- and large-scale industry, however, the private share of sales and employment was still below 40 percent in Poland and Hungary, although thanks to voucher privatization, this share was about 70 percent in the Czech Republic and over 60 percent in Russia.

In China, the central government still owns about the same share of the economy as in Eastern Europe and Russia, but the "non-state" sector

TABLE 3.1   Contribution of the Non-State Sector* to GDP and Industry
             in the Five Countries *(circa January 1, 1995, in percent)*

	GDP	Industry**
Poland	60+	40–
Hungary	60+	40–
Czech Republic	75	70
Russia	60	60
China	67	55

*Non-State Sector includes private corporations, joint ventures, unincorporated enterprises, cooperatives, enterprises owned by non-profit organizations, and, in China, firms owned by villages, townships, other local governments, and provincial governments.

**Excludes handicraft and small industry, the definition of which varies from country to country.

Source: Estimates by the authors, based on a variety of sources.

consists mainly of locally-owned firms, cooperatives, joint ventures, and small-scale farms and handicraft that lease land and buildings; full-blown private enterprise is still small, but growing. Industry owned by the central government now produces less than half of industrial output. Yet no large state-owned firm has been privatized.

In Poland and Hungary, the actual transfer of assets from state to private ownership accounts for only a small fraction of the large expansion of the private sector. Although internationally comparable data on such transfers do not exist, the indications are clear. In Poland, for example, employment in privatized industrial firms, excluding handicraft, was only 14 percent of private industrial employment in mid-1994, clearly indicating that new private firms accounted for the bulk of the private sector's expansion. And in Hungary, state revenues from privatization during 1990-1993 were only about 20 percent of the book value of state assets.

Large privatization can be achieved in two ways: through sales to outsiders with substantial funds, which, more often than not, means foreigners; or by giving away, or selling at subsidized prices, the majority of ownership shares to company employees and other insiders or to the public. A third method, leasing, can be used in cases where insiders may eventually be able to raise the necessary funds, but currently lack the liquidity and the credit to buy a firm outright. Each privatization method has advantages and disadvantages, economically as well as politically; none can claim a clear advantage on all counts.

Which of these various methods a country will employ depends on a number of factors. If it follows policies that appeal to foreign investors, a small economy like Hungary can rely much more on foreign investment than a large economy like Russia. Also important is the strength of the political influence of the "insiders," such as the managers and workers in state enterprises. Leasing is a means of accommodating insiders who lack the funds for outright purchase.

In *Poland*, the number of state enterprises declined by over one third during 1992-1994, mainly as a result of privatization, but by late 1994, state-owned firms still accounted for some 60 percent of industrial employment and sales, excluding firms with five or fewer workers. Organized labor has played a uniquely important role in Polish privatization policy. Polish labor has a long tradition of activism and was the principal base of the Solidarity movement. When Communism collapsed, workers' councils had acquired control over many state enterprises. Moreover, Polish workers tended to view themselves as the natural heirs of the state in the ownership of enterprises, and many Solidarity intellectuals at first advocated worker ownership, along the lines of the former Yugoslav model. Although more liberal views prevailed, and labor ownership as a primary approach was rejected, successive post-Communist governments were forced to compromise with powerful labor interests. Leasing was widely used to enable workers to gain ownership of small and medium-sized enterprises. Workers were given an important say in whether and how enterprises were to be privatized, and representation on the managing boards of those that were. A substantial ownership share for labor was assured even for enterprises privatized through the sale of stocks and through voucher privatization.

The fragmentation of the Polish Parliament among liberal and social democratic, labor-oriented groups in 1992-1993, followed by a government dominated by the Left, caused long delays in passing privatization legislation. Although the basic privatization law came into effect in June 1990, a liberal foreign investment law was not passed for another year, and the "mass" (or voucher) privatization" law (in committee for over two years) was passed only in mid-1993—though as of early 1995 it still had not been implemented due to delaying tactics by the Peasant Party Prime Minister.

In *Hungary*, less than 40 percent of employment in large and medium-sized firms was in private hands by the end of 1994. The most important reason Hungarian privatization has been fairly slow was the centralization of the privatization process, which created many "political" bottlenecks and delays. This over-centralization came about in March, 1990, when the State Property Agency (SPA) was established and was given practically all state property to administer and privatize.

Initially, the SPA tried to decide which firms to offer for sale, invited tenders, negotiated with potential buyers, and made the actual sales decisions. These tasks were too onerous in scope and complexity for a fledgling state organization to manage effectively. In 1992 and 1993, procedures were adapted to permit more initiative from below. Hungary is unique among the subject countries in being able to rely heavily on foreign investors to finance privatization, with net FDI of over $3 billion from privatization alone ($5.5 billion overall) during 1990-1993. Hungary financed about two thirds of its large-scale privatization from foreign sources during 1991-1992. This made it seem unnecessary to undertake voucher privatization or to engage in leasing on a large scale. In 1993, however, the share of foreign investment declined to 30 percent, partly because the best buys had already been picked out. The Hungarian government began to facilitate sales to domestic buyers through low interest loans (3-4 percent), employee buy-outs, and management leasing arrangements. These programs had little success, however, and the subsidized loan program was de-emphasized by the new government during 1994-1995. FDI picked up in 1994, as the left-wing government succeeded in selling some large utility companies, but its policies have generally discouraged foreign investors.

Led by Vaclav Klaus, Prime Minister since 1991, the *Czech Republic* is unique in the political dominance of economic liberals. Unlike the relatively weak Polish and Hungarian governments, the Czech government has been able to move rapidly with a generally consistent set of policies and few compromises. The central objective of Czech privatization policy was to divest the government of as many assets and responsibilities as quickly as possible. This was the fundamental rationale for organizing a massive voucher privatization program, beginning in 1991, very early in the transition process. It was also believed that voucher privatization would help attract foreign investment, but this was clearly not a primary goal. The government decided very early not to try to restructure state enterprises, except in a very few industries, and to leave that task to the eventual private owners. Thanks mainly to voucher privatization, the second wave of which has just been completed, the Czech Republic has increased the share of industrial assets in private hands from practically zero in 1990 to over 70 percent at the end of 1994. This was not the only privatization method used, however: thousands of privatization plans were prepared (several for each enterprise), each plan specifying one of several privatization routes. Although voucher privatization was the dominant route, almost all other methods were used to some extent.

Russian privatization policies began to be implemented very early in the transition process, before economic stabilization could be achieved and reasonably efficient markets created. This haste clearly does not reflect a political consensus: rather it appears to be motivated by Yeltsin's desire to weaken the institutional opposition to market reforms and to build some public support by giving people a stake in enterprises. Russian privatization virtually gave away majority ownership shares to workers and managers, and part of the remainder to the population at large. The privatization process was open and public to avoid the appearance of special deals. On paper, it has succeeded in transferring the bulk of state industry to private owners. In practice, the government is continuing to exercise considerable economic power, by retaining full control of some industries of national importance, by holding "golden" (i.e. controlling shares) of enterprises, or by controlling strategically placed units.

The institutional framework of privatization varies somewhat among subject countries. Poland and the Czech Republic have Ministries of Privatization responsible for planning and approval of the privatization process. Hungary and Russia have established partially independent government units with similar functions (the SPA in Hungary and the State Committee on Property, or GKI, in Russia).

Initially, the SPA was subordinated directly to Parliament, but since July 1990 its Board of Directors and Chairman are appointed by the Prime Minister. The Czech Republic had also established a National Property Fund (NPF) to act as owner and manager of enterprises during the transition period when they were engaged in a clear, approved privatization process, which had not yet been completed. Russia's Federal Property Fund (FPF) appears to have similar functions. In Eastern Europe and Russia, local governments and local units of the privatization ministry managed the privatization of small enterprises.

The following sections discuss and assess the main privatization routes: restitution to former private owners; small-scale privatization; sale to outside investors, both domestic and foreign, through either public sale of shares or negotiated sale; sale mainly to insiders—managers and workers; and "mass" or "voucher" privatization, which may involve both insiders and the general public. The main characteristics of these privatization methods, except for restitution, are summarized in Table 3.2.

Privatization Through Restitution

This was an important issue for the CE-3 countries, and each has handled it differently. In the *Czech Republic*, former owners were given strict time limits to make their claims. But once these were approved, privatization could not proceed until after a restitution agreement had been reached. Many houses were given back to their former owners, who invested heavily in the property. Former owners of larger establishments, such as factories, were given either shares in these enterprises when they were privatized, or other forms of non-cash compensation, such as government bonds. Apparently, restitution claims have not held up privatization.

In *Poland*, restitution became such a thorny political issue that no restitution law has been passed. To provide for possible future restitution suits, the government has been setting aside a small percentage of privatization revenues. Some restitution has been done through informal arrangements.

TABLE 3.2 The Matrix of Privatization Policies of Poland, Hungary, the Czech Republic, and Russia

	Poland	Hungary	Czech Republic	Russia
"Small" privatization	Locally managed; completed; successful; leasing widely used	Locally managed; completed; successful; auctioning of businesses, leasing of land	Locally managed; completed; auctions only	Locally managed; not completed; auctions, tenders, and leases
Public sale of shares	Few selected firms; 20% to workers; stock market boom	Few selected firms; 20% to workers; stock market improved	Spinoff from voucher program; large scale and booming	Spinoff from voucher program; just beginning
Other outsider sales	Limited scale; big FDI deals growing	Dominant mode of privatization; 70% FDI; formally tenders	Limited scale, except big FDI	Limited to firms with fewer than 1,000 employees
Insider sales	Buy/lease arrangements for existing managers and workers common in medium-sized firms	No special provisions	No special provisions	Workers/managers can buy 40–51% of shares free or at big discount
Voucher privatization	In organization phase; shares owned by Investment Funds (IFs) organized by government; adults get vouchers to buy into IFs; IFs have controlling interest in firms	No general voucher program; recent (1993) program of interest-free loans to all adults to buy vouchers for 5–15% of assets of privatized firms	Dominant method of privatization, 75% of state assets in 2 waves; first wave completed; share prices in vouchers calculated at computerized auctions; more than 70% of adult population participates; 2/3 of vouchers entrusted to IFs, which will control most firms	Used for all firms with more than 1,000 employees; vouchers used by adult population to buy shares not purcased by insiders; program started small and has grown rapidly

In *Hungary*, compensation vouchers were issued to those with valid compensation claims. The vouchers can be exchanged for shares in designated companies during privatization; in the case of land, they can be exchanged only for land and only by former owners or their heirs. The vouchers can be freely traded on the stock market. But because the shares of SOEs that will be made available for the remaining compensation vouchers have not yet been established, the open market value of the vouchers has been steadily declining.

Small-Scale Privatization

Privatization of small retail shops, service establishments, handicraft shops, and small construction contractors was generally managed quickly and effectively because the process was decentralized to local governments and organizations and many shortcuts were used. Foreigners were generally excluded from small-scale privatization. Programs for small-scale privatization were initiated in some East European countries without special legislation and took only a few months to complete. Few statistics are available on small-scale privatization, except for those showing a very rapid increase in the number of small private businesses, which do not distinguish between entirely new businesses, privatized businesses, and those that were merely leased by private parties from state-owned firms.

Each country's small privatization has some unique characteristics. In the *Czech Republic*, the properties were sold entirely at auction to the highest cash bidder. Leasing was considered, but rejected, because it would continue to involve government. Bank credit was made available to buyers, but nearly on market terms. In order to expedite the process, no questions were asked about the source of the funds—e.g., whether coming from former black market operations, former "nomenklatura" positions, and so forth. In addition, the assets were sold without any debt obligations, which were purchased by the government with part of the sales proceeds when the former state enterprise was legally liquidated. The substantial profits from "small privatization" were transferred to the NPF, which later used them to issue special bonds to add to bank reserves. The Czech approach was the cleanest and most profitable to the government among all the small privatizations in East-Central Europe.

In *Poland*, a mixture of methods were used, including auctions, but also widespread lease-buy arrangements, under which private parties take on what amounts to a multi-year mortgage on the property, or a lease with option to buy. This approach was considered more equitable because it enabled thousands who had been working in shops and other small establishments to take them over quickly. "Small-scale privatization" was not limited to small enterprises: it also included private purchases or leases of parts of large state trade and service enterprises that were broken up by the government. "Small-scale privatization" in Poland was very success-ful—by early 1991, the bulk of retail trade, restaurants, and consumer services were in private hands.

In *Hungary*, auctions were widely used, but with preferential terms for workers and managers of a firm, including lease-buy arrangements and price reductions. Because ownership rights to real property, such as land and buildings, often could not be transferred, businesses were typically sold while the space on which they operated was leased. Only citizens were eligible to participate.

In *Russia*, small-scale privatization covers both small enterprises (with employment below 200 workers) and some medium-sized firms (with employment of between 200 and 1,000). Larger firms scheduled for privatization must all become corporatized, and most of them have had to participate in the voucher program. Most sales took the form of auctions, but tenders were also used. Employees received price discounts and ex-tended payment terms and also were given leases with options to buy. In most cases employee groups were the buyers, although they sometimes acted as agents for private investors seeking concessionary terms. Progress under the program was uneven, depending greatly on the attitudes of local and regional governments. In some cities and areas, like Nizhnii Novgorod and Riazan Province, this process appears to have gone nearly as far as in the Central European countries, while in other locations, like Primorskii Krai and Ul'ianovskaia province, little was done. Overall, perhaps 70 percent of "small" enterprises had been privatized by July 1994, predomi-nantly in retail trade, restaurants and consumer services.

Sales to Outsiders

There are three basic ways to sell state-owned firms to private investors from outside the firm: public sale of shares, competitive bidding (auction or tenders), and negotiated sale to a particular buyer. In most, but not all, cases, state enterprises are first corporatized before being sold. Pure auctions are rarely used for large enterprises because other conditions besides the offering price—maintaining specified employment levels for a period of time, retraining workers, undertaking specified investments, undertaking environmental cleanup—are important. The distinction between tenders, negotiated sale, and issue of shares becomes blurred when only one bid is received or when an investor group wants to negotiate a purchase.

Among the subject countries, Hungary has relied most heavily on sales to outsiders because it was able to attract a large volume of foreign investments. In the Czech Republic and Russia, reliance on massive pro-grams of voucher privatization greatly limited the use of other outsider sales. In Poland, the issue of shares is the principal method of outsider sales, but the shares may be sold privately to "active investors."

The main problem with sales to outsiders has been the generally long delay—usually more than a year—between the initial approach and completion of the sale. During this time, the insiders, management and labor, are very uncertain about their future and are, therefore, prepared to take advantage of any short-term opportunities that may arise to increase their incomes, even at the expense of the long-term viability of the enterprise. In this inter-regnum, it is, therefore, important for the future owners to communicate effectively with current management and the workers so as to dispel unwarranted concerns and explain planned changes.

Public Issue of Shares. This was initially the preferred approach in Poland and, for a few large firms, also in Hungary because it was open and public, and therefore least subject to political criticism. Another advantage was that public issue of shares made it possible to develop domestic stock markets that could become important means of intermediating savings and investment. This method, however, is expensive and time consuming. First, the firm must be transformed into a state corporation. Then the firm's assets must be valued by outside experts, which, given the lack of domestic expertise, generally means expensive Western accounting firms. Third, a prospectus must be published. And finally, shares can be offered for sale. Each step requires approval from the Ministry of Privatization, or the equivalent organization. In Poland, the entire process takes 12-18 months. Another limitation is selectivity: in order to build public confidence in this form of privatization, some of the most profitable and best regarded firms were selected first. Thus, only some 30 enterprises in Poland and a similar number in Hungary were fully privatized through this method. In Russia, public sale of shares was used only as an adjunct to the voucher program.

Shares offered through public sale have been purchased by both domestic and foreign investors. In Poland and the Czech Republic, about half of the value of shares were purchased by foreigners. To make this method palatable to the workers' movement, Poland made 20 percent of the shares floated by an enterprise available to its workers at one half of the initial market price. It would appear, however, that many Polish workers did not take advantage of this option.

Competitive Bidding. In practice, foreign investors are most often the only outsiders with access to sufficient funds to purchase large firms outright. That is why this method has rarely been used outside Hungary. In the Czech Republic, public tender or public auction accounted for only 3 percent of the total property included under the first wave of privatization. In Poland, this method was not formally used. In Russia, its use was limited to small and medium-sized enterprises, the larger ones being covered by the voucher privatization program.

In Hungary, the sale of state enterprises legally requires competitive public tenders. The SPA must make a serious attempt to find more than one competitive offer. This choice is supposed to be made solely on the basis of business considerations, but politics is known to have been a factor. Enterprises to be sold are first corporatized. Then, after determining that the firm is ready to be sold—i.e., that no legal or financial obligations exist that might legally prevent the sale—the SPA negotiates the sale. During 1990-1991, the SPA initiated most sales, and searched for possible competing bids.

Beginning in 1992, a quicker, simplified procedure, in which the enterprise itself takes the initiative, was increasingly used for medium-sized and some large enterprises. Under such "self-privatization," the enterprise selects one of the SPA-approved consulting firms, which organizes and conducts the corporatization and the sale. The consulting firm enters into a contract with the SPA and acts as its agent. Because the consultants are paid when the company is sold, they have an incentive to expedite the process, but not to extract the highest price from the buyer. If the specified procedures are followed, the approval of the SPA is practically automatic.

Negotiated Sale. Negotiated sale to a particular buyer is the most politically sensitive method of privatization because of its potential for corruption. This method is illegal in Russia for large enterprises under the privatization program. In the Czech Republic, negotiated sales have to be approved by the Council of Ministers: they accounted for about 5 percent of the property sold in the first wave of privatization. In Poland, negotiated sale occurs by selling shares to "active investors." In Hungary, its use is limited to tenders in which only a single bidder can be found, even after a determined search.

In practice, sales of very large enterprises have to be negotiated because they require special conditions. For example, the sale of the Polish FSM automobile enterprise to FIAT provided for reserving a specified share of the Polish automobile export quota to the European Community for FSM/FIAT cars. Such negotiations are complicated, lengthy, and politically difficult. They are generally followed closely in the press.

Sale to Insiders

The first substantial privatizations in Poland and Hungary, were sales to existing managers of state enterprises and Communist Party officials during 1988-1989, when the Communist regimes were in retreat but post-Communist governments had not yet been formed and privatization policies had not yet been formulated. Enterprising individuals who controlled assets positioned themselves for a market-oriented economy by transforming profitable sections of state enterprises into private corporations, with a controlling position for themselves on the corporate board. This process, which came to be called "Spontaneous Privatization" in Hungary and Russia, and "Informal Privatization" in Poland, was widely viewed as involving an abuse of power by officials of the old regime and triggered a strong popular backlash after the political revolutions. This backlash led to a centralization of the privatization process in Poland and Hungary under legislation passed in 1990.

This centralization initially limited privatization in Hungary mainly to foreign sales. In Poland, however, the government had to accommodate workers' interests so that a compromise was reached—the process would continue to be controlled by the Ministry of Privatization, but workers and managers could take initiatives to take over their firm, would be given easy terms, and could use much simplified, faster procedures. Hungary took some similar steps in 1993, when privatization was slowing. Russia has also encouraged insider privatization, or at least provided for a major role for insiders in the voucher privatization program. In Poland and Russia, the consent of the workers is required for any form of privatization to occur.

The principal Polish program for sale of state enterprises to insiders is the so-called "privatization through liquidation under the privatization law," which applies to profitable enterprises. Between August 1990 and mid-1994, 933 Polish enterprises were put into the privatization process under this law and 842 were actually liquidated. All but a few of these enterprises were small and medium-sized. In contrast to privatization through sale of shares, "liquidation" of profitable enterprises took only a few months.

The bulk of the assets of enterprises privatized in this manner were leased by groups of workers and managers, with option to buy. Typically, the lease/buy contract required a 20 percent down payment, with the remainder paid over ten years at a moderate interest rate. Many newly leased firms have had financial difficulties because they found the lease payment burdensome. The terms have recently been liberalized. When a firm's workers acquire majority ownership, it is most often the manager who takes the initiative, persuades the workers to go along, and effectively runs the new firm.

There is both negative and positive evidence on the impact of insider takeovers. On the one hand, insiders have incentives to decapitalize firms so that they can take them over at low prices. On the other hand, once they become convinced that a viable long-term program under their control would improve their job and income prospects, they have clear incentives to support such a program. In Russia, workers were given the right to acquire a majority share of most state enterprises at a nominal price or through the use of vouchers, but managers have generally maintained effective control. Completion of the voucher program will increase the role of outsiders, especially investment funds, but this has not yet occurred.

Mass or Voucher Privatization

As mentioned earlier, the large-scale distribution of vouchers to the population free of charge, or for a nominal sum, is designed to give citizens a major share of large enterprises despite their lack of substantial capital. By the same token, this approach brings very little revenue into the national treasury. A potential weakness of voucher privatization is that the ownership of shares could become too dispersed for effective governance, or that control could be gained by some small group interested mainly in speculative profits. Indeed, there are evident conflicts between the objective of encouraging controlling investors with a long-term perspective and that of discouraging easy takeovers by speculators. The pros and cons of voucher privatization have been debated in all the subject countries. Two of them, the Czech Republic and Russia, established and implemented such a program. Poland is on the verge of starting its program. Hungary so far has rejected this approach, although in 1993 it introduced a smaller scale loan program, which was discontinued in 1994, under which Hungarian adult citizens could obtain shares in privatized enterprises with three-year, interest-free loans.

The Czech Republic. Czechoslovakia was the first country to undertake voucher privatization. As was mentioned, this was not the only route chosen for privatization. After small-scale privatization had been completed, each large state enterprise, except for those in certain designated industries, such as coal, steel, and public utilities, was required to submit at least one privatization plan. The basic plan was prepared by enterprise management, but competing plans from other insiders and potential outside investors were also solicited. To the surprise of the government, there were on the average four plans submitted per enterprise, although many of the competing plans involved only a part of the enterprise. Privatization plans could recommend not only voucher privatization, but also direct sale through various methods, as well as the giving away of assets. After review and recommendations by the responsible line ministry, the Ministry of Privatization decided among competing plans, with priority generally given to voucher privatization. Once the privatization plan had been approved, the enterprise became a state corporation controlled by the NPF.

Czech voucher privatization was divided into two waves. The first wave, in which about one half of large state enterprises throughout Czechoslovakia were included, was completed in 1993. The second wave, limited to the Czech Republic, was completed late in 1994. At the end of the second wave, only enterprises in selected sectors comprising some 20-25 percent of industry, will remain under state ownership.

The procedure is to first make vouchers available at nominal prices to all adult citizens. These can then either purchase company shares with the vouchers or entrust their vouchers to investment funds, who make the decisions for them. All companies participating in the program are transformed into corporations and issue shares, which are first valued at the original cost of the firms' assets. The aggregate initial value of the company shares, divided by the number of vouchers purchased by the population, establishes the initial value of each voucher, which is expressed in terms of "voucher points." Share prices are then raised or lowered in terms of voucher points in a series of computerized auctions until all the vouchers have been traded for shares.

The auctions were run efficiently on a country-wide basis, with over 70 percent of the eligible population participating. Investment funds played a much more important role than anticipated. During the two waves, they took control of over 60 percent of all shares. Many have a controlling interest in several firms, and others are cooperating to gain a controlling interest. Nine of the ten largest investment funds are owned by banks, and some banks have established investment companies that own several funds.

Poland. At the end of 1994, it seemed likely that Poland would finally begin to implement its "mass privatization" program, after nearly four years of failures and delays due to political opposition. The Polish program differs from the Czech program in three major ways. First, it places all firms in the program under the control of a small number (fewer than 20) of investment funds. Second, all adult citizens can buy vouchers for a nominal price, but can use them only to buy shares in the investment funds. Third, workers in companies undergoing "mass privatization" are guaranteed 19 percent of the shares and are represented on the supervisory boards of the privatized companies.

The program was designed to provide for patient ownership during the restructuring period. Each investment fund is given a controlling interest in a group of enterprises from the start, with other shares being distributed among the other funds. The fund directors are Polish citizens named by the President, but each fund contracts with Western companies to actually manage their accounts. The contracts are let under competitive bidding. Once the shares have been distributed among the funds, and the vouchers among the public, the funds will be able to trade their shares freely on the stock exchange and their own shares will also be traded.

Russia. The Russian voucher privatization program is a mix of insider sale and public distribution. First, Russian state enterprises undergoing privatization are corporatized, as in the Czech Republic. But the Russian program differs from the Czech one in several basic ways. First, it was a developing, not a clearly set, program, having started with a small number of firms and then rapidly expanded, rather than involving an massive group of firms simultaneously. Second, vouchers were distributed to the population free of charge and are marketable. Third, the majority of shares in most enterprises were sold to workers and managers (for cash or vouchers) before public bidding of vouchers and cash began.

Each enterprise under the program selected one of three options for insider participation. In the first option, selected by about one-fourth of the firms, workers receive 25 percent of the shares free of charge with an option to buy another 10 percent at a 30 percent discount, while managers may purchase another 5 percent. In the second option, chosen by nearly three-fourths of enterprises, employees may purchase 51 percent of the shares at 1.7 times book value. A third option, chosen by only 2 percent, is limited to firms of fewer than 200 employees. Only after these options have been exercised by workers and managers are shares offered for public sale.

Russian privatization under this program progressed very rapidly, with over 60 percent of industry having been formally privatized by the end of voucher privatization in June 1994. It is as yet unclear, however, who will exercise effective control of the privatized firms. Investment funds are permitted to buy shares. Over 600 of these have been formed and they hold some 23 percent of the vouchers. Presumably because of concern about possible fraud and to assure diversification, however, significant restrictions were imposed on the activities of the investment funds, including a prohibition against owning more than 10 percent of any enterprise, and investing more than 5 percent of their capital in a single enterprise (in the Czech Republic, these limits are 20 percent and 10 percent respectively). Unlike the Czech and future Polish funds, moreover, the Russian funds appear to be generally small, with little access to capital. With the investment funds still weak and constrained, foreign capital almost nonexistent, and the workforce of most enterprises owning a majority or a large minority of shares, it is likely that insiders will dominate Russian privatized enterprises in the foreseeable future. In practice, this almost certainly means that existing management will have its way, once it has made mutually satisfactory deals with the workers. So far, most Russian enterprises have not had to make very painful changes. What happens to management-worker cooperation if and when they do remains to be seen.

As mentioned earlier, the Russian government has kept a very important part of industry out of the privatization program for at least three years. This includes military plants, the entire energy industry, most raw materials, public utilities and some very large enterprises.

Assessment of Privatization Programs

Though "small-scale" privatization was successful in all the East European subject countries and in those Russian cities where it was supported by the government, the performance and prospects of large scale privatization are mixed. With regard to performance, available data are largely limited to the number, assets, and employment of firms under each program and the speed of implementation. There are also some data on profit rates, but these reflect the selection of firms for various privatization methods rather than the impact of these methods on post-privatization performance. Some interesting insights can be obtained from recent enterprise surveys and from expert opinion. With regard to prospects, a close examination of the various privatization methods reveals some major differences in the extent to which they satisfy the main criteria set forth in Chapter 1.

Speed and Extent. By far the fastest method of privatizing a large part of state industry is through voucher privatization. The Czech Republic and possibly Russia will have privatized a larger share of state industry in a year or two by using mainly this method than Poland and Hungary have privatized over four years, using other methods. The next fastest method of privatization is lease/purchase arrangements with insiders, but limited capital resources largely exclude the larger firms from such arrangements, unless the lease/purchase terms are highly concessionary, in which case they resemble voucher privatization. Sale to outsiders is severely constrained by domestic capital resources, and the process takes a long time. Hungary did well for the first two years by relying largely on foreign direct investment, but this is not a practical option for Russia.

Incentives. All forms of privatization create at least some incentive for restructuring and otherwise improving enterprises, although they vary with regard to the likely time perspective of the potential owners. Sale to outsiders is most likely to result in "real owners" who will work to increase the value of the enterprises. In Hungary and Poland, there is considerable evidence that enterprises privatized by this method underwent substantial changes after completing the process. Sale to insiders can also bring about major improvements if managers have the appropriate skills and can persuade employees of the necessity for such changes and of the potential benefits to them as owners.

Voucher privatization should also develop incentives for improving the enterprise where owners with effective control emerge, as in the Czech Republic. Czech investment funds began to play a major role in the supervisory boards of the enterprises under their future control, even before they had become full legal owners. Where ownership is dispersed and control remains with enterprise management, as is most often the case in Russia, incentives for change tend to be weak. Voucher privatization is an intermediate step: By itself it does not create "real owners," but it establishes mechanisms to this end.

Access to Capital. Only two forms of privatization appear to substantially increase the access of the enterprises to capital for restructuring and other investments with which transformation plans could be implemented. One of these is sale to foreign buyers, although the willingness of foreign owners to invest will depend on economic conditions and prospects. The other is ownership and control by large financial intermediaries as a result of voucher privatization. The larger Czech, but so far not the Russian, investment funds appear able to raise capital for investment in the firms they have acquired. The fact that most are owned by banks will help. The

Polish funds should also be capable of funding long-term restructuring programs. Insider privatization, however, is clearly not a good way to raise capital for restructuring—indeed, it may divert available funds into purchasing the firm. It is consequently likely to be effective mainly for relatively small, labor intensive firms that do not need much new capital to restructure. Public sale of shares may eventually enable some enterprises to finance new investments. In time, domestic, as well as foreign capitalists will be major sources of investment, if stable economic conditions exist.

Cooperation. In the transition economies, the powerful role of insider stakeholders has to be taken into account in privatization policies. Their cooperation is essential, even where outside parties become controlling owners. A great deal depends on the degree of uncertainty about the future role of insiders in the enterprise. Where this role is highly uncertain, insiders are likely to take a short-term perspective in which to maximize their incomes. But to the extent this role is clarified, insiders can gain incentives to cooperate with long-term transformation programs.

The record of insider cooperation with privatization through sale to outsiders is generally poor. First, there is a great deal of uncertainty during the many months of preparation for public sale of shares or negotiation for direct sale. Second, in the case of direct sale to foreigners, serious misunderstandings sometimes arise between the plans and commitments of the investor and the expectations of the workers. Several foreign investments in Hungary have run into difficulty because of resistance from the workers and disappointed expectations.

Sale to insiders places the burden of cooperation on relations between labor and management. In Poland, managers of many medium-sized firms apparently were able to work cooperatively with the employee organizations in planning and implementing restructuring programs. This is more difficult in large, bureaucratically complex, firms. Workers have even accepted large layoffs and other painful changes where they had become convinced that the alternatives were worse. In Russia, where many enterprises still do not face a convincingly hard budget constraint, management so far has been able to avoid hard decisions.

Owner-insider cooperation under voucher privatization has apparently been increasing in the Czech Republic and is showing some early favorable signs in Poland. In the Czech Republic, there were many early reports of asset stripping by managers in enterprises to be privatized, but apparently communication between managers and investment funds have been developing, leading to some cooperation. In Poland, managers of firms included in the "mass privatization" program are said to have already begun discussions with the investment funds and to feel fairly comfortable in their role.

Policy Credibility. Even the best designed privatization program will have little success if government policies are too unstable and are not implemented consistently enough to be credible. In this respect there is a huge difference between Czech and Russian privatization policies. In the Czech Republic, the objectives and general direction of these policies were clear from the start, although tactical policy adjustments were made—for example, accommodating a greater than expected role for investment funds. Voucher privatization was generally viewed as being fair and efficient, and there were few indications of serious fraud and corruption, even though securities regulation was slow to develop. In Russia, privatization policies varied from time to time, region to region, and even city to city. Despite a general policy of making the privatization of all large firms an open, public process, markets for shares were in fact highly segmented, often with limited access, thus creating vast opportunities for corruption. In 1994, moreover, calls by Russian politicians for reversing some privatizations have further undermined policy credibility.

In Poland, privatization policies have changed often, but more in detail than in general design. In Hungary they have been floundering and, with the interest of foreign investors apt to wane, future trends are uncertain.

Overall, despite the fact that all of the methods of privatization have disadvantages, the one that best meets all of the criteria for potential success is the Czech voucher privatization program. Sale of firms to foreigners in Hungary met most of these criteria, but, since the foreigners are willing to pick up only the most promising firms or those in which they have a long-term strategic interest, this leaves the bulk of state industry to be privatized by other means, including by a voucher program that is not now envisaged, or not at all. Poland also needs to get its long-delayed voucher privatization started, although foreign sales are increasing. Russia's privatization has been exceptionally rapid, although very messy and ridden with corruption. Even with most Russian firms formally "privatized," actual control in most cases is still in the hands of old line managers and/or the state.

In the long run, the key test of privatization methods will be their impact on corporate governance. The main benefits of voucher privatization stem from the fact that it forces many decisions that might otherwise be avoided or postponed and creates mechanisms that spur restructuring. Although the Czech and Russian voucher programs were completed only at the end of 1994, there are already signs of increased concentration of ownership away from passive individual and institutional investors, who initially benefitted from the distribution of vouchers at nominal prices, and toward active investors interested in improving the performance of firms through better management and restructuring. Active investors can include not only some of the investment funds and banks, but also, to an increasing extent, foreign investors and domestic capitalists, who have become quite wealthy by taking advantage of arbitrage and other opportunities during the early years of the transition.

Managing and Restructuring Remaining State Enterprises

Principal Issues

Even after several years of rapid private or non-state sector development and, in the subject European countries, intensive privatization efforts, 20 to 60 percent of large-scale industry in the subject countries is still state-owned. State ownership continues to predominate in fuels and power, raw materials, capital-intensive basic industries, such as steel and basic chemicals, and some finished products industries, such as military production. Moreover, many of the largest firms in all the countries remain state-owned. While many state-owned firms are slated for eventual privatization, especially in Poland and Hungary, where voucher privatization programs have not occurred, other state firms, and some entire industries, are to remain under state control for the foreseeable future.

In general, the remaining state firms face serious financial difficulties, even in China, where rapid economic growth has brought an increasing demand for the products of state-owned enterprises (SOEs). The profitability of state industry has been declining, and has been lower than in private industry in all the subject countries. The reasons for this are: first, that the most profitable firms have been privatized, except in China; second, that some major products of state industry, such as coal and oil, are still under price controls in Russia and China; third, that state-owned firms are often more heavily taxed, in part because they are less able than private firms to evade taxes; and finally, that these firms have rarely made fundamental structural adjustments because of weak incentives and lack of funds.

In the CE-3 countries and Russia, state-owned firms often lost a large part of their former markets and are producing far below capacity. Polish state-owned firms are barely profitable in the aggregate and most of those likely to remain after "mass privatization" (which is limited to profitable firms), is finally achieved, almost certainly will be unprofitable. In Hungary, most of the firms under the control of the State Holding Company (SHC), which was established to manage state firms not scheduled for privatization, are losing money. Even in China, 44 percent of state-owned, centrally controlled firms incurred losses during the first nine months of 1994, up from one third in 1993.[8] The declining profitability of Chinese state firms appears to be due both to increased competition from regionally and locally controlled firms and private firms and to the fact that the freeing of many prices in 1993 raised costs more than revenues for many state firms.

All the subject countries, including China, are beginning to mount major efforts to transform the remaining state-owned industrial firms. In the CE-3 countries and Russia, distinctions are beginning to be made between firms that should be privatized, but first need to be restructured and those that will remain under state ownership in the long-term. As of the end of 1994, Russia was only just beginning to deal with the management of firms that are to remain state-owned. China is still not contemplating privatization or liquidation of large state firms, but has introduced numerous approaches to improving their performance.

Most countries have transformed, or are transforming, all remaining state enterprises into corporations in which the state holds a controlling interest, but other parties may also participate as owners. The purpose of "corporatization" is to separate ownership from management and to create legal shares that can be transferred. Banks are acquiring ownership of nearly bankrupt firms through debt/equity swaps. Holding companies are being formed to combine government control over critical functions with decentralized operations.

Various incentive systems for management to undertake restructuring are being tried. These range from traditional, multi-goal contracts to management compensation in the form of company shares. Other major efforts include (except in China), the liquidation of entire firms, as well as the liquidation of sections of many firms. In some other industries, such as electric power, coal and steel, and very large firms, long-term restructuring plans are being implemented under government supervision.

Policies to deal with state-owned firms are characterized in Table 3.3 for all the subject countries. The following sections provide more detail on: the role of industrial policy; the attempts to separate ownership from management; the use of innovative managerial incentives for restructuring; the liquidation of unviable firms; and the planning and control of industries remaining under long-term state ownership. The final section provides an assessment of these policies.

Industrial Policy

Although, taken together, the kinds of policies listed above constitute implicitly a far-reaching "industrial policy," some of the subject countries claim not to have one. The very term "industrial policy" is anathema to the ideologically liberal Czech government, is avoided in Hungary, and was rejected in Poland until 1992. In principle, the only industrial policy in these countries was privatization until it became evident that large economic sectors would continue to require state resources and policy attention.

There are three broad approaches to industrial policy. From the least to the most interventionist, they are: creating a "framework," allocating resources according to some strategic concept, and "picking winners and losers." Most countries have elements of all three, and from time to time the emphasis may change, as was the case in Hungary during 1990-1993.

During 1990-1991, the "framework" approach prevailed in Hungary. The Ministry of Industry and Trade confined itself to defining a broad

TABLE 3.3 **Policies of Dealing with the Remaining State Enterprises in Poland, Hungary, the Czech Republic, China, and Russia**

	Poland	_Hungary_
Industrial policy	Not explicit until recently; now planned restructuring of some industries and very large firms	Has been shifting from very general to picking winners
Corporatization	Mainly a step toward privatization; otherwise motivated mainly by tax advantages	Becoming universal for large, state-owned firms; state corporations not being privatized are "owned" but not directed by single central organ
Management contracts	Limited use of management groups (incl. foreign ones) to restructure state firms; incentives from payment in shares	Not used in past; now considering contracts with investment stake and payment in shares
Liquidation	Fairly common for small and mid-sized firms; managed by branch Ministries; no time limit; new, smaller firms generally created after negotiated amounts paid to creditors	Common, except for very large firms; results from strict application of bankruptcy law since 11/92; clear rules and time limits; creditors in command; disruptive
Specific industries	Coal, steel, utilities, arms, very large firms still under Ministry control; restructuring plans; new organizational methods (i.e., holding cos.) being tried	Steel, utilities, arms, very large firms under single state organ; plans not yet developed

strategy for industrial development, carefully avoiding the suggestion of any kind of intervention. The document on industrial policy it published in 1991 devoted hardly any space to defining its tools: much of the document focused rather on what industrial policy should not do.

In 1992, as the situation of the state enterprises worsened, the Ministry of Industry and Trade switched to crisis management, and began to emphasize the importance of directing resources to well-defined ends. Its 1992 policy document stressed the experiences of the European Community countries and the desirability of developing similar types of policies in Hungary. However, the Ministry had practically no resources to dispose of to assist the restructuring of firms. Its role was mainly that of mediating between management, the commercial banks, and the Ministry of Finance.

During 1993, the picking winners and losers approach began to be applied in a limited way. The government identified 13 very large state enterprises (e.g., IKARUS, RABA, Pet Nitrogen Works), most suffering from the collapse of their traditional CMEA markets, but considered of

(Table 3.3 continued)

Czech Republic	China	Russia
Limited to 25% of industry; rest being privatized	Widespread use of credit and foreign exchange concessions; both central and regional government active	In flux; fuel, raw material, military, and most basic industries state-controlled; subsidized credit continues
Mainly a step toward privatization; status of remaining state firms being worked out	Increasingly used to give outside stakeholders part ownership of large firms; creates more flexibility	Required for large firms; methods of corporate governance not yet developed
Not used	Used widely earlier as alternative to directive planning; become simpler as markets develop	Not used yet
Tough bankruptcy law not applied until 6/93; will be used mainly for privatized firms	Bankruptcy law not applied to state-owned firms; some assets, but not entire firms, can be liquidated	Bankruptcy law on the books, but not yet applied
Coal, steel, utilities, arms, very large firms under state control for five years; plans and methods (i.e., holding cos.) being developed	Many industries still state-controlled; experimenting with new forms	Many industries still state-controlled; planning and new methods still at early stage of development

strategic importance. They are being assisted through special financial packages comprised of state credit guarantees, debt-equity swaps, and support schemes for the payment of interest.

In 1991 Poland began to undertake in-depth assessments of policy needs and options in a large number of specific sectors. About 30 so-called "sectoral" studies on specific industries like telecommunications, coal, electric power, iron and steel, shipbuilding, tractors, machine tools, cement, textiles, and beer, were contracted out, mainly to foreign companies. The studies analyzed the structure of the industry, the competitive position of its producers, domestic market and export possibilities and how these would be affected by alternative policies, such as reorganizations, export promotion, import protection, and foreign assistance.

In principle, such studies could have been used as a basis for developing coherent industrial policies. In fact, most of them died in ministerial files, either because the government did not want an integrated policy on a particular sector, or simply because the various bureaucracies with an interest in the sector were unable to agree. In time, such studies were used in telecommunications, coal, steel, petroleum and tractors, but at least two years were lost. Special studies were also produced for some very large enterprises, and restructuring plans are beginning to be implemented for a few of them. Some direct state subsidies, mainly in the form of subsidized investment credits, are going to state-owned firms being restructured under the supervision of special departments of the banks and subject to specific conditions.

In Russia, industrial policy is still in flux, but is likely to emerge as strongly interventionist, in view of the large size of the military-industrial complex and the fuel and raw material industries still under state control. The principal instruments of Russian industrial policy during the first two years of the reforms were the allocation of subsidized credits and imports and tax preferences.

Corporatization

The view that separating the ownership function from the management function of a state-owned firm could break the pattern of bureaucratic control and open the way to creative restructuring is widely held. In legal terms, this has been achieved by transforming state enterprises, which are in effect subordinate units of state administration, into state corporations (under various names), which issue shares and are governed by boards that represent the owners. All of the subject countries have introduced "corporatization," but not to the same extent. Hungary corporatized all the remaining state enterprises by year-end 1993; the Czech Republic corporatized some 80 percent of large firms in connection with privatization, but some firms left out of privatization programs retain enterprise status; Russia also corporatized the great bulk of its large firms as a step in its voucher privatization program; but Poland did not decide to corporatize state firms until 1994 and most of them still have enterprise status.

The impact of corporatization depends on how the ownership function is exercised and by whom, and on how the management function is changed. Where ownership still resides in a government bureaucracy, its impact depends on the power of the bureaucratic organization in relation to the firm's management. In some cases, the government organization which owns the shares, although incapable of providing much policy leadership, is jealous of its authority, which it uses to constrain management from doing much, as the SPA does in Hungary.

In other cases, as in Poland, an inactive central bureaucracy leaves effective control in the hands of the firm's insiders, with management generally having the upper hand. But, since the insiders do not have a clear long-term stake in the firm, they are more likely to try increasing their current income than to undertake long-term restructuring. On the other hand, corporatization can create opportunities to involve parties with a long-term interest in a firm's management, even where the central government continues to exercise majority control. So far at least, the experience of Poland and Hungary with corporatization has been largely negative, while that of China seems more promising. All the subject countries are experimenting with more flexible forms of control over "corporatized" firms, including holding companies, joint ventures, and "golden shares."

Poland. The basic problem with the Polish approach to corporatization is that the government was never able to decide whether it should be treated only as a step in the privatization process, or whether it should be exploited as an instrument for transforming the remaining state enterprises. Under Polish laws and regulations, the workers' council was disbanded when a state enterprise became a corporation, which potentially strengthened management at the expense of the workers. On the other hand, corporatization eliminated the "dividend tax" on the firm's fixed assets and reduced the tax on wage increases. According to Polish surveys, the main motive for corporatization at the initiative of the managers and workers was to more easily raise wages. The surveys also show that the corporatized firms made few, if any long-term improvements, unlike firms that were corporatized solely as a step to privatization.

As of mid-1994, most large Polish firms under state ownership still had the status of enterprises, employing over a million people. The left-wing government, however, made corporatization one of its main policy objectives, instead of treating it mainly as a step in the privatization process. State enterprise workers may now choose to corporatize without also being privatized, but must then submit a restructuring plan for approval.

Hungary. Unlike Poland, Hungary gradually transformed all state-owned firms into state corporations between 1988 and 1993. Controlling shares of the state corporations were given to the SPA, while the line industrial ministries were abolished. In 1992, as privatization slowed, a decision was made on a list of firms that would remain under complete or partial state control indefinitely. The SHC was established, and the shares of firms in such industries as public utilities, iron and steel, and military production, as well as those of very large companies, were transferred from the SPA to the SHC. The latter, however, will sell part of its shares to private parties. In mid-1995, the SPA and the SHC were merged into a new organization, the State Privatization and Holding Company (SPHC).

Corporatization in Hungary is widely viewed as having contributed little to the transformation of state firms. The state agencies are too bureaucratic and lacking in expertise, to be effective owners. State-owned firms have been run by their managers, but in an environment of great uncertainty (detailed in Chapter 6). As in Poland, a policy context for integrating the ownership with the management of state firms has been lacking.

Russia. Nearly all large state industrial enterprises have been corporatized. This was an essential preliminary step in the voucher privatization program. For firms remaining under state ownership, corporatization will facilitate the introduction of more flexible systems of ownership and control, such as holding companies and the use of "golden shares" that give the government effective control of firms that have marketed their shares widely.

China. China has been cautious, but creative in its use of corporatization. Although China established a Management Bureau of State Properties (MBSP), apparently along the lines of the Hungarian SPA, to hold shares of corporatized firms and represent the state, it has sought to diversify ownership widely. In effect, the "shareholder system" is becoming an ideologically acceptable substitute for privatization.

The "shareholder system" began to be used in the mid-1980s on an experimental basis, mostly in the coastal cities and SEZs. By the end of 1990, more than 3,000 firms had adopted this system, but most of these were non-state companies, in which local governments, other companies in China, and foreign companies held shares. Beginning in the late 1980s, firms whose shareholders were companies in different provinces of China with a mutual interest in cooperative ventures were developed.

Since 1991, the "shareholder system" has been used increasingly as a means of modernizing large, centrally controlled firms. Shareholders include not only the MBSP, but also domestic firms that are suppliers, customers, or partners, foreign firms, trading companies, and banks. In some cases, private parties can gain effective control by owning a minority of shares. Consequently, the Board of Directors represents organizations with a variety of real interests. In effect, corporatization in China involves a real change in the nature of corporate governance. It retains the government's power to intervene in and to guide policy, while substituting market-driven ownership incentives for bureaucratic ones.

Management Contracts

Perhaps the most difficult aspect of transforming state-owned firms is to create incentives for the managements to undertake long-term improvements and restructuring. Under the uncertain conditions of the transition, there are strong incentives for management and labor to maximize short-term income. The only way to substantially extend their time horizon is to give them an important stake in the financial outcome of transformation efforts. But the problem is that financial outcomes are difficult to measure or assess where capital markets are undeveloped and, consequently, the market value of a firm cannot be readily determined. Corporatization can help if shares are marketed publicly, but in thin stock markets, share prices by themselves may be poor indicators of success or failure.

China and, to a lesser extent, Poland, have used management contracts as restructuring tools. Hungary is beginning to consider a contract approach. Given the market limitations, there is obviously no single, best approach. Yet some approaches probably have had favorable effects.

China. China began to introduce a contract system of "management responsibilities" (CMR) in the mid-1980's and had extended it to nearly all large and medium-scale state enterprises by the end of 1988. Essentially, the CMR defined the rights and obligations of enterprises and tried to substitute multi-year contracts for detailed annual plans. Contracts specified production, some parameters of operational efficiency, profits, taxes, capital investment, and the use of retained profits. They generally covered periods of more than three years.

The CMR was an improvement over the previous system of annual plans. It gave enterprises stronger incentives to raise profits and cut costs. An increasing share of workers were hired under employment contracts that provided piece work or other incentive pay instead of the traditional "iron rice bowl" in which pay was only weakly linked to either skills or effort. Large enterprises under CMR also made organizational improvements by creating partly autonomous profit centers. On the other hand, the multiplicity of contract terms made it likely that inconsistencies would arise and ensured that enterprise management would artificially distort its priorities to assure contract fulfillment. At the same time, managers engaged in continuous bargaining with higher authority to obtain better contract terms. And even the multi-year contract period is likely to be too short for basic restructuring, especially when contract terms are likely to be modified even more often. These deficiencies were also apparent in Hungarian and Polish attempts at "parameter planning."

With the rapid expansion of free markets and the much restricted role of government price controls and product allocations, however, China has been introducing much simpler contracts. For some very large firms, contract obligations are limited to some overall multi-year profit goals—achievement of the goals is left entirely up to the enterprise, with no government interference. Other state firms can contract to take on most of the privileges and obligations of foreign joint ventures, including tax breaks and retention privileges for foreign exchange, but also the absence of subsidies in any form. And loss-making enterprises can contract for continued subsidies on a declining scale, on condition that an approved restructuring plan be implemented.

Poland. In Poland, industrial ministries have used management contracts to a limited extent to promote the transformation of state enterprises. Unlike those in China, the Polish contracts give management control to a new, outside management group, after selection through a competitive bidding system. Several forms of contracts exist. Under most of them, the management group is paid in part in the form of company shares. The contract covers at least a three-year period. In some of the contracts, the management group must invest some of its own capital. A severe constraint on this program has been the very limited number of competent management groups willing to get involved in contracts. Few foreign groups have been willing and few domestic groups have been considered competent enough. Consequently, only a few contracts have been let and the results are not yet in.

Hungary. Hungary is just beginning to seriously consider using management contracts. These involve management fees, or success fees, or equity investments with option to buy. The most creative Hungarian thinking is to privatize state firms incrementally—that is, to privatize the restructuring of a firm, where the entire firm cannot find a private market. This requires that the contract manager put up considerable capital of his own in return for a potentially high return on his investment. The problem, of course, is to ensure that the investment is used for restructuring, and not to maximize short-term income for the manager.

Liquidation

Even after financial and physical restructuring and reorganization, some state firms have little hope of becoming viable. In Eastern Europe and Russia, procedures exist for liquidating such firms. Poland and Hungary have liquidated fairly large numbers of state firms. The Czech Republic and Russia have only recently begun to apply their bankruptcy laws. In Russia, as of early 1994, only eight firms had been declared bankrupt. China, however, has been unwilling to go this far. It has dealt with hopeless firms either by continuing to subsidize them or by merging them with profitable firms. In the latter case, the objective is to gain economies through diversification and rationalization without having to lay off large number of workers. Loss making enterprises in China may liquidate some assets, but may not engage in mass layoffs.

Poland. Poland is unique among transition countries in that it has applied its bankruptcy law only to private firms and state corporations. For state enterprises a separate law that provides for "liquidation" under ministerial supervision has been applied. The reason for this choice is that it gives the government much more flexibility than does the bankruptcy law. In principle, liquidation proceedings can be initiated whenever an enterprise fails to pay its tax obligations to the government, especially the "dividend tax." In practice, however, liquidation was rarely begun until enterprises had accumulated large tax arrears and other unpaid debts and were running consistently large losses. Even then, the most important, very large enterprises were given much more leeway than the smaller ones, and none of the largest have been liquidated, despite their large losses and debt.

Another advantage of ministerial liquidation is that it bypasses the overburdened court system.

The procedure for ministerial liquidation is first, appointment by the ministry of a "liquidator" who takes over management of the firm. The liquidator then negotiates for relief from and payment of tax arrears, bank debt, and debt to other creditors. Finally, he tries to form a viable corporation from any remaining assets, for eventual privatization. Although a new corporation cannot be formed until the creditors of the enterprise are satisfied, its creation is clearly a major objective of the liquidation process: indeed, the Poles classify this kind of liquidation as a form of privatization. The total liquidation process takes a long time. Out of nearly 1,200 state enterprises that were put into the liquidation process during the July 1990 through June 1994 period, only some 250 were actually liquidated.

Hungary. As indicated earlier, Hungary applies a tough bankruptcy law to state corporations, into which virtually all state enterprises had been converted by the end of 1993. Of the 16,000 firms undergoing bankruptcy procedures between mid-1992 and late 1993, the great majority underwent some sort of restructuring process, either by agreement between the debtor firm and its creditors, or through court-ordered receivership. But relatively few of these firms were liquidated, partly because of long delays in the courts. In 1993, the tough bankruptcy laws were eased in several ways. For example, a 75 percent majority of debtors, compared with the former 100 percent, became sufficient to accept a restructuring plan; also, the minimum threshold of overdue debt required to trigger bankruptcy was raised.

The bankruptcy process has caused considerable, though temporary, disruption and has bogged down in the courts. This has led to many more informal arrangements among firms, banks, and other creditors. These arrangements include approved restructuring plans, partial sales of assets, debt/equity swaps, and other out-of-court arrangements. Consequently, the results of the Hungarian policies may not turn out to be fundamentally different from those of Poland.

Managing Industries Under Long-Term State Ownership

Poland, Hungary, Russia, and even the Czech Republic have effectively reserved some industries and some firms for long-term state ownership and control. As mentioned before, these include at a minimum public utilities, military industries, fuels and steel. In Russia they also include raw materials and some other basic industries considered important to the national security. Methods of state control for these industries are just beginning to be developed. In some cases, they combine long-term restructuring plans with partial privatization and with state ownership of key functions.

Coal. This is a large industry in Poland and the Czech Republic, with a fairly homogeneous product but a wide range of unit costs among mines, facing declining demand and overcapacity. In both countries, the objective is to phase down capacity in orderly fashion without too much labor unrest. In Poland, to avoid putting the burden of selecting individual mines for closure on the government, large regional state corporations are being organized, each with a balanced portfolio of high- and low-cost mines. Closures are then scheduled over a multi-year period within the broad framework of an agreed national plan. It remains to be seen whether the miners, whose wages and other benefits used to be far above the industrial average, but who have suffered big cuts in real incomes during the transition, will accept large layoffs without violent strikes.

Steel. The steel industry is less homogeneous and more complex than the coal industry, but it too faces the necessity of drastic cuts in capacity and employment. Poland and the Czech Republic are developing special policies for steel. These include a long-term plan and establishment of holding companies with majority government ownership and which in turn control a mix of government-owned and privatized firms.

Very Large Enterprises. Poland is beginning to restructure very large firms, such as the "URSUS" tractor plant, into holding companies in the framework of a reorganization plan in which some units are being sold, others are being modernized, and still others are being liquidated. Presumably, SPHC in Hungary will follow similar procedures. In the Czech Republic, the high-tech, military-oriented CKD Prague firm is also being reorganized along holding company lines.

Other Industries. Russia appears to be reorganizing some industries, such as the oil, gas and wood industry, using a holding company system in which the state maintains control of a critical function, such as marketing or R&D, while permitting mixed ownership of other units.

Assessment

Corporatization is a necessary step on the road to developing more effective ownership of a firm, but, if not followed by other steps, is likely to have either neutral or, under some circumstances, negative effects. It does not create incentives for long-term improvement of state enterprises unless it is viewed as part of a privatization process or of a longer-term state-sponsored restructuring process. Moreover, by itself corporatization brings no access to new funding.

Management contracts can yield significant improvements in enterprise performance under certain conditions, but are not effective substitutes for market driven property rights. The traditional types of multi-goal contracts used widely in China, are an improvement only over directive planning: they are too easily manipulated and negotiated, and, therefore, are likely to become tied to artificial measures of performance. Strong incentives for long-term restructuring are likely to require both a sufficiently developed capital market so that a firm's performance can be evaluated unambiguously, and the willingness of the managers under contract to put some of their own funds at risk. Such a system would also give the firm access to new sources of funding. Whether or not it would elicit cooperation from insiders depends on the terms and on how effective communication between the contract manager and the insiders would be.

Liquidation is a very difficult and painful task at best. On paper the Hungarian approach, which relies on the strict application of bankruptcy law, would seem to be the most efficient way to cull out inefficient firms. This approach sets out clear rules and time limits. If enforced, it creates very strong incentives for weak firms to reorganize and restructure in order to satisfy creditors and avoid liquidation. Such agreements may bring in new funds in the form of debt relief or debt/equity swaps. There is every reason for insiders to cooperate, even with very painful steps, in order to avoid a worse fate. Where liquidation occurs, it proceeds in a predictable manner. Unfortunately, in these countries neither the courts nor the financial institutions are able to manage the process well. So there are clear advantages in a more flexible, managed approach, such as Poland has followed in its liquidation law. This flexibility has bought time for firms to sort out their position in the market and has avoided overcrowded courts. On the other hand, it has not kept sufficient pressure on inefficient enterprises.

It is too soon to assess the effectiveness of the various methods for overseeing the management of firms that will remain under state control. One tentative conclusion is that large, central organizations, such as Hungary's SPHC, are too bureaucratic to be effective. The use of more flexible organizations, such as holding companies, will probably work better, particularly if they are combined with partial privatization, results-oriented management contracts, and some funds for restructuring.

In general, the record of the subject countries sheds considerable light on the merits in the long debate about whether privatization should come before or after restructuring. There is little doubt that rapid expansion of private enterprise, or of similar "non-state" enterprise as in China, is essential to a successful transition. Arguments can be made favoring continued state ownership of a relatively small number of firms in selected sectors so long as such firms operate in a predominantly market economy. But an effective, competitive market cannot exist without predominantly private (or non-state) ownership, and the faster this occurs, the better.

The state has a legitimate role, however, in assisting privatization and fostering improved efficiency by helping to restructure firms. Debt reduction on a large scale is often necessary. In addition, large firms that are losing money and can find no private buyers must be restructured with government help, either for eventual privatization or simply to keep them from continuing to be a drain on the budget. But large government restructuring programs should be undertaken mainly to deal with problems the private sector cannot or will not deal with, not as early steps in the transition.

Notes

1. The development of ownership rights, company law, contract law, bankruptcy law, and competition law in Poland, Hungary, and the Czech Republic is well presented in a series of studies by Cheryl Gray for the World Bank: *The Legal Framework for Private Sector Activity in the Czech and Slovak Republic*, Policy Research Working Papers, WAS 1051, November 1992; The *Legal Framework for Private Sector Development—The Case of Poland*, Policy Research Working Papers, WAS 800, November 1991; and *Legal Reform for Hungary's Private Sector*, Policy Research Working Papers, WAS 983, October 1992.

2. For 1986-92, data on FDI are from the IMF. For 1993 and projected 1994, they are from the Survey of China in *the Financial Times*, Monday, November 7, 1994.

3. China's industrial development is analyzed in a large number of IMF surveys and World Bank working papers. See also Donald A. Hay, et al., *Economic Reform and State-owned Enterprises in China, 1979-1987* (New York: Oxford University Press, 1994), pp. 301-312.

4. *PlanEcon* has regularly compared the levels and trends in purchasing power in all the East European countries by converting domestic currencies into U.S. dollars using both the official exchange rates and estimated purchasing power ratios. The results of these calculations are shown in all issues of the Czech, Polish, and Hungarian *Economic Monitor*, as well as in other publications. Although countries with relatively low per capital real incomes can be expected to have equilibrium exchange rates well below those calculated from purchasing power parities, the discrepancy is unusually large for these transition economies, ranging from slightly below to well above 2/1, with the Czech currency apparently being to most undervalued.

5. See, for example, Alfredo Thorne, *The Role of Banks in the Transition: Lessons from Eastern European Countries' Experience*, The World Bank, June 1992.

6. Several *PlanEcon* Reports deal analyze and assess the stock markets of Poland, Hungary, and the Czech Republics. Stock market results are also given in the Economic Monitors on individual countries.

7. See, for example, David Kemme, *Banking in Central Europe during the Protomarket Period: Developments and Emerging Issues*, paper prepared for the International Conference "Development and Reform of the Financial System in Central and Eastern Europe," Vienna, Austria, October 28-30, 1993.

8. Survey of China, The *Financial Times*, Monday, November 7, 1994.

4

Poland

A Brief Review of the Transition

General Characteristics

Among all the former Communist countries, Poland has the longest experience with the issues of transition from a centrally planned to a market economy. At the end of 1994, four years had elapsed since a new, non-Communist government committed itself to this transformation. Poland is also the former Communist country in Europe whose economy first began to recover from the disruptive effects of the transition. Although many serious problems remain, notably high unemployment, still numerous, unprofitable state enterprises and widespread public disaffection, which in turn is reflected in the victory of the left wing parties in the September 1993 legislative elections, Poland is rapidly becoming a "normal" country. The Polish experience with transition offers numerous lessons to other countries, such as Russia, that began their transition later.

Legacies from the Communist Era

Poland began the transition with some substantial advantages over the other European Communist countries, notably a larger private sector and strong foreign trade and payments links to the West. With some 90 percent of agriculture in private hands, the private sector in 1989 accounted for 19 percent of national income (30 percent if cooperatives are included) and 33 percent of employment (47 percent including cooperatives).[1] Outside of agriculture, the private sector employed some 1.4 million people, but nearly all were in very small-scale handicraft and service establishments and produced only 11 percent of the national income. Beginning at the end of 1988, private enterprise was given the same legal rights as state and cooperative enterprise, and the commercial code of the 1930s was revived.

About one half of Poland's foreign trade was oriented to the West. Foreign direct investment was permitted on a limited scale beginning in the early 1980s, and was encouraged from the end of 1988. To encourage the inflow of private foreign remittances from the Polish diaspora, the Communist government legalized the holding of dollar accounts in Poland, and by 1989 such accounts represented some 80 percent of the population's financial savings. The legal accumulation of dollars, together with increasing freedom for Polish residents to convert dollars into zlotys at a market exchange rate, resulted in a widespread use of dollars as a medium of exchange. At the same time, the liberalization of foreign travel greatly increased both personal contacts and informal trade with the West.

On the negative side, the Communist legacy in Poland also included a much more severe macroeconomic disequilibrium than in Czechoslovakia or Hungary. The Polish political revolution of 1989 was not a sudden occurrence; rather it was the outcome of the growing weakness of the Polish government and its declining ability to rule the country. In order to buy popular support, the Polish government, once Martial Law had been lifted, permitted wages to rise unchecked while greatly increasing budget subsidies to hold down prices, resulting in a 25 percent rise in real wages from 1985 to 1989 (9 percent in 1989 alone). This rise in real wages was not sustainable: inflation began to accelerate and the velocity of the circulation of zloty deposits began to increase. Then, in mid-1989, the last Communist government freed nearly all agricultural prices, thereby raising farm incomes, while permitting wages increases that more than compensated for the rise in the cost of living. By September 1989, when the Solidarity-led government took office, inflation had reached an annual rate of over 1,000 percent and the budget deficit had surpassed 10 percent of GDP.[2]

One consequence of the inflationary mini-boom of the late 1980s was to force the new non-Communist government to impose a severe macroeconomic stabilization program at the same time that it was launching policies of economic liberalization and structural and institutional change. Another consequence was to establish a generally misleading base for measuring the impact of transition policies. For example, in 1990 real wages fell 25 percent from the 1989 level, but only 5 percent in comparison with 1985.

Another distinctive feature of Poland's Communist-era legacy is the important role of organized labor in enterprise management and in national policy formulation. As enterprises were gradually given increased autonomy during the 1980s and as the ability of the government to make orders stick declined, workers' councils, first organized on a large scale during the rise of Solidarity in 1980-1981, again took hold in Polish firms and, in many of them, acquired a major say in management decisions. At the same time, labor developed strong political clout that any Polish government had to take into account in economic policy.

Unique features and distinctions aside, the Polish legacy from Communism resembled that of other former Communist countries far more than it differed from them. Structurally, the Polish economy favored heavy industry, although less so than Czechoslovakia or the Soviet Union. And its industrial firms were mainly very large (56 percent of industrial employment was in firms employing more than 1,000 workers and only 11 percent in firms employing less than 500 workers) and often monopolistic. Institutionally, systems of economic planning, management, and bureaucratic and political control were similar to those in other Communist countries, although the degree of control had been lessening for several years.

Polish Economic Policies During the Transition

Polish economic policies during the transition have been driven by events, a faith in free markets, a distrust of government intervention at the microeconomic level, and considerable public opposition to large-scale capitalism and foreign investment.[3]

As mentioned above, very high and accelerating inflation forced adoption of highly restrictive macroeconomic policies. These included major cuts in government spending, sometimes highly restrictive monetary policies, and punitive taxes on wage increases beyond norms that were far below inflation rates.

Faith in free markets gave rise to the "Big Bang" on January 1, 1990, which involved: freeing all but a small number of prices (mainly fuels, transport tariffs, utility rates and housing rents, which were all raised in steps toward market levels during 1990-1992); allowing full internal convertibility of the zloty; eliminating all quantitative restrictions on imports and nearly all those on exports; and setting some of the world's lowest import tariffs (nominal rates of 10–15 percent, but effective rates, after rebates, of nearly 5 percent). All at once, money counted and shortages disappeared.

Distrust of government micro-involvement is reflected in a refusal for more than two years to develop any formal "industrial policy," which meant that action-forcing micro-issues were dealt with on an *ad hoc* basis.

The need to accommodate widespread popular concerns about large-scale privatization and direct foreign investment caused lengthy delays in critical legislation. The general privatization law was delayed until mid 1990. A liberal foreign investment law did not get passed until mid-1991. The law on "mass privatization" was barely passed in April 1993, and has still not been implemented. A law on restitution of nationalized property has yet to be even presented to the legislature.

Because of these diverse and sometimes conflicting forces, the transition process has been highly uneven. Where the government, with its generally liberal philosophy and technocratic approach, has been able to act unilaterally, change occurred very quickly. This was the case for the removal of controls over prices and foreign trade, which did not require specific legislation, as well as the dismantling of the state economic control apparatus at the ministerial and sub-ministerial level. Growth of new private enterprise was rapid because the enabling legislation already existed and had broad support and there was little need for other government initiatives. But where legislation was required on politically sensitive matters, as on privatization of large enterprises and foreign investment, change took a long time.

Undertaking a severe macroeconomic stabilization at the same time that prices and foreign transactions were being freed created extremely difficult tradeoffs in the application of exchange rate, monetary, wage, and fiscal policy. To make internal convertibility credible, the zloty had to be devalued to near the free market exchange rate.[4] And to help bring down inflation after the initial shock, the exchange rate had to be fixed for at least several months—becoming a major anchor in the price structure. The downside of this policy was that an initially undervalued zloty, while stimulating exports, made imports too expensive to create competitive pressures on domestic producers, who therefore tended to automatically pass on cost increases. Then, when a fixed exchange rate in the face of still rapid domestic inflation inevitably caused the zloty to become overvalued (by the beginning of 1991), imports accelerated, the trade balance worsened, but competitive pressures on domestic producers quickly became much stronger. Not until May 1991, 17 months after the zloty became internally convertible at a fixed rate, was there a devaluation and a shift to an exchange rate policy based on a crawling peg.

Monetary policy was an important element in macroeconomic stabilization, but could be used only as a blunt instrument, not as a flexible tool and even less as means of redirecting credit from firms with weak to those with strong market prospects. Shock therapy took the form of a near cessation of bank lending in the first two months of the "Big Bang." Interest rates were raised sharply, as were bank reserve requirements, and the word went out that credit would be severely curtailed. New credit almost stopped and a liquidity crunch ensued. A smaller mini-shock occurred in early spring of 1991 to deal with rising inflation. But such extreme measures could not be sustained. Once the immediate crisis was past, the banks reverted to largely accommodating normal credit demand, with the sometimes positive real interest rates being factored in as normal elements of costs.

The limitations of monetary policy made it necessary to rely heavily on wage policy to control inflation. State enterprises were taxed at rates of 200-300 percent on wage increases in excess of norms that generally were set at 20-30 percent of the inflation rate. While few firms were able to afford such taxes during periods of credit shock, payments of this tax were quite large during the more normal periods of accommodating monetary policy. Not surprisingly, this tax (called the "popiwek") has been extremely unpopular in state enterprises and with organized labor and a major source of political contention. It was reduced in 1994 and will probably be eliminated in 1995.

Fiscal policy was intended to be restrictive and anti-inflationary, with declining government expenditures and sharp cuts in budget deficits. Initially, price liberalization was also a major deflationary factor because it resulted in a massive decline in subsidies to state enterprises, from 6.7 percent of GDP in 1989 to 2.2 percent of GDP in 1990. At the same time, tax revenues rose despite the fall in output because nominal enterprise profits were unexpectedly large (partly reflecting accounting lags, as explained later). Consequently Poland in 1990 was able to eliminate its budget deficit, and even to build a small surplus. But as the profits of state enterprises declined in 1991 and 1992, tax revenues from the state sector fell, while the growing private sector was able to largely avoid paying taxes, and the budget deficit began to grow again.

Although the fundamental Polish policy objective—to create an economic system similar to that of advanced West European countries with a view to eventually joining the European Community—has remained unchanged through the several post-Communist governments, emphasis on particular aspects of policy has changed in response to experience, external events, and internal political pressures. For example, the fact that "shock therapy" resulted in substantially higher prices and lower production than the government had projected was influential in permitting the banks to resume an accommodating credit policy while the exchange rate was fixed much longer than planned.

Also, as competitive pressure from imports became intolerable in early 1991, as a result of the increasingly overvalued zloty, the government backed off partially from its low tariff policy and increased average tariffs to about 15 percent, then to over 20 percent in 1994. Furthermore, disappointment with the slow pace of privatization of state enterprises led to a variety of programs to accelerate the privatization process (see below).

Finally, as the financial condition of state enterprises worsened and many faced imminent bankruptcy, the government experimented with a variety of techniques to delay or avoid closing down these firms, and began to make longer-term plans to develop or phase down particular sectors. Increased interventionism at the sectoral and micro level was a response to the unexpected severity of the problems of state industry and to political pressures from industrial interests and organized labor. Industrial policy issues are developed in more depth later.

Macroeconomic Trends During the Transition

The Polish economy is recovering rapidly from a severe decline that began with the "Big Bang" of January 1990 and ended in the first half of 1992. According to official statistics, GDP dropped 12 percent in 1990 and another 8 percent in 1991, began a recovery in 1992, and achieved growth rates of nearly 4 percent in 1993 and about 4.5 percent in 1994, the fastest growth in

TABLE 4.1   Poland: Macroeconomic Trends, 1985, 1990-1994

	1985	1990	1991	1992	1993	1994
Indexes: 1989=100						
GDP	90.2	88.4	81.7	83.0	87.5	91.4
Personal Consumption	90.0	84.8	91.0	95.8	101.1	104
Fixed Capital Form.	92.6	89.5	85.5	87.6	90.1	95
Industrial Prod.	88.5	75.9	66.8	69.5	74.4	83
Agricultural Prod.	95.1	97.7	94.1	87.5	84.7	---
Employment	100.8	97.3	91.6	87.7	85.7	85
Real Wages	80.9	75.6	75.4	73.3	71.4	72
Export Volume	83.2	113.7	111.0	108.1	105.5	118
Import Volume	82.2	80.6	113.1	128.8	154.5	172
Annual Percentage Changes						
Consumer Prices	---	586	70	43	35	33
Percent of Labor Force						
Unemployment*	---	6.3	11.8	13.6	16.4	16.0

* End of year.

Sources: 1985-93: CSO of Poland, *Statistical Yearbook, 1994*, Table 1; 1994: Author estimates, based mainly on CSO of Poland, *Statistical Bulletin*, No. 11, 1994.

Europe. In 1994, measured economic activity (GDP) was still some 10 percent below the 1989 level, but had about regained the 1985 (and 1980) levels; personal consumption was above pre-"Big Bang" levels; while fixed capital formation, although recovering in 1994, was still depressed, as shown in Table 4.1. There is little doubt that official economic aggregates exaggerate the severity of the recession because large amounts of private activity are unrecorded or under invoiced, even though otherwise legal, in order to avoid taxes. Estimates of unrecorded transactions range from 10 percent to 30 percent of GDP. There was also a "second economy" under Communism, but it involved mainly illegal diversion of goods from official to free market channels. According to Leszek Balcerowicz, the architect of Poland's "Big Bang," the real decline in GDP during 1990-1991 was only 5-10 percent, compared with the official 18 percent.[5]

The Polish economic recession was double-barreled. Output and real incomes dropped sharply during the spurt in prices triggered by the "Big Bang." The second drop occurred in early 1991, when a collapse of the former CMEA market coincided with a renewed credit crunch. Between and since these sharp declines, production and real incomes have trended slowly upwards. Since April 1992, industrial production has been above the same month of the previous year by substantial and generally increasing margins. For 1994 the growth of industrial production was about 11 percent.

Dramatic changes in the Polish economic structure have taken place. The share of GDP originating in industry in 1990 prices fell from 50 percent in 1989 to 38 percent in 1993, while that of trade and services increased correspondingly. This shift reflects the long-term decline in demand for many products of heavy industry that had depended mainly on the domestic and Soviet markets, the development of private business and consumer services, and the need to greatly expand sales, marketing and advertising far beyond what typical Communist-era trade markups could finance. The share of agriculture also fell, especially in terms of current prices, because relative agricultural prices on the world market, which has largely governed the Polish price structure during the transition, are far below the farm prices that had been set in the last few years of Communist rule.

Inflation continues to be rapid, but not out of control. The initial price liberalization brought an 80 percent jump in the cost of living in January 1990 and another 25 percent increase in February. Inflation trends then stabilized at monthly rates in the general range of 2-3 percent, except for a temporary acceleration in late 1990 and early 1991. In 1994 as a whole, both producer prices and consumer prices increased about one third.

Poland was successful in reorienting its foreign trade from the CMEA to the world market. Despite the collapse of the CMEA trade system in 1991 and the consequent decline of about 50 percent in Polish trade with the former Communist countries, the volume of total Polish imports is more than 70 percent above the 1989 level, and that of exports has increased almost 20 percent. Both exports to and imports from OECD countries have about doubled since 1989, with most of this growth involving West European countries.

Another benefit of the economic transformation policies was the willingness of Western official and banking creditors to reduce the Polish hard currency debt of about $45 billion by about 50 percent. Although the agreements will lead to some increase in Polish interest payments, as Poland meets its reduced obligations instead of capitalizing them, they will enhance Polish creditworthiness and increase access to commercial credit and portfolio investment. Through the end of 1993, however, cumulative direct foreign investment in Poland was still below $3 billion, although commitments were much larger and other large projects are in the negotiating stage.

Poland also received a considerable amount of foreign official aid, other than debt relief. Although much of this aid is not highly concessionary and only a fraction of the total has been disbursed, it has enabled Poland to launch programs of badly needed infrastructure investment and training in skills for a market economy, financed the use of many foreign experts, and established an Exchange Stabilization Fund of $1 billion that played a critical role in making exchange rate stability credible.

A major negative feature of the Polish transition has been the slide in recorded employment and the massive increase in unemployment to more than 15 percent of the labor force. Overall employment apparently declined about 15 percent during 1990-1993, as increases in recorded private sector employment failed to compensate for declines in the state sector. Employment in industry, construction and transportation fell the most (more than 25 percent), while employment in private services and trade increased. During 1994, total recorded employment leveled off and the unemployment rate began to decline slowly. It is generally believed that official data fail to record all private sector employment, especially in the case of part-time work, because of widespread tax evasion. For the same reason, recorded unemployment rates are almost certainly too high. According to a survey conducted in June 1994 by the Market Economy Research Institute in Gdansk, one half of the Poles registered as unemployed, and one of every three adult Poles, work without reporting their incomes or employment.[6] But although most major cities and the more industrialized regions have relatively low unemployment rates and many kinds of work skills in those areas are in short supply, there is clearly very severe unemployment in areas, mainly in eastern and northern Poland, where state firms have closed in small towns and cities and no alternative jobs exist.

Trends in living standards are clearly upward on the average, but a majority of Poles feel worse off than before the start of the transition. Data on household consumption suggest a downgrading of the diet in favor of inferior goods during 1990, as well as a postponement of expenditures for textiles and some durable consumer goods. Since 1990, the trend in consumption is steadily upward, and for durable goods, the increases are large. Inter-temporal comparisons are complicated by what was apparently a considerable increase in the inequality of income distribution—a distributional shift from unskilled and semi-skilled workers and farmers to entrepreneurs and skilled workers.

Institutional Change

The Polish record of institutional change in the transition is mixed, but impressive. Privatization of state enterprises has been disappointingly slow and has required different methods from those preferred by the government. On the other hand, the private sector has developed rapidly, the state's administrative control apparatus has collapsed, and most state enterprises have had to fend for themselves in the market.

The collapse of the Communist-era administrative control system began before the end of Communist rule and was generally complete by mid-1990. The entire network of industrial and other functional "Associations," which were in effect subordinate units of branch ministries, disappeared. This made it impossible for the government to exercise micro-economic control

TABLE 4.2   Poland: Percent Contribution of the Private Sector*

	Employment			GDP		
	1989	*1993*	*1994***	*1989*	*1993*	*1994***
Total Economy	47	59	60	30	55	57
Industry	29	43	46	16	36	39
Construction	37	75	78	25	82	85
Agriculture	88	95	96	---	88	90
Trade	73	93	94	---	56	60

* Includes cooperatives.
** Estimated by the authors
Sources: 1989 and 1993: CSO of Poland, *Statistical Yearbook, 1992, 1993,* and *1994,* and CSO of Poland, *Statistical Bulletin,* No. 11, December 1994.

over enterprises. It also eliminated some common service functions, such as R&D and marketing, that had to be picked up by the individual enterprise, or by new private firms, or not performed at all.

In 1994, the recorded private sector produced over 55 percent of GDP, compared with 30 percent in 1989, and accounted for 60 percent of employment, compared with 47 percent in 1989. These figures include cooperatives, which, like private firms, now have to operate without state aid or controls. They almost certainly understate the role of private economic activity because of under-reporting of private income and employment. A reasonable allowance for unrecorded private incomes would probably raise the private sector share of GDP to at least 60 percent. As shown in Table 4.2, the private sector, already dominant in agriculture under Communism, has become so in construction and trade, but still accounts for less than one half of industrial employment and about 40 percent of industrial sales.

Private sector development came from a variety of sources: creation of entirely new private firms; establishment of private businesses by leasing publicly-owned land and buildings; sale or leasing of sections of state enterprises; and the privatization of entire state enterprises. The relative importance of these activities can only be inferred, but it differs greatly among types of firms and economic activity.

The results of the institutional change are summarized in Table 4.3. The number of state enterprises has declined by about 40 percent since 1990, and almost 50 percent since the end of 1991. During 1990-1991, deconcentration policies had caused many state enterprises to split,[7] which increased the total number of enterprises, but reduced their average size. Corporations of all kinds almost tripled in number from 1990 to September 1994, but are generally much smaller than the state enterprises. Among the corporations, 72,000 were private domestic companies, and almost 19,000 were joint

TABLE 4.3   Poland: Number of Business Units, 1989-1994
   (Thousands, as of end of period)

Type of Unit	1989	1990	1991	1992	1993	1994*
State Enterprises	7.3	8.4	8.2	7.2	5.9	5.1
Communal Enterprises	---	---	0.7	0.5	0.6	0.6
State Corporations	0.2	0.3	0.4	0.5	0.6	0.8
Total State Firms	7.5	8.7	10.2	8.5	7.1	6.5
Foreign Corporations**	0.4	1.6	4.8	10.1	15.1	18.6
Private Domestic Corp.	15.2	33.3	47.7	57.0	65.1	71.8
Cooperatives	---	18.6	18.9	19.4	19.7	19.8
Total Private Firms	---	53.5	71.4	86.5	99.9	110.2
Individually Owned	813	1,135	1,420	1,631	1,784	---

* 1994 data are for 30 September.
** Including joint ventures.
   Sources: 1989-93: CSO of Poland, *Statistical Yearbook, 1994*; 1994: CSO of Poland, *Statistical Bulletin*, No. 11, December 1994, pp. 119-120.

ventures or fully owned foreign firms, more than 10 times the number in 1990. The number of state corporations began to increased rapidly in 1993-1994; there were about 800 by the end of September, 1994. In addition, there was more than a doubling in the number of unincorporated businesses and of private, non-profit organizations.

In 1990, private entrepreneurs and former employees of state enterprises purchased or rented space from local governments to establish retail, service and handicraft shops, which were generally small and unincorporated. They also set up numerous stalls and trailers on sidewalks and in markets, but, except for food markets, these were phased out as permanent private stores multiplied. In addition, cooperative establishments often became private and some large state retail trade and service enterprises were broken up. Small-scale privatization was managed by local governments and was rapid.

A substantial number of private corporations were established in the period between passage of the Enterprise Act of December 1988, which legalized two forms of private corporations, and the Privatization Law of July 1990, which regulated the entire privatization process. These firms were mainly spinoffs from state enterprises of specific service or manufacturing functions that were formed into private corporations at the initiative of managers or sometimes groups of skilled workers. Because the managers often owed their control over resources to the Communist Party, this form of privatization, called "nomenklatura privatization," generated strong political opposition and became illegal after July 1990.

TABLE 4.4   Poland: State Enterprises Privatized and Liquidated, 6/90 to 12/93

	Number	Percent of State Enterprises on 6/30/90
Total	1,046	12
Industry	358	13
Construction	356	23
Agriculture	64	4
Transport	37	13
Trade	143	26

Sources: Number of state enterprises privatized or liquidated: CSO of Poland, *Statistical Yearbook, 1994*, Table 1; number of state enterprises entering the privatization program on June 30, 1990: CSO of Poland, *Privatization of State Enterprises as of 12/31/92*, p. 25.

Many thousands of private corporations were also created on green field sites and in newly constructed or renovated buildings. They include hotels, banks and other financial institutions, trade and service organizations, and manufacturing and construction firms, often involving joint ventures between Polish and Western firms. The number of privatized state enterprises formed since 1990 is only a small fraction of the number of private corporations—about 1,000 out of more than 70,000—indicating that the bulk of these are "new."

The Privatization Law of July 1990 established most of the programs for transforming the ownership of 8,400 state enterprises, or nearly the total number in existence at that time. By mid-1994, some 4,400 enterprises (more than half the total) had been put into some sort of transformation process, including privatization, liquidation, conversion into state-owned corporations, and takeover by local governments. By the end of 1993, only 12 percent of the state enterprises existing in mid-1990 had been privatized or liquidated, which means either replaced by a private firm or closed down, as shown in Table 4.4. The proportion was higher (about 25 percent) in construction and trade.

Privatized enterprises are generally small or medium-sized. They include few of the large industrial firms, and only one of the giant ones. Many large firms, however, are scheduled for privatization under the "mass privatization" program, which has not yet begun. The various methods used for privatization are discussed below in the section on Privatization.

Trends in Enterprise Finances

One of the most difficult problems of transition has been the severe deterioration of the financial condition of enterprises. Since the latter part of 1991, about one half of enterprises have incurred losses after taxes, and a large number have been unable to pay all their tax obligations. Enterprise debt to government, banks, and other enterprises, has grown much more than receivables, and many firms would face bankruptcy if they were forced to meet their obligations on schedule. Both state enterprises and private firms have experienced serious financial difficulties. Official statistics show lower profitability for private firms than for state enterprises, but everyone believes that this reflects under-reporting of private incomes and that in reality the opposite was the case.

The financial deterioration did not begin right after market liberalization. Enterprises entered the new era with unusually high profits that developed during the inflationary mini-boom of 1986-1989. Then the short-term effects of price liberalization were to further increase profits despite the precipitous drop in sales. One reason was a surge in paper profits because the valuation of inventories and of fixed capital for purposes of depreciation calculations did not reflect the doubling or more of sales prices for several months. Another reason was the continued state control of the prices of fuels and electricity, which were important inputs in many industries. Finally, during the first few months of the transition, real labor costs fell as real wages declined more than labor productivity. During the first half of 1990, only a tiny number of enterprises incurred losses, and many had profits of 20-30 percent of sales.

The financial condition of enterprises deteriorated greatly in late 1990 and 1991, as maintenance of a fixed exchange rate despite high domestic inflation caused the zloty to become overvalued and brought a massive surge in competitive imports, and because of a collapse of the CMEA market. The deterioration continued through the first half of 1992, as a catch-up in previously controlled input prices, a continued but much slower appreciation of the zloty, and the rising financial costs of accumulating debt more than compensated for the favorable impact of higher tariffs in most industries. More than 40 percent of firms incurred losses after taxes, which essentially offset the profits of the other firms. With the start of economic recovery in 1992-1993, the financial situation stabilized thanks to rising sales, but at a very low level of net profits and a high level of debt. In 1994, enterprise profits slowly improved, but the net aggregate profits remained very low, providing little financing for investment.

The Politics of Transition

The Polish transition began on a wave of national consensus on the need to destroy an alien, imposed Communist system and replace it by a democratic political system, and a market-oriented economic system.[8] This consensus, however, did not include an acceptance of economic insecurity, a capitalist system of ownership of large firms, or foreign control over Polish land and major industries. As the economic costs of the transition mounted, in the form of lower real incomes, rising unemployment, growing income inequality, and declining farm terms of trade, the popular mood became more and more negative and pessimistic and popular confidence in government, and in politicians generally, fell steadily. For the past three years, public opinion polls show that an overwhelming majority of the population believe things have gotten worse and are pessimistic about at least the near future.[9]

Public disaffection and policy differences caused the Solidarity movement, which represented the anti-Communist national consensus in 1989, to break up and the system of political parties to become highly fragmented. Parties generally have weak organizations, depend mainly on a single leader, or a group of leaders, and have either narrow constituencies (e.g. farmers) or only a vague program. Constitutional issues, especially the relative powers of the President and the legislature, remain unresolved, pending agreement on a new constitution. Four governments have fallen since September 1989 and there were 29 parties represented in parliament prior to the September 1993 elections. These elections resulted in a victory for the left-wing parties, the former Communists and the Peasant party. Because of a change in the electoral system that established a threshold of 5 percent of the popular vote for parties to have representation, these two parties together have about two thirds of the seats in parliament.

There has been reasonable stability in basic policies in spite of frequent changes in government, but weak governments have been unable to adopt strong, coherent policies on contentious issues. Very little important new economic legislation was passed from the spring of 1991 to the fall of 1992. During this period, virtually nothing was done to deal with the rapidly worsening financial condition of state enterprises, or to develop new mechanisms for privatization (notably "mass privatization," which was repeatedly delayed). Progress continued from private sector initiatives and on the basis of existing laws, but developing problems worsened seriously. Political paralysis did not halt, and for a while may not even have slowed, the transition, but it threatened to slow the process in the future.

The September 1993 election results confirmed what public opinion polls had been showing for a long time—that the transformation had made life harder for the majority. The purchasing power of farmers and unskilled and semi-skilled workers declined; unemployment continued to increase despite the upswing in output; and many were afraid of losing their jobs. The fact that a minority became wealthy while the majority felt worse off, or at least more insecure, also caused resentment. Finally, successive governments did a poor job of explaining their economic policies to the population, reflecting long established habits of Polish intellectuals to talk down to ordinary people.

TABLE 4.5   Poland: Size of Public and Private Industrial Firms in 1993

	Average Number of Employees per Firm
State Enterprises	508
State Corporations	608
Private Corporations	28
Foreign Corporations	38
Cooperatives	107
Individual Proprietorships	2.6

Source: CSO of Poland, *Statistical Yearbook, 1994*, Table 1.

The left-wing government has not reversed the reforms that took Poland so far on the transition road, nor even made any fundamental changes in the direction of economic policy. Earlier fears that the government would adopt populist policies that would substantially increase the budget deficit, and thereby damage economic stability, have proved unfounded. Indeed, this government was able to satisfy IMF financial conditions and complete a debt reduction agreement with Western banks that had been under negotiation for over a year. However, the rate of privatization, which began to slow in 1993, has slowed even more, as existing programs lost momentum and new programs were delayed. State enterprises will be forced to transform themselves into corporations, but will have the right to remain state-owned if the firm's workers so decide. And implementation of the "mass privatization" program was stalled by Prime Minister Pawlak, who led the Peasant Party.[10]

In general, the left-wing government is favoring development of a policy consensus between government, labor, and business, over the more technocratic and authoritarian approach of the early transition governments. The so-called "Pact on State Enterprises," in which labor groups agreed to support the "mass privatization" program, national wage restraint, and some painful restructuring initiatives, in return for increased consultation and worker representation, and the elimination of the excess wages tax, will probably go forward.

The Behavior of State Enterprises

The Problem of Producers' Response

The most disappointing aspect of the Polish transition has been the alleged slow response of Polish producers to the freeing of markets. The slowness of the supply response is blamed for the unexpectedly large increase in prices following liberalization and for the renewed inflationary tendencies whenever banks provided enterprises with sufficient liquidity.

The image of the unresponsive state enterprise includes: passively adjusting product mix by producing to capacity what is in demand; passing on cost increases in the form of higher prices; continuing to deal with the same suppliers and customers; and holding on to labor despite falling demand and productivity. The reasons for this behavior include: the monopolistic or oligopolistic position of many state firms; the common interests of managers, workers, and sometimes government officials in avoiding painful change; and the sometimes still soft budget constraint facing state-owned firms, especially the larger ones.

The need to accelerate the producers' response to new market conditions is the central rationale for privatization policies. Although in theory state-owned enterprises could operate according the same market incentives as private enterprises if they faced a tight budget constraint, the political pressures on the government to intervene are difficult to resist. In addition to privatization policies, the Polish government has an anti-monopoly policy, based on legislation that permits government intervention to prevent a wide variety of both direct and indirect actions in restraint of trade. This section addresses the available evidence on the nature and extent of the adjustments of Polish state industrial enterprises during 1990-1993 in order to determine the conditions that either drove or impeded adjustment. It reviews the evidence from published information on production, employment and profitability of Polish industries and analyses the findings of enterprise surveys and other microeconomic information on enterprise behavior.

Trends in Industry

Polish industry underwent major structural changes during 1990-1993. Industry has become somewhat less concentrated. Among industrial firms employing more than 50 workers, the share of employment in the 200 workers and below category increased from 11 percent to 14 percent from 1991 to 1993, while that in firms employing 1000 to 5000 workers declined from 39 percent to 33 percent, although the largest firms, employing over 5000 workers, increased their share of total industrial employment from 17 percent to 20 percent. More importantly, there was a massive increase in the number of individual proprietorships (mainly handicraft and contractors), few of which employ more than 5 workers, and in the number of generally small private corporations.

Most of the large firms continue to be state-owned, with state industrial firms in 1993 employing about 500 workers on the average, compared with 28 in private domestic corporations and 38 in foreign-owned firms (Table 4.5). This great discrepancy in average size of firm results in part from the fact that private enterprise has concentrated in labor-intensive industries, where small firms can be efficient, has had little capital to invest, and has not

TABLE 4.6   Poland: Firm Size, Capital Intensity, and Share of Public
Ownership, 1993

Industry	Percent of Employment in Public Sector		Employment per Firm		Capital per Employee	
	Percent	*Rank*	*Thousands*	*Rank*	*Mil.zl.*	*Rank*
Fuels & Power	99	1	2,045	2	593	2
Metallurgy	86	2	2,388	1	803	1
Chemicals	61	3	456	3	572	3
Machinery	61	4	384	4	295	5
Minerals	56	5	273	7	343	4
Light Industry	42	6	289	5	150	9
Food	40	7	277	6	287	6
Wood & Paper	38	8	258	8	264	7
Other	33	9	186	9	181	8
Total Industry	**59**		**407**		**388**	

Source: CSO of Poland, *Statistical Yearbook, 1994*, pp. 328-329.

been willing to purchase state enterprises that are stuck with large, generally obsolete, plants and equipment. Table 4.6 shows that the state sector is
still dominant in capital-intensive industries, like fuels and energy and
metallurgy, while the private sector dominates in labor-intensive industries, such as wood and paper, light industry, and food processing. Indeed,
there is a very close correlation between the share of the public sector in
employment by industry and both average employment per firm and the
value of capital per worker. This relationship between degree of privatization
on the one hand and size of firm and capital intensity on the other hand,
would be even stronger if more detailed recent data on industrial branches
were available. Of the industries in Table 4.6, the most labor-intensive
branches—clothing and shoes in light industry, furniture and paper products in the wood and paper industry, fine glass and ceramics in the minerals
industry, and chocolate products in the food industry—are those with the
smallest average size of firm and are the most highly privatized.

A major difficulty in the analysis of industrial trends is distinguishing
long-term adjustment toward a production structure that is sustainable
under free market, competitive conditions from the short-term effects of the
severe contraction of domestic demand and of CMEA markets. Production
changes in 1990 were mainly responses to short-term demand shocks
resulting from the "Big Bang" and consequently are not indicative of likely
longer-term relationships. For the same reason, and because of lags in cost
accounting adjustments, relative profitability in 1990-1991 does not provide
useful indications of the likely long-term profitability of various Polish

TABLE 4.7   Poland: Industrial Production Indexes, 1990-1994 (1989=100)

	1990	1991	1992	1993	1994*
Clothing	76.0	73.6	83.8	111.3	133.9
Electron. & Instruments	83.9	62.6	89.9	111.1	132.1
Wood	74.8	74.6	86.2	108.2	126.4
Metal Products	74.4	65.4	70.5	85.2	107.8
Food	76.3	76.9	80.1	95.6	105.8
Transport Equipment	74.8	49.5	61.0	88.5	105.4
Paper	76.2	74.7	81.0	80.2	101.7
Construction Materials	80.0	78.1	76.6	86.2	100.5
Class	72.7	71.8	76.6	--	--
Fine Ceramics	78.4	70.3	68.9	--	--
Chemicals	75.4	65.2	69.6	70.4	96.1
Fuels	79.9	68.2	75.8	80.6	86.8
Elec. Equipment	79.8	66.4	71.3	78.9	85.8
Non-Elec. Machinery	80.4	64.2	60.0	63.2	71.5
Ferrous Metals	82.9	63.1	60.9	55.5	67.2
Nonferrous Metals	76.7	60.5	57.0	--	--
Leather	69.4	59.7	57.4	54.7	64.2
Electric Power	90.3	85.6	79.0	61.5	63.6
Textiles	60.4	49.8	50.0	53.8	63.3
Coal	68.2	68.8	62.6	55.3	55.3
Total Industry	**75.8**	**66.7**	**69.5**	**74.5**	**83.4**

Note: Because of a change in industrial classification, indexes for 1993 and 1994 are not fully comparable with those for earlier years. To gain approximate comparability, the following indexes were combined: Office Machinery and Computers, Radio, TV, and Communications Equipment, and Medical, Precision, and Optical Instruments were combined into an index of Electronics and Instruments; Chemicals and Rubber were combined into an index for Chemicals. At the same time, the index for Other Non-Metallic Mineral Products (shown in the table under Construction Materials) includes Glass and Fine Ceramics, and the index for Manufacture of Basic Metals (shown here under Ferrous Metals) includes Ferrous and Nonferrous Metals.

Sources: 1989-93: CSO of Poland, *Statistical Yearbook*, various issues; 1994: CSO of Poland, *Statistical Bulletin*, No. 11, 1994, pp. 124-125.

industries. By 1993, and especially 1994, the fourth and fifth years of the Polish transition, however, with the recovery in aggregate demand and a more stable policy and external environment, what appear to be important longer-term trends begin to emerge.

Production. Polish industrial production, which had fallen by one third from 1989 to 1991, had recovered to within nearly 15 percent of the 1989 level by 1994. An examination of production trends in the main industrial branches (Table 4.7) shows major changes in the composition of output, especially after 1991, when the economic recovery began. In 1991, production in all branches was far below the 1989 level, and in nearly all of them had fallen to a level 60 to 75 percent that of 1989, indicating that the big decline in aggregate demand was the dominant influence on industrial production. By contrast, after 1991, several branches drove the industrial recovery, while other branches continued to decline, resulting in a far greater dispersion of growth rates, and indicating clearly that industrial adjustment to the market environment was proceeding rapidly.

Most of the successful industrial branches have been labor-intensive and consumer-oriented: namely, clothing, wood products, consumer electronics, and some food products. On the other hand, production of metals, coal, leather and electricity continued to fall until 1994, when the strong overall expansion finally began to drag even the laggard branches along. Even so, production of coal in 1994 was only 55 percent of the 1989 level; textiles, leather and electricity were less than two-thirds of that level, while production in the fastest-growing branches had increased by about one-third.

There are large contrasts in performance within industrial branches as well. For example: production of household chemicals, cosmetics and plastic products has responded to increased demand, while that of basic chemicals continues to be depressed; furniture production is booming, while lumber production lags; clothing production is expanding rapidly, partly for export to the West, while production of basic textile yarn and fabrics has not recovered from the loss of the protected Soviet market.[11]

These structural trends partly reflect the strong recovery of consumer demand and the surge in demand for products that were virtually unavailable under Communism, such as high quality clothing, consumer electronics, and modern instruments. They also indicate a shift toward products in which Poland probably has a competitive advantage in the long term because of low labor costs and the low costs of certain skills. Nearly all the relatively successful industries use labor-intensive techniques that, with labor costs a fraction of those in Western Europe, give Poland an advantage. Clothing, furniture and processed foods are leaders in the growth of exports to the West. It is also easier for labor-intensive firms than for most capital-intensive firms to quickly change production mix in response to changes in demand. At the same time, Polish industrial firms are developing competitive niches even in more capital-intensive areas in which users can tolerate less than state-of-the-art technologies, as in the production of some metal products, shipbuilding, and various types of machinery and equipment.

Not surprisingly, the relatively successful industrial branches are also those in which privatization has gone the furthest and in which firm size is relatively small. This is, of course, both cause and effect. Firms in these branches have been the most attractive to private buyers and the least difficult to privatize, while there was little or no interest in buying unprofitable coal mines, steel mills, or plants whose main market had disappeared and which are saddled with large excess capacity. At the same time, privatization generally increased a firm's responsiveness and enhanced the chances for major restructuring, as discussed below.

Employment. Trends in industrial employment reveal a massive, but lagged adjustment to new demand conditions. Employment fell much less than output during the initial severe output drop, fell at an increasing rate in 1991, continued to decline slowly during 1992 and 1993, the first two years of economic recovery, and did not level off until 1994, the third year of output growth. The lagged response of employment to changes in output indicate that the amount of excess labor in industry, already considerable under Communism, increased greatly during the first two years of the transition. In 1991, average output per employee was only about 75 percent of the 1989 level. As output recovered but employment continued to fall, output per employee rose rapidly: it reached 88 percent of the 1989 level in 1992, met that level in 1993, and exceeded it by almost 15 percent in 1994. Rough estimates of trends in employment and output per employee by industrial branch, shown in Table 4.8, suggest that excess labor has largely disappeared, not only in the fastest-growing branches, but also in some branches where output is still depressed, such as textiles and leather, and at least in most parts of chemicals and machinery. Indeed, the only industries in which output per employee has not yet fully recovered are coal, electric power and metals, in all of which the firms are large, state-owned, and capital-intensive. Excess labor undoubtedly persists in individual firms in other branches, such as basic chemicals and heavy machinery, but it is apparent that enormous progress has been made in reducing this problem.

Profitability. Poland publishes detailed statistics by industrial and other economic branch on the elements of revenues, costs, taxes, and profits. Under Communism, revenues, costs and profits were severely distorted by price controls and other factors. Although controls have been lifted, except for public utilities and housing, however, profits are still poor indications of the longer-term viability of industrial branches. Even for 1993, they are poorly correlated with increases in production, and some branches with weak prospects, like non-ferrous metals, earn high reported profits, while some, like wood and clothing, earn low profits. Many of these anomalies are probably due to under-reporting of profits by private firms. For example, in 1993, the ratio of gross profits to revenues from sales in the economy as a whole was reported to be 4.3 percent in the public sector and 1.9 percent in the private sector. In reality, private firms were probably more profitable than state firms.

Despite under-reporting, profitability data do suggest at least the early stages of a sorting out process between profitable and unprofitable firms. A number of studies have classified firms into three groups in terms of

TABLE 4.8   Poland: Industrial Employment and Productivity, 1992 and 1994

	Employment		Output per Employee	
	1992	1994	1992	1994
Clothing	86	90	97	148
Electronics & Instruments	68	53	103	248
Wood	85	95	102	133
Metal Products	74	69	95	157
Food	102	96	78	110
Transport Equipment	70	66	87	160
Paper	78	72	103	140
Construction Materials*	87	78	88	129
Chemicals	81	76	86	126
Fuels	96	88	79	98
Electrical Equipment	59	53	121	161
Non-Electric Machinery	72	65	83	109
Ferrous Metals**	83	69	73	97
Leather	64	50	90	128
Electric Power	102	106	77	60
Textiles	55	48	91	132
Coal	76	66	83	83
Total Industry	**79**	**73**	**88**	**114**

Note: Industries are arrayed by rank of the change in output from 1989 to 1994 (see Table 4.7). Indexes: 1989=100.

* From 1992 to 1994, includes Glass and Fine Ceramics.

** From 1992 to 1994, includes Non-Ferrous Metals.

Sources: CSO of Poland, *Statistical Yearbook*, various issues; CSO of Poland, *Statistical Bulletin*, various issues; and Table 4.7.

profitability: those with positive net profits after income taxes; those with positive gross profits, but negative net profits; and those with negative net and gross profits. The proportion in the middle category has been declining, while that of both the clearly profitable and clearly unprofitable categories has increased. This suggests that, on the one hand, an increasing number of firms have found ways of achieving sustained profitability, but on the other hand an increasing number are also facing an unsustainable situation.

Sample data from industry surveys also show an increased dispersion of profitability among firms in all industries. This suggests that many firms have been finding profitable niches, regardless of the industry, and, until 1993-1994, despite poor macroeconomic conditions.[12]

Microeconomic Evidence of Enterprise Behavior

General. A wealth of literature exists on enterprise behavior in Poland, based on surveys of both public and private enterprises. Many of the surveys were conducted under the auspices of the Gdansk Institute for Market Economics; some by Warsaw University; and a major one by the World Bank.[13] The number of sample enterprises ranges from about 30 to 75 (the latter in the World Bank survey). This section is based on the findings of the surveys of state industry in 1990 and 1991, of state and private industry in 1992, and of trends in these enterprises over the entire 1990-1992. Studies dealing specifically with the impact of various forms of privatization are used mainly in the next chapter. The general picture of state enterprise adjustment that emerges from all the surveys follows below.

Over the entire period of the transition, state enterprises have made major adjustments in production, employment, marketing, and management. On the whole, small and medium-sized enterprises made more far reaching adjustment than large enterprises, and made them faster. Firms operating in competitive markets also made larger and faster adjustments than those in monopolized markets. The earliest adjustments (in the first few months after price and market liberalization) involved sales and included new marketing channels and a search for new markets. The most common adjustments in production were passive—producing to capacity items that were in strong demand and cutting production of those in weak demand. Substantial changes in production mix involved improvements in quality, packaging, and other features that are fairly easy to introduce. The introduction of new products and new technologies was considerably less frequent because of lack of funds for investment or lack of incentives.

Most firms steadily reduced employment, but avoided mass layoffs whenever possible, greatly preferring to accelerate attrition. Few firms underwent massive restructuring or reorganization, but many streamlined their production and organization by shedding (through sale, lease, or shutting down) peripheral functions, such as construction, health care, and other services. The majority experienced worsening financial conditions, although a group of the better firms prospered. Though nearly all borrowed from banks, few considered the banks to be helpful. There has been a trend, however, for increased bank involvement in enterprise activities, which is a good sign. Few firms attracted any foreign investment, and some were disappointed by the reaction of potential foreign investors to their efforts.

In general, expectations of obtaining help from the government diminished rapidly and, by 1992, had virtually disappeared. With few exceptions, firms behaved as if they had to fend for themselves. Very large firms, however, continued to get government help, in the form of unpaid tax obligations and continued bank credits despite a very poor financial condition. These firms acted as a "sponge" for direct and indirect assistance and also supported a number of subcontractors. The government began to come to grips with the problems of these very large firms, more than two years after these problems first became evident.

The Economic and Financial Environment. All firms felt under strong financial pressure in 1991 and 1992 and were acutely aware of constraints on their activities. For the great majority, profitability declined, the debt burden increased, and payables increased more than receivables. Perhaps one third of the firms were forced to follow survival strategies, doing whatever might help to stay alive.

Financial pressure was due partly to weak aggregate domestic demand and partly to increasingly competitive conditions. In 1990, competition was limited by the highly concentrated structure of industry and the high cost of imported goods due to an undervalued zloty. In 1991, massive competition came from imports, which were very cheap because of the overvalued zloty. In 1991 and 1992, competition also came from new private firms and from smaller state firms that had been spun off from the larger ones. In the 1992 survey, none of the sample firms claimed an absence of competition.

Purchasing and Marketing. The collapse of the command economy forced all firms to work hard to find markets for their products. Management attention shifted from production and acquisition to sales, marketing and finance. Within a few weeks after the liberalization of prices, state enterprises were looking for new sales channels, often finding the traditional state-owned outlets to be too rigid. They sold to new private middlemen and, in more and more cases, made direct sales to the ultimate user. Later, marketing departments were often organized and some firms began to advertise, although marketing and advertising are still weak by Western standards.

Firms were strongly interested in exports and almost all had programs to expand exports, but many of these programs could not be carried out because of lack of funds for investment. Exports were maintained or increased even when their current profitability was low or negative, because of a belief that export development would be a important aspect of modernization in the long-term.

None of the firms complained of difficulties in obtaining any supplies, which is not surprising, given the thoroughgoing nature of Poland's liberalization. About one quarter of the firms changed suppliers in 1990 and one half in 1991.

Production Adjustments. In all the surveys, enterprise managers were asked about the nature and extent of their production adjustments—specifically, whether they involved: new products and technologies; modifications of existing products and technologies; and changes in the output mix of existing products to reflect their relative profitability. In 1991 and 1992, most firms were able to modify their products, but a considerable number confined their adjustments to the passive process of adjusting assortment to demand and profitability. An increasing number of firms introduced new products in 1992, but they were still a fairly small minority.

All the surveys show that large firms were both slower to adjust and made less active adjustments than smaller firms. This is partly due to the relative inflexibility of large-scale production when substantial investment funds are not available for restructuring. In all firms, however, new product and new technology development was mainly hindered by lack of investment funds.

Employment and Labor Relations. Nearly all firms reduced employment gradually over the three-year period. Employment reductions occurred mainly through attrition, which was accelerated by means of a variety of measures, such as early retirement, paid leave, and individual persuasion. There was evidently a substantial improvement in labor discipline as a result of management's increased ability to fire individuals for cause. Only a small percentage of separations were officially for cause, but workers reacted to the possibility.

Mass layoffs were avoided whenever possible because they caused severe frictions with workers' councils and labor unions and were relatively expensive (involving double the amount of severance pay of individual separations). Generally, mass layoffs have been limited to enterprises that were closed down, were in a bankruptcy-type liquidation, or closed certain peripheral units, such as construction organizations, health facilities, and cafeterias. In the economy as a whole, they have accounted for about 20-25 percent of total layoffs since 1990.

Most managers consider that they have only partial freedom in their employment policy; they have to deal with both workers' councils and labor unions. In some firms, the workers' councils have been heavily involved in all important decisions, including layoffs. In other firms, managers take the initiative and workers' councils have no real influence. In 1992 the great majority assessed their excess labor supply at 10-20 percent, considerably less than in 1991, but indicating a potential for further declines in employment as sales increased. These survey findings are consistent with the overall trends in employment and output per worker discussed earlier. The rapid growth of labor productivity since 1992 suggests a disappearance of excess labor in the great majority of firms.

Most managers believe that their relations with workers' groups are cooperative on the whole. This is due partly to the widespread fear of ultimate bankruptcy, and consequently of much larger layoffs. It also reflects the fact that both workers and the managers can blame the government for limiting wage increases through the excess wage tax, instead of fighting each other.

Finance and Investment. There are signs that budget constraints on state enterprises are tightening. Although very few of the enterprise managers found the government or the banks "helpful," the many enterprises facing serious financial problems were able to survive by accumulating arrears on their payment obligations to the government, the banks, and other enterprises. Out of 25 state-owned firms in a sample, 13 were in arrears on tax payments, but only one of these was being liquidated. Moreover, these firms were continuing to receive short-term bank credits in spite of large overdue bank loans. This problem was especially severe for very large state enterprises. It is finally beginning to be addressed and is discussed in the next section.

Nearly all firms received credits for working capital, almost exclusively from Polish banks, but few obtained investment credits, and a substantial part of those were from foreign sources. The government provides some subsidized long-term credit to large state enterprises from special funds, but only to a very limited extent. Polish enterprise managers say that banks are beginning to get more involved in the enterprise so as to better assess its creditworthiness. Bank credit is being extended increasingly to firms that can provide mortgages as security or can show that they are following certain policy conditions. The best firms apparently have little difficulty getting credit. The other firms complain that banks are much too tight with their money.

The difficulties in enterprise finances have greatly limited enterprise investment. Decapitalization of Polish industry has certainly occurred, and is continuing. And unlike Hungary, Poland was been unable to attract much direct foreign investment until 1994. Foreign investments have been mainly small and few have been used for restructuring state-owned firms.

At the enterprise level, decapitalization has taken the form of the shutting down, sale or leasing of buildings, machinery and other assets, as well as of the depreciation of retained assets. Some social assets were given away to local governments. Productive assets were generally sold to subcontractors.

Privatization

Characteristics of Privatization Policies

Although all Polish post-Communist governments have aimed at an economic system in which private ownership was dominant, the actual rate of privatization has been disappointingly slow. Polish public support for privatization has cooled since the program began, with the ratio of positive to negative evaluations declining from overwhelming support to majority disapproval. The Polish people have never had any difficulty with small-scale privatization of trade, services, and construction, but are quite skeptical about privatization of large state-owned firms.

Policies to deal with state enterprises had to take into account the influential position of Polish workers, both inside the enterprises and in the legislature. In 1989 the Solidarity movement struggled with a fundamental debate over the role of workers in management. Many members of Solidarity, although supporting the freeing of markets, wanted a system of workers' management. The liberal intellectuals, however, argued that such a system would create too many rigidities, pointed to the unsuccessful Yugoslav policies to buttress their position, and were strongly supported by Western advisers and aid donors, including the IMF and World Bank. Although initially the liberals largely had their way, workers' rights had to be accommodated to get any major privatization laws through the legislature. And beginning in 1992, privatization policy has included increasing elements of industrial policy.

The Polish government has tried hard to control the privatization process. There was a political consensus when the Mazowiecki government came to power to prevent at all costs continued "nomenklatura" privatizations. The cost of doing so was to recentralize the process in the new Ministry of Ownership Transformation. Ironically, however, government privatization programs proved very difficult to implement and the most effective forms of privatization were those that depended the most on initiatives from below and required the least government control and decisions, such as the very successful privatization of small shops and firms in 1990.

Restitution to the original owners of property formerly nationalized by Communist governments has not been tackled, for fear of greatly slowing the entire privatization process. There is little chance that former private owners will get their original property back. In some cases, they may be offered alternative physical assets (e.g. land of about the same quality in a different location), but mainly are likely to receive some sort of financial compensation, perhaps in the form of privatization bonds convertible into shares of privatized enterprises, so as not to create an immediate burden for the state budget.

There have also been debates over another fundamental question, namely: What should be done to promote good management in enterprises that may not be privatized, at least in the relatively near term, because of their functions (e.g., public utilities), the absence of buyers, or the strong preference of their workers? Programs were introduced in some industries to deal with such enterprises, and legal forms for independent state firms exist, but a general policy covering the remaining state sector is still in the process of development. Policies governing the remaining state enterprises are assessed in the next major section of this chapter.

Methods of Privatization

General. Since July 1990, when the Law on the Privatization of State Enterprises was passed, the Polish government has distinguished between two main types of privatization: through the "capital route," and through "liquidation." The distinction is a purely legal one—under "capital privatization," the state enterprise is transformed in several steps into one of several kinds of private corporations, but keeps its legal identity, while under "liquidation," the state enterprise loses its legal identity, and one or more new private enterprises are formed from the assets of the former enterprise, if these assets are sufficient after paying off creditors. Privatization plans under either route can be initiated by the enterprise themselves or by government agencies, but decision-making authority is with the government agencies.[14]

The fundamental legal distinction among privatization routes obscures some major functional differences, especially for privatization through "liquidation." This kind of privatization takes place under two separate laws, which apply to entirely different types of situations. One of these is liquidation under the Privatization Law of July 1990, which can be used only for enterprises in at least reasonably healthy financial condition (in the remainder of this chapter we will refer to this approach as the recasting method, to distinguish it from what we will call the transformation method to refer to "capital privatization").

The other route is liquidation under the Law on State Enterprises of September 25, 1981, (amended in July 1991), which is a kind of bankruptcy law for state enterprises in poor financial condition, and that we refer to as real liquidation. A third kind of privatization was introduced in 1992 to organize the breaking up and sale of state farms.

Another important distinction is between "individual privatization" (one enterprise at a time), and "mass" or "general" privatization (with the use of vouchers for large numbers of enterprises). A great deal of controversy has surrounded "mass privatization," which is legally considered to be one of the methods of transformation through the "capital route."

The basic statistics on privatization through the several routes are presented in Table 4.9. They show a large surge in the number of enterprises entering the privatization process in 1991, followed by a slowdown in 1992-1993 and an even sharper drop in the first six months of 1994. Because of the substantial time required to accomplish privatization or liquidation of an enterprise, the peak rate of actual privatization and liquidation occurred in 1992, and has since fallen off. The firms that completed the privatization process during 1990-1994 made up nearly 45 percent of those put in process but only 23 percent of the latter's employment. As of mid-1994, employment in privatized firms was only 270,000, compared with 1.2 million workers in the firms put in process. In manufacturing, employment in privatized firms was 171,000—28 percent of firms under the privatization programs, but only 6 percent of total manufacturing employment. Among the various privatization routes, recasting successfully privatized by far the largest number of firms, but these are generally small, averaging fewer than 300 workers.

TABLE 4.9 Poland: Number of Nonagricultural Enterprises Privatized, 1990-1994

Program	1990*	1991	1992	1993	1994**	1990-94
In Process	130	1128	681	653	210	2803
Transformation	58	250	172	156	70	706
Recasting	44	372	246	203	68	933
Real Liquidation	28	506	263	294	72	1163
Completed	24	280	418	324	166	1212
Transformation	6	24	22	46	17	115
Recasting	15	227	307	184	109	842
Real Liquidation	3	29	89	94	40	255

* July-December
** January-June
Source: CSO of Poland, *Privatization of State Enterprises, Quarters I and II, 1994*, p. 18.

Privatization Through Transformation. This was the preferred approach to privatization for the initial post-Communist Polish government. It was patterned after the privatization methods in the United Kingdom during the Thatcher administration. The main steps of this approach are described below (Table 4.10).

The initial request is made by the enterprise itself, the so-called "founding organ" (the branch ministry), or the Ministry of Ownership Transformation, including whether to privatize the enterprise individually, or as part of mass privatization. After a positive preliminary government evaluation, the government engages an external consulting firm (most often a Western accounting firm) to assess the financial and market position of the enterprise and to estimate its value.

The enterprise is transformed, first into a "commercialized enterprise" (that is, an enterprise subject to the commercial code), based on preliminary government approval of the process, and then into a state corporation, 100 percent owned by the state treasury and registered as a corporation. At this point, the Ministry of Ownership Transformation becomes responsible for the new firm and may take steps to restructure or reorganize it.

Once the state corporation has been formed, it issues shares in accordance with a set of legal rules. Up to 20 percent of these shares may be sold to employees at one half the market price. The others are sold to "active investors," such as financial institutions or foreign corporations, managers, and the general public. Unsold share revert to the state treasury. The corporation becomes formally a private corporation when private parties acquire a majority of shares.

TABLE 4.10   Poland: Nine Steps of Privatization Through Transformation

Step 1: Initiation
The enterprise approaches the government and expresses an interest. In some cases, the Prime Minister can order privatization on proposal from Ministry of Privatization.

Step 2: Feasibility Study
Usually done by a consulting firm.

Step 3: Decision
To go ahead with process.

Step 4: Complete Documentation
- Formal application from either management or workers' council.
- Opinions from workers' delegation, founding body (e.g. Ministry of Industry).
- Proposal by workers' council on employee share ownership (up to a maximum of 20% of total shares).
- Draft of company statutes and proposed capitalization.
- Decision of anti-monopoly office.

Step 5: Additional Appointments (as required)
Advisors (chosen by tender to work on: auditing, legal analysis, business plan and valuation, privatization option.

Step 6: Ministerial Decisions
Minister decides on:
- Transformation with or without conditions.
- Company statutes.
- Selection of 2/3 of supervisory board (1/3 chosen by employees).
- Capital structure.

Step 7: Transformation
State-owned enterprise becomes a state-owned corporation governed by commercial code. Notary and court registration of company.

Step 8: Strategy
Decision of privatization strategy. Options:
- Trade sale, to one or more parties
- Public offer for sale of shares
- Management/employee buyout
- Some combination of the above

Step 9: Implementation
Advisors assist in such matters as: sales documents, auctions, selection of short-list of bidders, contract negotiations, prospectus, public relations, share distribution, and marketing.

Source: Documents prepared for prospective foreign investors by Poland's Ministry of Ownership Transformation (i.e., Ministry of Privatization), obtained through the Consulate of Poland, Chicago, Illinois.

This approach was considered to have several virtues: leading to clear-cut private ownership; potentially attracting foreign investment; adding to state treasury revenues; and creating the basis for a Polish stock market, on which corporate shares would be traded. Its main disadvantages were that it took a long time (more than a year on the average for the entire process) and was expensive, because of the high fees of Western accounting firms. As will be seen, privatization through this route was disappointingly slow, partly because foreign investment was small and partly because mass privatization did not develop. Indeed, the slowdown in the number of enterprises beginning the process during 1992-1994 is due in part to the very long delays in getting the "mass privatization" program, which had been expected to greatly accelerate the privatization of large firms, under way.

From July 1990 through June 1994, of the 706 enterprises that entered this transformation process, only 115 had been privatized. Most of those not yet privatized were corporations owned entirely by the state treasury that were to be sold individually to private owners (327) or were expected to participate in the "mass privatization" program (249). Beginning in 1993, however, some state corporations were scheduled to undergo restructuring without any commitment to privatization.

Most enterprises taking this route are large (about 1300 workers on the average); over 80 percent are in industry and they are found in all industrial branches. About 80 percent of these firms were privatized through sale to so-called "strategic investors"—in other words through negotiations leading to direct sale—with the remainder (17 percent) being privatized through public sale of shares. Foreigners purchased about one half of the firms that were privatized by the Transformation method. Workers took only 15 percent of shares, less than their preferential quota, and managers 4 percent. This method is the only one that contributed any significant revenues to the state budget. Such revenues have been increasing, but remain very small. They constituted less than 1.5 percent of total budget revenue in 1991-93, rising to 2.8 percent in the first ten months of 1994.

The Recasting Approach. This approach is most common for small and medium-sized enterprises of 50-500 workers, the average being about 300; it is simpler and takes less time than Transformation, and usually is initiated at the initiative of the insiders of an enterprise—its workers and managers. The steps are described below (Table 4.11).

First there is a proposal to liquidate from the enterprise, which specifies the manner in which enterprise assets will be disposed of and the ultimate form of the private enterprise. This is followed by a review by the government, leading to approval of the liquidation, coupled with a simplified evaluation of the firms's assets by an independent firm. Finally the assets of the former state enterprise are disposed through sale of assets, leasing, or creation of a new corporation.

TABLE 4.11   Poland: The Six Steps of Privatization Through Liquidation ("Recasting")

Step 1: Initiation
Enterprise or Founding Body decides to initiate the process, often with a consulting firm.

Step 2: SOE Decision
Workers' council presents opinion on whether to privatize. State-owned enterprise (SOE) chooses its preferred method (i.e. buy-out, asset sale, contribution into company). Business plan is drafted and Ministry of Privatization questionnaire regarding financial and legal data is completed. Documents are given to Founding Body (local government or branch ministry).

Step 3: Founding Body's Decision
- Founding Body appoints Preparatory Team to examine documents and renders an opinion on the application. If not satisfied, with valuation, can hire a different consulting firm.
- Preparatory Team discusses its opinion with SOE. Can chose a privatization method other than that preferred by SOE.
- Founding Body examines results of documentation submitted by Preparatory Team and renders an opinion and drafts a decree on privatization of SOE.
- Documentation and decree is submitted to Ministry of Privatization

Step 4: Ministerial Decision
Ministry of Privatization reviews documents and evaluates the financial and legal status; approves or disapproves of privatization plan.

Step 5: Implementation
Founding Body administers liquidation process, or resolves any problems in cooperation with Founding Body.

Step 6: Methods
- Asset sale.
- Contribution into Company. A new company is created between Treasury and domestic or foreign investors.
- Management/Employee Buy-out. Requires 20% down payment, the rest on installment.

Source: Documents prepared for prospective foreign investors by Poland's Ministry of Ownership Transformation (i.e., Ministry of Privatization), obtained through the Consulate of Poland, Chicago, Illinois.

About 60 percent of the enterprises involved in recasting were leased by their employees, usually in cooperation with the director, becoming internally held private corporations. Because of funding limitations, financing of these transactions typically involved a lease of about 10 years, generally with 20 percent down payment—in effect, a leveraged buy-out. Leasing often became very burdensome and caused the profitability of the enterprises to decline. In 1993 and 1994, leasing terms were liberalized by reducing the down payment to 10 percent in some cases, by reducing or waiving some payments if the money goes for investment, and by transferring ownership rights to the lessee after payment of only one third of the value of the property. The latter concession helps to expand the supply of mortgage instruments that can provide security for long-term bank loans.

In a few cases, the property was purchased outright by domestic and foreign buyers. In other cases, the enterprise went out of business and its assets were sold. A combination of methods was also used. On the average, the market value of the assets of enterprises privatized through recasting was only about one quarter of their book value.

As mentioned earlier, this approach has been much faster than the transformation method. It has been a favorite method in construction and fairly important in industry, but only in relatively small firms. Uses of this approach hit its peak in the second half of 1991, and has since slowed to a crawl, mainly because the bulk of the smaller, profitable firms had been privatized.

Real Liquidation. Real liquidation involves the disposal of the assets of a state enterprise in poor financial condition—that is, those unable to pay the "dividend tax," or making losses even if they are exempted from the tax—through private sale of assets and/or transfer to a new corporation. Real liquidation is initiated by the founding ministry, with the approval of the Ministry of Ownership Transformation. It constitutes an administrative bankruptcy procedure, not under court control, designed to reorganize and restructure a loss-making enterprise with a view to insuring the survival of at least a portion of it.

Once Real liquidation is approved, the founding organ appoints a "liquidator" (a kind of receiver) to manage the enterprise. The "liquidator" has wide authority to negotiate with creditors, including the government, for debt reduction or forgiveness, to sell redundant or unprofitable assets at auction, to pay off creditors with the proceeds, and to lay off workers. Once the enterprise is in Real liquidation, the workers' council is disbanded. The liquidator's main objective is to recast and generally to downsize the loss-making enterprise into a potentially profitable corporation, which can find private investors.

About 1200 state enterprises have entered the Real liquidation process, but only about 255 of these have completed this process, which is time consuming because of the difficulties of finding buyers for assets and negotiating debt relief. Real liquidation has been confined mainly to small enterprises—in mid-1994, average employment in state enterprises undergoing Real liquidation was only 41. A few larger ones are also being liquidated, however, as is described in the next major section of this chapter.

Mass Privatization. Privatization through citizen ownership has had a long intellectual life in Poland, but has experienced a rough political ride. The first concrete "mass privatization" plan for Poland was developed by Lewandowski and Szomburg in 1989, debated in and out of the government, first proposed officially in November 1990, and then revised on several occasions, until it was finally passed by the Legislature in April 1993.

There has been a fairly broad consensus in favor of some sort of mass privatization among Poles who did not want the government to continue managing most large industrial enterprises. It was always assumed that domestic capital was insufficient to purchase most of the large enterprises outright, and this view was reinforced by the slow progress of individual privatization by transformation. But there were sharp debates over how mass privatization should be handled and the role of institutional investors and foreign advisors. The proponents of mass privatization saw it not only as accelerating the privatization process, but also as giving the population at large a personal stake in the capitalist system, hopefully giving rise to more positive attitudes and broader investment opportunities.

Table 4.12 outlines some of the elements of the Mass Privatization Law. Some 450 generally large and profitable state enterprises (a reduction from an originally planned 600) will be transformed into corporations and will issue shares. The enterprises that are to be transformed have been identified and include some of the best enterprises in Poland.

Up to 20 intermediate institutional investors, called National Investment Funds (NIFs), will be formed. The NIFs will be managed by Western investment companies, but their directors will be Polish citizens and the chairmen of the supervisory boards will be appointed by the President of Poland. Each NIF will hold what is expected to be a controlling interest (one third of shares) in some 30 companies, the remainder of shares being distributed among the other NIFs (25 percent), the employees of the enterprise (19 percent, distributed free of charge), and the state treasury (30 percent). All Polish adult citizens will receive equal shares in the NIFs for a nominal charge after these have been listed on the Warsaw Stock Exchange. NIF shares will then be freely bought and sold.

The Poles hope the NIFs will act as real owners with a long-term perspective. The management companies of the NIFs will have management and performance contracts that hopefully will create strong incentives to increase the value of the companies. The main objections to the plan have been that the NIFs could become another form of government bureaucracy, that the people will sell their shares for "beer money" to speculators, and that the government will lose income it badly needs by giving away instead of selling strong enterprises.

The left-wing government in power since late 1993 has supported mass privatization in principle, but Prime Minister Pawlak, head of the populist

TABLE 4.12   Poland: Mass Privatization Program (MPP) in Brief, circa 1993–1994

• The program gives all adult citizens the opportunity to obtain an equal stake in the privatized enterprises through the acquisition of Share Certificates (SCs) in National Investment Funds (NIFs).

• NIFs will take the form of closed-end funds registered as joint stock companies. Up to 20 NIFs will be created. Each of these will be managed by a firm or consortium selected through competitive bidding from among the most reputable investment banks, funds and management organizations from many countries.

• NIFs will have supervisory boards representing the interests of their owners. These owners will be Polish citizens who acquire SCs, and the State Treasury, which will initially retain 15% of shares for use as part of the compensation package for fund managers.

• MPP includes about 600 (now 450) large and medium-sized Polish enterprises, primarily manufacturing plants.

• The commercialized joint stock companies formed from the original state enterprises will have the following share holding structure: 33% by a "lead" NIF; 25% distributed evenly among all other NIFs; 30% retained by the state treasury; and 19% distributed free of charge to enterprise employees.

• The "lead" NIF in each company will be chosen through a draft line process by the 20 NIFs; each NIF will have in its portfolio a "lead" shareholding in 30 companies.

• The Fund Management Companies managing the NIFs will have a management and performance contract which provides strong financial incentives to manage these funds in such a way as to maximize the long-term value of the NIF fund in the interest of the shareholders through restructuring, modernization, and refinancing. It is expected that NIFs will exist for 10 years.

• After one year of operation and preparation of prospectuses, the NIFs will be listed on the Warsaw Stock Exchange (WSE). Soon after that, Polish citizens will be able to obtain SCs in bearer form at a nominal fee of approximately U.S. $25 (10% of an average monthly salary). These SCs give Polish citizens the right for at least four years to trade both within and outside the official market for one share in each NIF listed on the exchange. The trading procedure for NIFs will be the same as for all WSE stocks.

Source: Documents prepared for prospective foreign investors by Poland's Ministry of Ownership Transformation (i.e., Ministry of Privatization), obtained through the Consulate of Poland, Chicago, Illinois.

Peasant Party raised a variety of issues, evidently as a delaying tactic. As of January 1995, it appeared that the program would finally go forward. The participating firms and NIFs had been selected.

Effectiveness of Privatization Methods

The purpose of privatization is to increase the long-term profitability of formerly state-owned enterprises through improved management and restructuring. The record is too short to draw firm conclusions and is, of course, strongly biased by large differences in the condition of enterprises entering different privatization routes. Some insights can be gained, however, from industry surveys that examine a small number of firms undergoing various forms of privatization during 1990-1992. Polish surveys of privatizing firms[15] find considerable differences in firm behavior, depending on the privatization route. Their principal findings are the following.

Firms privatizing through transformation tend to make few efforts to reorganize or restructure until after the process has been completed, or is close to completion. In the early stages of transforming into a state corporation, the firm's longer-term policies are not clear. This is partly because the ultimate owners may not be known and partly because the purpose of and need for the change was not made clear to the workers, and sometimes even the managers. Many of these firms, however, do make substantial changes after the transformation is completed. Of the 10 firms that were privatized through this route and listed on the Warsaw Stock Exchange, all undertook restructuring, including reorganization of head offices, introduction of new production and sales methods, and cuts in employment.

Firms privatizing through recasting tend to make more changes before than after privatization. This reflects the direct involvement of managers and workers in the preparation for the Recasting. Typically, managers draft the initial proposal, then discuss it in depth with the workers' council. By the time it is submitted to the government, not only has it been thoroughly vetted among the insiders, but action has already been taken. The fact that most firms using this route are small or medium-sized undoubtedly facilitates communication between labor and management. The capital for the down payments in leasing arrangements is obtained from the retained earnings of the firm, and often from managers and the managing director, who thereby gain substantial ownership shares. Funding did not come from financial institutions. Leasing rates were generally set late in the process, and often became an undue burden on the enterprise. After privatization, the power of management, especially the firm's director, apparently tends to increase, though outsiders are playing an increasing role in supervisory boards. Employee ownership shares have declined as a result of sales of shares to managers and outsiders. Most recast firms have been profitable, but their liquidity has been cut by the fixed leasing payments and there have been few funds for investment. This method of privatization has been overwhelmingly popular with both labor and management.

Firms that have become state corporations without any clear privatization agenda, made the fewest changes. Managers and workers appear to view achievement of this status alone mainly as a means of raising wages (because they are no longer subject to the excess wages tax) as a quid-pro-quo for eliminating the workers' council. The tendency, however, is to avoid any upsetting actions, pending a longer-term solution.

The kinds of changes introduced by most privatizing firms include: widespread changes in marketing; changes in the mix of production; slow declines in employment (except in firms under real liquidation, wherein employment fell 75 percent); fairly deep changes in organization; increased wages (except for those under liquidation); and changes in managing directors, although more before than after privatization.

The government bureaucracy was perceived as passive and unhelpful. Because of bureaucratic delays and sometimes unclear property rights, it often took months for the enterprise to sell or lease physical assets, such as buildings. The ups and down of government privatization policy were deplored. Banks were said to be of no help in the privatization process, but this was before the major bank reforms of 1993-1994. Enterprise directors usually played the key role. The workers' councils were active and generally helpful as transmission belts to the workers in efforts to develop common positions. Labor unions were moderately active.

The main conclusions about privatization in Poland are, first, that it is important to clarify property rights quickly. When the privatization process takes a long time, and even more when there is uncertainty about the eventual outcome, managers and workers have little incentive for change, except for changes designed to raise their immediate incomes. Second, it is important to involve those with insider rights (managers and workers), in the privatization process from the beginning. Even when a buyer is found for an entire enterprise, insiders' cooperation is necessary because they can sabotage any attempted change or alternatively can be very helpful in bringing change about. Finally, wherever possible, initiatives should come from below, not from the bureaucracy. Insider privatization, such as leveraged buy-outs, can be effective when large amounts of capital are not needed to improve the performance of a firm.

Transforming the Remaining State Enterprises

General

As it became apparent that the formal privatization programs were leaving the bulk of large-scale state industry in the public sector and that the financial condition of state enterprises was deteriorating, the government initiated a variety of programs designed to improve the efficiency of state enterprises, so that they might become better candidates for privatization, or at least able to survive.

In 1991, Management Contracts, under which managers were given personal incentives to improve and restructure the enterprise, were introduced. Also in 1991, a large program of sectoral assessments, designed to serve as a foundation and spur for privatization or restructuring of major industries, was initiated. Although initially unsuccessful, this program was revived in 1993-1994 in the form of specific policies for developing or phasing down certain industries.

In 1992, as the finances of state enterprises continued to deteriorate and it became evident that large amounts of overdue debt were uncollectible and were severely constraining banking operations, the Polish government began to work on large-scale debt relief programs, together with the recapitalization of banks.

Beginning in 1993, the government belatedly began to deal more forcefully with the problems of large, unprofitable firms to force major restructuring, downsizing or, in extreme cases, closure. In 1994, the new left-wing government set out to transform all remaining state enterprises into state corporations, but it is not yet clear where this step will lead.

These various programs, which together require considerable government intervention, are a belated recognition that privatization policies alone could not bring about a sufficient transformation of large-scale Polish industry in an acceptable time period. As of June 30, 1994, state enterprises still employed about 1.5 million people, some 25 percent of total employment outside government and private agriculture, but only 18 percent of the employment of over 8 million in state enterprises when the privatization program began in 1990. Since employment in privatized enterprises and in state corporations was only about 900,000 in mid-1994, it is evident that a massive erosion and downsizing of state enterprises, on the order of 70 percent, has occurred.

Very few of the remaining state enterprises are at an advanced stage of privatization, liquidation, or restructuring. A larger number are in preliminary stages of transformation as shown in Table 4.13. In mid-1994, over 60 percent, with two-thirds of the workers (about one million), had not yet undergone any formal organizational changes. As indicated earlier, the bulk of these enterprises were in heavy industry, notably coal, steel, electric power, and heavy machinery and chemicals. Some of them were suffering heavy losses, but the majority were profitable, which will make future transformations easier. By early 1995, the number of enterprises with no privatization or restructuring plan had declined to about 2,000 as another 200 firms entered the "mass privatization" program (making the total in this program 450) and other measures were taken.

TABLE 4.13   Poland: Status of State Enterprises as of 6/30/94

Status	No. of Enterprises (thousands)	No. of Employees
Total	4,629	1,536
in liquidation	417	14
being privatized	45	4
in insolvency*	466	18
being restructured	321	108
being "administered"**	80	34
awaiting division	29	20
awaiting amalgamation	4	1
awaiting liquidation	247	55
awaiting restructuring	272	198
awaiting transfer to local govt.	54	15
undergoing financial restructuring by banks	144	110
not subject to formal changes	2,668	1,038

*Under real liquidation
**By the branch ministry
Source: CSO of Poland, *Privatization of State Enterprises, Quarters I and II, 1994,*
p. 64.

Strengthening Enterprise and Bank Finances

The Polish government has begun to come to grips with the poor
financial condition of a large part of state industry, especially the massive
accumulation of overdue debt. It is likely that many loss-making and over-
indebted enterprises are salvageable, although others should eventually be
closed down. Unfortunately, very little was done during 1991 and 1992, as
bad debt was allowed to pile up. The only major step was government
issuance of $5.5 million in foreign currency-denominated bonds in mid-
1991 for recapitalizing two large banks that had suffered severe foreign
exchange losses. Belatedly, some major debt relief programs are being
implemented, especially since the Debt Restructuring Program was introduced in February 1993.

Rules have been established for the financial restructuring of enterprises
and debt relief through such measures as:[16] debt-equity swaps, in which the
creditors of an enterprise agree to accept ownership shares once the enterprise has become a corporation; debt restructuring at reduced interest rates
and with longer maturities and partial debt write-down; sale of assets; and
new medium-term loans at below-market interest rates, financed through
the state budget, for enterprises that abide by specified conditions, such as
restructuring and privatization.

The country's nine large commercial banks were recapitalized so as to enable them to write down part of their loan portfolio without serious risk to their own viability. The total amount of the capital enhancement is about $1.3 billion, which is covered by using the $1 billion stabilization fund that Poland has not drawn on and some World Bank credits.

Other steps have been taken to improve internal banking procedures and credit practices. Loans are more carefully categorized and reserve requirements for various categories of questionable and non-performing loans have been established. Clearer credit guidelines were set, and there is some indication that these are beginning to make a difference. Bank loans to problem debtors were prohibited, except as part of approved debt workout programs. Commercial banks established special departments to deal with loss-making enterprises, work out their bad debts, and channel subsidized government credit. Two large state banks were privatized in 1993 and two more were to be privatized in 1994. Unfortunately, a political storm occurred over the privatization of the first of these (shares of Bank Slaski were sold initially for a small fraction of the subsequent market price, triggering accusations of fraud), which has set back the entire process.

In general, the Polish government hopes to greatly increase the role of banks in the restructuring and privatization process. As indicated earlier, this role had been very small in the past, because of financial constraints on the banks, poor training and management, and the fact that banks have found it more profitable to buy government bonds at positive real interest rates than to lend to firms that are either heavily indebted or lack a track record. All of these problems are being addressed and progress is being made. In early 1994, among the firms with serious debt arrears at the end of 1991, half of the non-performing bank loans were in firms that had signed conciliation agreements, one quarter were being partially serviced, 19 percent were being fully serviced, 13 percent had been repaid, 10 percent were in bankruptcy proceedings, 5 percent had been sold, and 3 percent had been liquidated. The fact that two thirds of firms that had reached conciliation agreements through the banks were making net profits before interest payments indicates a large potential for salvaging debt-ridden firms.[17]

The future demands on Polish banks will be large indeed. Polish banks may take equity positions in enterprises, within certain exposure limits, and consequently may become heavily involved in enterprise management. They may also purchase shares in the NIF's, once these are established and their shares are publicly marketed. They have become major players in the restructuring and write-down of debt for firms that are being transformed and eventually privatized. And, most important, they are expected to use their enhanced capital base to expand credit to deserving private and state-owned enterprises. Considering how ineffective and passive Polish banks have been in the past, it is highly questionable that they can perform all these functions well. On the other hand, the record of centralized organs in managing the restructuring of loss-making enterprises in other countries, notably Hungary, is poor.

On balance, the Polish government is probably right to use a decentralized approach, in which banks make the micro-level decisions to restructure and help to privatize state enterprises. But it is essential for the banks to be fully independent of the government, and this can only occur through privatization, a process that is under way. The sooner the banks are privatized the better.

Management Contracts

The use of management contracts is based on the recognition that some firms must be restructured before any privatization becomes possible. Management and business contracts were first developed in the second half of 1991. Polish and foreign managers were encouraged to bid for the right to manage enterprises by submitting business plans for the firms' reorganization and future development.[18] The Ministry of Privatization selects the winning bids. Both sticks and carrots are provided in the contract—a down payment requirement of around 5 percent of the value of the firm can be partly or wholly withheld if the program is unsuccessful; and the managing group is paid partly in stock options, from which it can keep the capital gains if the program is successful. The contract period can cover several years, during which time the managing group is typically given considerable flexibility for restructuring the enterprise.

Unfortunately, it has proved difficult to find enough good Polish managers and interested foreign managers to allow this program to develop on a large scale. At the end of 1992, officials at the Ministry of Privatization hoped to conclude no more than 40 such contracts during 1993.

The Sectoral Approach

Under the Sectoral Approach, analyses of entire sectors, such as coal, steel, cement, petroleum, and machine tools, were to be used to facilitate and accelerate the privatization and restructuring of all the enterprises in the sector. Initially introduced as another approach to privatization, it eventually became both more selective and of broader application. The basic steps follow below (Table 4.14).

First, the government selects a sector on the basis on national importance, development potential, and investor interest. Next, a project manager drafts terms-of-reference for competitive bids from investment banks and consulting firms, who prepare written proposals. The ministry selects a winner, who is named the sector advisor. The sector advisor prepares a comprehensive analysis of the sector, based in part on on-site visits to most of the firms in the sector. The sector advisor then develops a policy for

TABLE 4.14   Poland: The Sectoral Approach to Privatization, in Brief, circa 1993-1994

Choosing a Sector

Government identifies sector to be privatized. Selection criteria are: Positive potential of sector; investor interest; eagerness of firms to privatize; and national economic importance of sector.

Choosing an Advisor

- Sector assigned to project manager by Ministry;
- Project Manager drafts terms-of-reference outlining goals and questions to be addressed;
- Competitive bid is organized targeting investment banks and consulting firm, often forming consortia and joint ventures;
- Firms submit proposals; talks held to clarify proposals;
- Ministry chooses Sector Advisor from among competing firms;
- Ministry decides on financing, which may come from Ministry budget or foreign aid (e.g. PHARE, USAID or World Bank).

Phase I: Analysis

Sector Advisor prepares a comprehensive analysis of sector, including a study of the individual companies, based partly on on-site visits.

Phase II: Strategy Development

- Based on previous analysis, Sector Advisor develops a restructuring/privatization policy for sector;
- He also works out concrete strategies and action plans for individual companies, choosing between: Trade sales, IPO's, Auction; and Management/Employee buy-outs;
- Sector Advisor contacts potential investors to ascertain the extent of their interest in this sector and helps them understand the privatization process;
- He reports to the Ministry.

Phase III: Implementation

- Advisor conducts privatization of major companies in sector.
- He assists smaller companies in liquidation.
- He works with government agencies to develop ideas for restructuring other companies.
- He makes available his knowledge to interested parties and funding organizations.

Source: Documents prepared for prospective foreign investors by Poland's Ministry of Ownership Transformation (i.e., Ministry of Privatization), obtained through the Consulate of Poland, Chicago, Illinois.

restructuring and privatization, including strategies and action plans. He also contacts potential investors. Finally, the sector advisor advises, assists in, or conducts privatization and restructuring measures.

The initial plans for this approach called for a study of some 30 sectors, and bids were sent out to foreign and local groups. Sectoral studies were prepared for some 20 industries, including communications, petroleum, steel, coal, cement, pulp and paper, and heavy chemicals. In the judgment of experts who have been directly involved in this process, however, only very few of these have been useful—the others were relegated to the back files of the ministries.

Such studies are expensive. To be useful, they must feed into a wide range of policy decisions concerning the sector. These include not only privatization techniques, but also management of the enterprises while they are still under state ownership, the need, if any, for tariff protection, use of foreign credits, and sometimes more direct government involvement. Apparently, the approach was used successfully for communications and petroleum, both areas in which government involvement would continue to be large in any case. In these cases, moreover, the government was able to reconcile inter-departmental differences and develop a coherent policy, whereas this did not happen in many other cases.

Variants of this approach are being used in the coal and the steel industries, both of which suffer from large excess capacity in the long-term and face the closing of many mines and plants and the laying off of many thousands of workers.

The coal industry, using a Polish study, plans to cut employment by half over ten years. The industry is being reorganized with a holding company at the top, under which six regional state-owned corporations, with balanced holdings, will actually make the specific decisions as to which mines to shut down in accordance with the overall policy. The government will provide some special funds for the closing of mines and World Bank financing is being sought.

The steel industry, using a Canadian study, plans to cut capacity and employment by half or more over a decade. This plan's implementation, however, will be much more decentralized than that for coal. The industry has been organized into 26 independent corporations, some of which may be privatized (Huta Warszawa has already been purchased by an Italian firm). The government has established an inter-ministerial "Council for the Restructuring and Privatization of Polish Steel" and an independent "International Trade Bureau for Steel." The long-term plan is apparently being discussed with the workers' organizations, but it is not clear how coherent government policy will be.

Dealing with Losers

Sooner or later, post-Communist governments must deal with the losers in the economic transition—with the firms that, even with considerable assistance and time, probably cannot become competitive. The glib advice that these firms should just be closed down so that their resources can be reallocated to more productive uses ignores the enormous social and political costs of such moves on a large scale. It is simply not possible to close down firms employing thousands of workers, and on whom thousands more depend in contracting firms, without at least a lengthy process of adjustment. This painful problem of dealing with the bankruptcy of large firms is common to all transition countries. What distinguishes Poland is that it has grappled with it for five years.

In effect, Poland has dealt with bankruptcy differently for firms of different size. There has been no state interference, of course, with the bankruptcy and exit of private firms. Thousands of small unincorporated firms have failed to compete in the market and closed down, but these were more than offset by the entrance of new private firms. A fairly large number (about 250) of generally small and medium-sized state-owned firms have also been allowed to close under the Real Liquidation law. Since 1993, legal bankruptcy proceedings have been taken against some 900 small state-owned firms that had been transformed into corporations. But thousands of firms are still losing money, and the largest among these are accumulating tax arrears and piling up debt. So far, none of the very large firms has been closed down.

In Poland, the bankruptcy law has been applied only to companies, regardless of ownership, that operate under the commercial code (they may or may not be issuing shares). Under bankruptcy, when a firm cannot pay its debt obligations, a court first sets a time limit for negotiating a solution with the creditors. Failing an agreement, the court appoints a receiver to pay off creditors in order of priority and then close down the firm. For state enterprises, however, the Poles have used the more flexible process of real liquidation before the enterprise was formally "commercialized," as was described in the section on types of privatization above. The Law on State Enterprises of September 25, 1981, specifically spells out the conditions under which unprofitable state enterprises may be liquidated. The main advantage of this process is its relative flexibility and the fact that it remains under government, rather than court control. But to deal with the largest enterprises, the government has also been using *ad hoc* methods of restructuring. The following examples of liquidation/restructuring are based on interviews conducted by the author in May 1993. One of the firms was under formal liquidation procedures and the other was not.

The wool fabrics firm "Lodex" in Lodz, formerly with over 1000 employees, was under Real Liquidation. The Director had been appointed by the Ministry of Industry to act as "liquidator." He hoped to organize a much smaller firm, with perhaps one quarter of the capacity of the existing firm, that would produce higher quality fabrics at lower cost and become profitable. He was paying off debts—in order of priority, first to the workers, second to the budget, and third to other creditors. Debt to the government was being negotiated; bank debt had mainly been paid off. He was selling many assets. The workers had initiated the request for liquidation after three years of unprofitable operations, during which more than half of the workforce had been laid off. The alternative was to close down entirely.

The tractor enterprise URSUS is one of the largest in Poland, formerly with over 10,000 employees. It had lost money on a large scale for more than three years, producing at 10-20 percent of capacity. Enormous unpaid debts and tax arrears had accumulated. URSUS was under "Commissariat Administration" since September 1991—a form of reorganization supervised directly by the Ministry of Industry.

In 1992, a government council was established to restructure the tractor industry, in which URSUS is the dominant firm and the only final assembler of tractors. An in-depth Sectoral Study was prepared, and the director of that study was appointed Managing Director of URSUS. He had taken, or planned to take, several major steps, including: transformation of URSUS into a holding company, which will hold stock in ten or more corporations (this was still on the drawing board); debt reduction and restructuring and debt-equity conversion; the closing down of old facilities and unneeded assets; sale and leasing of assets; and probably, obtaining low interest credits to modernize the remaining facilities, although the source of such funds was unclear.

The fact that actions are being taken, albeit after excessive delays, to restructure large loss-making enterprises is encouraging. Nevertheless, it will still take a long time to determine which parts of these enterprises to close down and it may or may not be possible to find funding to restructure the rest. Subsidies for industrial restructuring have constituted a minute and declining share of the state budget—0.2 percent in 1993. Government policy is to use many instruments to deal with the problem little by little, salvaging a few enterprises, closing down a few, and breaking up or restructuring others.

Foreign investors are likely to make an increasing contribution to the restructuring of large Polish industrial firms. Although FDI was less than three billion dollars through 1993, of which less than one half took the form of purchases of existing firms,[19] it is certain to increase considerably as some major projects in such industries as automobiles (FIAT and General Motors), food processing, cement, and chemicals, are implemented. In addition, implementation of mass privatization would greatly expand the opportunities for FDI in existing firms.

Evaluation of Policies on the Remaining State Enterprises

In general, Polish policies to promote the restructuring, downsizing, and closure of the remaining state enterprises have had little success. It has proved very difficult for Polish governments to develop coherent industrial policies; instead, the various bureaucracies have constantly fought with each other. The strong clout of organized labor, both at the enterprise level and in national politics, has constrained whatever policies the government could agree on. Although more has been done in the past two years than in the first three years of the transition, it is difficult to be optimistic about any Polish government's ability to solve such difficult problems as the fundamental restructuring of the coal industry and of very large enterprises, like URSUS, in the foreseeable future.

Problems with policy formulation reflect both political differences within the government and inadequate mechanisms for policy coordination. In some cases, the Economic Council, a high-level inter-ministerial council, has made decisions, but the Council has virtually no staff, and consequently deals with only a small number of issues. Moreover, there has been more competition than cooperation between the staffs of the Prime Minister and those of the President.

Even when clear policies are established, in the virtually unanimous view of Poles and foreign observers in Poland, most government ministries, including especially the Ministry of Industry and Trade, are not competent to make micro-decisions affecting a firm. Polish managers consider the ministries to be passive and unhelpful. This suggests that the implementation of any policy decision should be left to the firm, and oversight mainly to independent institutions, such as banks, once these have been privatized. The government, however, can and should clarify regulations and property rights, and generally create a stable, predictable environment for firms.

The left-wing government's policy of corporatizing the remaining state enterprises will not solve anything by itself, but may have useful effects if combined with other policies, such as going ahead with Mass Privatization and privatizing the banks so that they can better deal with loss-making firms.

Yet it is difficult not to be optimistic about the future of the Polish economy—about the prospects that the transition to a market economy will be successfully completed over the next few years. In spite of often ineffective government policies, the economy is recovering strongly, the private sector is booming, privatization is continuing, and, most importantly, the remaining state enterprises are steadily being eroded. And these trends almost certainly will continue.

Why will these trends continue? The basic reason is, of course, that Poland has a market economy, with free prices, open to foreign trade, and with developing markets for labor, capital, and management. But there is another reason—the government and all but a small number of firms face a hard budget constraint, and consequently have no choice but to adjust and restructure. Severe constraints on government spending have been imposed by the IMF and Poland's foreign bank creditors. Fiscal order is also a long-term condition for admission to the European Union—something the great majority of Poles want. Consequently, the Polish government, like those in Western Europe, has had to limit its direct or indirect subsidies to a small number of firms. And even these firms have come under a tightening budget constraint, and consequently have felt increasing pressure to restructure. It is no wonder, therefore, that the Polish state sector has been steadily eroding, shedding workers and functions, even in the absence of positive government action.

Notes

1. Official Polish economic statistics are from publications of the Central Statistical Office (CSO). The principal CSO publications used for data on income, production, employment, trade, and economic units are various issues of: *Rocznik Statystyczny (Statistical Yearbook); Biuletyn Statystyczny*—monthly (*Statistical Bulletin*); *Zatrudnienie I Wynadrodzenia W Gospodarcze Narodowej*—annual (*Employment and Earnings in the National Economy*); *Przemysl* (*Industry*); and *Handel Zagraniczny* (*Foreign Trade*).

2. An excellent economic history of Poland in the Communist era is found in Ben Slay, *The Polish Economy: Crisis, Reform, and Transformation* (Princeton University Press, 1994).

3. A large number of books and articles describe and assess Polish post-1989 reform policies. Some of those this author found most useful are: World Economy Research Institute, *Transforming the Polish Economy*, Warsaw School of Economics, Warsaw, 1993; World Economy Research Institute, *Poland: International Economic Report 1993-94*, Warsaw School of Economics, Warsaw, 1994; The World Bank, *Poland: Reform, Adjustment and Growth, A World Bank Country Study*, Vols. I and II, 1987; Polish Policy Research Group, Department of Economics, Warsaw University, *PPRG Report on the Economic Policy of Poland*, 15 July, 1993; Jeffrey Sachs,, "Building a Market Economy in Poland," *Scientific American*, March 1992; OECD, *Industry in Poland: Structural Adjustment Issues and Policy Options*, Paris 1992; OECD, Poland, Paris, 1992; Kazimierz Poznanski (ed), *Stabilization and Privatization in Poland*, University of Washington, International Studies in Economics and Econometrics, Volume 29, Kluwer Academic Publishers, Boston, Mass., 1993; and Stanislaw Gomulka, *Economic Reform in Poland, 1989-91: Aims, Policies and Outcomes*, The World Bank, Research Paper Series Number 19, July, 1991.

4. The Polish foreign exchange market was much broader than that in Russia at the same stage of transition. Consequently, although the free exchange rate initially greatly understated the internal purchasing power of the zloty, the extent of the understatement was much less than for the rubles.

5. From Balcerowicz's chapter "Lessons from Economic Transition in Poland for Central and Eastern Europe" in *International Economic Report* listed above.

6. *Gazeta Wyborcza* No. 227, 29 September 1994.

7. Blaszczyk and Dabrowski, "The Privatization Process in Poland" (see Note 14 below).

8. For background on Polish political history and attitudes, see Roger A. Clarke (ed), *Poland: The Economy in the 1980s*.

9. Here again, Ben Slays's book, *The Polish Economy*, is very useful.

10. See Ben Slay, "The Polish Economy Under the Post-Communists," *RFE/RL Research Report*, Vol. 3, No. 33, 26 August 1994. Also, an article by Danuk Zagrodzka, "Marooned Economy: PSL/SLD Coalition Record," *Polish News Bulletin Weekly Supplement*, September 29, 1994.

11. Leszek Zienkowski (ed), *Polish Economy in 1990-92: Experience and Conclusions*, RECESS, Warsaw, 1993, especially chapter 8.

12. Brian Pinto, Marek Belka, and Stefan Krajewski, "Transforming State Enterprises in Poland: Microeconomic Evidence on Adjustment," World Bank, Policy Research Working Papers, WPS 1101, February 1993. Also, Ian M. Hume and Brian Pinto, Prejudice and Fact in Poland's Industrial Transformation, World Bank, *Policy Research Working Papers*, February 23, 1993.

13. In addition to the World Bank survey listed under Note 12 above, the following Polish industry surveys were used: Janusz M. Dabrowski, Michal Fedorowicz, and Anthony Levitas, "Przedsiebiorstwa Panstwowe w Roku 1990—Wyniki Badan" (State Enterprises in 1990—Survey Results), *Institute for Surveys on the Market Economy*, No. 11, Warsaw, January 1991; Janusz M. Dabrowski, Michal Fedorowicz, and Anthony Levitas, "Przedsiebiorstwa Panstwowe w Drugim Roku Transformacji Gospodarczej—Wyniki Badan" (State Enterprises in the Second Year of Economic Transformation—Survey Results), *Institute for Surveys on the Market Econom*y, Gdansk-Warsaw, 1992.

14. This section draws heavily on studies produced for an International Workshop on Privatization Experiences in Eastern Europe on 21-22 May, 1993 in Budapest, Hungary: Barbara Blaszyczyk and Marek Dabrowski, "The Privatization Process in Poland"; and Jan Mujzel, "Privatization in Poland—Its Achievements." Privatization statistics are mainly from Main Statistical Administration (GUS), *Prywatyzacja Przedsiebiorstw Panstwowych* (Privatization of State Enterprises), which provides systematic data semi-annually. The Ministry of Ownership Transformation also publishes detailed information on the steps followed in the various privatization routes, as well as *Prywatyzacja*, a monthly review of privatization legislation, regulations, and activities.

15. See: *Report Warunki Pobudzania Mechanizmow Podazowych w Przedsiebiorstwach Przemyslowych w 1992: Dla Przedsiebiorstw Panstwowych I Prywatnych* (Report on the Conditions for the Awakening of Supply Responses in Industrial Enterprises in 1992: for State and Private Enterprises), Institute of Development and Strategic Studies, Warsaw, May 1993; OECD Advisory Group on Privatization, Seventh Plenary Session, *Performance of Privatized Enterprises: Corporate Governance, Restructuring and Profitability*, Moscow, 29-31 Martch, 1995, articles by Marek Mazur, "Assessment of the Situation of Privatized Enterprises and Banks in Poland: Case Study," and Jacek Bukowski, "Performance of Polish Small and Medium-Sized Enterprises Privatized Through Leveraged Buyouts."

16. This section on the role of banks is based partly on interviews with World Bank and Bank of Poland officials. The main publications used are: Alfredo Thorne, *The Role of Banks in the Transition: Lessons from Eastern European Countries Experience*, The World Bank, 1993; and David Kemme, "Banking in Central Europe During the

Protomarket Period: Developments and Emerging Issues," paper prepared for the International Conference *Development and Reform of the Financial System in Central and Eastern Europe*, Vienna, Austria, October 28-30, 1993.

17. "Debt as a Control Device in Transitional Economies: The Experience of Hungary and Poland," by Hubert L. Baer and Cheryl Gray, papers presented at a joint conference of the World Bank and the Central European University Privatization Project, *Corporate Governance in Central Europe and Russia*, 15-16 December 1994, Washington, D.C.

18. Ben Slay, "Poland: The Role of Managers in Privatization," *RFE/RL Research Report*, March 19, 1993.

19. *Foreign Privatization in Poland*, Wladyslaw W. Jermakowicz, Project Director, Center for Social and Economic Research, Studies & Analyses 30, Warsaw, October 1994.

5

The Czech Republic

A Brief Review of the Czechoslovak Transition

General Characteristics and Legacies

In comparison with Poland and Hungary, the transition of Czechoslovakia, and especially of the Czech Republic, toward a market economy has been an orderly process, based on an integrated set of policies. In some respects, however, the process is still behind that in Poland and Hungary— notably, some of the most painful aspects of state enterprise restructuring are only beginning to be addressed.

The "velvet revolution" of November 1989 brought a sudden, dramatic turn in the economy and policy of Czechoslovakia. Unlike Poland, where there was a substantial and growing private sector and a wide opening to the West in trade and payments, or Hungary, where even the state enterprises had developed wide autonomy for decades, Czechoslovakia still had a traditional, centrally-planned economic system, in which state-owned units produced more than 95 percent of GDP. Consequently, the private sector had to be built virtually from scratch. More than 60 percent of Czechoslovak foreign trade was oriented to CMEA countries, with the Soviet Union accounting for about one third. And its economic structure was even more dominated by heavy industry, especially steel and heavy machinery, than in most other Communist countries, reflecting a comparative advantage within the CMEA, but not on Western markets.

While such inherited characteristics put Czechoslovakia at a disadvantage in undertaking the transition, other characteristics were obvious assets: a long industrial tradition, comparable to Germany's, reflected in good technical training and traditions of workmanship; a relatively good physical and technical infrastructure; and the absence of any severe macroeconomic imbalance. In addition, lack of a strong workers' movement and the non-confrontational tendencies of the Czech people made it easier for strong pro-market policies to be adopted and implemented.

Czechoslovakia's comparatively advanced technological level has been a two-edged sword: it provided a strong human capital base; at the same time, it created an industrial structure that made the transition particularly difficult because the high-technology industries are the least competitive in Western markets and the most costly to bring up to world market standards.

Avoidance of any severe macroeconomic imbalance during the late Communist era was a great advantage to the post-Communist transition government. During the late 1980s, inflation was only 1-2 percent annually, the budget deficit 1.2 percent of GDP, and foreign debt 15 percent of GDP (versus 60-70 percent in Poland and Hungary). Although there were shortages of many products and substantial price subsidies, queuing was rare for basic consumer goods. The absence of severe macroeconomic imbalances was owing in part to the increased role the central bank had acquired in economic policy making. Consequently, post-Communist Czechoslovak governments were able to quickly bring the destabilizing effects of price and exchange rate liberalization under control, whereas in Poland and Russia macroeconomic imbalances constantly threatened to derail the economic transition process.

The balance of positive and negative inherited factors is substantially more favorable for the Czech Republic than for Slovakia, in the wake of the dissolution of the joint state in January 1993. The Czechs benefit from a much longer industrial tradition, proximity to Germany, and a more diverse economy and export mix. The Slovaks have inherited a disproportionate share of plants that depended on the Soviet market.

Transition Policies

Czech economic transition policies have been consistently based on liberal (in the European sense) principles, as reflected in the views of Vaclav Klaus, the Prime Minister of the Czech Republic and former Finance Minister of Czechoslovakia. Considering the complexity of the task, Czech policies have been surprisingly consistent and coherent. Their common, single-minded goal has been to free the economy from government micro-level influence as fast as possible.

It took about a year after the "velvet revolution" for these policies to gel, during which time a great deal of essential legislation was passed[1] (Table 5.1), and some preliminary economic measures were taken, such as breaking up the state economic control apparatus, beginning to break up state-owned firms, and eliminating food subsidies. The first post-Communist year was also one in which political forces competed and debated over the main goals and methods of economic policy. Although the debate between the liberals, led by Klaus, and those who favored a more gradual, social-democratic approach, was not completely resolved during 1990, Klaus was clearly in the ascendancy toward the end of the year. Since then, the liberals,

**TABLE 5.1   Czech Republic: Major Federal Economic Reform Legislation
in 1990 and 1991**

1990
- Small Property Restitution Law (No. 403)
- Small Scale Privatization Law (No. 427)
- Revisions to the Civil Code (Nos. 87, 105, 116)
- Amendments to the Labor Code of Dec. 5
- Joint Stock Company Law (No. 104)
- Amendment to the Foreign Activities Law (no. 113)
- Foreign Exchange Law (No. 528)
- Copyright Law
- Private Entrepreneurs Act (No. 105)
- Power Sharing Act (No. 296)
- Prices Act (No. 44)
- Personal Income Tax Law (No. 389)
- Corporate Income Tax Law Amendment (N. 214)
- Turnover Tax Law Amendment (No. 107)
- Wage Limit Law (No. 108)
- Intellectual Property Law (No. 527)

1991
- Customs Act (No. 5)
- Large Property Restitution Law (No. 87)
- Land Law (No. 229)
- Large Scale Privatization Law (No. 92)
- Revisions to the Civil Code ((Nos. 87, 509)
- Bankruptcy Law of July 11
- Anti-Monopoly Law (No. 63)
- Small Business Law (No. 455)
- Insurance Law of April
- Law on the Transfer of State Property of February
- Agricultural Cooperatives Transformation Act of December 21
- Bank Act of December 20

Source: Richard Judy, *The Czech and Slovak Republics: Two Paths for Eastern Europe*,
Hudson Institute Country Report No. 1, August 1992.

with Klaus as Prime Minister, have dominated Czech politics, especially
after the break with Slovakia. In sharp contrast to Poland and Hungary,
where a large majority of the population have been strongly dissatisfied
with government policies and leadership, Klaus has been receiving a
positive popular rating of over 70 percent.

The Czech government has tried to make money count and to find "real
owners" for firms as quickly as possible. In this drive to improve economic

efficiency, the Czechs made far fewer compromises to considerations of social or economic equity than the Poles and Hungarians. For example: when small enterprises were put up for sale, no questions were asked about the sources of the money; leasing was rejected as a means of privatization because it continued a government involvement; and no special provisions were made for labor participation in enterprise ownership and management. The policy compromises and adjustments the Czech government has made—such as postponing application of the bankruptcy law, and continuing state control of and support for some industries and large plants—appear to have been mainly tactical.

The main lines of Czech economic transition policies have been:[2]

Price Liberalization. One year after Poland, Czechoslovakia eliminated most price controls. The share of regulated prices in GDP fell from 85 percent in December 1990 to 15 percent in January 1991, then declined to about 5 percent by the end of 1991.

Exchange Rate. The crown was drastically devalued in real terms and free internal convertibility into hard currencies was introduced. The crown-dollar exchange rate has been stable since January 1991. At this exchange rate, Czech wages are lower in dollar terms than those in Poland and Hungary, although Czech productivity is higher. This contributes to the attractiveness of the Czech Republic for foreign investment, but also strongly favors labor-intensive production.

Foreign Trade. Imports and exports were generally freed of licensing requirements and quotas. Exceptions were arms, oil, goods under quota in trade agreements or imposed by trade partners, and goods in temporary barter agreements with Russia and other former Communist countries.

Monetary Policy. As in Poland, monetary policy during initial price liberalization was extremely tight as banks virtually stopped lending. As prices stabilized, lending resumed, with mildly positive real interest rates.

Fiscal Policy. Sharp reductions in subsidies and cuts in the bureaucracy and the military moved the state budget from a small deficit to a surplus. Revenues from enterprises remained large because of fairly high profitability, which, however, may decline in the future.

Wage Policy. Wage policy has been an important anti-inflationary tool. Real wages were held down by temporary wage freezes, a high tax on above-norm wages, and country-wide wage bargaining. Wage controls were eased slowly in 1992, largely removed in the first half of 1993, then partly reintroduced in July 1993 for firms employing more than 20 workers. For the remainder of 1993 and in 1994, firms could raise wages by the rate of inflation plus 5 percent without paying any penalties.

Privatization. Privatization has had an extremely high priority since 1991. It has involved "Small Privatization"—the sale of retail trade, service and other small enterprises—which is complete, and "Large Privatization"—

the conversion of the larger state enterprises into private corporations through several methods, the most important of which is distribution of vouchers to the population. An independent National Property Fund (NPF) has been the sole recipient of revenues from privatization and the sole source of financing to facilitate privatization.

Industrial Policy. The Czech government has no overall industrial policy. It has, however, pursued an active policy of industrial de-concentration, used a variety of financial tools to prepare firms for privatization, established long-term policies for such branches as communications, oil and gas, coal, and steel, and provided *ad hoc* assistance to very large firms that were in financial difficulty.

Bank Reform and Regulation. Banks are expected to play a major role in the restructuring of Czech industry. They are being privatized, steps are being taken to bring bank regulation up to the needs of a market economy, and many are being recapitalized.

Economic Performance

The Czech economy on the whole has performed better than those of other former Communist countries during the past three years.[3] The break with Slovakia caused disruptions in 1993 and 1994 and delayed economic recovery. Some major statistical indicators are shown in Table 5.2.

TABLE 5.2   The Czech Republic: Economic Trends, 1990-1994

	1990	*1991*	*1992*	*1993*	*1994**
1989=100					
GDP	98.8	84.7	79.1	79.9	81.9
Personal Cons.	106.6	80.7	88.2	89.5	94.0
Fixed Investment	97.8	80.5	85.6	78.8	82.7
Industrial Prod.	96.4	72.9	62.9	58.2	59.0
1990=100					
Exports**	--	71.8	72.4	80.1	83.7
Imports**	--	87.0	96.7	108.7	120.5
Annual Percent Change (December to December)					
Retail Prices	15.3	65.2	12.6	18.1	10.0
Percent of the Labor Force					
Unemployment	0.8	4.1	2.6	3.5	3.2

* Estimated by the author, based partly on PlanEcon estimates.
** Includes Slovakia. From 1990 to 1991, calculated from monthly dollar values. From 1991 through 1994, based on data in constant Czech crowns.
Source: PlanEcon Report, Volume X, Numbers 31-32, September 28, 1994, "Czech Economic Monitor."

GDP fell 20 percent between 1989 and 1993, although as in many other transition economies the actual decline was almost certainly smaller than the measured decline because of large unrecorded private transactions. Economic activity leveled off in late 1993 and has since begun to recover. GDP growth was slightly over 2 percent in 1994. Industrial production, after falling 38 percent, began to exceed the monthly levels of the previous year in March 1994.

Inflation has been under control. Since an initial spurt in prices of 26 percent in January 1991, when most prices were liberalized, the rate of growth in consumer prices has been near a 10 percent annual rate, if some brief price spurts, due to such one-time events as the elimination of remaining price controls and the introduction of a value added tax, are considered. Growth of producer prices has been in the single digits—about a 6 percent annual rate since early 1993.

Personal consumption fell 20 percent from 1989 to 1991, according to official data (which almost certainly exaggerate the decline). But then it increased sharply in 1992, and more slowly in 1993 and the first half of 1994. Real wages fell sharply at the beginning of 1991, but have since trended upward.

Investment dropped sharply in 1991 and again in 1993, but apparently increased in 1994. The only dynamic part of investment has been private construction, which is booming. Employment trends are mixed. Excluding small-scale enterprises, registered employment declined about 30 percent from 1989 to 1992. During the same period, there was an increase of 1.2 million in the number of private registered self-employed. Employment in industrial firms with more than 25 workers continued to fall in 1993 and the first half of 1994, which, together with rising output in the latter period, indicates a recovery in labor productivity.

Unemployment is very low in the Czech Republic (about 3 percent of the labor force, by far the lowest rate in Europe) and has never exceeded 4.5 percent since the transition began. The trend in unemployment was up in 1991, down in 1992, up in 1993, and down again in 1994. The rapid expansion of private activity, part of which is unrecorded, the low level of wages, and a well organized system of job placement and retraining have all contributed to low unemployment.

Both exports and imports have increased since 1990, in spite of a 50 percent drop in trade with the former USSR, a 25 percent drop in trade with Slovakia, and smaller drops with other former Communist countries. Trade with the West has grown steadily. The shift to Western markets has brought a major shift in the composition of exports away from machinery and equipment (down from 40 percent in the late 1980s to less than 30 percent of the total) to mainly semi-manufactured products, such as steel and chemicals, and light industrial products.

TABLE 5.3   De-concentration in the Czech Republic: Number of State Enterprises in Selected Industries in 1990

Industry	1/90	4/90
Machinery and Equipment for Heavy Industry	5	77
Machinery and Equipment for Agriculture, Trade & Services	4	58
High-tension Products for Industry	9	16
Low-tension Products for Industry	2	30
Metal Products for Industry	1	21
Flat, Building and Technical Glass	5	14
Printing and Publishing	6	30
Fish and Game Products	1	15
Construction	2	49
Restaurants and Catering	1	17

Source: Joshua Charap and Alena Zemplinerova, "Restructuring in the Czech Economy," European Bank for Reconstruction and Development, Working Paper No. 2, March 1993.

Policies in Dealing with State Enterprises

General Characteristics of Policies

Czech policy to deal with state industrial enterprises had three primary objectives: privatization, de-concentration, and restructuring. Privatization has been the dominant objective and instrument for achieving a more efficient economy. De-concentration began first, in 1990, but has since become a by-product of privatization. Restructuring is expected to largely follow privatization—it is considered to be the responsibility of the new private owners, not of the state. In practice, however, the government has been forced to take some restructuring measures before privatization, especially financial restructuring.

De-concentration

Czechoslovakia had one of the most concentrated industries among the Communist countries. In 1989, only 430 state industrial enterprises were registered, compared with about 2,200 in Poland. By August 1992, out of 16,852 industrial enterprises, 2,258 had more than 25 workers.[4]

De-concentration occurred first by breaking up—or spinning off units from—large state enterprises and establishing new state corporations. In 1991-1992, it became an integral part of the privatization process.

The first wave of breakups occurred in early 1990, often being initiated by plant managers, with the approval of the line ministries. As shown in

TABLE 5.4   Czech Republic: Number of Industrial Units Before and After Approval of Privatization Projects

Branch	Number Before Approval	Number After Approval
Fuel and Energy	11	27
Power Plants	10	23
Ferrous Metallurgy	13	25
Non-Ferrous Metallurgy	6	13
Chemicals and Rubber	24	40
Machinery	186	325
Electronics	45	111
Building Materials	55	108
Wood Processing	46	106
Metal Products	10	20
Paper and Pulp	11	27
Glass, China and Ceramics	29	51
Textiles	41	91
Apparel	7	20
Leather	8	24
Printing and Publishing	16	19
Food Processing	97	239
Tobacco Products	5	5
Other	12	20

Source: Joshua Charap and Alena Zemplinerova, "Restructuring in the Czech Economy," European Bank for Reconstruction and Development, Working Paper No. 2, March 1993.

Table 5.3, the number of state enterprises in selected branches of industry increased about eight-fold between January and April 1990. The breakups were strictly organizational in nature—that is, they split multi-plant units into several production units, many of which were still large enterprises. Multi-enterprise regional trusts that had become super-enterprises were split up. In other cases, subcontracting enterprises became independent from the central assembly enterprise.

De-concentration was given a new boost by privatization procedures. As will be explained in more detail later, privatization projects were presented on every enterprise and many of them entailed the separation of various parts of the enterprise into new corporations or other units. This process increased the number of independent firms by factors of two or three, as shown in Table 5.4. At the same time, the number of private corporations in industry grew rapidly to about 10,000, some of which are new rather than offshoots of former state enterprises.

The combined results of these forces was to make Czech industry much less concentrated than before the revolution. Table 5.5 shows that a great

TABLE 5.5   **Czech Republic: Number of Industrial Enterprises by Employment Group**

Number of Employees	1989	1990	1991	1992
25-29	---	---	---	549
100-149	---	---	129	216
150-299	---	---	397	522
300-599	48	459	394	409
600-1,199	84	207	348	260
1,200-2,499	175	250	383	195
2,500-4,999	74	74	137	78
5,000+	49	29	29	29

Source: Joshua Charap and Alena Zemplinerova, "Restructuring in the Czech Economy," European Bank for Reconstruction and Development, Working Paper No. 2, March 1993.

many small and medium-sized enterprises (of between 25 and 1,200 employees) were created. In addition, some 250,000 craftsmen and other unincorporated businesses involved in manufacturing were added. The table also shows, however, that there was little progress in de-concentrating very large enterprises. Indeed, industrial enterprises with more than 5,000 workers show increased concentration.

Privatization Policy

The Czech government has tried to transfer as much of the economy as possible to private ownership as quickly as possible. Most of the necessary legislation had been passed by early in 1991, although it was not until June 1991 that the NPF began operations. As in Poland and Hungary, small enterprises, especially in trade and services, were privatized under different procedures than those for large enterprises. But there were major policy differences from those followed in Poland and Hungary. Because the Czechs wanted to privatize quickly, they put great stress from the start on a voucher distribution program and encountered much less political opposition to such a program than in Poland, and did not have to make preferential provisions for workers. And Czechoslovakia is unique in having clarified the politically difficult restitution issue before even starting privatization.[5]

By early 1995, 80 percent of the former state business assets had been de-nationalized. About one-half of these de-nationalized assets underwent a formal privatization process. The rest consisted mainly of restitution (10 percent), transformation of collective farms and cooperatives (15 percent), and transfer to municipalities (25 percent).[6]

Restitution. Unlike the Poles, the Czechs were able to clear up the issue of restitution to pre-Communist owners early. The main restitution law was passed in February 1990, covering assets expropriated through nationalizations that began in 1948, or whose former owners were subsequently forced to make a gift of their property to the state. Reimbursement of approved claims is made through return of the actual property, ownership of shares, or financial compensation. A great many houses and apartments have been returned to their original owners. In the case of industrial firms, the claims of former owners have been given priority in privatization projects.

"Small Privatization." "Small privatization" began early in 1991 and was essentially complete by the end of 1992. Focused mainly on retail stores and service establishments, it was administered on a local level by Privatization Committees of about 20 people. The method was straightforward—the auctioning of state property to the highest bidder. The possibility of offering leases was considered, but rejected, because government policy was to break all ties with the former state enterprises. Concerns about problems of equity were raised, since many of those with the most money to bid were likely to be the former members of the "Nomenklatura" and others who had taken advantage of opportunities on the black or grey market. Nevertheless, the decision was made not to question the sources of funds and to accept inequities in order to proceed quickly and without leaving lingering governmental responsibilities. Many purchases were financed with bank credits of four-year maturity at then slightly subsidized interest rates of 15-17 percent.

The government did facilitate the sale of small enterprises by selling their assets on a gross basis, without liabilities. The liabilities remained in the old state-owned enterprise, and were paid out of the proceeds as part of a liquidation process. Even after paying off debts, the "small privatization" yielded net earnings to the government of 33 billion crowns ($1.2 billion), which were transferred to the NPF.

"Large Privatization." The process of "large privatization" is highly structured. Preparation began in 1991, but most of the necessary action occurred in 1992-1994. Large privatization was organized in two waves: the first, involving nearly 2,800 enterprises, is complete; the second, involving 851 enterprises, was completed in early 1995. Together, the two waves cover some 70 percent of the property of all large state enterprises, worth some $40 billion, including 80 percent of those in industry.

Large privatization follows a procedure that begins with privatization projects initiated by enterprises and other interested parties, which go through a review, selection and approval process, and then are implemented either ad hoc or through the voucher program.

Types of Large Privatization. Though Czech privatization is best known for the use of vouchers, several other privatization methods are also used:

TABLE 5.6   Czech Republic: Information Required by Authorities in Privatization Projects *(circa 1993-1994)*

1. The enterprise's name, and property for privatization;

2. Information on how the State acquired the property to be privatized;

3. Identification of the property unusable for business purposes (i.e., debts, unusable fixed assets and stocks);

4. Valuation of property to be privatized (usually book value, except in the case of Foreign Direct Investment, in which case an official assessment of "market value" is required);

5. Manner of transferring the property to be privatized, including the settlement of claims of entitled persons;

6. When establishing a commercial company, the definition of its legal forms;

7. When establishing a joint-stock company, the distribution of stock shares and their value or type, as well as information on whether and how investment vouchers will be used;

8. If local property is to be sold, the location and method of sales, pricing, and the conditions and terms of payment;

9. In some cases, the proportion of the privatization process proceeds to be handed over to the NPFs of the republics;

10. The manner of transfer of intellectual property rights, which must be discussed in advance with the Federal Bureau of Inventions;

11. The privatization project implementation schedule.

Source: Michal Mejstrik, "Vouchers, Buyouts, Auctions: The Battle for Privatization in Czechoslovakia," International Workshop on Privatization Experiences in Eastern Europe, May 21-22, 1993, Budapest, Hungary.

1. Public auction of the entire enterprise or, more often, part of it—the highest bidder wins.
2. Public tender, in which other criteria besides price—employment, investment commitments, environmental cleanup—are considered in closed bids.
3. Direct sale to a predetermined buyer, domestic or foreign.
4. Commercialization of a state enterprise into a state corporation, generally as a precondition to voucher privatization.
5. Privatization of an existing state corporation.
6. Unpaid transfer of assets to municipalities, pension funds, banks, or savings banks.

Vouchers are used only for privatizing state firms (4 and 5). Restitution, or sale combined with restitution where the current value of an enterprise exceeds the interest of the former owner, must be worked out before privatization. For many enterprises, a combination of methods is used.

TABLE 5.7   Czech Republic: Originators of Privatization Projects Through
1993

Originator	Number of Projects	Percent
Enterprise Management	2,804	25.1
Subordinate Management	416	3.7
Interested Buyer	4,379	39.2
Original Owner	397	3.6
Ministry	22	0.2
Consulting Firm	334	3.0
Local Privatization Council	760	6.8
Other	1,451	13.0
Local Founding Institution	431	3.9
Trade Union	19	0.2
Not Listed	153	1.4

Source: Karel Cermak, *Czech Republic Ministry for the Administration of State Property and
its Privatization*, Prague, 1993.

Privatization Projects. Every enterprise entering a wave of privatization
is required to submit at least one basic privatization project, but competing
or supplementary projects are also considered. A privatization project must
provide the information listed in Table 5.6, including the identification and
valuation of the property to be privatized, the privatization method to be
used, and the schedule for implementation.

The number of projects submitted was much larger than expected. While
2,776 enterprises were included in the first wave, over 11,000 privatization
projects were submitted. Besides the basic projects submitted by enterprise
managers, there were numerous projects submitted by interested buyers,
middle-management, consulting firms, and various levels of government
(Table 5.7). For the most part, the basic projects proposed commercialization leading to privatization through vouchers, and most interested buyers
proposed direct sale. Many of the competing projects apparently proposed
selling or giving away parts of enterprises. The unexpected growth in the
number of projects forced the government to modify its original policy of
relying predominantly on voucher privatization. It also caused slippage in
the initial deadlines for submission and review of projects in the first wave.

Once submitted, the projects were first reviewed by the branch ministries, which were to give their recommendations to the Ministry of
Privatization within two weeks. The Ministry of Privatization then made
the decision (except in the case of direct sale), approval for which had to be
obtained from the Council of Ministers. The government decided to first
review the projects that were intended for voucher privatization so that the
first wave of that process could be started on time (May 18, 1992). In the first

**TABLE 5.8   Czech Republic: Approved Privatization Projects
              as of January 19, 1993**

Method of Privatization	# of Units (mil.Kcs)	Share of Property	Value	Share
A. Public Auction	336	8.60	3902	0.80
B. Public Tender	308	7.88	10,924	2.25
C. Direct Sale	1,005	25.72	25,955	5.35
D. Commercialization into Joint-Stock Structure	1,028	26.31	289,524	59.65
E. Privatization of Existing State-owned Joint Stock Co.	191	4.89	130,670	26.92
F. Unpaid Transfer*	1,040	26.61	9,689	2.00
Voucher Privatization (out of D and E)			238,041	49.05
Write-offs and Other			14,682	
TOTAL	3908	100.00	485,343	100.00

* Transfer to municipalities, pension funds, banks, or savings banks.
Source: Karel Cermak, *Czech Republic Ministry for the Administration of State Property and its Privatization*, Prague, 1993.

wave, out of 8,600 projects that were reviewed, slightly less than 2,000 were approved. The approved projects created 3,900 business units out of 1,900 enterprises, thus greatly promoting de-concentration. About half of the property of the approved projects was included in voucher privatization in the first wave (Table 5.8).

Implementation of the privatization projects is the responsibility of the NPF. The NPF became the interim owner of enterprises that had been "commercialized," but not yet privatized, such as is the case with those in the process of voucher privatization. The NPF also became part owner of many privatized enterprises and majority owner of some enterprises that had been commercialized.

By the end of the second wave of large-scale privatization, 65 percent of covered state assets had been privatized through the voucher system and 35 percent through traditional methods, such as auctions and direct sale.

Voucher Privatization

Basic Design. Czechoslovakia was the first post-Communist country to undertake a massive voucher privatization program. Each citizen over the age of 18 could purchase investment vouchers, each voucher being worth 1000 "investment points," for a nominal registration fee of 1000 crowns (about 25 percent of the average monthly wage). With these vouchers, Czech citizens could buy shares of any company under the program or transfer their vouchers to an Investment Privatization Fund (IPF), a kind of closed end mutual fund, that makes the decisions on how to allocate the points. The average book value of the assets purchasable with a voucher was about 70,000 crowns.

As mentioned earlier, voucher privatization, like other forms of "large privatization" occurred in two waves. The process of transferring ownership of the corporations included in each wave from the state to private owners involved several rounds of bidding. Before the bidding starts, there is a so-called "zero-round," in which voucher holders have the opportunity to delegate their points to the IPFs. When the bidding rounds begin, IPFs and individuals bid on the same basis. The vouchers themselves are not tradeable. Foreigners may not acquire vouchers.[7]

Each round takes about one month. Voucher holders may spend their points in any or all of the rounds. Orders are placed in local registries and orders are processed centrally through a computer network. Up to date information on orders placed and filled and on prices (in terms of number of voucher points) is available to all.

The initial prices of company shares are based on book values. Prices are raised or lowered in each round to balance supply and demand. Where a company's shares are oversubscribed by more than 25 percent, the vouchers are returned and the price is raised in the next round. Where they are oversubscribed by less than 25 percent, enough vouchers are returned to IPFs to balance demand with supply. Where they are under subscribed, the vouchers are all returned, and a lower price is set in the next round. All unsold shares remain the property of the NPF.

Role of the Investment Privatization Funds. In all the economies in transition, governments have been concerned about how enterprises privatized through the mass distributions of coupons or vouchers could find owners with a sufficient stake to provide strong policy direction to management. With few nationals having sufficient funds to acquire a controlling interest over large enterprises, financial intermediaries are needed. The question is how these should be created and regulated. In sharp contrast to Poland, which wants to establish and structure the intermediaries through government action, Czechoslovakia allowed them to enter the market and to develop freely. For the most part, IPFs are owned by investment companies, many of which are themselves parts of banks, and an investment company may have several IPFs.

The role of IPFs quickly became far greater than had been expected. 430 IPFs were registered early in 1992 and began to compete for vouchers.

TABLE 5.9   Czech Republic: Supply, Bids and Sales of Shares in the First
Wave of Voucher Privatization *(in millions of shares*)*

	Round				
	1	*2*	*3*	*4*	*5*
Supply of shares	299.4	210.0	132.1	99.6	62.5
Bids for shares	235.7	148.2	273.9	106.8	47.4
Bids by IPFs	175.2	92.5	122.2	53.4	20.8
Bids by individuals	60.5	55.7	151.7	53.4	26.5
Sold to IPFs	69.9	50.6	19.6	17.0	18.8
Sold to individuals	19.5	27.2	12.9	20.0	22.1
Sold in round	89.4	77.8	32.5	37.1	40.9
Cumulative sales	89.4	167.4	199.8	236.9	277.8
Percent of total sold	29.9%	55.8%	66.9%	79.1%	92.8%

*One share is valued at 1,000 Kcs of book value.

Source: Karel Cermak, *Czech Republic Ministry for the Administration of State Property and its Privatization*, Prague, 1993.

Some, notably the so-called "Harvard Fund," advertised widely with promises to redeem the vouchers at large multiples of their face value. This campaign greatly stimulated public interest in the program, resulting in an unexpectedly large participation rate of three quarters of eligible citizens. Over 70 percent of all vouchers were transferred to IPFs in the first wave. Among these, the 15 largest controlled 43 percent of all investment points. The five leaders, and nine of the ten largest IPFs, were banking institutions, the Harvard Fund being the only non-bank fund in this top group. Banks in the Czech and Slovak Republics, like those in Poland, are permitted to own shares in enterprises. Some banks formed investment companies that in turn owned several IPFs. In the second wave, the degree of concentration declined slightly. The 349 IPFs that competed (in the Czech Republic alone) obtained 64 percent of all voucher points, and the 15 largest ones obtained 41 percent. Although IPFs were forbidden to invest more than 10 percent of their capital on one security, or to own more than 20 percent of the value of a firm's securities, they, or the investment companies that owned several IPFs, were able to acquire a controlling interest over most privatized firms, singly or by cooperating with each other.

Implementation of the Voucher Program. The first wave of the voucher program proceeded smoothly. Five rounds of bidding were held between June and December, 1992. The percentage of shares sold was 30 percent in the first round, increasing sharply to 56 percent in the second round, and reaching 93 percent after the fifth round (Table 5.9). Nearly 99 percent of the total number of voucher points were used to purchase the shares. IPFs tended to invest most heavily in the early rounds and in the more expensive shares, and ended up in control of two thirds of total property value. Unsold shares remained in the possession of the NPF. In the Czech Republic alone, 987 enterprises with a book value of more than 200 billion crowns were privatized in the first wave.

The second wave of voucher privatization, which is limited to the Czech Republic and to Czech citizens, covers 861 enterprises with a book value of 155 billion crowns.[8] The first two auctions took place in April 1994, and the last in November 1994.

Strengthening Enterprise Finances

Czech state enterprises, like those in Poland and Hungary, have accumulated heavy indebtedness to banks and to other enterprises. Unlike those in Poland, they have not become heavily indebted to the government—apparently tax obligations have generally been met.

During the early months of 1991, when the Czechoslovak version of the "Big Bang" occurred, cash flow constraints gave rise to a massive increase in inter-enterprise debt. These constraints resulted not only from very tight credit policies, but also from non-payment of large receivables from the former Soviet Union. Many state enterprises became technically insolvent and widespread bankruptcies were feared.[9] Inter-enterprise debt continued to increase through 1991, reaching 150 billion crowns in December, compared with 50 billion crowns in January, but the growth slowed in 1992. To ease liquidity problems, the government took a series of actions involving reductions or cancellations of enterprise debt and re-capitalization of banks.

The first step was to relieve enterprises of some of the burden of debts to commercial banks incurred under the Communist regime, and consequently assumed to have been outside their control. A special "Consolidation Bank" was formed and 110 billion crowns ($4 billion) of loans were transferred to it from the commercial banks. The loans were then consolidated into 8-year loans at low (8 percent) interest rates.

Another step was to recapitalize the banks to help them relieve enterprises entering voucher privatization of bad debts. The NPF issued 50 billion crowns ($1.7 billion) of bonds, but left the management of the funds in the hands of the banks. The banks may take such measures as writing off uncollected receivables and promoting debt-equity swaps.

A third step was an attempt to cancel out inter-enterprise debt by tracing chains of mutual indebtedness so that cancellations can benefit all parties. This program did not succeed in canceling out much debt.

These programs all benefit from the establishment of NPF to oversee privatization and related activities. The NPF is the source of all the funding for debt relief and these expenditures are paid out of the proceeds from the sale of state property.

Bankruptcy and Restructuring

While debt relief is designed to help firms with liquidity problems that may be solvent (that is, profitable in the longer term), there remain large numbers of firms that will eventually be considered insolvent. The number of enterprises making a loss increased from 735 in the first half of 1991 to 1,202 in the first half of 1992, about 20 percent of all enterprises. The financial position of enterprises apparently stabilized in 1993-1994, although some economists believe that accounting conventions (especially the valuation of capital assets at acquisition cost for depreciation purposes) greatly over-state profits and understate losses.[10]

Government policy is not to subsidize insolvent enterprises, although fear of widespread closings and massive unemployment have led to excep-tions being made. By and large, loss-making enterprises have not been included in voucher privatization. Other forms of partial privatization in some cases may lead to their liquidation.

The Czech government has not yet used legal bankruptcy as a major instrument of economic restructuring. A tough bankruptcy law was passed in early 1992, but its application was then suspended until April 1993. Even since then, the law has been applied only to private firms and apparently with considerable caution. Priority was given to completing voucher privatization before firms became vulnerable to bankruptcy proceedings. Even where such proceedings are begun a firm has up to three months to negotiate a restructuring agreement with creditors before its assets are liquidated. In practice, a few large firms, including three banks, but many small firms, have been declared bankrupt.

The Residual Role of Government

In the wake of the two large privatization waves, the Czech government has retained a small direct ownership of large-scale firms, and considerable indirect influence. Some 500 enterprises, employing over 100,000 workers, were kept out of the privatization programs and remain under the supervi-sion of the branch ministries.[11] The very large enterprises have generally remained intact and are not in the process of liquidation. For example, the high-tech compressor firm, CKD Prague, which used to produce advanced components for the Soviet space and military programs, is not yet ready for privatization, although one of its main subordinate companies is in the second wave. Like other large enterprises, it is preparing restructuring plans under the supervision of the responsible branch Ministry.

The government has also maintained control over the adjustment pro-cess in certain industries, including petroleum, telecommunications, coal, and steel, as well as military industries.[12] The approach is to develop a long-term plan for development or phasing down of the industry, with the help of foreign consulting firms, and to implement the plan with a mix of state-owned and private firms operating in a state-controlled framework. Both these regulated industries and the very large firms appear to be organizing holding companies, in which the government has a controlling ownership, to guide the subordinate companies in accord with national policy.

The government is capable of exercising influence over privatized enterprises in which it retains a substantial minority share, which is often as large as 20 percent. Government shares are owned by the NPF, which has chosen not to take an active role on the firms' governing boards, but the potential for greater intervention exists. Finally, the government will continue to exercise considerable indirect leverage on firms so long as it owns a substantial share of the banks that own the largest IPFs, and that in turn have controlling interests in the majority of privatized firms.

Evaluation of Czech Policies

Results

The two main criteria of success for policies designed to transform and restructure state enterprises are how much restructuring was achieved and at what economic and social cost. As to the first criterion, the Czechs seem somewhat behind the Poles and Hungarians. By the second criterion, the Czechs are clearly doing better than either of the other countries. It is likely that the pain will increase as restructuring proceeds, but the prospects for a favorable outcome seem good.

As indicated earlier, the Czechs have suffered about as large a drop in output as Poland and Hungary. Apparently, the greater damage due to the collapse of the Soviet market on the average compensated for a less severe macroeconomic imbalance. Although the available data are unclear, employment in state industry appears to have declined somewhat less than in Poland. With production only beginning to recover, labor productivity is still below pre-transition levels, suggesting that some excess labor persists. There is thus a potential for substantial additional layoffs after privatization. On the other hand, success in stabilizing prices and balancing the budget lays a sound foundation for a sustained economic recovery.

Although reported accounting data on profits and losses of enterprises probably present too rosy a picture, and the Czechs will face a serious problem of dealing with loss-making enterprises in the future, this problem appears much less severe than in Poland, Hungary, and especially Russia. This is due in part to greater macroeconomic stability and in part to prompt action by the government to ease the debt problem of enterprises that have severe liquidity problems but may become profitable in the long-run.

It is also very encouraging that unemployment rates are so low at this stage of the transformation process. Apparently, the growth of employment in the small-scale private sector has offset the decline in employment in the state sector. It is likely that the Czechs have been far more efficient at finding jobs for the unemployed than have the Poles and Hungarians. Computerized data bases on job offers and job seekers presumably have been helpful. And maintenance of an exchange rate that undervalues the crown has made Czech labor very inexpensive in terms of hard currencies and consequently has stimulated restructuring and helped minimize unemployment.

Privatization policies to date must be rated a success. From a technical standpoint, the voucher system was handled very well, in fact, remarkably so given its complexity and the absence of prior models or experience. The fact that the program was adopted early, when most enterprises were still profitable and the government had considerable credit with the population, was probably helpful. The extremely wide popular response to the offer of vouchers indicates generally optimistic expectations for the economy.

By mid-1994, the share of the state sector in production and employment of firms employing 25 or more workers had already been reduced to 40 percent in industry, 15 percent in construction, and 10 percent in trade. Smaller firms were almost exclusively private, so that the private sector was producing about two thirds of GDP. With completion of the second wave of voucher privatization, the private share of GDP will increase to about three quarters.

Even though most large firms under privatization are being almost given away, the government has gained substantial revenues from the privatization of small enterprises and from foreign investments. The use of a single, independent fund, the NPF, to oversee and finance privatization and financial restructuring has been a positive feature of Czech policy, especially by imposing financial discipline on the process.

In spite of an efficient privatization process, most Czech industrial enterprises, and particularly those in heavy industry, have a long way to go before they can be internationally competitive. The managers of enterprises being privatized waited for the new owners to emerge and decide on new policies. There was a hiatus of a year or more between the submission of privatization projects and the actual arrival of new owners, when the enterprise is still "owned" by the NPF, but led by no one. During this period of "limbo," enterprise managers have incentives to enhance their personal financial situation, often at the expense of the long-term health of the enterprise. It is reported that instances of various forms of asset stripping by managers are frequent. Moreover, because many managers had a personal stake in the privatization process and submitted bids for at least portions of firms, they had strong incentives to take actions that would depress the value of the enterprises.

An even more basic constraint on enterprise restructuring has been the lack of funds for investment. Many state enterprises have no internal funds for investment. Where they do, managers often have no incentive to invest for the longer-term when ownership is not yet clear. And neither the banks, nor the government, nor so far the NIFs, have provided substantial funds for investment. Government policy has been to facilitate privatization, but then to let the private owners invest in the restructuring of enterprises. Large funds have been spent for debt relief, but not for investment.

Foreign direct investment has been an important source of funds for the Czech Republic, which ranks far behind Hungary and about equal to Poland as a net recipient of FDI, with over $3 billion during 1990-1994. About half of this amount went to purchase existing enterprises and assets. FDI dropped in 1993, presumably because investors were waiting for completion of voucher privatization. At the same time, portfolio investment increased from almost nothing to $900 million in 1993, and the Czech Republic became the first among former Communist countries to receive an investment-grade rating for its bonds.

The Roles of the Principal Actors

The principal actors in the transformation and restructuring of state enterprises—management, labor, banks and financial intermediaries, and government—have influenced the process quite differently in the Czech Republic than in Poland, Hungary, or Russia. Specifically, the role of labor has been much smaller; the role of financial intermediaries promises to be large; and that of the government seems more timely, more coherent, and better organized.

Management. Management plays a key role in the Czech Republic, as it does in the other countries. Although the Czech approach imposes more constraints on management initiatives than in Poland and Hungary, these initiatives prevail in most cases. For example, enterprise managers initiated and presented more than 60 percent of approved projects in the first wave, representing an even larger portion of the value of assets. These projects included not only the "basic projects" for enterprises, but also proposals for selling or giving away parts of enterprises.

Managers have continued to negotiate with government agencies and the banks for debt relief and other advantages and have continued to determine enterprise policies, pending the arrival of new owners. Managers also still hold strong cards because of their unique knowledge even after the new owners arrive.

Labor. The role of labor has been small, both in enterprises and at the political level. Workers' councils, never strong in Czechoslovakia, were eliminated in 1990. Unions have some influence and serve as transmission belts between management and the workforce, but have almost always been passive. For example, they initiated only 19 privatization projects, of which one was approved. At the political level, labor-oriented, social-democratic political parties and groups have had only small effects on the design and implementation of the privatization/restructuring programs, and appear to be weakening. Very unlike Poland, there is no labor representation on enterprise supervisory boards in the Czech Republic.

Banks. As in Poland, Czech banks have played a generally passive role in the transition. Credits have been predominantly short-term, although substantial medium-term credits were provided to help finance "small privatization" and a few larger projects. Banks have also made *ad hoc* decisions concerning restructuring and reduction of enterprise debt. The criteria they used are not clear, and probably included the "importance" of an enterprise, as well as its long-term credit worthiness. With their capital enhanced, the banks are expected to play a more active role in the future. Moreover, most of the large IPFs are owned by banks, and their role will be crucial to the country's future transition. More stringent regulation of banks is necessary and is proceeding.

Other Financial Intermediaries. The IPFs have acquired a controlling interest in nearly all the enterprises under voucher privatization. Even where a single IPF cannot control an enterprise by itself because of the 20 percent limit, several IPFs together generally have control if they cooperate. This gives them a potentially leading role in the restructuring process. The question is how soon and how effectively they can play this role.[13]

Czech officials and outside economists see signs that IPFs are already beginning to take on the responsibilities of principal owner. They are sending representatives to meetings of both management and advisory boards in order to assure that their interests are well protected. Indeed, such representation has become a major burden on the personnel of investment companies and of the parent banks, since the IPFs themselves are inadequately staffed for this purpose. Typically the large IPFs are represented on the boards of dozens of companies.

It is still unclear, however, that the IPFs have as yet begun to undertake major restructuring. They face many constraints, including lack of funds for investment. In the case of bank-owned IPFs, there are conflicts of interest between the commercial banking interest in expanding loans and avoiding debt writeoffs, and the ownership interest in guiding firms toward long-term profitability. Some fund owners hope to sell their holding to large foreign investors and are reluctant to undertake difficult and expensive changes in the interim. The trend in the wake of voucher privatization is for an increasing concentration of ownership of Czech firms in favor of the larger IPFs and large foreign investors, both of which have the incentive and the resources to undertake restructuring.

Government. Although Czech transformation policy has tried to minimize the direct role of the government bureaucracy at a micro level, the government has been clearly in control of the transformation process. Its policies have been coherent and consistent and its credibility high. Government has passed the laws and set the rules for privatization and other transformation processes. Nearly all of the important laws and rules were established before the main economic transformation measures were taken, which contributed to a relatively smooth process.

There has been less direct intervention than in Poland. One reason for this was that privatization followed a fairly coherent set of policies that changed only in detail after the process began. Another reason was a decision to cut out the branch ministries, notably the Ministry of Industry (MOI), from most important decisions. The Ministry of Privatization made the final selection of privatization projects and the Fund for National Property (FNP) managed the program. Bureaucratic infighting exists, of course. For example, the MOI claims that the FNP lacks the expertise to guide enterprises while they are awaiting final privatization and, consequently that MOI experts will have to do the job. Branch ministries retain effective control over enterprises that are not yet being privatized, such as the very large firms and those in certain industries, like coal and steel.

Conclusions

The main conclusion on the Czech transition is that it is working relatively well to date, that the painful stages yet to be entered can be managed, but that painful effects will persist for a long time. The structure of Czech industry will be very difficult to adapt to global market conditions without a large loss of real income. The bulk of Czech industry is highly capital-intensive. It is also skill-intensive, but many labor skills cannot be used without complementary capital investments. The trouble is that these investments are not being made and the prospects for obtaining sufficient investments to quickly restructure Czech heavy industry are not good.

So far at least, the principal adjustments in Czech production have involved a shift toward labor-intensive goods and away from technology-intensive goods, such as machinery and equipment. The expansion of capital-intensive exports, such as steel, to the West, which occurred in 1990-1991, did not continue because of unfavorable overall demand trends and importing country restrictions. Machinery producers have found some growing niches, some substantial Western investors, notably Volkswagen, and an expanding export market, mainly in Germany, for low-tech components. But the former CMEA market is unlikely to recover much and, consequently, the industry is likely to continue producing well below pre-transition levels. The situation is much better in labor-intensive consumer goods, such as shoes and food products, as well as in some simpler machines and metal products, because of very low labor costs at the current exchange rates.

TABLE 5.10   Czech Republic: Ranking of Sectors by Average Price per Share in the First Wave of Voucher Privatization (*in Kcs; nominal face value per share = 1000 Kcs*)

Above 1000 Kcs		Below 1000 Kcs	
"Hot" Sectors		*"Mediocre" Sectors*	
Beer & Malt	3740	Textile Products	950
Financial Services	3480	Building Materials	950
Hotels & Spas	3460	Retail Trade	930
Motion Pictures	2420	Trade: Drugs & Chemicals	920
Liquor & Soft Drinks	2040	Apparel	900
Misc. Fabricated Prod.	1700	Utilities	860
Misc. Food & Tobacco	1670	Engineering Services	850
Printing & Publishing	1620	Instruments	800
Trade:Fuels	1580	Trade: Raw Materials	780
Business Services	1510	Trade: Equipment	770
Glass & Ceramics	1500	Repair Services	770
Fuels	1480	Metalworking	760
Minerals & Stone	1480	Woodworking	720
Sugar & Confectionery	1380		
"Solid" Sectors		*"Junk" Sectors*	
Chemical Products	1310	Heavy Construction	680
Dairy Products	1250	Primary Metals	640
Trade: Cons. Goods	1250	Machinery & Equipment	630
Leather & Footwear	1240	Transport Services	620
Fruit & Vegetables	1210	Surveying Services	620
Architectural Services	1180	Agriculture	600
Meat & Poultry Prod.	1170	Transportation Equipment	590
Bread & Bakery Prod.	1130	General Construction	580
Personal Services	1120	Research	560
Grain Products	1050	Trade: Food, Farm Prod.	550
Furniture	1050	Automotive Repairs	460
Paper Products	1050	Electrotechnical Prod.	400
Storage & Warehousing	1020		

Source: PlanEcon, "Results of Czechoslovak Voucher Privatization," Part I, December 31, 1992, and Part II, February 16, 1993, *PlanEcon Report*, Nos. 50, 51, and 52, 1992, and Nos. 7-8, 1993 (Washington, DC).

These basic trends can be seen in the results of the bidding for the shares of Czech and Slovak companies in the first wave of voucher privatization in late 1992. The shares of most service and consumer goods companies sold at a premium over book value, while engineering and most other heavy industry shares sold at large discounts (Table 5.10). Production of most companies in relatively high demand requires relatively unskilled labor, while that in companies in low demand is clearly more skill-intensive. Although demand for some skills, such as knowledge of English, computer software, and environmental protection, has increased, other skilled workers will have difficulty finding jobs at anywhere near their previous real wage. Without much larger investments for restructuring heavy industry than appear likely, therefore, the Czech Republic probably faces several years of reduced per capita real incomes.

In the long run, however, the outlook for large-scale restructuring is favorable. At the level of the firm, it seems likely that the Czech Republic is moving toward a form of corporate governance of the West German type, although it is still far from having developed such a system. As in Germany, there are large cross-holdings of shares among the investment funds and the banks, as well as among the banks themselves. The banks are still in a transitional stage, with the government, in the form of the NPF, owning substantial, potentially controlling, shares, although not taking an active management role. As private ownership of bank shares increases and eventually predominates, Czech banks will be forced to behave much more like their German counterparts. Banks and investment companies are likely to increasingly divide control of large Czech industrial firms with foreign direct investors, who can bring in new funds the Czech financial institutions lack.

Notes

1. The listing of relevant legislation is from: Richard Judy, *The Czech and Slovak Republics: Two Paths for Eastern Europe*, The Hudson Institute, Hudson Country Report Number One, August 1992. An excellent analysis of the development of Czech business and commercial law is found in Cheryl Gray, *The Legal Framework for Private Sector Activity in the Czech and Slovak Federal Republic*, The World Bank, Policy Research Working Papers, WAS 1051, November 1992.

2. See, for example, *OECD Economic Surveys: Czech and Slovak Republics*, OECD, Paris 1991.

3. The economic statistics used in this chapter are from various publications of the Czech Statistical Office, including especially the *Quarterly Statistical Bulletin*, and *Selected Economic and Social Indicators of the Cz*. The charts are taken directly from *PlanEcon Report* Nos. 31-32, September 28, 1994, "Czech Economic Monitor."

4. An excellent review and analysis of these issues is found in: Joshua Charap and Alena Zemplinerova, *Restructuring in the Czech Economy*, European Bank for Reconstruction and Development, Working Paper No. 2, March 1993.

5. Much of the material on privatization is based on information and analysis in papers delivered at the International Workshop on Privatization Experiences in Eastern Europe, 21-22 May 1993, Budapest, Hungary. Most widely used was a paper by Michal Mejstrik of the Center for Economic Research and Graduate Education in Prague, *Vouchers, Buyouts, Auctions: The Battle for Privatization in*

Czechoslovakia. Two other useful papers from this workshop are those by Otakar Turek, *Interconnections Between the Macroeconomic Policies and Privatization—The Case of Czechoslovakia,* and by Ales Capek and Alena Buchtikova, *Privatization in the Czech Republic: Privatization Strategies and Priorities.* Other useful sources on this topic were: A lecture by Tomas Jezek, Director of the National Property Fund in *Privatization and the National Property Fund,* CERGE, Prague, 1992; the *Annual Report of the National Property Fund of the Czech Republic,* various years; and Karel Cermak, *Czech Republic Ministry for the Administration of State Property and its Privatization,* Prague 1993.

6. Data on the results of the privatization program through early 1995 are available in Roman Ceska, "The Czech Republic's Experience," OECD Advisory Group on Privatization, *Performance of Privatized Enterprises: Corporate Governance Restructuring and Profitability,* Moscow, March 29-31, 1995.

7. A detailed, two-part analysis of the voucher program can be found in "Results of Czechoslovak Voucher Privatization," Part I December 31, 1992 and Part II, February 16, 1993, *PlanEcon Report*
Nos. 50-51-52 1992 and 7-8 1993.

8. Information on the second wave of voucher privatization is found in: Sharon Fisher, "Czech Economy Presents Mixed Picture," *RFE/RL Research Reports,* Vol 3, No. 29, 22 July 1994.

9. See, for example, Kamil Janacek, "Widespread Insolvency of State-owned Firms," RFE, *Report on Eastern Europe,* August 2, 1991.

10. According to Professor Matejka of the Center for International Management Studies of the Higher School of Economics in Prague, only 45 billion crowns out of the reported 155 billion crowns of gross profits in 1991 were real, the remainder being fictitious. Taxes were levied on fictitious profits, thereby weakening the longer-term financial position of enterprises.

11. See *Coping with Hydra-State Ownership after Privatization: A Comparative Study of Hungary, Russia, and the Czech Republic,* by Katherina Distor and Joel Turkewitz, a paper presented at the Conference on Corporate Governance in Central Europe and Russia, on 15-16 December, 1994, in Washington, D.C.

12. A good review of Czech policies to restructure state enterprises is found in UN/ECE, *Economic Survey of Europe in 1993-1994,* chapter on "Restructuring Policies."

13. An excellent study of IPFs in the Czech Republic, including not only their role in voucher privatization, but also their subsequent efforts to manage privatized firms and the linkages between IPFs, banks, and firms, is found in *Investment Privatization Funds: The Czech Experience,* a paper by John C. Coffee, Jr., presented at the conference on Corporate Governance in Central Europe and Russia on 15-16 December, 1994, in Washington, D.C.

6

Hungary

This chapter has five parts. The first section gives a brief background on Hungary's economy, focusing mainly on the economic reforms introduced through 1989. The next section reviews macroeconomic policies and performance between 1989 and mid-1995. The third section describes those key economic institutions and policies during the first five years of the transition that have particularly important direct effects on SOEs: privatization, the banking system, enterprise finance, and corporate governance.

The fourth part reviews the responses of SOEs to the institutional arrangements and policies discussed in the preceding section, namely, responses to import liberalization and to the large decline in aggregate demand, to monetary policy and credit conditions, and to corporate governance arrangements. The last section summarizes restructuring's accomplishments and the remaining tasks.

The Economy Through 1989

Basic Features

Level of Development. Comparisons of dollar per capita GDP, based on purchasing power parity (PPP) type convertors (which are preferred over prevailing exchange rate convertors) or on physical indicators, show that in the late 1980s Hungary's level of development was approximately one-third that of the U.S.A. and about 50 percent of that of Austria or the average of Western Europe. Among the European historically planned economies (HPEs), Hungary's level of development was behind those of the former Czechoslovakia and German Democratic Republic but higher than those of the rest of the countries in the region.[1]

During the 1980s the position of each European HPE had deteriorated relative to the economic progress achieved, on average, by the countries of Western Europe.

Regional Differences. Although Hungary is a small country, it has large regional differences in development levels, differences that have become accentuated since the late 1980s. Budapest and the Western part of the country are areas directly linked to the developed part of Europe. The population in these areas is more highly educated, and most members of the workforce possess multiple skills and are therefore more flexible in the kinds of jobs they qualify for.

The least developed region is the northeastern part of the country. Not well suited for agriculture, it is dotted with industrial factories that used to serve mainly the CMEA and domestic markets. Also suffering great hardship are the eastern, southern, and southeastern peripheries that border on Romania and Serbia. These areas have been disadvantaged by the negative spillover effects of the war in the former Yugoslavia and the weakness of Romania's economy.

Economic Structure

The combination of postwar economic policies and system features left the legacy of a misdeveloped economic structure: an overexpansion of capacity, employment and output in industry, especially heavy industry, and an underdeveloped service sector. Low employment in services was due in part to the modest role that commercial, business and financial services had played under the old system.

Hungary also inherited an obsolete technological and production structure, a situation that deteriorated during the "lost decade" of the 1980s. Not only was industrial growth slow, but there was also not much structural change in this sector, macro or micro.[2]

During the 1980s, industry became seriously undercapitalized. During 1980-89, investment growth in real terms was negative in a number of important sectors; gross real overall industrial investment in 1989 was almost 20 percent below its 1980 level, with mining, capital-intensive chemical industry, and iron and steel gaining somewhat larger shares of a shrinking pie. The slowness and even reversal of structural changes during the 1980s thus "prepared the ground" for the dramatic crisis that followed in the early 1990s.[3] Although a multitude of reform steps were taken (discussed below), they were insufficient in scope and effectiveness to offset the absence of a target-oriented and effective industrial policy.[4]

Industrial organization was also skewed. Due to the widespread application of labor- as well as energy-intensive mass production, based on obsolete technology and production processes that often yielded poor-quality products, production was dominated by large enterprises employing large numbers of workers. Generally absent were small and medium-sized specialized manufacturing and service establishments. During much of the postwar period, infrastructure continued to deteriorate, except for housing between the mid-1960s and mid-1970s. Another legacy was large foreign indebtedness: by 1989 more than $20 billion gross and $15 billion net, with annual interest payments to service the debt amounting to about 4 percent of GDP.

One relatively bright spot in the economy was the expansion of agricultural production between the mid-1960s and late 1970s. To increase the production of cereals and livestock, agriculture relied on production systems and machinery imported from the West, much of it from the United States. Even more important for the success of agriculture was that, beginning in the 1960s, an effective working arrangement was established between labor-intensive agricultural activities, rewarded under private incentives, and the socialist sector, which performed the capital-intensive tasks and provided the political "cover" for the spread of market mechanisms in agriculture and in the industrial and service activities that became linked to this sector. Agriculture was able to provide the population with ample and affordable food and generated about 25 percent of total foreign-currency earnings.

Reforms[5]

Summarized below are reform measures that had substantial importance for the operation of SOEs and the behavior of their managers.

Planning. The essence of the New Economic Mechanism (NEM), introduced in 1968, was the replacement of compulsory plan directives with two kinds of less formal methods of enterprise control: a simulated market mechanism and "persuasion" by the authorities. Enterprises formally became free to prepare their annual plans. The reform blueprint said that SOEs should strive for profit maximization. But in a small economy in which all kinds of controls remained on prices, especially on factor prices, and in which most enterprises faced little domestic and no foreign competition, profit maximization could not really be allowed to guide decisions. Nor was it the intention of the authorities to permit it to do so.

Controls on SOEs were exercised through less formal mechanisms than compulsory planning. Enterprise managers had to discuss their plans with the authorities and were expected to comply with their expectations concerning such matters as increasing exports to the West, helping to eliminate domestic shortages, and giving preference to imports from the CMEA to help achieve a desired bilateral trade balance. And since enterprise managers were appointed by bureaucrats at the industrial ministries who also set the managers' bonuses, and since SOEs continued to depend on the authorities to help secure key supplies, imports, investments and bank credit, informal controls remained powerful. To be sure, the arbitrariness of those controls was kept in check by Hungary's heavy dependence on Western imports and thus also exports, and by the slow but steady expansion of the cooperative and private sectors, which were generating some competition for SOEs in certain consumer goods and services.

Prices and Trade. The NEM established three price categories: free, maximum and controlled. This certainly was a step forward. In 1980, the so-called competitive price system was introduced, which had two key features. First, the domestic prices of energy and raw materials were anchored to dollar world market prices, converted to local currency at the prevailing exchange rate. Although this helped create a more rational structure of domestic prices, cost-plus pricing was essentially retained. Second, SOEs whose convertible-currency exports represented at least 5 percent of their total sales had to apply a pricing formula on their domestic and CMEA sales that tied profitability on those sales to the profitability of their Western exports. This was an example of attempting to simulate how a market would have worked if it existed. Because this pricing rule gave rise to all kinds of undesirable manipulation on the part of the enterprises (e.g., eliminating less profitable exports to the West, either to increase the profit *rate* on the remaining exports or to force Western exports below the 5 percent threshold), the system was abandoned in 1987.

Recognition that there is no substitute for real market forces led to the introduction by the reform Communist government of a three-year (1989-91) program of rapid liberalization of imports and domestic prices. The implementation of the program was completed, as scheduled, by the government that was formed after the 1990 elections.

Price and trade liberalization were two of the key areas in which Hungary had a head start in transformation, even compared with Czechoslovakia and Poland.

Industrial Organization. In 1980, three industrial ministries were combined into a single *Ministry of Industry*, with a view toward encouraging a less interventionist (enterprise- or product-specific) industrial policy. This goal, however, was not achieved, because the new ministry's personnel, and their modus operandi, came from the old ministries, essentially unchanged. There was no substantial and favorable industrial restructuring during the 1980s, as was noted.

More significant was the *deconcentration* between 1980 and 1985 of Hungary's highly concentrated industrial and trade structures. The number of monopolistic enterprise conglomerates (trusts) was reduced from 24 to 9 and more than 4,000 new enterprises emerged either as their successors or as newly independent units of state enterprises.

Enterprise Management. The 1985 Act on Enterprise Management Boards granted increased autonomy to SOE managers. SOEs were divided into three categories: (1) firms of strategic importance, for which there was no change in management; (2) other large enterprises, where formally independent management boards were established; and (3) firms employing fewer than 500 people, where the general assembly of all employees, or a council elected by them, became the top decision-making body.

Enterprises in the second and third categories were called "self-managed enterprises." But the reality was that in most such firms top management gained the dominant role. This was a distinguishing mark of Hungary's reforms, in contrast to Poland's, where labor had played a more important role, and Czechoslovakia, where the state had retained its commanding role until the system changed.[6] Soviet reforms under Gorbachev were rather similar to those in Hungary.

These reforms have had both positive and negative implications for transformation. One positive implication is that it had forced managers not only to pay attention to the authorities but also to take into account market conditions and market forces. The reforms also helped prepare managers, and perhaps also the workers, for the possibility that eventually they may take over as their enterprise's new owners. On the other hand, the devolution of certain ownership functions to enterprises hindered transformation because the state must fully control all property rights before it can sell them to their new owners.

Getting back to the 1985 Act, management boards (sometimes called enterprise boards) were made up 50 percent of directly elected representatives of the work force and 50 percent by the designated representatives of management. Enterprise directors were selected on the basis of *tenders* submitted by those who aspired to be become general managers. The tenders had to include a proposed business plan. But since appointments to the management boards could be vetoed by the authorities, the change was less fundamental than the reformers intended.

Optimistic expectations that this further devolution of authority to enterprises generally and to their management specifically would significantly improve management and enterprise performance were generally not met because

- managers became partly dependent on employees for maintaining their position, so that managers and workers formed an alliance to pressure the authorities to help provide the resources needed;
- firms continued to depend on the authorities in many respects (for example, the uses to which after-tax profits could be put remained centrally controlled);
- there were frequent, and in some cases retroactive, changes in the "regulators";
- real owners, meaningfully representing the interest of the suppliers of capital, were absent.

In this environment, management and directors serving on enterprise boards formed redistributive coalitions. That is, the priority objective became short-term increases in compensation to themselves and to the work force. Although compensation increases were constrained by supposedly uniform rules, in reality the application of the rules to specific enterprises was often subject to bargaining. Bargaining over the rules was often as important for the managers and the workers as improving the rate of return on investment and implementing a viable business strategy.

Enterprise Organization. Three important legal changes in *enterprise organization*, with substantial combined effects on the behavior of managers, were put in place during 1988-1989:

1. The Company Law (also called the Law on Economic Associations, or Corporation Act), which came into effect in 1989, defined and made possible the transformation of the traditional socialist enterprise into two other forms of quasi-state enterprises: the joint stock company and the limited liability company (Box 6.1). The Act provided legal guarantees to owners, in conformity with international standards.

2. The Foreign Investment Law (also called the Law on Entrepreneurship with Foreign Participation), adopted in 1988 and amended in 1990, made possible up to 100 percent foreign ownership of enterprises, guaranteed the repatriation of profits, and provided important tax benefits for joint ventures.

3. The Law on Enterprise Transformation, which came into effect in 1989, made it possible (then necessary) for SOEs to transform themselves into a corporation or a company, with 20 percent of the shares to be set aside for insiders, who could purchase them at substantial discounts of up to 90 percent. This provided a strong inducement to undervalue the assets of the enterprise to be transformed.[7]

The combined effect of these laws—together with other, generally market-oriented "liberalization" measures introduced in the late 1980s—was to trigger all kinds of initiatives by managers of SOEs. These involved one or more of the following: reorganizing into corporate form; privatizing; and

---

BOX 6.1   Joint Stock versus Limited Liability Companies

A *joint stock company* (RT) may be closed (all shares purchased by the founders), or open (shares publicly traded). Its minimum capital requirements were relatively large: HUF 10 million ($100,000). A single-owner RT does not have to call a stockholders' meeting.

A *limited liability company* (Kft) is a "share" company whose shares are not publicly traded. (In Hungarian terminology, a Kft's shares are called "quotas.") Its minimum capital requirements are smaller: HUF 1 million ($10,000). A Kft must employ a professional bookkeeper.

selling shares to, or forming some kind of alliance with, foreign investors. These types of deal making became known as *spontaneous privatization*.

Many large enterprises, consisting of a complex set of establishments, reorganized their units into independent joint stock or limited liability share companies, with the headquarters becoming de facto holding companies. This typically involved a cross-ownership of shares, i.e., the shares of the now independent units were held by the holding company, while the shares of the holding company were given to the newly independent units and/or to the banks, exchanging equity for a reduction or elimination of the former company's debts. The Company Law restricted the ownership of such newly created companies to institutions. The Company Law thus permitted the establishment of a peculiar hybrid between a market-economy-type of company and a socialist enterprise.

Joint stock and limited liability companies could be created in two ways. The first, particular to Hungary in the late 1980s, was the method just described: a peculiar arrangement through which a SOE could contribute a portion of its assets to one or more newly created companies, in exchange for shares in the new company(ies). An important feature of the Company Law was that it made the creation of the new companies formally independent of the government. In this way the state lost control over a large (indeed, often the best) portion of the assets. One motive for pushing through "spontaneous reorganization" was management's desire to solidify its control over the firms and to gain greater independence from the state. In this way, management could "shield" certain assets and have more freedom of operation (e.g., to enter into contracts with other entities). The beneficiaries typically were management itself, participants in the second (private) economy, and foreign investors. Another purpose was to reduce, through debt-for-equity swaps, the often onerous debts enterprises owed to commercial banks. Still another was to obtain foreign capital from suppliers, customers, or third parties, or to find foreign joint venture partners. Motives for seeking foreign partners ranged from strategic business considerations, to tax advantages, to gaining private benefits in some form.

The second way in which non-private joint stock or limited liability companies could be formed—in Hungary and in all other transition economies (TREs), following the demise of the Communist system—was through *corporatization*. Undertaken in most cases at the initiative of the state, SOEs are transformed into share companies to serve one or both of the following purposes. One purpose was to legally sort out—in effect, for the state to take back—the often obscure or tangled ownership, control and other entitlements that earlier decentralizing reforms (in Hungary and Poland) had devolved to other parties. The other purpose was to provide the legal and practical means to privatize, fully or partly, a SOE by selling or transferring its shares from a government agency to another party.

Financial and Tax Reforms. In 1983, a bond market (government and corporate) was created, enabling the population to invest a portion of its savings in this new financial instrument.

In 1987, the monobank was partitioned into a central bank and a network of five commercial banks. Each new commercial bank was given a portfolio of assets (loans outstanding) and liabilities (deposits). Several previously existing specialized financial institutions continued their existence.

The establishment of a set of independent commercial banks meant that what traditionally were *intrabank* transactions, became *interbank* transactions upon the creation of a dual banking system. This required the establishment of an interbank payment system which has turned out to be a daunting task. Eight years after separate commercial banks had been created (in 1995, as this chapter is being written), the payment system still operates inefficiently; it often takes weeks to have a check cleared or a payment credited to the firm's account. Insufficient customer orientation (a legacy), insufficient competition (major commercial banks are still state-owned), inadequate technology (computer systems), and poorly trained bank personnel are contributing factors. Securities legislation was codified in 1988, and in 1990 a small stock exchange was reopened in Budapest.

Tax reform measures introduced during 1988-89 replaced the earlier, highly variable (between sectors and product groups) system of sales taxes with a West European-type value added tax. Also, new and more uniform profit tax as well as personal income tax systems were introduced. However, both business and personal income tax rates were set high, one factor behind growing tax evasion. Although the levels of the profit tax on business and of the income tax on individuals are comparable to those in Western Europe (which means they are high), especially onerous are the value-added tax (VAT) rates that everyone pays and the social insurance contributions levied on business. The steep early progressivity of the profit and income tax rates is also a problem.

The main reason for Hungary's high tax rates is the role of the state budget in redistributing close to 60 percent of GDP, an unusually high share in international comparisons, especially considering the country's level of development. This share did not change significantly in the 1980s, nor has it changed even to date. Although in the late 1980s and early 1990s, production and consumption subsidies were substantially reduced, the role of the state budget in the economy has not diminished, owing to the substantial decline in the GDP (reducing the denominator); growing expenditures for unemployment, welfare, housing and other social programs; the state assuming responsibility for a large volume of bad debts of enterprises and banks (discussed below); and the as yet unreformed system of transfer payments (pensions, disability, family allowances) and social provisions (free health care and education). The main problem with transfer payments is not the extravagance of the expenditures but the fact that they are given, as entitlements, to all citizens rather than targeted to the needy.[8]

Significance of Pre-1990 Reforms for Transition. The significance of the reform measures introduced in Hungary through 1989 is to be found *not* in decisive improvements in economic performance. Outside agriculture, such improvements were modest, owing to the flawed concept of the reforms, the political constraints on their implementation, uninspired economic policies, and the unfavorable external environment. But economic reforms became cumulatively significant because by the late 1980s they created an environment that provided considerable independence for SOEs, a sizable private sector, and certain comfort with non-dirigiste methods of influencing economic activity. This legacy gave Hungary a head start and permitted more gradual transformation policies than either in Poland or in Czechoslovakia.[9]

Macroeconomic Policies and Performance, 1989-1995

Legacies of the 1970s and 1980s

Hungary's economic system, economic policies, and rapid changes in the external environment to which the economy was not able to adapt smoothly had, by the late 1970s, created an unbalanced economy in serious disequilibrium. The structure of the economy revealed misdevelopment (relative to the structures of comparable market economies).[10] The high and rising foreign indebtedness and continuous problems in the balance of payments showed that the economy was in more or less permanent disequilibrium. For these reasons, macroeconomic policy in the 1980s was characterized by two- to three-year cycles of "stop and go": accelerating economic growth quickly caused severe domestic and external disequilibria, forcing the authorities to give priority to macrostabilization. A fundamentally similar pattern continued during the first half of the 1990s, as detailed next. Superimposed on this pattern were the temporary dislocations of systemic transformation.

Transition Coincides with Large Economic Shocks

The economies of all of the European HPEs—especially their industrial sectors where most SOEs are to be found—have had to absorb a series of shocks that have exacerbated the legacies of the Communist economic system. The main external shock was the collapse of trade with the former CMEA countries, particularly of import demand by the USSR. At the same time, the reorientation of these countries' trade to Western Europe resulted in a new wave of competition for Hungary's industry. Moroever, after a period of EC liberalization, protectionist trends reappeared in Western

Europe, reinforced and made worse by West Europe's economic stagnation during 1992-93. The demise of the CMEA and its pricing mechanism has contributed to a more than 10 percent decline in Hungary's terms of trade during the early 1990s, causing a 3 to 4 percent loss of GDP that could be domestically absorbed.

These external shocks had multiplier effects in the domestic economy. The unavailability of relatively cheap energy and raw materials and the loss of CMEA markets had large adverse affects, especially on industrial production, and also contributed to an acceleration of inflation and unemployment. To bring inflation under control and to be able to continue to service Hungary's large foreign debts, monetary and fiscal policies were tightened, which reduced real wages and the population's total purchasing power and wealth. At the same time, as consumer subsidies were phased out, the relative prices of food and other basic consumer goods increased. Because the demand for these goods is more inelastic than the demand for industrial products, light industry as well as construction were hurt especially badly. Also, the liberalization of Hungary's imports during 1988-90 exposed its industry to much greater competition, representing a further shock. The generally outdated structure and quality of output—a legacy of decades of central planning—contributed to the severity of output contraction. At the same time, fundamental systemic changes, such as in ownership and the legal system, caused further economic dislocations. And contributing to the severity and long duration of economic decline were serious mistakes of economic policy: the excessively optimistic assessments of short-term economic accomplishments and of the economic situation generally; the underestimation of problems; and the delayed or inconsistent implementation of essential economic policy measures.

1989-1991: Economic Stabilization

In 1989 the (by then quite liberal Communist) government introduced a three-year program of economic stabilization, whose key elements were tight (but not excessively tight) monetary policy (including a positive real rate of interest); prudent fiscal policy, which meant a government budget close to balance; controls on wage increases in the state sector (imposing steeply progressive wage taxes on compensation increases that exceeded inflation); and a modestly appreciating real exchange rate.

Top priority was given to restrictive demand management to maintain Hungary's ability to service its large foreign debt, to control inflationary pressures, and to promote the restructuring of enterprises by making the budget constraint harder. The main macroeconomic objectives were by and large realized; restructuring much less so, partly because Hungary did not have an effective industrial policy and partly because of various constraints on enterprises, to be discussed.

Between 1989 and mid-1992, a number of key macroeconomic indicators—inflation, exports, the balance of payments, the inflow of foreign investment, net foreign debt, and central bank reserves—showed impressive improvements. One factor was the steep fall in production, which cut imports and promoted exports, especially since many companies faced an export or die situation. Another factor was the booming German economy, Hungary's main export market. Economic policy was generally sound. Monetary and fiscal policy remained somewhat restrictive during 1991. Household savings increased impressively in real terms, generating sufficient savings to finance simultaneously the government's budget deficit and the enterprise sector's net credit demand. Inflation peaked in mid-1991 and began to slow during the second half of the year, although unemployment rose to double-digits.

1992-1994: Economic Policy Mistakes

The government faced strong domestic political and social pressures to "get the economy moving again," to achieve a positive rate of growth and to improve the standard of living. Prompted by these pressures, and gaining increased confidence as the indicators of macro-stabilization had improved, beginning in the second half of 1992, the authorities made a series of policy misjudgments that are easy to identify by hindsight.

The government remained sanguine about the large and growing budget deficit in 1992, and again in 1993 as well as in 1994, expecting that continued large household savings would be able to finance them. That assumption turned out to be wrong, in no small measure owing to the interest rate policies of the central bank. By early 1992, the real rate of interest became unusually high: the nominal rate was around 30 to 35 percent, the consumer price index temporarily stabilized in the mid-20s range, and the producer price index around the mid-teens. This meant that businesses that could obtain credit had to pay nearly a 20 percent real rate of interest, which constrained business expansion and thus economic growth. The central bank then tried to push down the price of money by substantially reducing the interest it paid on government bonds. That, in turn, forced down the interest rates on household bank deposits to negative levels in real terms. This contributed to the large decline in household savings. At the same time, the real rate of interest that the banks charged to business borrowers had remained high (for reasons noted below and discussed in one of the Blue Ribbon Commission's policy studies[11]). Large budget deficits, financed by household savings, and increasingly by foreign borrowing, preempted the financing that should have gone to support domestic business expansion.

Policies on agriculture were inept. The combination of restitution-compensation policies, the rapid decline of financial support to the farm sector, and the dismantling of import barriers in the face of the EU's continued high level of agricultural protectionism and export subsidization have all contributed to the severe problems of agriculture in Hungary (Box 6.2).

Foreign economic policy also had problematic aspects. Between mid-1992 and mid-1993, the exchange rate of the forint had appreciated substantially in real terms, undermining export competitiveness while promoting imports, contributing to a substantial worsening of the trade balance during 1993 and 1994. During the early 1990s, import restrictions, especially in areas where Hungary had potentially competitive domestic capacity, were removed, perhaps a bit too hastily.

Between mid-1992 and mid-1994, the main economic policy mistake was that the government tried to stimulate economic growth primarily by easing monetary and fiscal policies and *not* via measures designed to improve the supply response and the competitiveness of Hungary's producers. Specifically, with respect to the supply side:

- The strategy and tactics of privatization were modified several times, causing uncertainty and many missed privatization opportunities, as will be detailed;
- Neglected completely the efficient management of SOEs—still a dominant sector in the economy—whether such firms remained under state control temporarily or permanently, as discussed below;
- Paid scant attention to rectifying the large and pervasive operating inefficiencies of the banking system, except for by and large solving, by year-end 1994, the banking system's bad debt problem (detailed on pp. 184-193);
- Pushed business taxes and taxes on personal incomes to extraordinarily high levels, in comparison with the tax burdens in other countries. This created a difficult dilemma for the business sector, especially in Hungary's recessionary environment: Pay the taxes fully and thus have meager internal funds to replace fixed assets and expand business, or cheat on taxes and hide part of the income, thus encouraging consumption, capital flight, and a short-term orientation, among other negative consequences. Taxes in Hungary are high, among other reasons, because of the unwillingness of successive governments to fundamentally reform the expenditure side of the budget,[12] and because of the pervasiveness and scope of tax cheating, which has been placing an ever larger burden on those who are unable or unwilling to cheat.

1994-1995: A New Crisis Prompts New Austerity Measures [13]

Policy mistakes during 1992-1994, an unusually long period of economic policy paralysis that followed the national elections of mid-1994, and unfavorable developments in the external environment helped trigger an economic crisis in Hungary in early 1995. "Crisis" did *not* mean Hungary was on the verge of defaulting or rescheduling its large external debt, or that it was facing some kind of an unavoidable economic catastrophe. Hungary faced an economic crisis in the sense that unless there was a speedy and decisive change in the direction in which the economy was heading, some

BOX 6.2   Hungary's Compensation Policies and Their Economic Impacts

Decisions on restitution or compensation affect a large subgroup of the citizenry, as well as SOEs and privatization. After lengthy and acrimonious debates in Parliament—restitution vs. compensation, full vs. partial, and who was to be eligible—restitution was rejected (except for some former church properties). The law provided for partial compensation of those citizens (or their descendants) whose private property was confiscated after 1947 and to those persecuted on political grounds.

Partial compensation is to be paid on a degressive scale, with the maximum limited to HUF 5 million (cca $50,000). Total "marketable" compensation of HUF 220 billion (cca $2 billion) of face value had been issued in the form of vouchers. The owners of the vouchers may sell them, or they may use them to purchase state property reserved for this purpose, including government-owned apartments by those who reside in them. Those who have reached retirement age may convert the vouchers into an annuity. Through March 1995, HUF 57 billion ($450 million) in face value had been exchanged by the SPA and the SHC for property, and certain amounts by other public bodies (such as local authorities selling apartments), leaving cca HUF 120 billion (about $1 billion) in circulation. Because the value of the property that could be purchased with the vouchers had declined and future policies on converting the vouchers for real assets remained uncertain, their market value declined to about 25 to 30 percent of face value by spring 1995. How to absorb the compensation vouchers without undermining privatization has been a difficult economic and political issue that is not yet fully solved.

Peasants whose land was confiscated or transferred (forcibly or not) to collective farms after 1947 were given inscribed vouchers that could be used only by the designated person or his descendants, and only to purchase agricultural land put aside at or near the original parcel. Agricultural cooperatives, which in 1988 controlled two-thirds of the country's cultivated arable land, were obliged to register all of their land under the names of the cooperatives' members (active or retired). Eligible people were then given the right to bid for land with vouchers—but, for the time being, without the right to sell it. Considering that only some of those eligible to bid wish to farm (but given the small parcels and depressed product prices, farming would require an uneconomically high investment in machinery and implements), while others would like to obtain high rent and still others would like to sell, there has been tremendous uncertainty over land ownership and use.

Thus, along with a severe drought, the collapse of domestic and foreign markets, the withdrawal of subsidies, the faster rise of input than output prices, and the unavailability of reasonably priced credits, the essentially politically motivated approach to compensation was a fundamental factor in disrupting Hungary's agriculture and causing a widespread paralysis in the sector during 1990-1994.

Source: Figyelő, March 30, 1995, p. 27; conversations with Ellen Commisso and János Hrabovsky helped clarify several issues.

kind of an economic catastrophe would, sooner or later, occur. The most visible signs of an approaching crisis were the rapid worsening of the current account of the balance of payments, a substantial rise in net foreign debt, an acceleration of inflation, and public criticism by the IMF of Hungary's economic policy course.

In May 1994, Hungary's second post-Communist elections were won by the Socialists (many Party members had been associated with the ruling liberal Communists of the late 1980s), taking over from an unpopular conservative (in domestic and foreign political matters) cum populist (in economic matters) government. They formed a coalition with the market-oriented Free Democrats, thereby commanding more than a two-thirds majority in Parliament. Hopes were high that a technocratic government would move quickly to implement the Socialists' campaign pledge to stabilize the economy, place it on a sustainable growth path, and complete transition to a market economy by the end of its term in 1998. Instead, the first nine months brought constant bickering within the government and the coalition, a slowdown of privatization, a string of dismissals or resignations of top economic officials, and continued inattention to Hungary's rapidly deteriorating economic health.

Given the country's heavy dependence on foreign investment and finance, confidence in its economic management is crucial. In early 1995, foreign confidence began to evaporate as the new government dithered, and as the HungarHotels controversy was reported in the Western press. (The essence of the HungarHotels case was that after the deal had been signed, Prime Minister Horn stopped the sale of the hotel chain to a foreign strategic investor, apparently for domestic political reasons.) The situation became especially serious after Mexico's economy crashed. Headlined the *Financial Times*: "Hungary Next?" An increasing number of Hungarian economists also pleaded with the government to change course. When in early 1995 the IMF and private lenders made it clear that they would stop doing business with Hungary until the government put its own economic house in order, a crisis was triggered. Prime Minister Horn had little choice but to appoint and to back the policies of two competent and tough-minded experts: György Surányi as president of the Central Bank and Lajos Bokros as Minister of Finance. In March 1995, the Bokros-Surányi team announced a stringent economic stabilization program, slashing in half the projected $3 billion (10 percent of GDP) budget deficit by cutting spending by about $1 billion and raising $500 million in additional taxes. They also devalued the currency substantially in real terms, moved to a crawling peg exchange rate system with pre-announced devaluations, added a customs-duty surtax of about 8 percent, and pledged to accelerate privatization.

These actions by the Horn government are necessary but not sufficient conditions for successful stabilization *and* sustained economic growth. The right policy is not to choose between economic stabilization *or* growth (a pattern that Hungary appears to have been following for about two decades) but economic stabilization *and* also laying the other foundations of sustained economic growth. Sustained growth requires not only a low level of inflation and a sustainable balance of payments position, but also a set of coordinated measures to strengthen the supply response and the competitiveness of domestic as well as foreign producers in Hungary. Several important such measures that should be taken were already mentioned (p. 164, second paragraph).

The Economic Performance of Hungary
vs. the Czech Republic and Poland, 1989-1994

For all three countries, the peak year for GDP was 1989. Measured GDP declined by roughly one-fifth during the next two to three years:

	Maximum Cumulative GDP Decline
Hungary	18%
Czech Republic	21%
Poland	18%

The only significant difference was in the timing of the decline. In Poland the largest decline occurred in 1990, there was a further smaller one in 1991, with good growth rates registered since 1992. In Hungary and in the Czech Republic, the largest declines came in 1991, with further declines in 1992 and 1993; modest turnarounds began only in 1994.

Because the three countries had significant differences in initial conditions as well as policies, these data suggest that the "transformation depression" was caused primarily by the strong external shocks hitting domestic economies that were unsuited to absorb them easily, and not mainly by the different economic policies the countries had pursued during the early years of the transformation. Poland's shock therapy affected mainly the timing of its decline and recovery, and not the magnitude of the decline, relative to the other two countries—which, in different ways, followed more gradualist economic policies.

Maximum declines in industrial output, while exceeding those of GDP, were also about the same in the three countries:[14]

Hungary	31%
Czech Republic	33%
Poland	31%

One notable difference among the countries is industry's contribution to GDP, which in the late 1980s was around 50 percent in the Czech Republic,

40 percent in Poland and 30 percent in Hungary. That these differences did not cause larger discrepancies in GDP performance is probably explained, in the case of Hungary, by the very large declines in agriculture and construction. In each country the expansion of the service sector has mitigated the depressed performance of these other sectors. There were large differences among the countries in their inflation rates, measured by the consumer price index (CPI), but the rates appear now to be converging (Table 6.1).

Poland and the Czech Republic dealt with their combined repressed inflation and price-liberalization-induced open inflationary pressures via shock therapy. Hungary had freed its prices earlier and more gradually over the years and did not need shock therapy to bring inflation to manageable range as additional prices were freed.

Comparative trends in unemployment rates (Table 6.2) show further important similarities as well as differences in economic policies. One similarity is that declines in employment have been considerably smaller than declines in GDP. One difference is that while policy makers in the

TABLE 6.1   Annual Inflation Rates in Hungary, the Czech Republic, and Poland, 1989-1994 *(Percent)*

	Hungary	Czech Republic	Poland
1989	17	1	251
1990	29	10	600
1991	35	57	70
1992	23	11	43
1993	22	21	35
1994	19	10	32

Source: CSOs of the respective countries, as published in *PlanEcon Reports,* various issues.

TABLE 6.2   Unemployment Rates in Hungary, the Czech Republic, and Poland, 1990-1994 *(Percent)*

	Hungary	Czech Republic	Poland
1990	2	1	6
1991	8	4	12
1992	12	3	14
1993	13	4	16
1994	10	3	16

Source: CSOs of the respective countries, as published in *PlanEcon Reports,* various issues.

Czech Republic have been emphasizing limiting unemployment, for social and political reasons (for example, by going easy on bankruptcies), policy makers in Hungary have allowed unemployment to rise, with their policies on bankruptcy (to be discussed) probably contributing to it. Poland's situation is probably explained in part by the rapid increase in new entrants into the labor force.

BOX 6.3   Policy Mistakes and Hungary's Business Environment

In spite of the mistakes in economic policy, the indigenous private sector has expanded rapidly and foreign investment has also grown impressively, year after year. How can one reconcile the policy mistakes and poor macro-economic performance on the one hand with the rapid growth of domestic private business and foreign investment on the other?

The growth of the private sector, in terms of the number of new business starts, has indeed been impressive. A significant number of business starts are, however, desperation "shoe-string" ventures by the unemployed or the underemployed, with little chance of long-term survival. Many new ventures are phantom undertakings, either shell companies whose purpose is to hide personal income and expenditures, or to "park" at a new location the assets of purposefully or unintentionally bankrupt businesses. While it is quite common in any market economy for business start-ups to have a high failure rate, what *is* unusual in Hungary is how few of the small businesses undertakings have been able to grow into mid-size or large businesses during the past five years. And many of those that have grown did so by finding ways to pay little or no taxes. Furthermore, the size of Hungary's hidden (unreported) economy is quite high, which means that real macro-economic performance, in terms of production and consumption, has been significantly better than that indicated by official statistics (details on p. 178).

Throughout the first half of the 1990s, Hungary had remained a *comparatively* attractive host country for foreign investors interested in this region. This is explained by Hungary's decades-long head start with economic reforms as compared with the other Central and East European countries; Hungary's traditions of entrepreneurship and long-established business contacts with the West; a privatization strategy that sought mainly to sell, not distribute, the assets; and continued improvements since 1990 in the legal-regulatory framework as well as in the physical infrastructure. In sum, throughout the first half of the 1990s, Hungary's business environment had remained comparatively more attractive, especially for foreign investors, than what might be suggested by its official data on macro-economic performance (Charts 6.1, 6.2, and 6.3) or by the government's economic policy stance. To be sure, the "business environment" and the "foreign business perception" advantages that Hungary had so clearly enjoyed vis-à-vis the other CEE countries during 1989-1991 have declined, but probably have not disappeared entirely by mid-decade.

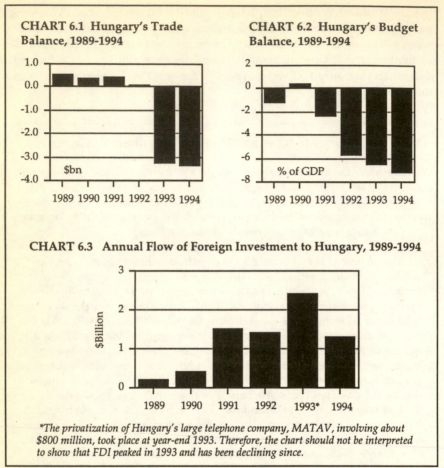

CHART 6.1 Hungary's Trade Balance, 1989-1994

CHART 6.2 Hungary's Budget Balance, 1989-1994

CHART 6.3   Annual Flow of Foreign Investment to Hungary, 1989-1994

*The privatization of Hungary's large telephone company, MATAV, involving about $800 million, took place at year-end 1993. Therefore, the chart should not be interpreted to show that FDI peaked in 1993 and has been declining since.

Sources: Prepared by the authors, based on CSO of Hungary, *Statistical Yearbook 1994*.

Key Institutions and Policies Affecting State-owned Enterprises

Privatization

Legal-Institutional Aspects. Hungary was the only CEE country where "spontaneous privatization" had begun already in 1989 on a substantial scale. To accelerate the process while making it more systematic and transparent, and to prevent abuses, legislation was passed in 1989 to establish the State Property Agency (SPA), to be in charge of privatization, subordinating it directly to Parliament. The SPA commenced operations in March 1990, just before the elections.

Soon after the new government was formed, Parliament changed the law and placed the SPA under direct government control. The government began to rail against spontaneous privatization, ostensibly because the procedure lent itself to self-dealing and fraud, of which there were a number of well-publicized cases. A further important reason for turning against spontaneous privatization was that the new government and its supporters did not like the fact that the program's initiators and administrators were in many cases the economic leaders of the old regime, and that privatization's typical beneficiaries were the managers, the technocrats, and other members of the previous establishment. After a strong media campaign against spontaneous privatization, the replacement of key SPA officials, and the cancellation of several preliminary agreements already signed (some involving foreign partners), the managers of SOEs became uncertain and cautious, and the pace of privatization slowed considerably.

In one important respect, however, there was policy continuity. The basic strategy of privatization had remained unchanged: selling to those who could afford to purchase the assets rather than giving them away. (Compensation vouchers and subsidized credits were the exceptions.) The rationale of this strategy was that it is important for the future viability of privatized businesses to be run by owners who have risked their own capital.

The SPA then assumed the initiative to privatize all but small businesses.[15] During the second half of 1990 and into 1991, the SPA created packages of companies it wished to privatize, sought investors, negotiated with them, and made the decision if there was an offer. However, SPA-initiated privatization was exceedingly slow, for which the government was criticized.

To speed up the process, beginning in mid-1991 more and more work was delegated to consulting firms. In 1992 a new version of enterprise-initiated privatization was introduced, the so-called "simplified procedure," also called *self-privatization*. Consulting firms approved by the SPA helped prepare each deal, in behalf of the SPA. The Agency of course had to approve each proposal. It had also retained its discretionary right to intervene in the process, at any stage.

Once an enterprise is transformed into a company, the SPA receives the state's shares and exercises its ownership functions. This includes the supervision and the right to replace management, as well as the appointment of thousands of people to serve on the boards of the hundreds of companies owned by the SPA. The dismissal and appointment of managers and board members has been an area in which political influence has been at work. Athough the extent of politically motivated firings and appointments is difficult to assess, competent people have been dismissed or room was otherwise made for political appointees, especially to the boards.

In 1992, Parliament established lists of companies over which the state wished to retain either full control (100 percent ownership) or hold onto the majority or a minority of the shares. The ownership, management, and partial privatization of these companies was then placed into the hands of a newly-created state organization, the State Holding Company (SHC; often referred to by its Hungarian initials, AV Rt). The political background for creating a separate institution was that the then Minister of Finance, Mihály Kupa, wanted to gain formal control over the entire privatization cum state property management process. But the then Prime Minister, József Antall, decided that such an arrangement would concentrate too much power in another person's hands. Therefore, a compromise was reached, justified as follows: property to be fully privatized would remain with the SPA, which was to be a temporary agency, while property in partial, permanent or semi-permanent state ownership would be managed by the newly established permanent agency, the SHC. Both property agencies would report to the Minister of Privatization, a newly created post filled by a close confidant of the Prime Minister.

The creation of a separate agency, though seemingly justified, caused confusion and delays and was not a good move from the point of view of expediting economic transformation. Both agencies had two quite similar functions: (1) to manage the property owned—whether the assets are controlled temporarily or permanently, partly or fully; and (2) to privatize as quickly as possible what can be sold. Because it took time for the new bureaucracy to get its objectives established and its operations under way, the transfer of firms from the SPA to the SHC involved further uncertainty for management and delays in completing the pending deals.

Because Hungary's privatization strategy was to sell rather than to distribute state property, foreign buyers who had the money were, inevitably, in a preferential position to pick and choose what they deemed to be worth acquiring. Not surprisingly, during 1990-92, four-fifths of privatization revenues were generated from sale to foreigners. This was favorable from the point of view of obtaining sizable foreign investment inflows, but it also contributed to a political backlash against the rapid growth of FDI. Responding to political concerns, in 1993 the government instituted programs to grant subsidized credits to domestic citizens who wished to acquire property through privatization.

During the last year, and especially during the first half of 1994—the last several months of the government led by the Democratic Forum Party—many abuses of preferential privatization reportedly had occurred, with the government allegedly favoring its political supporters. One of the primary campaign promises of the Socialist and Liberal parties elected in 1994, which formed a coalition government, was to enact quickly a new basic law on privatization in order to eliminate the problems and alleged abuses. The government coalition had a sufficient majority in Parliament to pass the bill, but disagreements about what to do stalled it for nearly a year. Although the legal framework of the old law permitted continued privatization, the uncertainty about how the law would be changed, and the dramatic intervention of Prime Minister Gyula Horn in his government's first major privatization deal—that of selling the HungarHotels chain to the highest-bidding foreign investor—*de facto* paralyzed major privatization deals.

Finally, on May 9, 1995, Parliament passed the third basic Privatization Law (208 votes for, 86 against, and five abstentions), without making any *fundamental* changes in privatization strategy. A key new provision is the premium put on cash purchases over such preferential forms of privatization as management-employee buyouts, sale against compensation coupons, and subsidized credits for domestic entrepreneurs. The 1995 Law states that preferential privatization techniques may be used only "if no valid *cash* bid reaching or exceeding the limit price [set by the state] is received." This provision again gives a competitive edge to foreign investors.

The Law also merged the SPA and the SHC into a newly named State Privatization and Holding Company (SPHC; often referred to by its Hungarian initials, APV Rt) to be operated under the Minister without Portfolio in Charge of Privatization (who in May 1995 was Tamás Suchman). The SPHC is to be run by a board of directors and overseen by a supervisory board, each comprising 11 members. Members of both boards are appointed by the government. Regrettably, during 1994-1995 many experienced experts were fired or decided on their own to move to the private sector. Some of them were replaced by less qualified political appointees.

The Law also introduced *simplified privatization via public auction* of the 800 or so small and medium-sized companies remaining to be sold. To be included, such firms must have registered equity below HUF 600 million (cca $5 million) and employ fewer than 500 people.

The Law stipulates, further, that transparency is to be improved by publishing detailed bidding guidelines and financial records when a company's privatization is announced, and an explanation is to be provided after a decision was made. To be sure, such procedures were by and large already followed voluntarily during the four years (1990-1993) when Lajos Csepi was head of the SPA.

Prompted by the clamor over the HungarHotels fiasco, the new Law specifies that the ultimate decision about companies of *national importance* (to be defined) rests with the government, not with the SPHC. This seems like a retroactive justification of the Prime Minister's intervention into the sale of HungarHotels.

During 1990-1994, the four years of the first post-Communist government, 50 laws were passed and 100 regulations issued that had an impact on the SPA's policies. Although the intentions of the lawmakers and bureaucrats were, in the majority of cases, commendable, trying to respond to real or perceived problems, the constantly changing legal and regulatory framework clearly reduced privatization's efficiency and speed.

The first *basic law* on privatization was enacted in 1990, the second in 1992, and the third in 1995. The primary change in the 1992 law was to make it easier for Hungarians to acquire property on preferential terms; that of the 1995 law (discussed earlier) was to reduce the citizens' preferences.

Since 1990, each year Parliament is supposed to pass an "annual guidelines for privatization" to supplement and interpret the general language of the basic law. During 1991-1995 the guidelines were often not issued until well into the year. They generally specify eight to ten priorities, several contradictory, for example, to encourage domestic ownership of privatized assets and to promote foreign direct investment.

The Politics of Privatization. The main implication of the foregoing sketch of the legal and institutional changes in privatization procedures is that in practically every year since 1988, managers of SOEs were confronted with changing privatization policies, prompted by politics. Together with the many other twists and turns in law and regulation and in economic conditions and policies, politics was the cause of a great deal of uncertainty in the environment. This had a paralytic effect on many managers, reinforcing the short-term orientation of their decisions, on which there is considerable evidence in the Hungarian literature. This finding was also confirmed during the interviews that two of this study's authors had conducted with former CEOs of large SOEs as well as with current and former officials of the SPA and the SHC.

A key political issue is whether to offer restitution or provide compensation to those whose properties were confiscated and those who had suffered serious injustices from Communist authorities. If offered, what form should it take? Who should have what claim over property not yet lawfully in private hands? How this was decided in Hungary, and what economic impact it had, especially in agriculture, where restitution-compensation was particularly important, are discussed in Box 6.2.

The reason politics is unavoidably so important for privatization is that the pocketbooks of many interest groups are affected by the outcomes. Chart 6.4 provides an overview of the numerous interest groups that have a direct or indirect say in privatization as well as in the management of SOEs.[16] It elaborates on the simpler, more generic Chart 2.3 in Chapter 2. Although the institutional details and relative power of the various parties involved differ from country to country, both charts show the political complexity of privatization and state property management. Chart 6.4 lists the many competing stakeholders in Hungary who were involved in privatization—directly or indirectly—circa 1993-1994. These include the various agencies of the state; the political parties that elect or appoint responsible officials, whose priorities often differ greatly; the citizens, who influence the politicians through public opinion and elections; the media, whose reporting, especially of real or alleged corruption, helps shape public

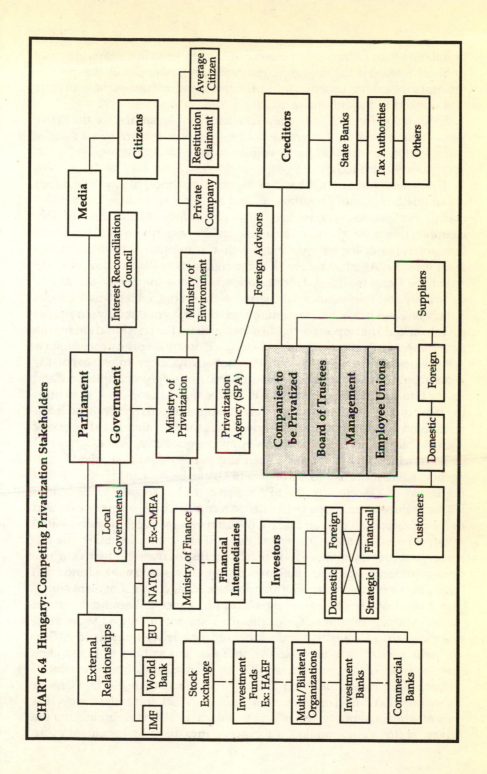

CHART 6.4 Hungary: Competing Privatization Stakeholders

opinion and the behavior of politicians; foreign economic, financial, and political interests; the creditors, customers, suppliers, and prospective buyers of the enterprise that is to be privatized; and, of course, the managers and workers of the enterprise itself.

Focusing on the SPA (the analysis would be quite similar for the SHC), let us highlight some of the more politically motivated pressures that the privatization agency and the government were facing during 1993-1994, and probably also today.

The general public ("Citizens" in the chart) is almost always suspicious about any large-scale privatization, and for several reasons. Most politicians, as well as the average citizen, do not fully understand the issues—for example, that even giving away a loss-making enterprise to a competent investor is better for the public purse than continued subsidization and asset erosion. Another reason is that privatization—which involves the redistribution of wealth and income opportunities—inevitably gets caught up in envy and thus politics. Furthermore, the media, which tends to focus mainly on cases of alleged corruption, thereby sways public opinion against privatization. The opposition parties then pick up the chase and charge the government with allegedly unfair dealings. How much of any accusation is just politics or media sensationalism is not always clear. In any event, the general public is left with the impression that undue political influence and corruption are shaping many deals. To be sure, there is no system of privatization that can be fully protected from subjectivity, political interference, and corruption. The only question is the prevalence and degree of such problems—a matter on which opinions, of course, differ.

To conclude, political pressure remains ever present as a privatization agency makes its decisions. As of mid-1995, the situation in Hungary is that the Board of Directors of the SPA's successor organization, the SPHC, whose members are appointed by the government, must approve each and every privatization deal and take a position on any major strategic initiatives proposed by the management of an SPHC-controlled SOE. The bureaucrats supervising management, who transmit management's suggestions or present to the Board their own proposals, are overworked and often have little or no business backgrounds or experience. Most of them supervise dozens of companies and thus have no chance to become experts in "their" companies' affairs. Given the environment in which they operate and the desire of many to preserve their unusually well-paying jobs (they are paid handsomely to make the staff less susceptible to graft), they function more like the bureaucrats they are than strategic business owners.

Data and Trends in Privatization and the Private Sector. One of transformation's most important economic, political, and social issues is the pace at which the public sector's contribution to GDP is shrinking and the private sector's is expanding. This can be measured by benchmark estimates, of the respective shares of the two sectors, in the economy overall as well as in the main branches, at various points in time.

There are basically two ways to estimate the relative importance of the public and private sectors. One is to consider changes in their respective shares of economically productive *assets;* the other, to estimate their shares in *current production.* The share of the private sector in *current production* (GDP) will generally be larger than its share in business *assets* because the private sector tends to be less capital-intensive than the public sector and because the private sector dominates the growing *unreported economy.*

The private sector's *share* of the economy's assets and output may increase through the establishment of new and the expansion of existing private businesses by domestic investors; through the privatization of state assets to domestic and foreign investors, including joint ventures; and through greenfield investment by foreign investors. The first of these has been the most important in Hungary.

The public sector is not synonymous with the state sector. The public sector includes state-owned economic units, economic units owned by local authorities, by the social security fund and other public funds, and forcibly established (nonvoluntary) cooperatives. The latter had existed in Hungary only up to 1992.[17]

The availability and reliability of comparable data for the public and private sectors leave a great deal to be desired, even in Hungary (whose statistics are considered better than those of most transition economies). Only ballpark estimates can be given of changes in the relative sizes of the two sectors. This section presents the best estimates available as of May 1995, with brief descriptions of the statistics and caveats about their interpretation. According to official statistics, the changing contributions of the main ownership sectors to Hungary's official GDP during 1980-1992 were as shown in Table 6.3.

TABLE 6.3   Contributions of the Public, Private, and Foreign Sectors to Hungary's GDP, 1980-1992 *(As percent of the total)*

	1980	1985	1989	1990	1991	1992
Public sector	90	85	80	76	70	56
Domestic private sector	10	15	20	23	27	36
Foreign-controlled sector	0	0	0	1	3	8

Source: János Árvay and András Vértes, *The Share of the Private Sector and the Hidden Economy in Hungary* (Budapest: GKI Economic Research Company, 1995), p. 18.

TABLE 6.4   Contributions of the Public, Private, and Foreign Sectors
to Hungary's "Extended" GDP, 1980-1992

	1980	*1985*	*1989*	*1990*	*1991*	*1992*
Public sector	83	79	74	70	63	50
Domestic private sector	17	21	26	29	34	42
Foreign-controlled sector	0	0	0	1	3	8

Source: Árvay and Vértes, p. 25.

A pioneering research project (sponsored by the joint Hungarian-International Blue Ribbon Commission, the government of Canada, the OECD, and the GKI Economic Research Company) estimated the size of Hungary's hidden economy, which is defined as unreported activities that add to "socially useful" economic value—i.e., excluding criminal activities. Using a variety of approaches that provided checks on each method's findings, the project then added to official GDP that part of the hidden economy which was not included in the official GDP,[18] generating what the researchers call "extended GDP" and what we may call "adjusted GDP." As a result, in 1992 official GDP was adjusted upward by 16 percent, as were the official growth rates of the early 1990s by an annual 1.5 to 2 percent.

One notable finding is that while the role of the hidden economy is indeed most significant in the private sector, all sectors of the economy, including the public and foreign-owned sectors, contribute to the generation of hidden incomes. Table 6.4 shows the changing contributions of the main ownership sectors to Hungary's "extended" (adjusted) GDP, during 1980-1992. Thus, according to the best available estimates, by 1992, 50 percent of Hungary's GDP had originated in the private sector, nearly one-fifth of which was foreign-controlled. By 1994, the private sector's share in GDP is estimated to have grown to about 55-60 percent.[19]

Turning to the ownership shares of business *assets*, the best estimate is that at year-end 1989, just before transformation began, 90 percent of such assets were state property, 10 percent private property. The *book value* of all SOEs (which, according to the accounting system of a planned economy, excludes the value of real estate and of intangible assets, such as patents, brand names, and copyrights) was about HUF 2,000 (about $30 billion).[20]

Making estimates for subsequent years of the HUF or dollar values of public and private assets, and their respective shares in total business assets, is fraught with difficulties. Especially troublesome is trying to estimate the value of business assets that remain state owned, because the equity of SOEs not yet privatized is stated at *book value*. Box 6.4 enumerates the conceptual and statistical problems that should be considered in interpreting HUF data on changes in state and private property shares during privatization.

BOX 6.4   Problems in Estimating the Degree of Privatization of SOEs

1. The book value of SOEs tends to significantly undervalue assets relative to their current value because it is not adjusted for inflation, which during 1989-94 moved into the 20 to 40 percent annual range.

2. The market value of not-yet-privatized state property has been declining rapidly because of inattention by the State as owner, and because the property that has remained with the privatization agencies is generally less desirable than the property already sold. So the resulting ratio of sales price to book value appears to decline over time from the 20 percent noted in (3) below. Such a decline in the market value to book value ratios suggests a smaller share of total assets for the private sector, resulting in an apparent slowing rate of privatization. However, this apparent trend may itself be misleading, owing to inflation, by which the book value of all assets should be adjusted upwards. Thus, the bias mentioned in (1) works in the opposite direction from that noted here.

3. Actual sales are recorded at *market value*, which can be higher or lower than book value. From March 1990 to March 1993, privatization sales revenues accounted for about 20 percent of 1989 book values. But because in those early years the SPA at first sold the generally more attractive property— whose sale price was, on average, about twice the book value—the 20 percent figure (whose numerator is computed at market prices) overstates the degree to which state-owned assets have been privatized.

4. In recent years, a growing share of privatized assets has been sold not for cash (HUF or foreign currency) but on credit, extended on highly subsidized terms, and against compensation vouchers, as shown in Table 6.5. Even assuming—unrealistically—that all credits will eventually be repaid, the *net present value* of sales on credit is considerably less than the sale price (the value at which the privatization transaction is actually recorded). Furthermore, sales against compensation vouchers are recorded at the vouchers' full face value, even though in early 1995 the market value of the compensation vouchers was fluctuating around 25 to 40 percent and generally declining. The real value of assets so privatized is only around 25 percent of the reported transaction value.* Thus, the ratio of non-cash sale price to book value will overstate not only the degree of privatization but also the share of privatized assets that in any given period is sold *not for cash* as compared with the share sold for cash. For example, although data in Table 6.5 indicate that in 1994 only about one-fifth of privatization sales were for cash, the real value of what the cash buyers obtained was almost certainly greater than just one-fourth of the value obtained by the non-cash buyers.

5. There is also the problem of how to account for partly privatized and liquidated SOEs.

*Based on information in Csillag and Tömpe, *Figyelő*, p. 18. Another article in the same issue (p. 20) estimates the value of property held by the SPA (only) as HUF 280 billion (cca $2 billion).

TABLE 6.5   **SPA's Annual Revenues from Privatization by Type of Payment, 1990-1994** *(in billion current HUF)*

	1990		1991		1992		1993		1994	
	HUF	*%*	*HUF*	*%*	*HUF*	*%*	*HUF*	*%*	*HUF*	*%*
Cash Sales*										
Foreign exch.	0.5	83	24.6	84	41.0	70	25.5	63	6.1	30
HUF	0.1	17	4.8	16	17.5	30	15.3	37	14.1	70
Total Cash	0.6	100	29.4	100	58.5	100	40.8	100	20.2	100
Cash + Non-cash Sales										
Foreign exch.	0.5	83	24.6	81	41.0	58	25.5	32	6.1	6
HUF	0.1	17	4.8	16	17.5	25	15.3	19	14.2	15
On credit**	---	---	1.0	3	9.1	13	21.7	27	30.2	32
Comp. vouch.	---	---	---	---	2.5	4	16.9	21	44.9	47
Total Revenues	0.6	100	30.4	100	70.1	100	79.4	100	95.3	100

*Excludes dividend income.
**Includes cash down payment.
Sources: Based on SPA, *Privatizációs Monitor*, February 28, 1995.

For all the reasons enumerated in Box 6.4, the SPA cooperated with the World Bank to develop a methodology for estimating the degree of privatization of state property held by the SPA and the SHC. The approach is to estimate the 1989 book value of state assets that were "affected" by privatization. Table 6.6 shows that from early 1990 to mid-1994, 47 percent of state property was affected by privatization, meaning that control over it was exercised by the private sector. Although privatization slowed considerably during the second half of 1994, our best estimate is that by year's end—after five years of transition—approximately 50 percent of state property had been privatized. Given the rapid growth (though from a small base) of the indigenous private sector, by the end of 1994 considerably more than half of the economy's total business assets were privately controlled.

To conclude: Although no precise figures can be given on the relative importance of the public and private sectors in the Hungarian economy, it can be stated with confidence that by the end of 1994, well over half of the country's GDP originated in the private sector, which also controlled well over half of the country's business assets. Some estimates may put the private sector's share as much as two-thirds, but that is probably too high.

The sources and disposition of the *number of SOEs* handled by the SPA during its first five years (between March 1990, when it was established, and February 1995) are shown in Table 6.7. One striking fact is that about 25 percent of the SOEs were liquidated through bankruptcy and related

TABLE 6.6 Method of Calculating Share of State Assets Affected by Privatization (*as of June 30, 1994*)

Item	Billions of HUF
+ Total net assets of companies sold 100%	229
+ Total net assets of companies transferred to majority private ownership	202
+ Proportionate share of net assets of companies in minority private ownership	91
+ Small privatization (called "pre-privatization")	17
+ Net assets of organizations (being) liquidated	316
+ Miscellaneous other transactions	89
= Net assets of the SPA and SPHC affected by privatization	944
Degree of privatization (944/2000) x 100	47%

Source: SPA, "Report on the Activities of the State Property Agency...." (Budapest: September 1994), Annex II, Table 1.

procedures.[21] This is a much higher ratio than in the Czech Republic, and even than in Poland, which is explained by Hungary's unusually tough 1992 bankruptcy law, discussed below.

Hungarian versus Foreign Participation in Privatization. The SPA's 1990-1994 annual revenues from privatization by type of payment (shown in Table 6.5) reveal that during the first two years of the transformation, more than 80 percent of the revenues came from foreign investors and less than 20 percent from domestic investors. This is understandable in light of Hungary's fundamental initial strategy of selling rather than distributing state assets and the limited financial capability of its citizens. The Blue Ribbon Commission (BRC) had established that while in 1990 the book value of all SOEs was around $30 billion (HUF 2,000 billion), the then current annual flow of private savings in currency that *could* be available for purchasing assets (other than real estate) was approximately $300 million (HUF 20 billion). At that rate of domestic savings, it would have taken Hungarians 100 years to purchase all SOEs.[22] For that reason—and also because of declining foreign interest in the property the government was then willing to sell, as well as to keep at bay the economic and political backlash against the preferences that "rich " foreigners enjoyed over "poor" Hungarians—the following special programs were established, strengthened, and increasingly relied on by the Antall government between 1992 and mid-1994:

1. The "existence" loan, or E-loan, was originally introduced to support the micro ventures of small entrepreneurs by providing them with subsidized credits. In 1992, the average loan was HUF 200,000 to

TABLE 6.7   Sources and Disposition of State-Owned Enterprises by the SPA
              (as of February 28, 1995)

Number of state-owned enterprises handled by the SPA
(March 1990-February 1995)

Operating in Hungary in 1989			2,000
Received by the SPA in 1990			1,848
Of which:	Transferred by SPA to other public agencies	210	
	Liquidated	437	
	Corporatized by the SPA	1,196	
	Remained SOE	5	
	TOTAL	1,848	

Number of companies handled by the SPA (March 1990-February 1995)

SOEs corporatized by the SPA (from above)			1,196
Newly established or transferred to the SPA*			257
TOTAL			1,453
Of which:	Transferred to other state organs	66	
	Liquidated	97	
	100% sold (privatized)	670	
	Privatization to be completed	620	
	Of which: Majority-owned	342	
	Minority-owned	278	
	TOTAL	1,453	

*Many companies were established before the SPA was set up in 1990 and
subsequently transferred to the SPA.
Source: SPA, *Privatizációs Monitor*, February 28, 1995.

500,000, or about $2,000 to $5,000. By 1993, the average ranged from
$50,000 to $1.5 million, many obtained to buy privatized assets.

2. The Small Investor Share-Ownership Program (known by its Hungarian initials, KRP), launched in the spring of 1994 just before the general
   elections, was a five-year program under which, when a state-owned
   company is floated on the Budapest Stock Exchange, its shares will be
   offered, on preferential terms, to small Hungarian investors who had
   pre-registered for the program, and to the holders of compensation
   vouchers. The program was "suspended" by the new government in
   1994, pending a policy review.[23]

3. Lease/buy-out schemes that offer the shares of a company to its
   management and workers on preferential terms, such as a 20 percent
   down payment on book value and the rest paid off, as a direct loan
   would be, over several years.

TABLE 6.8 **Types of Assets Remaining to Be Privatized**
(*as of April 1995*)

Asset type	Estimated Value as Percent of Total
About a dozen large SOEs (infrastructure, public utilities, banks, and SOEs with substantial domestic market shares)	70%
Around 400 to 500 mostly medium-sized SOEs still being controlled by the state	15 to 20%
Minority equity shares owned by the state	10 to 15%
Total state property to be privatized	100%

Source: Based on I. Csillag and I. Tömpe in *Figyelő,* April 20, 1995, p. 19.

As a consequence of the government's growing reliance on these special programs, the structure of privatization revenues has changed, as shown in Table 6.5. However, because cash and non-cash revenues are not really comparable (Box 6.4, paragraph 4), the percentage shares understate the relative importance of cash sales and overstate those of non-cash sales.

The Privatization Law enacted in May 1995 has reinstated the new government's preference for cash sales, as was noted. This was prompted, first and foremost, by the pressing need in 1995 to obtain privatization revenues and FDI to help finance unsustainably large budget and balance of payments deficits. The alleged abuses by the previous government in granting preferential credits, and the growing involvement of speculators in acquiring compensation vouchers with which to buy state assets, also played a role in the reorientation back toward cash sales.

Types of Assets Remaining to be Privatized. Table 6.8 shows the three main categories of assets that had remained to be privatized as of April 1995, and the approximate relative importance of their values.[24] It is evident that controlling interests in enterprises in the *first category* must be sold or leased to foreign investors because only they have the capital to acquire such firms at market prices and to make the sizable further investments needed to improve the efficiency of their operations. The main constraint of their privatization is the not yet fully developed legal-regulatory framework (for example, the ownership of real estate; the enforcement of commercial contracts; the normal collection of debts, such as by calling in collateral; predictable taxation; the pricing of the services provided by private public utilities; rules of competition; and prudential supervision) that would be appropriate to guide large firms in a market economy. Up until now (May 1995), direct political and/or bureaucratic intervention into the operation of large firms has remained more the rule than the exception. The exact provisions of the regulatory framework, and the prospects that the state would be able to, and would be inclined to, intervene *directly* into the operations of such firms, will largely determine whether the right type of foreign investors would be interested, and also the price such an investor would be willing to pay. Although the privatization of a few of these large firms, such as the state telephone company, MATAV, is well under way, the preparation and implementation of selling all or most of the companies in this category will take several years. And they will be privatized only if political will succeeds in overcoming the opposition of vested interests against further privatization in these sectors.

Enterprises in the *second category* can be, and should be, privatized as soon as possible—approximately within a year. Those that can not be sold or given away should be liquidated quickly. But two types of vested interests have been constraining their rapid privatization. One group is represented by those, mostly in the private sector, who obtain commercial benefits from the continued erosion of these companies' assets. For example, many of their suppliers are private. Many private firms are obtaining (unreported or under-reported) labor services from those whose main job and employment benefits are provided by these SOEs. The assets of these firms (such as real estate, buildings, machinery, tools, and marketing contacts) often yield benefits to individuals in the private sector, whether legally, semi-legally, or illegally. This is possible because they have no real owners who would stand up against the rapid erosion of their properties' values and because the SOEs still have softer budget constraints than have private firms. The two factors are, of course, interrelated.

The other group that opposes their rapid privatization are those in the political establishment and government bureaucracy who obtain certain tangible or intangible benefits by controlling or influencing the affairs of these firms. Thus, looking ahead, the fundamental question, again, is the strength of the government's political will to keep special interests at bay.

The *third category* is minority equity shares already in the hands of the state, plus further minority shares that the state would initially retain when privatizing SOEs in the first category. An appropriate privatization policy would be some combination of (1) periodically auctioning off some shares, especially those listed on the stock exchange; (2) distributing shares to individuals against compensation vouchers and to public agencies, such as the social security fund; and (3) selling them to the enterprise workers on preferential terms. Ultimately, these decisions, too, are political.

The Banking System and Enterprise Finance

Because Hungary's capital markets, especially the stock market, have as yet remained quite underdeveloped, commercial banks have remained of overriding importance for enterprise finance. Though more than 30 commercial banks are operating in Hungary, competition—which would be expected to improve the quality of bank management as well as customer service—so far has remained limited, owing to the high degree of market segmentation.[25] In 1987, the accounts of most SOEs were divided among, and still remain with, the largest state-owned banks, each of which was assigned to specialize in servicing enterprises in given sectors. The small and medium-sized banks, to which most foreign-owned banks belong, are, in turn, competing to provide banking services to the perhaps hundred or so truly profitable firms, be they state-owned or private. Households and small enterprises form still a separate sector and are the clients mainly of the country's giant savings bank system (the OTP) or the savings cooperatives, which often enjoy a local banking monopoly. Competition among the banks has been primarily for funds, not in the quality of the services rendered.

Non-performing Enterprise Debts to the Banks. Commercial banks have acquired nonperforming assets in three ways:

1. Some assets were already bad when the portfolios of assets and liabilities were transferred to the newly created commercial banks in 1987.
2. Many more outstanding debts became nonperforming as the collapse of trade with the CMEA and other shocks hit Hungary during 1990-93.
3. Further bad debts have accumulated as new loans were provided to SOEs as well as to private firms that proved not to be creditworthy. Such loans were given because in many cases the banks were not in a position to, or neglected to, assess creditworthiness. If old loans would not be refinanced, they would have to be written off. The managers of state-owned banks often preferred to postpone this so that large losses would not be reported while they remained at the helm.

By 1992-1993, the quality of the debts to the banking system, especially to many of the state-owned banks, had deteriorated to such an extent that many of the most important banks—and the banking system as a whole— lost all equity and even a large portion of the depositors' money. One reason was that decades earlier, Hungarian SOEs were established with little capital strength, so most of them were forced to rely continuously on relatively large loans, not well cushioned by equity.[26] Large state intervention thus became inevitable in order to avoid massive bank failures and the disastrous consequences for the economy.

The Banking System Is Rescued. At some point, a once-and-for-all cleaning up of the financial sector's bad debts is essential.[27] If only a portion is paid, if no line is drawn between old bad debts and new ones (created by imprudent new lending), then bank managers will know that the state will have no choice but to bail out the banks again and again. This gives rise to a "moral hazard" problem for bank managers: The easiest course of action may be to continue to finance loss-making enterprises.

At what point is it possible "to draw the line"? It probably cannot be done at a very early stage, while the transformation depression is running its course, because it is difficult to establish immediately which enterprises have survival potential. The true financial condition of debtors is also clouded by an accounting and financial reporting system that is not yet in conformity with the requirements of a market economy.

There are also political reasons why drawing a line once and for all between old and new bad debts is so difficult. Few governments anywhere are apt to allow one or more of their country's large commercial banks to go bankrupt and thus undermine the country's financial system and confidence in its economic management. So large banks know that ultimately the government really has no choice but to bail them out. And few governments in a democracy will stand idly by when several large enterprises are facing bankruptcy, especially if they are located in areas where they are the principal employer—which is often the case in Hungary and the other TREs. And if the state owns and controls nearly all the large banks—again, as in Hungary—then debtor lobbying for financing or refinancing will likely be effective. Furthermore, the state is a poor owner of businesses, including banks. Several of the large Hungarian banks have found ways to finance political parties (mostly by contributing to "not-for-profit" political foundations), which has helped secure the positions of management, irrespective of performance. In sum, large non-performing loans can perpetuate the inherited symbiotic relationship between SOEs and the state-owned banks. Such relationships also reduce the banks' ability to play a fully constructive role in corporate governance and enterprise restructuring.

On the other side of the coin, there is pressure on the government as well as on the banks to reduce, and eventually solve, the problem of bad debts. As long as the problem is not solved, it is likely to snowball and increase the future cost of the cure. In the meantime, economic recovery is thwarted, among other reasons, because bad loans crowd out potential good loans, and add to inflationary pressures. And the partial or full privatization of at least some of the banks, most likely to foreign buyers—which is desirable in order to improve the banking system and to bring in foreign capital— remains doubtful because few buyers are likely to be interested in, or pay a good price for, a bank with negative equity. International financial institutions have also been pressing the authorities to solve the bad debt problem and have offered modest financial assistance.

A basic issue in handling the bad debt problem is: Who should absorb the net balance-sheet losses that arise when debts are not paid? Whatever approach or combination of approaches is employed—privatization, work-out, restructuring, debt-equity conversion, or liquidation of the debtor—

society at large ultimately bears the brunt of the burden, through higher current or future government expenditures. An alternative is paying low real interest rates to savers and charging high real interest rates to borrowers, which penalizes the actual and potential users of banking services.

Spreads in interest rates—the difference between what borrowers pay and what depositors receive—rose from about 5 percent during 1991 to upwards of 10 percent during 1992-1993. The main reason was to provide a source of revenue to commercial banks from which to help finance the losses arising from nonperforming loans. Such large spreads have imposed a burdensome tax on savers and investors, caused financial disintermediation, and helped choke the long-awaited economic recovery.[28]

Direct aid to the banking system cost the government some $3.4 billion—equivalent to about 9 percent of 1993 GDP.[29] The banking system was "saved" by the state employing a combination of approaches (Box 6.5).

BOX 6.5   Recapitalizing Hungary's State-Owned Banks , 1991-1995

> *Note on Converting HUF values to Current U.S. Dollars*
>
> *Whenever possible, we tried to use the average annual exchange rate of the HUF for the year to which the data refer. Establishing the dollar value of cumulative flows and stocks, such as total bank recapitalization or the total debt relief granted to enterprises, is especially thorny. Depending on the exchange rate used, the dollar values quoted in various sources could differ significantly.*

1991 - The government issued guarantees for HUF 21 billion ($280 million) of doubtful loans—one-half of the doubtful loans that had been transferred to the commercial banks in 1987, when they were created out of the monobank. It was agreed that in 1992 banks would pay only small dividends into the state budget, to enable them to gradually improve their capital base.

1992 - Under the Loan Consolidation Program, the government swapped HUF 105 billion ($1.2 billion) of 15 state-owned commercial banks' and 69 savings cooperatives' problem loans for approximately HUF 80 billion ($1 billion) in state bonds. The replacement ratio of bonds for debt was set at 50 percent for loans made before 1992 and 80 percent for loans made during 1992. The debts of four large SOEs designated by the SPA and the SHC were replaced fully with government bonds. Of the HUF 105 billion in debt, approximately a third was transferred to a new institution, the Hungarian Investment and Development Company. (HID). The remainder stayed temporarily (for about 1.5 years) with the banks, which were to serve as collection

(continued)

(Box 6.5 cont'd.)

agents for the Ministry of Finance. In reality, nothing happened in most cases; the banks simply sat on the nonperforming loans. HID was to serve as a collection/workout agency, with a mandate to restructure debtor enterprises, "where possible." However, HID did not perform as an effective restructuring agency.

1993 - Under a Bank Recapitalization and Loan Consolidation Program, the government issued state bonds worth HUF 171 billion (about $2 billion) to eight problem banks. Of this, HUF 114 billion (almost $1.3 billion) was direct capital infusion, ostensibly to bring the assisted banks' capital-asset ratios (CAR) up to 0 percent. HUF 57 billion (nearly $700 million) involved government purchases from the banks of the loans of 16 large ailing enterprises (plus a large number of agricultural cooperatives) that had been explicitly targeted for rescue.

1994 - In May, another HUF 16 billion ($170 million) was injected into five of the eight banks, to raise their CARs to a purported 4 percent. In December, HUF 20 billion ($200 million) was injected into these banks to bring their CARs to at least 8 percent. In the same year, an Enterprise Debt Consolidation Program was introduced. Its essence is to arrange "workouts", outside insolvency procedures, between volunteering debtor enterprises and their creditors, led by a lead commercial bank. Commercial banks sent notices to 13,000 enterprises, owing a total of HUF 200 billion (close to $2 billion) to the banks, to consider participating in the program. A total of 2,000 enterprises had volunteered. During 1994, only about 10 percent of the cases had been resolved, involving some combination of interest and/or partial debt forgiveness, rescheduling, and debt-equity conversion. Since most debtors also owed to such government agencies as the tax authorities, the social security administration, and the customs office, these agencies also participated, giving debt relief in a variety of ways.

1995 - In February, the Ministry of Finance announced a deadline of June 30, 1995 to participate in the Enterprise Debt Consolidation Program. All negotiations must use a "simplified procedure," which means that the workouts involve only the debtor firm and its creditors, without the presence of any government officials.

Sources: Herbert L. Baer and Cheryl W. Gray, "Debt as a Control Device in Transitional Economies: The Experiences of Hungary and Poland," paper presented at the World Bank-Central European University Conference on Corporate Governance in Central Europe and Russia, Washington, DC, December 15-16, 1994, p. 15; *Financial Sector Reform and Enterprise Restructuring in Hungary.* Policy Study No. 4 of the Joint Hungarian-International Blue Ribbon Commission (Indianapolis: Hudson Institute, 1994); *Heti Vilaggazdasag,* January 22, 1994, p. 76; *Figyelő*, March 22, 1995, p. 14; *Privinfo* (periodical of the State Property Agency), Vol. 4, No. 5 (March 1995), p. 6; Mark E. Schaffer, *Government Subsidies to Enterprises in Central and Eastern Europe: Budgetary Subsidies and Tax Arrears* (London: Center for Economic Policy Research, Publication No. 1144, March 1995); and discussions with Hungarian banking experts.

These were not carefully planned in advance, but arrived at as ad hoc compromise solutions, technically not always the best. Yet, even with better planning and execution, the order of magnitude of what it cost the state to rescue the banking system probably could not have been substantially reduced. Rather, the main problem is that the efficiency of the banking system had improved much less than it was desirable and would have been possible.

On the positive side, during 1992-1994, the entire portfolio of Hungary's banks (not just their outstanding debts) was professionally evaluated during 1992-1994 by a team led by a respected international accounting firm, fully in accord with international rules and standards. To the best of our knowledge, Hungary is the only HPE where this has been accomplished as of mid-1995. Although bank portfolios still contain large non-performing and doubtful assets, the equity plus bad debt reserves of each of the large banks, as well as of the banking system as a whole, cover those assets fully. With the exception of one or two small financial institutions, no important bank has negative equity. And uniquely among the HPEs, all of Hungary's large banks had capital-asset ratios (CARs) of at least 8 percent by early 1995. And the CAR of the banking system as a whole was well above 10 percent! The amount of bad debt reserves that had to be created during 1994 was significantly less than in previous years and the required reserves could be set aside without causing significant net new losses. Although a few of the large banks are still loss-makers, in 1994 the banking system as a whole was profitable. Banks participating in the Loan Consolidation Program have begun to work on the financial restructuring of debtor enterprises. To be sure, banks differ greatly with respect to the quality and speed with which they are moving forward in this area.

In sum, by the end of 1994, a line had been drawn between old and new bad debts and the program of "consolidating" (taking care of) the bad debts of the banking system had essentially been completed. This is quite an achievement, generally not well recognized in the country, or even by foreign experts. This is because a series of banking problems, many of them quite visible, have remained as yet unsolved.

On the negative side, as payment to the banks for taking over a further portion of the bad debts, the government created large new debts (which is acceptable), but without providing for a revenue stream to cover the cost of servicing them (which is a problem). It means that future taxes, budget deficits, or both will have to be larger to cover the obligations. The realization of these facts by the international financial community probably contributed to the weakening of Hungary's creditworthiness in early 1995.

Bank Operations and Enterprise Relations. Two major and interdependent problems are that little improvement has taken place in the internal operation of the state-owned banks and that customer service is generally poor throughout the banking system. Although the banks are somewhat differentiated in this regard, the management and operation of state-owned banks has, on the whole, changed little as yet.

Parallel with the implementation of the various bank and loan consolidation programs (Box 6.5), the authorities were unable to come up with a concept, and therefore a program, of bank modernization, so that loan consolidation was not coupled with rapid modernization. The ultimate reason for this neglect is state ownership. During 1990-1993, the state's ownership functions were exercised mainly by the SHC (AV Rt), an agency entirely unsuited for the task. The same is true for the Ministry of Finance, which became a co-owner of the banks as a result of taking over some of the banks' non-performing loans, in exchange for bank equity. Individuals appointed (often on political grounds) to serve on the board of directors or on the supervisory boards of the state-owned banks were generally left to their own devices. Since no one guided or checked on their performance, they essentially did not perform the tasks that persons in such positions would be expected to perform in a market economy.

As a consequence of this state of affairs, the systematic financial restructuring of SOEs with nonperforming loans has been delayed much too long. Even now, as of mid-1995, financial restructuring is still proceeding rather haphazardly and slowly, thus delaying general economic recovery. State-owned banks, holding a large part of enterprise debts, have been doing little because no real owners stand behind bank management. The state agency (HID), responsible for handling some of the nonperforming loans of enterprises, has not been equipped to ferret out which enterprises could become viable after partial or full debt-forgiveness and which ones should be pushed into bankruptcy. Nor has HID been willing to contract out this task to the private sector, as the Blue Ribbon Commission and others had recommended.[30] Even in those cases where one of the owners or creditors has initiated financial restructuring or bankruptcy proceedings, there was often little coordination among the owners (such as the SPA or the SHC, the HID and the banks), among the creditors (the banks and—in the frequent case of enterprise payment arrears—the tax authorities, the social security administration, the customs office, and the suppliers), or between the owners and the creditors as stakeholder groups with different interests. Only now are restructuring issues of debtor SOEs *beginning* to be systematically addressed, by the banks, first and foremost. Several banks have established subsidiaries to try to collect or renegotiate the debts enterprises owe them and, in some cases, to try to arrange the restructuring of the debtor enterprises.

Bank Privatization. Privatizing the banks has been delayed partly because, given their poor financial shape, most state-owned banks could not be readily marketed to foreign strategic investors, at least until 1995. An equally, if not more important reason has been the reluctance of the authorities to sell controlling interest to foreign strategic investors. One influential opponent of privatization is bank management that knows or surmises that a private owner would change the management quickly. Of course, management's main argument to the politicians and to the general public is that selling a large bank to a foreign investor would not be "in the national interest." An apparent case in point is that in 1994, and again in 1995, two successive Hungarian governments, each of different political persuasion, rejected offers by George Soros, one of the world's richest financiers and a native of Hungary, to buy a controlling (25 percent) interest in Hungary's largest bank, the OTP, promising to quickly improve its operations and customer service.

There is one important exception to the generalization that the authorities are by and large not supportive of bank privatization: the 1994 sale to a strategic foreign investor of Hungary's fourth largest bank. The unusual circumstances of that sale are summarized in Box 6.6.

BOX 6.6   The Sale of Hungary's Fourth Largest Bank to Foreign Strategic Investors

In 1994, Hungary's fourth largest commercial bank, the Hungarian Foreign Trade Bank (Hungarian abbreviation: MKB) was sold to the Bayerische Landesbank Girocentrale, Germany's sixth largest bank, headquartered in Munich. The German bank—whose purchase decision reflected growing trade ties between Germany and Hungary, as well as MKB's knowledge of, and long-established contacts with, the other former CMEA countries—took a 25 percent stake, while the EBRD bought a 17 percent stake, in a deal valued at HUF 5.8 billion ($58 million).

Several unusual circumstances made it possible to privatize this bank, and so far this bank only. One, the MKB is a solid financial institution, generally considered to be a pearl among Hungary's state-controlled banks. That the MKB is different has come about because the Bank, established in the 1950s to finance East-West barter and switch transactions, was allowed to be professionally managed, given its crucial importance as an earner of convertible currency. The Bank's management took advantage of its relative freedom to operate almost as if it were a private bank and expanded to the domestic market also. Furthermore, the management of the Bank, not worried about its position under a prospective private owner, was fighting for, not against, privatization. Yet, even after the deal was arranged, it took several years and the combined efforts of a patient foreign strategic investor, a determined management, and skillful pressure by the EBRD to convince the Hungarian authorities to approve it.

Sources: Wall Street Journal, July 18, 1994; Financial Times, July 18, 1994; The Banker, July 1994; and interviews with the management of MKB.

Most of the shortcomings of the banking sector enumerated in the preceding paragraphs can be laid to the doorstep of the authorities, ultimately, to the ineptness of Hungary's political leadership. Between mid-1990 and mid-1995, political ineptness manifested itself in giving low priority to economic issues, in the reluctance of the political parties to move toward a policy consensus on fundamental economic issues, and in the unwillingness of successive prime ministers (Antall, Boros, and Horn) to allow a single, well-qualified expert to design and coordinate a purposeful economic policy.[31]

Bankruptcy. Bankruptcy laws serve several related functions in a market economy.[32] First, they provide a mechanism to liquidate inviable enterprises and repay creditors' claims according to agreed priority rules. Second, if the debtor's operations are potentially viable, bankruptcy procedures provide a framework for negotiating binding agreements to revalue assets and liabilities and to reorganize operations. Third, the threat of bankruptcy imposes a degree of financial discipline on enterprise managers. In sum, bankruptcy laws are important promoters of restructuring. All three of these functions played a role in the 1992 decision in Hungary to introduce tough bankruptcy laws. Especially important was the determination to impose more financial discipline, which was getting out of hand with the rapid increase in inter-enterprise debts—"queuing," in Hungarian terms.

Several factors have made many SOEs decide during 1990-1992 to help finance themselves by stretching out or not paying the bills of their suppliers. They had also accumulated arrears in customs duties, social security contributions, and taxes.[33] One factor was the impact of the economic shocks to which enterprises were exposed during the early 1990s. Another was the impact of a tight monetary policy through mid-1992 that was designed to bring down inflation and facilitate the continued servicing of Hungary's foreign debts. A third factor was their growing indebtedness to commercial banks as more and more loans became nonperforming. Nonpayment by customers to suppliers caused an ever larger and longer "queue" of mutual indebtedness among enterprises.

Partly to stop this snowball, in 1992 Hungary instituted one of the world's toughest bankruptcy laws. Any business owing as little as HUF 1 (about a penny) for more than three months had to self-initiate bankruptcy procedures, even if the creditors had no desire to take the debtor to court. The management of the debtor firm then had 90 days to submit a restructuring/refinancing plan. Only if 100 percent of the creditors accepted it could liquidation be avoided.

The Bankruptcy Law provides for three alternative procedures: "bankruptcy," "liquidation," and "final settlement."[34] *Bankruptcy* as a category corresponds, for all practical purposes, to what in the West is called reorganization procedure. The debtor enjoys a payment moratorium of 90 days (which may be extended for another 30 days) during which the debtor is free to manage its assets and the rights of the creditor are limited. At the creditors' option, the court may nominate a bankruptcy supervisor (trustee), who, however, has no right to actually intervene. If all the creditors do not agree with the reorganization plan submitted by the debtor, the bankruptcy procedure is automatically transformed into a liquidation procedure. *Liquidation* can be initiated either by the creditors or the debtor, if the debtor is determined to be insolvent. It involves selling the enterprise's assets because the assets appear to be worth more that way than if the business would continue to remain a going concern. *Final settlement* is a procedure for the voluntary termination of a company for reasons other than insolvency. Thus, the approach is somewhat different from the two former procedures.

Predictably, during 1992-1993 an avalanche of more than 10,000 bankruptcy cases swamped the fledgling bankruptcy courts. To be sure, most of those were small private ventures, many of which were paper corporations whose finances were often manipulated to avoid paying taxes, or for other reasons. Nevertheless, the unusually tough law forced even solvent but illiquid enterprises into bankruptcy. At the same time, procedural delays of a year or more often made it impossible for creditors to collect any revenue before the remaining assets were used up or squandered. There was also much uncertainty, which contributed to the paralysis of business decision making. A portion of the 1992-1993 decline in GDP can be attributed to the impact of bankruptcy laws and procedures.

In 1993, several provisions of the law were changed and bankruptcy conditions and practices became more lenient, bringing them more in line with those found in market economies. On the positive side, the growth of the queue of mutual indebtedness was stopped and a good number of unviable enterprises were liquidated, though perhaps at a higher cost than was necessary.

Corporate Governance

Definitions. Corporate governance concerns two sets of issues. The first asks: Whose interests should the activities of a corporation serve? Those of its owners, the stockholders? Or those of its multiple stakeholders—owners, managers, employees, suppliers, customers, creditors, the local community, and the nation state? If society places a high value on the efficient use of scarce resources, then theory tells us that the corporation should try to serve mainly the interest of its owners—subject, of course, to not neglecting the interests of its other stakeholders. (This is sometimes called "satisficing" the owners, which means providing at least an adequate, but not necessarily the maximum, rate of profits in the short run.) To be sure, ownership is not just a legal concept. People can be motivated to intelligently exercise ownership functions, for example, through contracts, profit-sharing arrangements, and, in some cases, by providing longer-term employment security. Societies differ in their preferences among alternative corporate governance arrangements. The second issue is how to align the divergent interests of managers, who wish to assure the continuity of their position and maximize their own income, and of owners, who wish to maximize the net present value of their investment.

Textbook versus Reality. A textbook answer provided to these two questions in countries representing (or strongly influenced by) the Anglo-Saxon tradition is that once the majority of SOEs have been privatized, competitive market conditions created, and market institutions established, competition and attempted profit maximization by owners forces managers to maximize the value of their firm.

In TREs, however, several arguments would seem to support more active policies toward corporate control than relying solely on the Darwinian process of natural selection through competition and bankruptcies. These are related to the economic, social and political costs of uncontrolled market failures in a situation in which many firms face distress simultaneously, often for reasons that are not of their own doing. If effective corporate control is lacking, managers can erode shareholder wealth to the point at which creditors' capital is endangered and bankruptcy becomes a threat. Bankruptcy as a selection process is costly because it is designed to serve creditors, not owners, and because if bankruptcies become too widespread, managers become discouraged and may not try hard to avoid it. And if creditors have insufficient interest in protecting the value of their assets, then managers have even less constraint on allowing the erosion of the firm's assets. In all these cases, society pays a high price because its accumulated productive resources will be consumed. To the degree that corporate control mechanisms can prevent the waste of capital, the costs to society are correspondingly reduced.

When bankruptcy threatens many firms simultaneously, the associated employment losses and social costs might be so large as to threaten the stability of the government. In extreme cases, even the continuity of the reform or the transformation process may be undermined. In these cases bankruptcy regulations or enforcement are likely to be softened and other means of supporting distressed enterprises found. Hungary during 1992-93 was a case in point.

Alternative Governance Models. Market economies have developed two basic alternative models of corporate control: (1) the Anglo-American model (with which the U.S. is most closely identified), and (2) the Continental European-Japanese model. Each has many variants. In the first model, changes in share values on the stock market supposedly reflect management's performance. If a company's stock performs poorly, the company will be a target for takeover, after which management will be replaced. The threat of takeover is supposed to serve as a stick; rising share values, benefiting top managers who are given generous stock options, are said to be the carrot. The interests of owners and managers are thus presumed to be aligned. Whatever the validity of these arguments in developed countries, the Anglo-Saxon model is not—or at least, not yet—a realistic option for TREs, primarily because of their underdeveloped stock markets.

Under the Continental European-Japanese model, share ownership is concentrated. In Germany, for example, ownership functions are exercised mainly by creditor banks that own part of the stock and also vote the proxies assigned to them by other stockholders. In Japan, the main creditor banks, the suppliers, the customers and other companies that are members of the "kereitsu" group jointly exercise ownership functions over their members.

Options for Transition Economies. Whether commercial banks can play a role in corporate governance in TREs similar to what they play in Germany is an open question. Those who argue in favor of such an arrangement point out that there is probably no other institution that can effectively exercise ownership functions over the SOEs. The other side of the argument is that as long as the main commercial banks are government owned or controlled, they are unlikely to have either the motivation or the realistic opportunity to act as tough owners vis-à-vis state-controlled corporations. Hungary to date is a case in point, as was discussed.

Another option would be to temporarily privatize the management of those SOEs that are slated for privatization but have no current buyers. Their management could be privatized through asset-management holding companies or through management contracts. Such holding companies would be in joint public-private ownership. The state would contribute the shares of the state property to be managed, but temporarily relinquish control to the private partners. Private investors would contribute cash and intangible assets and be granted the right to manage the property for a period of years. Management contracts would be drawn to provide incentives for increasing asset values as well as to privatize quickly. While privatizing the management of "temporary" state property may not solve all problems of corporate governance, it would almost certainly be an improvement over the SOEs drifting and their assets rapidly eroding. The Blue Ribbon Commission recommended to the government of Hungary to put in place this new form of corporate governance, but the recommendation has not been implemented widely.[35]

Although corporate governance is an issue for the larger private firms as well as for SOEs, in Hungary the issue concerns mainly SOEs because privatized firms are generally in the hands of owners who actually control them. But in countries where SOEs are privatized via the voucher method, the corporate governance issues raised here also concerns such "private" companies.

Developments in Hungary Through 1995. Through May 1995, Hungary still had not developed a clear, consistent, and effective policy on corporate governance for SOEs. One reason may be overly optimistic projections at the beginning of transformation about the likely speed of privatization. Another likely reason is a general lack of awareness of the importance of effective corporate governance. Ultimately, the legacies of a centrally directed economy, entrenched vested interests, and the broader problems of economic policy are the fundamental reasons.

The amended Transformation Law provided that every SOE had to be corporatized, that is, made into a share company by (after the deadline was extended) the end of 1993. Management was obliged to work with any one of more than a hundred authorized consulting firms, representing the SPA, many employing experts from one or more of dozens of countries, each firm and individual consultant with its own ways of doing things.

Upon corporatization, the old enterprise boards (which management itself helped create and staff) were replaced with two new boards, a board of directors (in charge of strategic issues) and a supervisory board (to report to the general assembly of stockholders about the affairs of the company and to exercise internal control; one-third of its members are elected by the employees). In many cases the new boards involved a complete change of personnel, who were not necessarily knowledgeable about the company's affairs; some members could simply be political appointees.

In 1992, enterprises that were permanently to remain fully or partly state-owned were transferred to a new government agency, the SHC, and there were other ownership changes as well. The managements of the affected companies thus had to deal with new "owners." Of the approximately 300 mostly large companies transferred to the SHC, 74 top managers were let go during the first year.[36] Hungarian Electricity Works, the business group with the largest total assets in the country, had three ownership changes during 1990-1993.

If a company has been or is to be privatized, managers face uncertainty about their personal future. Will the new private owner retain their services?

Responses by State-owned Enterprises

Three sets of principal impulses influenced the behavior of SOEs between 1990 and 1995: (1) the decline in aggregate demand and import liberalization; (2) the government's tight monetary policy until 1992 and credit conditions generally; and (3) frequent changes in the formal and informal mechanisms of corporate governance. The impact of these impulses and the responses of SOEs are discussed next.

To Import Liberalization and Decline in Aggregate Demand

Overview. It is difficult to distinguish between the effects of the collapse of exports to the former CMEA countries, the decline in domestic demand, increased competition from imports, and changes in relative prices. For many SOEs (as well as private firms), the shock from the East was the strongest. Cut-backs of exports by one firm have caused it to reduce purchases from domestic suppliers. The liberalization of domestic prices and the elimination of subsidies for food and energy had altered the pattern of domestic demand away from certain industrial consumer goods and raised the costs of energy and energy-intensive inputs.

Dramatically reduced CMEA and domestic demand for many products, and to a lesser extent tight monetary policy, have made many firms illiquid and a good number of them became insolvent. The most typical response was to grant each other inter-enterprise credits and to reduce or stop servicing their debts. Reinforcing this attitude was the well-founded belief that banks will not take action against enterprises in arrears on their long-term obligations, uncertainty regarding the nature of the budget constraint that enterprises were really facing, and the fact that Hungary's capital market offers no ready means to refinance firms in ways that would temporarily ease their debt burden.[37] The introduction in 1992 of exceedingly tough bankruptcy laws changed the external environment suddenly and significantly.

Import Liberalization. By the end of 1991, 90 percent of imports were liberalized (no import license was required). In 1989, 15 percent of industrial production faced import competition; by 1993, the number was 78 percent.[38] Average tariff rates are modest and Hungary has not been employing an extensive array of nontariff barriers. Because rapid import liberalization came at the time when the economy was reeling from other shocks, and because Hungary has many industries, enterprises, and products in which it could not conceivably have a comparative advantage under an open trading system, certain enterprises were particularly strongly affected. Domestic consumer electronics practically disappeared, owing to import competition, and those producing detergents, textiles, shoes, and building materials were hit hard.[39] In some cases import competition took the form of a foreign producer acquiring key units of the wholesale or retail disribution chain, which (together with a strong advertising campaign) put the foreign competitor in an advantageous position to take market share from domestic producers. To be sure, import liberalization and the introduction of de facto currency convertibility for Hungary's enterprise sector had a favorable impact. It gave producers ready access to imported parts, components, and equipment.[40]

Plummeting CMEA Demand. Corporate restructuring involves a wide range of possible steps. Some restructuring may be forced by circumstances, others take place at management's initiative, or both influences may be at work. An example is decreased dependence on the former CMEA markets, which was largely imposed, and reorientation toward trade with the West, which requires strategy and effort.

During 1989-1992, Hungarian firms were, on balance, remarkably successful in reorienting exports to the West. Many firms accomplished this by entering into joint-venture type arrangements with Western partners. Within a few years, the number of joint ventures with foreign partners increased from fewer than 2,000 in 1989 to more than 10,000 by 1993. The positive role of joint ventures in the rapid expansion of exports is well documented. Western partners were sought to provide marketing networks and expertise, as well as the investment and the know-how needed to produce, package, and deliver products on terms acceptable in the West. The extensive business contacts that many Hungarian firms had built up in the West since the early 1970s was one of Hungary's advantages over the other CEE countries, and it was quickly translated into a spectacular early export success, especially from mid-1990 until the end of 1991. The 1990-91 boom in West Germany, the liberalization of EC imports and negotiating in 1991 the terms of obtaining association membership in the EC were important contributing factors. And since maintaining employment became the overriding concern of managers, and exports to the West were often the only means of obtaining revenue, exports were pushed as long as their marginal costs could be covered.

During 1992-1994, exports showed a declining trend while imports continued to increase, turning the trade surpluses of 1990-1991 into growing deficits. These developments reflected the combined impact of deepening economic recession in Western Europe during 1992-1993 (which hit in particular three of Hungary's main trading partners: Germany, Austria, and Italy), increased protectionism in the West, the absent recovery in intra-regional trade, and the unusually high and growing import-intensity of Hungary's economy, partly explained by the timing, extent, and speed of the 1989-1991 import liberalization. A further important factor was the continued substantial real appreciation of the HUF (until the devaluation in September 1993), which made Hungary's exports and labor (subcontracted by firms in Western Europe) less competitive.

To Monetary Policy and Credit Conditions

One consequence of tight monetary policy during 1990-92 was to force many SOEs and private firms to rely on inter-enterprise debts rather than on bank credit. Restructuring efforts were hampered by making it difficult to acquire funds for investment. The reduced availability and the high real cost of bank credits prompted SOEs to rely on low-cost or zero-cost inter-enterprise credits, mostly to finance working capital.

Two factors made the real cost of bank credit high. One was the unusually large spread (around 10 percent) between the rates paid by borrowers and to depositors. In addition, there was a large difference between the rate of increase in the consumer price index (CPI) and the producer price index (PPI). For example, in 1992 the CPI increased 9 percent *faster* than the PPI. (One reason was the establishment of normal trade margins, which were close to zero in the old system.) Since much of the economy's net savings are provided by households, the interest rate paid to them must be linked to the CPI. The margin added to the deposit rate determines the interest rate charged to business borrowers. But the inflation rate that is relevant to a business borrower is that of the PPI—hence, the universal complaint from private firms and SOEs alike that business cannot afford the interest rate charged. The bankruptcy law put a stop to the growth of inter-enterprise debts, but it also endangered the financial status of many SOEs.

Case studies do not suggest that the growth of inter-enterprise debt and the shortage of working capital hampered production unduly by restricting the SOEs' ability to purchase inputs. But many firms reportedly could not obtain the funds essential for restructuring investment. The difficulty of raising money domestically increased the attractiveness of Western firms as joint venture partners and investors. At the same time, the accumulation of short-term assets of dubious quality has made privatization more difficult because it weakened the firms' financial situation.

To Changes in Corporate Governance

From 1989 to 1995, managers of SOEs faced many unsettled questions of corporate governance, frequent changes in managements, and frequent changes in policies by the supervising state agencies and by the government. Consider the "environment" (elements of which are highlighted in the next several paragraphs) in which managers of SOEs found themselves during 1990-1995.

SOE managers had no clear marching orders as to what their priorities should be. They were told that "spring cleaning" of personnel was needed (1991), or that privatization came "first and foremost" (1992), or that "protection of jobs" was paramount (1993), or to "wait" for the election results and then "see" what the new government wants to do (1994). The objective of *accumulating wealth* was always driven to the background. Instead, the opposite happened: The economic and financial systems, as well as politics, tolerated a behavior that *eroded capital*.

Many of the new appointees to the boards of directors and the supervisory boards, who were supposed to represent the state shareholders, in many cases turned into representatives (lobbyists) for the company vis-à-vis the state, because in most cases the state agencies that legally owned the company gave no clear guidance as to what they wanted to achieve.

Top management is not supposed to make any important decision without getting approval from the person in charge of the company at the SPA or the SHC (as of June 1995, the SPHC). To be sure, there was no clear policy on which questions management or the owner's representative would have the final say.

A frequent complaint is that the staff of the government agencies think and act like good bureaucrats; they do not approve anything for which they could later be held responsible. They often automatically forward for approval by the SPA's or the SHC's own board whatever requests are made by the firm's management. More generally, major or minor officials of these two institutions (as well as their counterparts in the ministries who control dozens of business units directly) have the right to merge, break up, rescue, or bankrupt the firms, or dismiss management overnight—all without personal liability or (in many cases) business expertise—in the name of better or worse political considerations and privatization concepts.

Managers have also faced numerous other barriers to restructuring. One is the formal and informal political and social pressures by the authorities against laying off workers and shutting down work places. Such pressures are especially strong in "company towns" outside Budapest where the employment effects of shutdowns would be severe. Another barrier managers have noted is that tax laws did not make downsizing attractive because the financial benefits of reducing the wage bill often accrued to the government, not to the firm.[41] Nevertheless, few SOEs could avoid downsizing their workforce. In many cases this was the result of the voluntary departure of (often the most productive) employees, who were taking positions with better-paying domestic private or foreign firms. But there were also significant layoffs and some bankruptcies, reflected by the rising unemployment figures. The national average unemployment rate was 13 to 14 percent during 1993 and only somewhat lower during 1994, hiding large regional variations.

Changes in product structure were undertaken by virtually all firms interviewed or on which case studies could be found. Financing was a problem for many firms, as was insufficient familiarity with Western market conditions or how best to adopt to them, especially during transition's early years.

One generalizable finding is the evident disinclination of management to think about restructuring in a strategic way. This conclusion is based on the rarity of finding any mention of a long-term strategic plan, the desire for investment without undertaking a careful cost-benefit analysis of its expected rate of return, and the rather ad hoc way in which many Hungarian companies seemed to have searched for Western joint venture partners and entered into agreements with them. Rare is the case in which the partners' strategic fit was considered.[42]

The declining trend in investment resulted in a dramatic under-capitalization of many industrial firms. At the same time, loss-making production was maintained at many SOEs, using the firm's assets to cover current losses because the strategic priority has been the survival of the enterprise at almost any price.[43]

The most typical situation and outcome is "drifting," which was said to have characterized the behavior of around 60 percent of Hungary's industrial firms still in state hands in 1992.[44] Drifting means that the enterprise does not invest on a large scale on account of its liquidity and debt problems, and it is also slow to shed labor. The main concern is day-to-day survival, tied to the similar fate that many other SOEs are facing. Managers hope that the authorities will not allow the simultaneous collapse of many, or that their firm will be privatized on terms advantageous to management. Even a significant number of the firms that have had to declare bankruptcy were able to continue drifting, due to the long delays in the process of reaching an agreement with the creditors.

Restructuring: Accomplishments and Tasks

The restructuring that has taken place after several years of transformation can be analyzed from various macro, mezzo, and micro perspectives. These include *changes* in the structure of the macroeconomy; in the branch composition of industrial production and employment; in productivity and levels of technology; in foreign trade composition; in the size structure of business units; and type of ownership. Representative case studies of individual firms offer micro perspectives. It is useful to speculate about the impact of government policies and other factors on the outcomes.

Restructuring the Macro Economy

At the time of writing, only selective data were available on restructuring and only through 1993. Some of the changes are highlighted through a separate analysis of the 1989-1991 and 1991-1993 periods:[45]

1. While between 1989 and 1993, the total output of the economy had declined by about 18 percent, the decline had occurred mainly in the production of goods. The output of the service sectors stagnated during 1989-1991 and grew during 1991-1993.

2. In the sectors where output declined, employment also decreased, but with a lag. Particularly large were the job declines in agriculture (employment in 1993 stood at less than 40 percent of that in 1989). However, a part of the decline was due to the reclassification of "alien" activities (industrial, construction, and service) from agriculture to the other sectors.

3. During the four years, industrial output declined by 35 percent, with large variations among the branches. Hurt especially badly were mining,

TABLE 6.9   Sectoral Composition of Hungary's Current-Price GDP in 1989 and 1993 *(As percent of the total)*

Sector	Composition		Changes in	
	1989	*1993*	*Volume*	*Price*
Goods and related services	71.4	60.8	-7.0	-3.6
Agriculture	12.8	6.7	-2.2	-3.9
Industry	32.9	26.5	-3.4	-3.0
Construction	7.8	5.3	-1.8	-0.7
Trade	9.9	13.3	-0.2	+3.6
Transport	8.2	9.0	-0.8	+1.6
Other services	28.6	39.2	+8.9	+1.7

Source: Éva Ehrlich and Gábor Révész, "Structural Changes in Hungary's Economy During the First Phase of Transition, 1989-1993," International Conference on Structural Changes in Central and Eastern Europe, Weimar, Germany, April 27-29, 1995, Table 2/a.

metals, machinery, and textiles. The relative winners (smaller declines) were the food, wood-working and electricity industries. The declines in mining and metal-fabricating are desirable, given that the attempt to maintain these large, loss-making, autarchic industries, and failure to modernize them, have been acute problems of industrial policy for decades. The interpretation of the large declines in the machinery and textile branches is more ambiguous. Several sub-branches in both have long performed well, boasting of a long tradition of excellence, considerable intellectual capital, and some advanced technology. Part of the reason they also suffered was the absence of an industrial policy designed to aid in the survival of those sub-branches where Hungary had a comparative advantage.

4. *Changes* in the sectoral composition of GDP in 1989 and 1993, computed in current prices, are presented in Table 6.9. Also shown is how much of the shifts in the contribution of the sectors is attributable to changes in the volume of output and changes in relative prices. It is revealed that the decrease in the *relative* prices of the output of the "material" sectors explains much more of the decline in the share of these sectors' contribution to GDP than the decline in production volume.

5. As to the *use* side of the GDP, Table 6.10 presents shifts in its composition and the effects that are attributable to changes in volume and to changes in relative prices. The table shows that during 1989-1993, domestic absorption declined by about 10 percent, considerably less than domestic production dropped. Hungary's "excess consumption" was financed by turning an export surplus (mostly with the CMEA countries, not readily convertible into goods or cash) into a large import surplus with the West. It is noteworthy that while the economy was shrinking and transformation to

TABLE 6.10 Changes in the Uses of Hungary's GDP, 1989-1993
(Indices or percent)

	Volume Indices			Composition		Changes in	
Type of Use	1991/89	1993/91	1993/89	1989	1993	Volume	Price
Indiv. consumption	91.0	100.8	91.7	63.7%	70.2%	0.7%	5.8%
Public consumption*	99.8	106.7	106.5	9.4%	11.0%	1.6%	0.0%
Gross fixed K-form.	83.2	99.0	82.4	24.3%	17.7%	-2.2%	-4.4%
Domestic use	88.1	103.0	90.7	100%	100%		
Export surplus (+)				3.4%			
Import surplus (-)					-5.3%		

* Excludes large import of military equipment from Russia in 1993, obtained as settlement of certain Soviet debts to Hungary.

Source: Éva Ehrlich and Gábor Révész, "Structural Changes in Hungary's Economy During the First Phase of Transition, 1989-1993," International Conference on Structural Changes in Central and Eastern Europe, Weimar, Germany, April 27-29, 1995, Table 5.

a market economy was proceeding, the volume of public consumption grew by 6.5 percent. Overall, the share of capital formation declined considerably (as its volume declined, although changing relative prices were even more important). These trends helped sow the seeds of Hungary's deteriorating external creditworthiness by 1995.

6. Foreign trade has been successfully reoriented from East to West. By 1993, 75 percent of trade was with the West (including the developing countries), and 25 percent with the East. Trading more with the West provides obvious benefits to the economy, but the cost of reorientation includes a large deterioration in Hungary's terms of trade (changes in export prices relative to changes in import prices). This has contributed to the rising import surplus and external debt.

7. One major change in the commodity structure of exports was the 44 percent decline in the volume of machinery exports between 1989 and 1993, explained mainly by the severe damaging of trade relations with the former CMEA countries. Only a small part of such machinery exports could be reoriented to the West. Also striking is the decrease in the volume of food exports. In addition to trade disruption with the CMEA countries, the damage caused to Hungary's agriculture by government policies (Box 6.3) and protection by the European Union were further significant factors.

8. On the import side, most striking is the 20 percent volume growth in food and the 66 percent (!) volume growth of industrial consumer goods between 1989-1993, at a time when the economy was in a transformation depression. Policies that favored consumption over investment, far-reaching import liberalization at a time when many domestic producers were facing major external and domestic policy shocks, and the real appreciation

of the Hungarian currency (vis-à-vis a basket of leading currencies) were some of the factors behind the growth of imports.

Changes in the Size Structure of Firms

The size structure of business units has changed in a rather unusual way. For any economy, the size structure of its business units can be depicted in a chart that shows the percent of a country's total labor force employed in enterprises of various sizes. Small enterprises are at the bottom of the chart, medium-sized firms are in the middle, and large enterprises are at the top. Chart 6.5a shows the typical size structure in a well-functioning market economy: the largest percent of the work force is employed at relatively small businesses (say, those that have fewer than 50 employees); a substantial percent is employed at mid-size firms (say, those with fewer than 500 employees); and only a relative small percent finds employment with the very large firms. Chart 6.5b depicts the typical pattern of a centrally planned economy, similar to that of Hungary in the 1960s. The shape is inverted, indicating that the largest part of the labor force finds employment at very large firms and only a relatively few work for small ventures. Chart 6.5c depicts Hungary's current pattern, which resembles a vase.[46] The broad base indicates the large number (tens of thousands) of small businesses that have been established. The new shape of the head reveals that many of the very large SOEs have disappeared—through downsizing, being broken up,

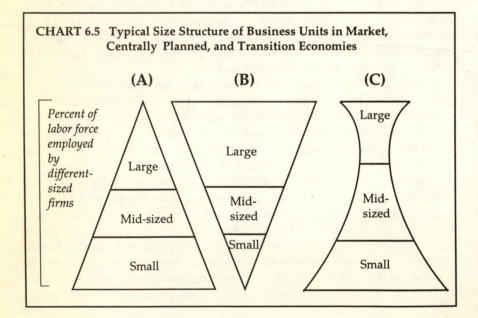

CHART 6.5 Typical Size Structure of Business Units in Market, Centrally Planned, and Transition Economies

(A)   (B)   (C)

Percent of labor force employed by different-sized firms

Large
Mid-sized
Small

Large
Mid-sized
Small

Large
Mid-sized
Small

liquidation, or privatization. For example, after Hungary's mammoth light source producer, Tungsram, was sold to General Electric, the work force was reduced by 50 percent, from about 20,000 to 10,000, while output and productivity increased greatly.[47] What is unusual in Chart 6.5c is the narrow middle, showing the continued small percent of the work force employed by medium-sized enterprises.

In Chart 6.5c, the broad base is explained mainly by the rapid expansion of private enterpreneurship during transition. To be sure, many small units are hopeless ventures, set up with meager investment only to flee unemployment. Many business units remain small so as not to catch the eye of the tax collector. The fact that the head is still larger than that for a market economy indicates the slowness of privatization of the largest firms, as well as the slow pace of restructuring enterprises that have remained state controlled. The continued small number of mid-size firms shows the absence of specialized suppliers. This reflects, in addition to the factors mentioned, the unavailability or high cost of business finance and Hungary's unusually high level of business taxation, which constrain the growth of all business.

Changes in Ownership Structure

Despite the somewhat sluggish pace of privatizing medium-sized and especially large firms during 1990-1994, the ownership structure of the economy's business units was dramatically transformed. Though precise computations are not feasible (Box 6.5), careful estimates show that the share of the private sector in the ownership of business assets had increased from roughly 10 percent in 1989 to well over 50 percent by the end of 1994. In bringing about this impressive structural change, as important as privatization has been the rapid growth of the private sector as well as the continous erosion of the assets of the state sector, through various legal, semi-legal and illegal means.

The Tasks Remaining

The main conclusions in Chapter 8 about the experiences of the TREs studied, based partly on the Hungarian experience, represent the most general evaluation of policies, so they will not be repeated here. But a few additional concluding observations may be made.

Along with other TREs, the new government of Hungary faced immensely difficult and complicated tasks. The economy, burdened with a large foreign debt and accelerating inflation, had to be stabilized; market institutions had to be created or strengthened; the size, ownership, production, and foreign trade structures of the enterprises had to be fundamentally changed. And all this had to be done while facing major external economic shocks, by a government that had no apprenticeship in the art of governing.

Read in this light, then, the achievements of 1990-1994 are considerable: domestic social peace (though not political or social harmony) has been maintained; a legal framework and other market institutions have been created or strengthened; the size, ownership, and foreign trade orientation of enterprises have been fundamentally changed; shortages have been eliminated; large foreign investment inflows have been obtained; and foreign economic relations have been liberalized and reoriented toward Western Europe.

These achievements notwithstanding, Hungary could be further along the road toward a strong market economy. And it could have traveled the road in the last four years with less social sacrifice, if authorities had paid more consistent attention to macroeconomic stabilization and had formulated and implemented better strategies and policies in defining the proper role of the state, improving economic policy consistency and coordination, and paying more attention to corporate governance.

Redefine the Role of the State. It seems that the state has remained or entered into areas of the economy in which it is not the best agent to accomplish things, and neglected to concern itself with problems and solutions in other areas in which it has an important role to play.

The state budget still redistributes too large a share of GDP, and as of early 1995, the expenditure side of the budget has not been fundamentally restructured. This is one reason why tax rates are too high and since tax evasion (partly because tax rates are high) is extensive, there is a large and growing budget deficit, whose financing is crowding out the financing of the private sector.

The state continues to own and control all but one of the country's main commercial banks. This is a big obstacle to the development of efficient financial intermediation.

The government has had no clear industrial policy for at least 15 years, which is one cause of the drifting of many SOEs.[48] SOEs are vitally affected by whether a country does or does not have an industrial policy. During 1990-1994, Hungary did not have one—certainly not a consistent one.[49] To illustrate, the former CEO of Hungary's mammoth tire and rubber product company, Taurus, said in his 1994 interview with the authors:

> Ever since the World Bank funded a thorough assessment of our company by a world class consultant orgnaization, in the 1980s, it has been clear that Hungary cannot maintain an economically viable tire industry. The authorities need to make a decision: Should Hungary, for some strategic or political reason, have a tire industry, or should it not have one? If a tire industry is desired, then let's provide it the subsidy or the protection needed. If we don't need this industry, then let's save the specialty rubber products that Hungary is able to competitively manufacture and adopt a plan of phasing out the rest. But no one is willing to make a clear-cut decision. Therefore, the company continues to drift.

There also seems to be no policy on how to jump-start the struggling private sector, which faces adverse economic conditions at home and abroad, unaffordably high real rates of interest, and a financial system that does not serve well its business needs. In sum, supply side measures have generally been neglected

Make Policies More Consistent. Privatization guidelines have changed frequently, which has engendered a degree of paralysis on the part of managers of SOEs as well as prospective investors; more consistency is needed.

Whereas countries typically establish their industrial policies first, to which privatization, foreign trade, foreign investment, and competition policies are adjusted, Hungary has done it backwards. It first liberalized imports, then signed an association agreement with the EU that enjoins Hungary from taking protectionist measures. But in Hungary's small, open economy, it is not possible to have an effective industrial policy without relying on *selective and temporary* protection. Hungary needs better coordination between industrial, trade, competition, and privatization policies.

Improve Corporate Governance. The oft-noted absence of long-term strategic thinking by managers of SOEs has two possible explanations: managerial ineptitude and large, multiple uncertainties in the environment. The latter has been by far the more important factor, we believe, owing mainly to the many unsettled questions of corporate governance of SOEs. Having effective corporate governance means that the owner—in this case, the state—has a strategy of what it wants to accomplish and then puts into place mechanisms that will motivate management to work hard to achieve those objectives. The best strategy, we believe, is rapid privatization, especially in light of Hungary's current political culture, which seems to emphasize debate more than reaching and implementing a consensus.

Notes

1. Éva Ehrlich and Gábor Révész, *Hungary and Its Prospects, 1985-2005* (Budapest: Akadémiai Kiadó, 1995), Table 1, p. 142.

2. Josef C. Brada et al., "Firms Afloat and Firms Adrift: Hungarian Industry and Economic Transition," special issue of *Eastern European Economics,* January-February 1994, pp. 1–112.

3. *Op. cit.,* p. 26.

4. *Ibid.*

5. For sources and additional details, see János Kornai, "The Hungarian Reform Process: Visions, Hopes, Reality," *Journal of Economic Literature,* December 1986, pp. 1,582-1,612, which presents a comprehensive analysis of reform ideas, policies, and their impact on economic performance through the mid-1980s. Gábor Révész, *Perestroika in Eastern Europe: Hungary's Economic Transformation, 1945-1988* (Boulder, CO: Westview Press, 1989), offers a broader and less technical account. Paul

Marer, "Economic Reform in Hungary: From Central Planning to Regulated Market," in *East European Economies: Slow Growth in the 1980s*, Vol. 3, Country Studies in Eastern Europe and Yugoslavia (Washington, DC: U.S. Government Printing Office, 1986), pp. 480-505, provides still another perspective on the reform process.

6. Brada et al., *op. cit.*, p. xiii.

7. Edmund S. Phelps at al, *Needed Mechanisms of Corporate Governance and Finance in Eastern Europe* (London: EBRD, Working Paper #1, March 1993), pp. 10, 44.

8. *Hungary's Welfare State in Transition: Structure, Initial Reforms, and Recommendations* (Indianapolis: Hudson Institute, Policy Study #3 of the Joint Hungarian-International Blue Ribbon Commission, March 1994).

9. For additional details, interpretations, and references, covering the period through mid-1994, see Paul Marer, "Hungary During 1988-1994: A Political Economy Assessment," in *East-Central European Economies in Transition*, papers submitted to the Joint Economic Committee, Congress of the United States (Washington, DC: U.S. Government Printing Office, 1994).

10. Keith Crane, "The Costs and Benefits of the Transition," paper presented at the Wilson Center Conference on the Economies of Central and Eastern Europe, Washington, DC, May 1994.

11. *Financial Sector Reform and Enterprise Restructuring in Hungary* (Indianapolis: Hudson Institute, Policy Study #4 of the Joint Hungarian-International Blue Ribbon Commission, 1995).

12. *Hungary's Welfare State in Transition: Structure, Initial Reforms, and Recommendations* (Indianapolis: Hudson Institute, Policy Study #3 of the Joint Hungarian-International Blue Ribbon Commission, 1994).

13. This section is based on two articles by Ákos Balassa, "Van-e válság, és ha igen, miféle?" ["Is There a Crisis, and If Yes, What Kind?"], *Népszabadság*, October 29, 1994; and "Egyensúly vagy növekedés?" ["Equilibrium or Growth?"], *Népszabadság*, June 3, 1995.

14. Based on the official statistics of the three countries.

15. The privatization of small businesses, mostly retail establishments, was accomplished quite quickly and efficiently during 1990-92.

16. This chart was made in cooperation with Stephen C. Eastham, a member during 1994-95 of the USAID's Transaction Support Team attached to the SPA.

17. János Árvay and András Vértes, *The Share of the Private Sector and the Hidden Economy in Hungary* (Budapest: GKI Economic Research Company, 1995), p. 10.

18. *Ibid*, p. 6.

19. Éva Ehrlich and Gábor Révész, "Structural Changes in Hungary's Economy During the First Phase of Transition, 1989-1993," paper presented at the International Conference on Structural Changes in Central and Eastern Europe, Weimar, Germany, April 27-29, 1995.

20. *Hungary in Transformation to Freedom and Prosperity: Economic Program Proposals of the Joint Hungarian-International Blue Ribbon Commission* (Indianapolis: Hudson Institute, 1990), p. 26. Certain independent experts preferred to quote HUF 3,000 (about $45 billion). The reason for the discrepancy is the uncertainty of asset valuation. Some adjust the original book values upward to better reflect presumed market values.

21. A total of 534 SOEs were liquidated—437 before corporatization and 97 after. The SPA originally received 1,848 SOEs, to which 257 companies were added through new transfers or by being newly established, for a total of 2,105 units. The ratio of 534/2,105 is 25 percent.

22. *Hungary in Transformation, op. cit.*, pp. 26-27. A similar figure is cited in Csillag andTömpe, *op. cit.*

23. "Small Investor Share-Ownership Program (KRP)," report by the KRP Project Management Group, in *Mass Privatization: An Initial Assessment* (Paris: OECD, 1995).

24. István Csillag and István Tömpe, "Business Transactions or Private Dealings by Public Servants?" (in Hungarian), *Figyelő*, April 20, 1995, p. 19.

25. Éva Várhegyi, "The Modernization of the Hungarian Banking Sector," in István P. Székely and David M. G. Newbery (eds.), *Hungary, an Economy in Transition* (Cambridge, U.K.: Cambridge University Press, 1993), p. 154.

26. Lajos Csepi and Mária Illés, "Performance of Privatized Enterprises in Hungary," paper presented at the OECD Conference, "Performance of Privatized Enterprises: Corporate Governance, Restructuring, and Profitability," Moscow, March 1995.

27. This and the next paragraph follow closely the text of Paul Marer, "Hungary During 1988-1994," *op. cit.*, pp. 494-495.

28. This and other issues are discussed in *Financial Sector Reform and Enterprise Restructuring in Hungary,* Policy Study #4 of the joint Hungarian-International Blue Ribbon Commission (Indianapolis: Hudson Institute, 1994).

29. Herbert L. Baer and Cheryl W. Gray, "Debt as a Control Device in Transitional Economies: The Experiences of Hungary and Poland," paper presented at the World Bank-Central European University Conference on Corporate Governance in Central Europe and Russia, Washington, December 15-16, 1994, pp. 15-16.

30. *Privatizing the Management of Temporary State Property* (Indianapolis: Hudson Institute, Policy Study #2 of the Joint Hungarian-International Blue Ribbon Commission, June 1993).

31. A detailed interpretation can be found in Paul Marer, "Hungary During 1988-1994," *op. cit.*

32. Cheryl W. Gray, et al., "Legal Reform for Hungary's Private Sector," Working Paper No. 983, Country Economics Department, the World Bank, 1992.

33. Details in Mark E. Schaffer, *Government Subsidies to Enterprises in Central and Eastern Europe: Budgetary Subsidies and Tax Arrears* (London: Center for Economic Policy Research, Publication No. 1144, March 1995).

34. Éva Hegedüs, "The Hungarian Framework for Bankruptcy and Reorganization and Its Effect on the National Economy," in *Corporate Bankruptcy and Reorganization Procedures in OECD and Eastern European Countries* (Paris: OECD, 1994).

35. *Privatizing the Management of Temporary State Property,* Policy Study #2 of the Joint Hungarian-International Blue Ribbon Commission (Indianapolis: Hudson Institute, 1993).

36. *Heti Világgazdaság*, July 1993, p. 89.

37. Josef Brada et al., "Firms Afloat and Firms Adrift: Hungarian Industry and Economic Transition," special issue of *Eastern European Economics*, January-February 1994, p. 56.

38. *Ibid.*

39. *Figyelő*, April 7, 1994.

40. *Currency Convertibility for Hungary: When and How to Introduce It*, Policy Study #1 of the Joint Hungarian-International Blue Ribbon Commission (Indianapolis: Hudson Institute, 1992).

41. Csepi and Illés, *op. cit.*, p. 12.

42. Marjorie Lyles, "An Evaluation of the Private Sector in Hungary: A Study of Small/Medium Joint Ventures and Enterprises," study sponsored by and prepared for the U.S. Agency for International Development and the Blue Ribbon Commission, September 1993.

43. How and why the managers of SOEs have been causing the erosion of their enterprises' assets and thus net present value is discussed by Lajos Csepi and Mária Illés, *op. cit.*

44. Chapter by Adám Torök in Brada et al., *Firms Afloat...*, p. 70.

45. The data below, in paragraphs marked (1) through (8), are based mostly on Éva Ehrlich and Gábor Révész, "Structural Changes in the Hungarian Economy in the First Phase of Transition, 1989-1993," paper presented at the Conference on Structural Changes in Central and Eastern Europe, Weimar, Germany, April 27-29, 1995. Their data, in turn, are based on revised official statistics, published in 1995. Official statistics on production and consumption incorporate only a portion of the estimated unreported economy.

46. The analogy to a vase was made in Ehrlich and Révész, *ibid.*

47. Paul Marer and Vincent Mabert, "GE's Pioneering Purchase of Tungsram: The First Five Years," in *Trends and Policies in Privatization* (Paris; OECD, forthcoming).

48. Josef Brada et al., "Firms Afloat...," p. 57.

49. *Review of Industry and Industrial Policy in Hungary* (Paris: OECD, 1995).

7

Russia

Despite a remarkable (by Russian standards) openness that has prevailed in Russia for several years now, studying the Russian economy may have become more difficult than it has been for quite some time. First, while a great deal more information is available and access to various sources has improved greatly, the reliability of that information is highly questionable. This is usually due to measurement and methodological problems rather than to conscious attempts by the statisticians to mislead. (A great deal of "misleading" is, of course, done by the enterprises and entrepreneurs in order to evade taxes, among other things.) Second, it has become extremely difficult to generalize from whatever information is available because of the great variety of economic phenomena and types of economic organizations in today's Russia. Third, the process of transformation which is taking place in the former Soviet Union and Eastern Europe is unique and so far lacks any accepted "general theory."

The economics of Russia's state-owned enterprises (SOEs) is a particularly challenging and, so far, a relatively poorly studied topic. Until recently, large and medium SOEs constituted the bulk of Russian industry. Many of the newly privatized enterprises are still partly owned by the state and act similarly to their completely state-owned brethren. Even after the ambitious Russian privatization program is completed, the state will preserve substantial ownership of industrial enterprises in the foreseeable future. SOEs represented the main target of structural reforms in Russia. For these reasons, the behavior of the SOEs and their newly privatized counterparts in the new environment will ultimately determine the outcome of the reform process.

The importance of understanding the effect of reforms on the SOEs has been relatively well understood by researchers and politicians. What has been somewhat less appreciated is the effect of SOE behavior on the outcomes of reform policies. Meanwhile, economic policy in Russia is and should be a two-way street, in that policy often has to be changed in response to enterprise behavior rather than simply forcing enterprises to change their ways according to the wishes of the reformers.[1] Without restructuring and significant changes in the mode of behavior of the SOEs, the Russian economy will not stabilize and will continue to experience significant problems.

This chapter analyzes the Russian reform process, putting particular emphasis on its effect on SOE behavior and on the feedback from SOE actions in the changing environment to reform policies. Section two summarizes reform attempts in the USSR between the early 1960s and 1991, and presents the basic features of the Russian economy on the eve of the introduction of Gaidar's reform package in 1992. Section three describes this reform package, including the details of the privatization program. Section four characterizes the major macroeconomic trends that resulted. These trends were strongly influenced by the peculiar behavior of SOEs in response to reform policies. The governance structure of SOEs and its evolution during the 1992-1994 period is examined in section five. The external relationships of SOEs are analyzed in section six. Section seven explores the relationship between major reform policies and SOE behavior since the beginning of 1992. This section also assesses the early signs of economic adjustment by the SOEs and recently privatized enterprises (RPEs). The major institutional changes in enterprise environment that took place in 1994 and the immediate effects of large-scale privatization are described in section eight. Finally, section nine provides an assessment of Russian economic reforms as of late 1994.

The Economic Legacy and the Economy in Late 1991

The Pre-1992 Reform Efforts and the 1991 Economic Situation

The Soviet Union undertook a number of more or less important economic reforms after the mid-1950s. The main feature of these reforms was that they never seriously attempted to change the systemic characteristics of the economy. The Soviet system proved to be stubbornly consistent in that it seemed impossible to change an important part of it without radical changes of the entire system. The constant stream of ultimately meaningless reform measures prompted Gertrude Schroeder, a well-known student of the Soviet economy, to refer to this process as a "treadmill of reforms."

Perhaps the most ambitious pre-Gorbachev reform undertaking was the 1965-1967 attempt to introduce market criteria, such as profitability and volume of sales, for evaluating enterprise performance. In the end, however, the reforms did not change much because other elements of the system, particularly state controlled prices, state ownership of virtually all assets, and the resulting power of the ministries and central allocation of important supplies, had remained unchanged. Perhaps the ultimate constraint was the Soviet government's realization that genuine reform of the system would seriously threaten its power.

The treadmill of reforms continued, perhaps because the Soviet leadership understood that the system was not functioning well. None of the governments prior to Gorbachev's, however, had been willing to gamble on losing its power. Meanwhile, Soviet economic performance continued to deteriorate. Finally, Gorbachev's perestroika (restructuring) reforms proved the previous Soviet leaders' worst fears about radical reforms.

Gorbachev's initial attempts to change the economic mechanism in the country did not differ in principle from many earlier reform endeavors. The major difference was in the political aspect of Gorbachev's program, the policy of "glasnost" (openness). Eventually, it was the political changes brought about by glasnost that allowed (or even forced) his reforms to continue beyond the point at which any earlier government would have turned back. Initially, Gorbachev probably did not realize that he would preside over the fall of the Soviet empire. And when he did realize this, it was too late to prevent it.

The most important economic component of Gorbachev's reforms was the Law on State Enterprise adopted in 1987 and enacted in January 1988. This law gave a large measure of independence to the state-owned industrial enterprises without, however, imposing anything close to a hard budget constraint on them. Also, the formal ownership of enterprise assets remained with the state and prices continued to be formally controlled by the central government.

The Law on State Enterprise, combined with the fast development of new crypto-private cooperatives, made it significantly easier to convert enterprise balances at the state bank (*"beznalichnye"* or "non-cash" money) into cash. This quickly exacerbated the problem of inconsistency between the fixed retail prices and the growing cash incomes of enterprises and the population. Also, the increased independence of enterprises was in conflict with the continuing existence of the branch ministries which retained responsibility for enterprise performance.

At the same time, glasnost and the general deliberate devolution of central power by the Gorbachev government brought into the open the independence aspirations of various nationalities of the Soviet empire. Eventually, the central government lost much of its control over both enterprises and the republics.

By 1991 the gap between the volume of money in the hands of the consumers and the value of consumer goods offered for sale at state-determined prices (the so-called monetary overhang) became intolerably large. In April, Prime Minister Ryzhkov instituted a round of price increases in order to reduce the monetary overhang and the state budget deficit. Even though consumer prices for the year increased by about 90 percent and wholesale inflation reached almost 140 percent, regulated price increases did nothing to address the underlying problems of the economy such as the inconsistency between the *de jure* state ownership of most productive assets and the *de facto* management control of most enterprise activities.

Economic and political developments fed on each other and culminated in the August 1991 coup which ultimately resulted in the Communist party being completely discredited and losing power. After the defeat of the coup, the government of the USSR lost virtually all of its enforcement power, not only in the peripheral republics, but also in Russia. In December, the breakup of the Soviet empire became official. The collapse of the Soviet Union did not help the Russian economic situation, which became critical as neither the state bureaucracy nor the market performed coordinating functions in the economy. Radical market-oriented reforms were the only feasible alternative which did not involve large scale repression. The time available for putting together a reform package, however, was quite limited. Although serious mistakes were made by the reformers, overall reforms that began in January 1992 could be considered a success under these extraordinarily difficult circumstances.

In evaluating the effect of the 1992 reform package, one must have an understanding of the pre-reform situation. To a significant extent, market-oriented reforms brought into the open many of the problems, such as inflation and unemployment, that existed in a repressed or implicit form prior to reforms.[2] In addition, the effect of the long-term legacy of the Soviet system must be taken into account. Any economy's performance depends on its physical capital, human capital, and the institutions which coordinate economic activities, allocating inputs and outputs and providing economic agents with information and incentives. While reforms set out to change the institutions over a relatively short period of time, the stock of the available physical and human capital will influence Russian economic performance for years to come.

Physical Capital and Industrial Structure

Russia has inherited a large amount of obsolete physical capital.[3] Moreover, the structure of the capital stock was heavily distorted by the investment decisions of Soviet planners who used to emphasize investment into heavy industry and defense-related industries at the expense of consumer-related sectors, especially services.[4] The Russian economy was misdeveloped to produce many goods for which the demand will be low in the near future (the comparative structure of output and employment in the USSR and the U.S. is shown in Table 7.1). In addition, a large proportion of all investments was tied up in unfinished projects, many of which will never be completed.

Excessive capital stock in some areas (e.g., metal cutting machines and many other types of heavy equipment) coexists with low capital endow-

TABLE 7.1 The Structure of Output and Employment in the U.S. and the USSR
(percent of total)

Sector	Output		Employment	
	USA	*USSR*	*USA*	*USSR*
Industry	23.5	48.9	17.6	28.9
Electricity	3.3	2.2	0.8	0.6
Fuel	2.3	5.0	0.7	1.2
Metallurgy	1.1	3.7	2.1	1.5
Chemical	2.2	3.1	1.7	1.4
MBMW	8.7	15.1	6.3	13.0
Wood and Paper	1.7	2.1	1.7	2.1
Construction materials	0.6	2.1	0.5	1.9
Light industry	1.0	6.1	1.8	3.7
Food processing	2.4	8.1	1.5	2.4
Other industry	0.3	1.4	0.3	1.3
Construction	6.1	10.7	4.6	11.5
Agriculture	1.9	9.3	2.7	19.3
Transp. and communication	5.8	10.1	4.0	7.2
Trade and distribution	11.2	6.1	22.2	8.0
Other	1.5	0.8	1.4	0.6
Services	5.0	13.9	47.6	24.5

a. Data for the USSR are for 1988. Data for the U.S. are for 1986;

b. Output is measured as value-added in domestic currency;

c. "Transportation and communications" category includes passenger services as well as freight.

Source: Kwon (1992) as quoted in Lipton and Sachs (1992), p. 217.

ments in other areas. Particularly important for the development of the market economy is the poor state of Russia's transportation and communications networks.

The main characteristic of the Soviet industrial institutional structure was the dominance of state ownership. Production by SOEs accounted for 96 percent of all industrial output. This figure, of course, disregards the illegal second economy production, which was considerable but was concentrated outside industry. The state owned 22,000 industrial enterprises, leaving fewer than 1,000 for other forms of ownership. Out of these, 70 were private and 922 were in "collective" ownership.[5] State enterprises employed the overwhelming majority of the labor force as well (Table 7.2).

Russian industry is commonly characterized as highly concentrated and monopolized. According to Kroll (1991), the average number of employees per enterprise in 1987-1988 was 813. Almost 75 percent of the labor force worked in enterprises employing more than 1000 workers. The very

TABLE 7.2. **Employment in Enterprises and Organizations of Various Forms**
of Ownership *(annual average, 000s of employees)*

	1990	1991	1992*	1991 as % of 1990	1992 as % of 1991
State-owned	61,380	55,766	48,764	90.9	87.4
Leaseholds	2,764	5,590	4,891	202.2	87.5
Joint-stock	182	860	2,115	472.5	245.9
Associations	100	238	230	238.0	96.6
Private (ex. farms)	50	323	1,114	646.0	344.9
Joint ventures	65	140	181	215.4	129.3
Cooperatives	2,567	1,779	918	69.3	51.6
Kolkhozes	3,979	3,847	3,653	96.7	95.0
Private farms	7	133	592	1,900.0	445.1

* Estimate.

Source: Rossiia-1993 (1993), p. 211.

large enterprises with more than 10,000 workers employed 21.6 percent of the labor force. Also, 80 percent of the output of machine building was produced by monopolists, and 77 percent of machine building enterprises were monopolistic.[6] According to the World Bank, 77 percent of the 7,664 product groups whose distribution was administered by Gossnab were produced by monopolists.[7] The problem of monopoly has been greatly exacerbated by immense distances and the poor transportation and communications networks that partitioned the country into regional markets.

Human Capital

The composition of human capital in Russia is also highly distorted relative to what is needed in a market economy. The country has too many engineers and technicians, and too few competent accountants, economists, marketing specialists, lawyers, etc. On the positive side, the Russian population possesses good basic skills necessary to adapt to a changing environment. Presumably, people with such basic skills can adjust much easier than the machines. The high educational level of the population represents one of the most important resources of the Russian economy.

The 1992 Reform Package

Overview

By 1991 it had become clear to most observers that the traditional, Soviet-type system was no longer functioning in Russia. The old, hierarchical coordinating mechanism was disintegrating and had to be replaced with a new system. To some extent, such a replacement was taking place spontaneously as enterprises, entrepreneurs, and the population at large were adapting to the new environment. Nonetheless, the formal existence and inertia of the old system were creating confusion, obstructing the adjustment processes, and preventing the emergence of effective markets. A radical reform became virtually unavoidable. In a speech on October 28, 1991, President Yeltsin outlined the goal of economic reforms as achieving transition to a market economy and macroeconomic stabilization.

While many of the important laws and regulations were adopted prior to 1992, the implementation of the main reform package began only on January 2, 1992. The main features of this package included liberalization of most producer and consumer prices, radical reduction of government investments and subsidies to enterprises, introduction of the new system of taxation, relatively tight credit policy, partial liberalization of foreign trade, creation of the new administrative and institutional structures for development and implementation of economic policy, and removal of most wage controls and other direct controls over SOEs. In addition, the government put forth an ambitious privatization program which, however, was not scheduled to start until later in the year, continuing through 1993 and beyond. The next several sections describe elements of the 1992 reforms in greater detail.

Price Liberalization

On January 2, 1992, the Russian government stopped setting wholesale prices for about 80 percent of output and retail prices accounting for about 90 percent of all sales (measured in 1991 relative prices).[8] Virtually all of the remaining controlled prices were sharply increased. In particular, energy prices, which were still controlled by the state, were raised five-fold. Most of the other regulated prices, including those for consumer necessities, were raised by 300 to 500 percent.[9] More prices were deregulated or further increased later in the first half of 1992.[10] According to official statistics, consumer prices more than tripled in January, but went up only by 24 percent and 21 percent in February and March, respectively. In May the rate of inflation fell to 11 percent per month. (Table 7.3 presents the wholesale price indices by branches of industry and retail price indices for 1991 and 1992.)

Price liberalization transformed repressed inflation into open inflation. For this reason, price indices, particularly those dealing with consumer prices, calculated in a conventional manner, do not tell the whole story. First, throughout much of the country, many consumer goods were not available at all at state-controlled prices. When more or less desirable goods were available, consumers had to stand in long queues to obtain them. Official price indices do not take into account either the degree of availabil-

TABLE 7.3   **Russian Inflation Rates, 1991-1992**
(Monthly percentage change unless otherwise indicated)

Branch or Market	Within 1991	Jan 1992	Feb 1992	Mar 1992	Apr 1992	May 1992	Jun 1992	July 1992	Aug 1992	Sep 1992	Oct 1992	Nov 1992	Dec 1992	Within 1992
All industry (whsl. prices)	236	382	75	28	17	23	36	17	13	14	27	27	20	3,275
Electric energy	110	269	55	49	35	32	92	49	19	5	5	32	17	5,409
Fuels	129	394	26	28	6	108	228	9	1	5	113	36	20	9,166
Ferrous metallurgy	237	361	60	25	33	27	24	11	8	4	12	14	7	3,525
Nonferrous metallurgy	233	500	57	67	12	27	37	42	9	8	26	28	45	5,120
Chemicals	165	502	78	33	34	25	22	17	8	9	31	22	15	3,791
Petrochemicals	149	696	37	20	34	16	38	23	8	1	23	33	32	5,248
Machine building	212	412	63	33	16	15	9	15	16	11	17	28	22	2,621
Forestry, timber processing and pulp and paper	242	371	123	26	10	10	12	11	10	5	17	14	23	2,921
Construction materials	215	382	69	13	15	15	30	22	12	11	29	27	14	2,714
Light industry	371	230	61	16	6	8	8	7	7	13	11	39	26	1,198
Food processing	314	365	25	18	19	9	23	12	14	28	35	27	24	2,628
Composite consumer goods and services	146.1	245	38	30	22	12	19	11	9	12	23	26	25	2,509
Foodstuffs (excl. alcohol)	n/a	306	20	18	17	11	13	8	6	11	26	27	26	2,033
Nonfoods	n/a	211	48	42	25	12	12	10	10	13	20	26	27	2,573
Services to population	79	130	87	34	31	18	39	21	11	11	29	23	19	3,258
State and cooperative trade	152	245	24	21	15	11	13	7	n/a	n/a	n/a	n/a	n/a	n/a
Kolkhoz market	281	53	15	16	7	5	-2	-13	-15	12	17	30	33	731

Annual indices represent percentage increase over December of previous year.
Source: Koen and Phillips (1993), pp. 32-33.

ity or the extent of queuing and search costs which were dramatically reduced with price liberalization. Roberts presents calculations which suggest that the radical reduction of queuing and searching costs due to price liberalization probably led to a gain in consumer welfare that offset the apparent drop in output of consumer goods.[11] Note that in early 1992 inflation in the kolkhoz and black markets was much lower than official price inflation in early 1992. Lower shopping costs not only save leisure time but leave more time available for work that can, in principle, result in greater supply of consumer goods and increase welfare even further.[12]

The reduction in shopping costs is the most obvious and immediate effect of price liberalization. Its other major positive impact consists in providing the feedback from consumption to production. Only prices that reflect the interaction between demand and supply can make conventional markets work properly. In the traditional Soviet system the lack of feedback from consumption to production presented the major problem for economic coordination.

Despite these positive features price liberalization has not been uniformly welcomed. The main reason for this lies in its significant distributional consequences. Prices set below market-clearing levels usually serve as a subsidy to the poorer groups of the population.[13] However, the partial breakdown of the official distribution system by the end of 1991 made both the positive and negative effects of the Russian price liberalization less pronounced. To the extent that goods were already *de facto* distributed through the unofficial markets, some benefits and costs of flexible prices had been incorporated in the system before the 1992 reforms.[14]

Fiscal Policy

The government's main fiscal policy goal at the beginning of 1992 was to reduce the budget deficit.[15] In fact, the initial budget draft for the first quarter of 1992 provided for balancing the budget. Even after the changes introduced by the legislators, the budget deficit was to be drastically reduced by eliminating most subsidies through price liberalization, reducing military expenditures, and curbing investment financed out of the federal budget.

At the same time, however, the traditional Soviet system of revenue collection was collapsing, largely because its main sources of revenue were not appropriate for a market economy.[16] The centerpiece of reform in revenue collection was the introduction of a 28 percent value-added tax (VAT). The VAT collections started out much slower than expected with only 63 percent of the planned target collected in the first quarter. The original revenue estimates did not account for the fact that many of the deliveries made during the first quarter were contracted for at pre-VAT prices, and the tax was not supposed to be retroactive. In addition, the initial administrative confusion and the emerging non-payments crisis contributed to slow collections.

Later in the year, however, VAT revenues increased because the ability to pay taxes improved for many enterprises due to a temporary success of mutual cancellation of inter-enterprise debts carried out by the government (see discussion below) and some unorthodox measures making it difficult for the enterprises to claim deductions against VAT. Revenues from the profit tax also trickled in slowly at first but held strong during the rest of 1992, presumably helped by high inflation combined with lagging depreciation allowances and by limiting deductions for wages. Nonetheless, the federal budget deficit which remained modest during the first quarter began to balloon in the second quarter (Table 7.4). The main reasons for this were the proliferation of inter-enterprise debt in arrears and sharply increasing government expenditures.

Monetary Policy

Reformers understood that liberalization of prices and elimination of various other controls over the SOEs, unaccompanied by tightened monetary policy, would lead to high inflation. The Central Bank of Russia (CBR), which extended huge amounts of cheap credits to Soviet enterprises in 1991, began the year by raising its interest rates from 6 to 20 percent per year and limiting the amount of credits to commercial banks. The credit rate was raised to 50 and then to 80 percent later in the year. The CBR also phased in a 20 percent reserve requirement for short-term commercial bank deposits.[17] These were steps in the right direction, although given the monthly inflation rates of 7 to 31 percent during 1992 real interest rates remained highly negative. The CBR, however, could not resist the demands for credit from the SOEs, and by the end of the first half of 1992, it channelled R457 billion of finance credit through commercial banks to enterprises.[18] This amount was roughly equal to the stock of high-powered money in the beginning of the year.[19] Credit creation accelerated further in the second half of the year.

In addition to channelling credits to enterprises, the CBR continued to issue credit to other republics of the former Soviet Union (FSU). Also, each republic had its own central bank capable, at least in the first half of 1992, of creating ruble credits virtually on its own. Such a system could not function well due to incentives for each of the individual states to free-ride by issuing ruble credits at the expense of the rest of the system.

Additional problems facing Russian monetary policy in the first half of 1992 included the subsidization of other republics of the FSU mainly through the underpricing of energy exports, remaining limitations on convertibility of the ruble, lack of central bank independence, an inefficient banking system, and huge inter-enterprise arrears.[20]

TABLE 7.4 Russian State Budget Balance, 1992-1994
(*Billion rubles*)

	Jan & Feb	Mar-Apr	May	Jun	Jul	Aug	Sep	Oct	Nov	Dec	1992	1993	1994
INCOME													
Consolidated	196.6	417.1	211.1	216.3	374.9	375.7	516.1	1022.9	813.4	1183.8	5327.9	74,093.0	230,445.0
Federal	114.9	241.4	111.5	99.1	193.6	198.0	290.7	612.4	446.4	713.4	3021.4	23,911.0	79,753.0
Local	81.7	210.1	115.8	139.4	194.7	202.2	255.9	437.9	390.9	643.8	2672.4	29,029.0	109,839.0
EXPENDITURES													
Consolidated	184.4	404.2	253.1	415.3	524.7	675.7	394.2	675.3	851.5	1591.1	5969.5	82,376.0	291,226.0
Federal	116.1	293.1	181.7	277.3	385.2	525.0	187.1	429.8	535.3	1048.6	3979.2	39,742.0	127,835.0
Local	68.3	145.5	87.6	160.2	152.9	175.2	237.6	272.9	340.1	715.9	2356.2	27,558.0	109,072.0
BALANCE													
Consolidated	12.2	12.9	-42.0	-199.0	-149.8	-300.0	121.9	347.6	-38.1	-407.3	-641.6	-8,283.0	-60,781.0
Federal	-1.2	-51.7	-70.2	-178.2	-191.6	-327.0	103.6	182.6	-88.9	-335.2	-957.8	-15,831.0	-48,082.7
Local	13.4	64.6	28.2	-20.8	41.8	27.0	18.3	165.0	50.8	-72.1	316.2	14,71.0	767.3
BALANCE AS % OF GDP													
Consolidated											-3.5	-5.1	-9.6
Federal											-5.3	-9.8	-7.6
Local											1.7	0.9	0.1

Note: In addition to the federal and local budgets, the consolidated budget includes income and expenditures of the extra-budgetary funds such as the national pension fund.

Source: 1992: Rossiiskaia (1993), p. 64; 1993: *Russian Economic Trends* (1994), *Rossiia–1994* (3), p. 35, and *Rossiiskaia* (1995), pp. 56-58.

Liberalization of Foreign Trade

Russian foreign trade was essentially decentralized but not liberalized even prior to 1992. A host of important restrictions remained in place and had to be dealt with. The 1992 reform package included adoption of more realistic exchange rates; all import duties were abolished[21] and the number of goods for which import licenses were needed was reduced; export tariffs were introduced on many goods, although a number of regions and enterprises were given exemptions, significantly reducing revenue collections. As a form of a separate export tax, Russian exporters were required to surrender 40 percent of their hard currency revenues to the government at a special low exchange rate, and to sell an additional 10 percent at a market rate. At the same time, the government reduced the number of goods for which export quotas or licenses were required.[22]

A special problem for the Russian government was how to deal with the republics of the FSU. While significant trade restrictions were put in effect for trade between them and Russia, the porousness of the Russian borders impeded enforcement. Also, Russia continued to subsidize many of these republics by selling them oil and other natural resources below world market prices.

New Administrative Structure

In early 1992, Russia's administrative structure for implementation of economic policy was split into two parts: the executive branch of the government (hereafter, the government) and the institutions under the oversight of the Parliament. The main government agencies in charge of economic policy and implementation were supervised by the First Deputy Prime Minister and included the Ministries of Economy, Finance, Industry, Trade and Material Resources, the Committee for Management of State Property, and the Committee on Anti-Trust Policies and Support for New Economic Structures.[23] Another Deputy Prime Minister was responsible for social policy and foreign economic relations and supervised the Ministries of Labor and Social Affairs, Education, Social Protection, and Foreign Economic Relations. The Parliament was overseeing the CBR and the statistical agency Goskomstat, both of which were formally independent from the government.

The Ministry of Finance controlled the preparation and implementation of the budget, submitted for approval and amendments to the Parliament. Revenue collection was performed by the State Tax Service. The CBR was responsible for monetary policy, credit policy, cash emission and banking supervision. The Ministry of Economy handled macroeconomic programming, public sector investments, pricing policy, and the conversion of the military industrial complex.

Several agencies had overlapping responsibilities for external economic relations. Most importantly, the CBR was ultimately responsible for determining the exchange rates and foreign exchange regulations, while tariffs, taxes, licenses and quotas in international trade were under the supervision of the State Customs Committee and the Ministries of Finance and Foreign Economic Relations.

In the direct relationships with industrial enterprises, the main role was played by the Ministries of Industry and Fuel and Energy. The Ministry of Industry appointed and contracted with the directors of industrial SOEs, and both ministries distributed some export quotas to enterprises and contracted for (non-obligatory) state orders. The Ministry of Foreign Economic Relations auctioned export quotas to enterprises and distributed export licenses. A somewhat less important Ministry of Trade and Material Resources oversaw the system of wholesale distribution and trade with the former republics of the Soviet Union.

Removal of Controls on SOEs

As a result of 1992 reforms, SOEs experienced a radical change in their economic environment. In addition to price liberalization, the new fiscal and monetary environment, changes in foreign trade regime, and modified administrative structure, virtually all direct governmental controls over the internal functioning of enterprises were lifted. Enterprises became free to decide on their own the size of their work force, wage levels, suppliers and customers, volume and timing of purchasing inputs and producing output. In short, enterprises acquired almost complete managerial autonomy in day-to-day decisions. At the same time, the government no longer had responsibility for providing them with inputs and investment resources, advancing automatic credits, and so on. With the exception of a few priority areas such as energy production and conversion of military enterprises, the government committed itself to allocating only limited financial resources for pilot projects and disseminating information to enterprises.

Wages were largely deregulated, along with prices. The speed of increases of wages and income in general, however, did not keep up with the price index in January 1992. During February, however, income growth exceeded the rate of inflation. Real disposable income remained stable in March and April, and fell back slightly in May.[24] Also note that the drop in real wages only brought them back to 1987 level.[25] Basically, the extra money paid out in 1988-1991 was not "real" in the sense that it was not backed up by increases in productivity.

Privatization Program

The major area where the government retained significant responsibilities vis-à-vis enterprises was the implementation of the privatization program. Although implementation of this program with respect to the medium and large SOEs did not begin in earnest until 1993, the legislative framework for it was adopted in 1991-1992.

Russia's privatization program discussed in detail below was largely modelled on the Czech approach, modified to account for the large size and regional structure of the Russian economy and to gain the support of the politically powerful managers of SOEs. Naturally, given the enormous scale of the undertaking, Russian privatization was a rather messy process accompanied by widespread irregularities, corruption, favoritism, bending of rules, and so on. Nonetheless, it was the official framework that to a large extent determined the basic outcomes.

The most important features of the Russian program included heavy reliance on tradeable privatization vouchers distributed to all citizens, compulsory corporatization and privatization of most large SOEs (those employing between 1,000 and 10,000 people), and generous privileges given to the insiders. In addition, the Russian program was implemented mostly by regional authorities, relied almost exclusively on auctions for privatization of large enterprises and, unlike its Czech counterpart, emphasized uniformity of corporatization and privatization procedures.

According to the program, some government property deemed to have "strategic" imporance was not subject to privatization, some could be privatized only with the permission of the appropriate agency of regional or federal government (the agency was determined based on the type of property involved), while other designated property had to be privatized.[26]

The first category included mineral rights, forests, water resources, some broadcasting systems, roads and communications. The second category consisted mainly of the extra large enterprises employing over 10,000 people, enterprises dominating a particular market or industry, defense enterprises, energy, fuel and mining enterprises, foreign trade associations, printing and publishing enterprises, local public transportation. Compulsory privatization covered enterprises in wholesale and retail trade, catering, consumer services, food processing, construction and construction materials industry, frozen and delayed construction projects. Also, lossmaking enterprises had to be privatized unless their privatization was prohibited by other provisions of the program.[27]

Depending on the type of property, privatization procedures were managed by the federal State Committee on Property or by regional and municipal committees on property. Most of the small shops were to be sold for cash by the local governments while the larger enterprises went into the mass privatization program.

Small enterprises (those employing fewer than 200 people and with a book value less than one million rubles as of January 1, 1992) were to be sold at auctions or through similar bidding procedures. If a partnership consisting of at least one third of the enterprise employees bid for the enterprise, it received a 30 percent discount and was allowed to pay for the enterprise in installments over three years.

Large enterprises (those with at least 1,000 employees or book value greater than R50 million as of January 1, 1992) were supposed to be privatized through their transformation into a corporation (joint-stock company) of an open type, i.e. the shares of which could be traded publicly. Corporatization of large enterprises was a rather simple compulsory procedure with enterprises given only a limited time to comply. While many firms managed to stall their corporatization significantly beyond the required period, most firms complied within a reasonable timeframe. One of the strong incentives for proceeding rapidly was the rule preventing enterprises from choosing their privatization option prior to corporatization. Medium-sized enterprises could be privatized using any of the procedures allowed in the Privatization Program. Privatization through creating a corporation of a closed type was prohibited. Moreover, corporations of a closed type, formed with government's participation prior to the adoption of the program, had to be transformed into openly held corporations.[28]

Corporations created from state-owned enterprises initially had 100 percent equity owned by the government. These corporations established their corporate charter and selected a board of directors. The board of directors consists of representatives of the government, the management, the workers, and the representatives of suppliers and customers. At the time of corporatization, some divisions of state firms have the right to split off from the main holding enterprise and gain independence. While such splitoffs occurred often they did not seem to become a mass phenomenon.

After an enterprise had been corporatized it had three privatization options, each giving certain privileges to the employees of the enterprises.[29] The *first option* gave 25 percent of the shares to the employees free of charge. These shares, however, were non-voting. The employees had the right to purchase an additional 10 percent of the common shares at a 30 percent discount of face value.[30] In addition, management had the right to purchase up to 5 percent of the common stock at face value. Thus, under this option employees could acquire up to 40 percent of all shares under privileged conditions.

The *second option* allowed the employees to purchase up to 51 percent of the common shares by subscription prior to the public offering. In this case no discounts were given relative to face value.[31] The managers and workers could acquire another 5 percent of the shares after privatization at low prices through an arrangement resembling employee stock ownership programs used in the U.S.

Under the *third option*, a group of enterprise employees (with the approval of the majority of the work force) entered into a short-term contract (up to a year) with the State Committee on Property to privatize the enterprise and provide a certain level of enterprise performance. If they fulfilled this contract, they could acquire up to 20 percent of common shares of the enterprise at their face value. In addition, all employees were eligible to purchase up to 20 percent of all common stock at a 30 percent discount to its face value and pay for them in installments over three years. This option was available only to enterprises with more than 200 employees and a book value of between R1 million and R50 million (as of January 1, 1992).

In order to choose options 2 or 3, more than two-thirds of the enterprise employees had to vote for them; otherwise, the first option was used. Despite the apparent government's preference for the first option, less than 25 percent of enterprises ended up using it. By far the most popular option in the voucher stage of privatization was the second. It was chosen by about 75 percent of enterprises. Virtually no enterprises used the third option.

Under all options the shares remaining after distribution to employees were given to the federal State Committee on Property or to corresponding regional committees, which could sell them to the public at market prices, put them in a trust fund, or retain them. Large enterprises had a right to establish a privatization fund financed out of profits to help employees buy their shares. Proceeds from privatization (selling shares by the State Committee on Property or auctioning small enterprises) were distributed to the local, republic, and federal budgets and to the State Committee on Property.

To facilitate the privatization program, the government decided to issue privatization vouchers with the face value of R10,000 to every citizen of the Russian Federation. These vouchers could be traded in the open market or used to buy shares of privatizing enterprises. The vouchers were issued at the end of 1992 and expired on July 1, 1994.

After the managers and workers had selected a privatization option, they submitted a detailed privatization plan describing how the rest of the shares were to be sold. During the voucher stage of privatization, a certain percentage of the corporation's shares had to be sold at a voucher auction. This required percentage, which varied in the course of privatization, did not include the vouchers used by the management and workers to acquire enterprise shares. This rule, however, was often violated in the regions.[32]

The shares that were sold for vouchers were sold through a subscription auction which worked in the following way.[33] The subscriber could submit two types of bids. A bid of the first type consisted of a commitment to use a certain number of vouchers to purchase enterprise stock at whatever price came out of the auction. The bid of the second type specified a maximum price in terms of vouchers per share that the subscriber was willing to pay. The equilibrium price was determined in such a way that all the bids of the first type were satisfied, and all the bids of the second type with the specified price below the equilibrium price were also executed.

When shares of stock or entire enterprises were sold for cash, the sale was supposed to be conducted either through a regular "open" auction or through a "closed" auction where tender bids were submitted in a sealed form. The form of the auction is determined either by the State Committee on Property or by the local committees on property, depending on the type of property involved (federal, republican, or municipal). Open auctions are used to sell assets of liquidated enterprises, small enterprises (less than 200 employees), and shares of joint-stock companies. Entire large enterprises and blocks of shares of joint-stock companies are sold at closed auctions.

The enterprise did not have to auction off all of the shares remaining after allocation (mainly for vouchers) to management and workers. Some of these shares could be sold by the state property committees to recover the expenses of privatization, some could be sold through investment tenders to domestic or foreign investors for cash, vouchers, or investment commitments. In practice this has often amounted to giving away shares to relatives and friends of management and workers.[34] Finally, some shares remained in the hands of the government's property funds.[35] The proportion of these shares has been typically around or under 20 percent.

Privatization of small enterprises has been taking place particularly fast. Such enterprises are privatized mainly through commercial bidding [kommercheskii konkurs] (45 percent of all enterprises privatized in 1993), exercise of the purchase option for leased enterprises (42 percent), and auctioning off (11 percent).[36]

The privatization process has been accompanied by some anti-monopoly measures (breakup of the monopolists prior to allowing their privatization). Also, the government has decided to keep certain important industries under its control for the time being, including communications, electricity generation and distribution, oil and natural gas, arms production, distilleries, rail, water, and air transport, among others.[37] The government reserves the right to hold on to the majority of shares of enterprises in these industries for three years after their partial privatization. Also, the state holds a veto power on certain ownership decisions in other companies which require the federal government's permission for privatization. This is accomplished by issuing the so-called "golden share" of the stock of these firms to the state.

In early 1995 it remained unclear how the Russian government was going to use its ownership in all these firms. But these arrangements do provide the government with the tools for implementing its industrial policy.

Macroeconomic Trends Since the Beginning of Reforms

With the notable exceptions of the privatization program and the absence of an exchange rate "anchor," the Russian reform package resembled that introduced in Poland in January 1990. Nevertheless, while the experience of Poland and other East European countries in reforming their own economies was useful, there were significant differences between these countries and Russia. Compared to Poland, Russia's economy was much larger and more distorted, its legal market institutions were considerably less developed, its special relationship with the republics of the FSU created both problems and opportunities, and Russia was probably less unified politically in its quest for market reforms.

As the description later in this section demonstrates, there were both similarities and important differences between the initial outcomes of Russian and Polish reforms. First, however, a word of caution is necessary about serious measurement and methodological problems involved in interpreting the available data.

A Note on Measurement Problems

It must be emphasized again that the 1992 reforms were only one factor in determining the economic developments described in the following section. Many of the trends such as industrial output decline and inflation began prior to 1992, although some of them were partly hidden. Also, many of the problems faced by the Russian economy, such as a substantial weakening of economic ties with the countries of the former Council for Mutual Economic Assistance (CMEA) and the breakup of the Soviet Union, had nothing to do with the reform package. In fact, as was argued in section two, market reforms were aimed at alleviating the breakdown of the old system.

Another important general consideration is that the available data describe only the officially recorded part of the economy. Meanwhile, a great deal of economic activity in Russia, both now and in the past, has been taking place underground. And this underground economy appears to be growing fast.[38] Even legal private economic activities, particularly of newly created private enterprises, often are not properly reflected in the official statistics. The unrecorded operations of private businesses are probably greatest in light and in food processing industries, as well as in services and in residential construction. Keeping this in mind, the 1992 economic statistics presented below are treated as essentially reflecting the performance of the SOEs. For later years, the industrial statistics reflect the activities of the RPEs and SOEs.

A different bias in the output statistics has to do with changing incentives in statistical reporting. Under the traditional Soviet system there were strong incentives to overreport output in order to improve the SOE performance relative to the plan. In the reforming Russian economy, high taxes create even stronger incentives to underreport output. Such underreporting is particularly difficult to detect in the case of final goods, especially consumer goods. For example, in December 1991 household expenditures on goods and services as shown in the monthly household budget survey exceeded the volume of retail trade and paid services reported by Goskomstat by about 4 percent. This difference jumped to approximately 24 percent in January 1992 and 36 percent in June 1992.[39] Even these numbers probably underestimate underreporting since the Russian household budget survey is notorious for missing second economy transactions.[40]

Comparison of the current Russian statistics with the pre-reform period also suffers from a severe index number problem. For example, officially, real GDP declined by 18.5 percent as measured in 1991 prices. According to some recent research, however, real GDP fell only 15 to 16.5 percent in 1992 prices and 13 to 14 percent in world prices.[41] The choice of prices has this effect mainly because the (greatly underpriced) output of the Russian energy sector declined less than output of the rest of the economy.

Even when the data themselves are reliable, their interpretation is often problematic. For example, relatively high employment at an enterprise may be either a sign of its successful performance in the new environment, or evidence of its reluctance to fire superfluous workers. Similarly, a drop in output could be a result of successful downsizing or of lack of demand for the enterprise's products. Only a review of several different indicators in their dynamics would allow one to construct a reliable picture of enterprise or industry performance.

Macroeconomic Trends During 1992-1994

This section reviews overall economic trends during the entire 1992-1994 period. A discussion of the interaction between economic policies and enterprise behavior, particularly in 1992, is pursued later in the chapter.

The major macroeconomic indicators presented in Table 7.5 reflect a rather dismal record of sharply falling output, persistently high inflation, and falling investments.[42] The relatively high employment level in the environment of declining output testifies mostly to the slow pace of restructuring. While Poland by the third year after its "Big Bang" experienced some improvement in its economic performance, Russia continues to exhibit a declining pattern.

Particularly noticeable is the accelerating drop in industrial output. Even taking into account the caveats of the previous section, the industrial output decline looks dramatic. It implies that enterprise behavioral adjustment has been mostly passive, involving reductions of output of goods in low demand without significant increases in production of more marketable goods. This is confirmed by the continuing decline of investment volume. It should be noted, however, that Russia's industrial output structure prior to reforms was particularly inconsistent with market priorities, more so than in most other former socialist countries. For this reason, it is natural to expect a sharper fall in output in Russia. Another reason for the protracted

TABLE 7.5   Major Macroeconomic Indicators, Russia
(constant prices, % over previous period)

	1990	1991	1992	1993 6 mos.	1993 Year	1994 6 mos.	1994 Year
GDP (current prices, trn. rub.)	0. 626	1.27	18.1	43.14	162.3	234.3	630.0
GDP	98.4	91.0	80.8	86.8	88.1	83.1	85.0
Industry	99.9	92.0	84.4	83.6	83.6	72.5	79.0
Agriculture	96.0	95.0	90.6	n/a	96.0	95.0	91
Investments	100.1	84.5	60.3	94	84	72	75
Real income	n/a	n/a	56	135.6	114	112	114
Household consumption*	99	86.5	63.7	n/a	110	n/a	91
Retail trade turnover	107.4	94.0	61.0	110**	102**	100**	100**
Inflation (%)	106	160	2,509	210	840	80	220
Registered unemployment (%)	n/a	n/a	0.69	0.84	1.0	1.5	2.1

* Calculated based on household consumption shares in GDP and changes in GDP.

** Retail trade turnover and paid services.

Sources: Most of the data for 1990-1992 are from *IMF* (1993). Nominal GDP for 1992 as well as the data for 1993 and first half of 1994 are from *Rossiia-1994* (3). Information for entire 1994 is obtained from Goskomstat reports summarized in *Izvestiia* no. 9 (24368), January 18, 1995, pp. 1,2 and *Finansovye izvestiia* no. 3 (132) January 19, 1995, p. 1.

TABLE 7.6   Structure of GDP by End-use
(% of total GDP)

	1990	1991	1992	1993	1994
GDP	100.0	100.0	100.0	100.0	100.0
Consumption	69.5	61.7	53.6	60.1	68.3
Households	47.7	42.1	35.9	42.1	43.9
Public	21.8	19.6	17.7	19.8	24.5
Gross accumulation	30.3	38.0	32.0	25.8	27.2
Fixed investment	28.9	24.4	20.4	20.5	23.6
Stock building	1.4	13.6	11.6	5.3	3.3
Net export	0.2	0.3	12.2	12.7	3.4
Statistical discrepancy	0.6	2.9	2.2	1.4	6.5

Source: Popov (1995), p. 8; *Rossiia-1995* (1).

nature of output decline is that Russian industrial SOEs were slower in cutting output in the first year of reforms than their Polish counterparts, as witnessed by a 15 percent output drop in Russia in 1992 versus a 25 percent decrease in Poland in 1990. The initial delay necessitated sharper cutbacks later in the reform process.

A large drop in investment in the initial stages of reform was also predictable (see Table 7.6 for the structure of Russia's GDP). In the highly uncertain economic and political situation in the country, enterprises and private entrepreneurs could not have been expected to compensate for a large decrease in centrally allocated investments. Russia differs from other reforming economies in that the decline in investment continued and even accelerated through the third year of reform. The continuing inconsistencies in reform policies and general political instability are partly responsible for this outcome. The underdeveloped credit and capital markets, relatively low depreciation allowance due to inadequate revaluation of fixed capital stock, and the incongruence of the structure of investment demand and the existing capacity of investment goods production also contributed to the drop in investment in Russia.[43]

The changes in the structure of investments appears to be consistent with market priorities. The decline has been especially large in "productive" investment—that is, investment aimed directly at enhancing the production potential of the economy. The share of such investment had declined from 65 percent in 1992 to less than 60 percent in 1994. Particularly steep had been the decrease in investment in the agro-industrial complex, equipment manufacturing, electronics, chemical, and petrochemical industries. At the same time, investment in oil and gas, car manufacturing, and communications increased. The share of investment going to housing and other "nonproductive" purposes also increased. The flow of direct foreign investments in Russia has exhibited large fluctuations since 1992 but at no time has it been significant. Most foreign investments have gone into the fuel and energy sector.

Lower demand for investment goods together with a sharp drop in defense orders were the major factors in the changing structure of industrial output. The output of the defense complex enterprises dropped by 23 percent in 1992 and the share of military related production[44] declined from 38 percent in 1991 to 19 percent. The rate of decline of military production continued in 1993-1994, reaching 30 percent during 1993 and accelerating to around 35 percent in the first three quarters of 1994. During 1992-1993 the drop in military output of the defense complex was accompanied by a much slower decrease in civilian output. In 1994, however, the rate of decline in civilian production of defense enterprises was approximately the same as in their military output. Other structural changes within industry included the rising importance of the energy sector and nonferrous metals, and the

TABLE 7.7 **Structure of Industrial Output**
  (1991-1992 in current prices, 1993-1994 in 1993 prices; %)

	4Q 1991	1Q 1992	2Q 1992	3Q 1992	4Q 1992	1993	1994
Fuel and energy	11.8	12.1	20.4	25.5	26.6	25.4	29.7
Metallurgy	11.9	17.8	19.3	20.6	17.7	15.9	18.9
Chemical/petrochemical	7.2	9.7	10.2	9.1	8.8	7.2	6.5
MBMW	25.3	24.3	21.4	19.8	20.4	20.2	15.4
Wood/wood products	5.6	7.0	4.9	4.3	4.4	4.3	3.9
Construction materials	3.1	2.8	2.7	2.6	2.4	4.6	4.2
Light industry	17.1	13.7	9.1	5.2	7.1	5.1	3.6
Food processing	13.4	9.2	9.3	9.4	9.4	15.2	15.6
Other branches	4.6	3.5	2.8	3.6	3.6	2.2	2.2

Source: 1991-1992, *Rossiiskaia* (1993), p. 84; 1993–1994, *Rossiia-1995* (2), p. 115.

declining role of the machine building and metalworking sector (Table 7.7).

In more general terms, the share of industrial output has been declining, but the share of services in GDP has increased sharply from less than a third of GDP in 1992 to slightly over one half in 1994.[45] Household consumption has been rising as a share of GDP by end-use from about 35 percent in 1992 to close to 45 percent in 1994. Consumption by the government has been increasing at similar rates. The share of gross investment has declined correspondingly.

With respect to inflation, Russia's comparisons with other reforming countries look even worse. Not only was inflation in Russia much higher in the first year of reforms, but it remained in the hundreds percent per year three years later. By contrast, Polish inflation fell below 50 percent in the third year after price liberalization. Moreover, the year-to-year declines in inflation in Russia mask its upturn by the end of 1994 when it reached double digit monthly rates after a period of relative stability. Due to rising inflation, the official real interest rates, after staying close to zero during much of 1994, turned highly negative again in the last quarter despite the increase in the CBR refinancing rate from 180 to 200 percent. High inflation continued in early 1995 (18-20 percent in January), but declined significantly later in the year.[46]

Because of its increasing share in the economy (Table 7.6), the decline in household consumption during 1992-1994 period has been smaller than that of the entire GDP. Moreover, household consumption did not decline nearly as much as the official GDP figures seem to suggest.[47] Apparently, Goskomstat very substantially undercounts output of consumer goods and services in its calculations of real GDP. In 1994, Goskomstat revised its estimates of retail sales and paid household services without, however, revising the published GDP series.[48] While the old data indicated that in 1992 retail trade declined by 35 percent, the revised estimates suggest that it declined by only 3.5 percent. The discrepancies for 1993 and 1994 are much smaller but still non-negligible, with the old series showing small declines each year and the new estimates reflecting increases of 2 and 4 percent, respectively. The alternative estimates of real GDP and its components which incorporate this and some other revisions are presented in Table 7.8.

The trends in living standards can normally be gleaned from real disposable money income data. The 1991-1994 real income data for Russia, however, only add to confusion. To begin with, a spectacular drop in measured real income in 1992 was largely, if not entirely, a consequence of the artificially low pre-1992 official prices rather than a reflection of a real decline in living standards. Less obvious are the reasons for 14 percent per year increases in real disposable income reported for 1993 and 1994. In part, these increases, that took place despite the drastic decline in measured output of the economy, are a result of the rising share of household consumption in GDP. The real disposable income trends, however, appear to be inconsistent with either the old or the new household consumption estimates described above, particularly given no dramatic increases in savings rate over the 1992-1994 period.[49]

TABLE 7.8   Alternative Estimates of Trends in Real GDP and its Components
(billion rubles; 1990 prices)

	1990	1991	% of 1990 1992		% of 1991 1993		% of 1992 1994[a]		% of 1993
GDP	639.9	599.2	93.6	515.4	86.0	476.6	92.5	433.5	91.0
Consumption	444.4	396.9	89.3	360.7	90.9	350.0	97.0	342.1	97.7
Households	305.0	289.6	95.0	274.7	94.9	271.3	98.8	275.2	101.4
Goods[b]	265.0	256.5	96.8	247.5	96.5	252.2	101.9	261.3	103.6
Services[c]	40.0	33.1	82.8	27.2	82.2	19.0	69.9	13.9	73.2
Public	139.4	107.3	77.0	86.0	80.1	78.7	91.5	66.9	85.0
Gross investment	194.1	199.5	102.8	153.9	77.1	124.1	80.6	88.7	71.5
Fixed[d]	184.9	156.3	84.5	109.4	70.0	95.2	87.0	74.2	77.9
Inventory	9.2	43.2	470.0	44.5	103.0	28.9	64.9	14.5	50.2
Net exports	1.4	2.8	200.0	0.8	28.6	2.5	312.5	2.6	104.0

[a] Projection.
[b] Based on revised Goskomstat retail sales series.
[c] Based on revised Goskomstat retail paid services series.
[d] Including capital repairs.
Source: Gavrilenkov and Koen (1994), p. 12 and percentage changes implied therein.

Moreover, in interpreting published data one needs to keep in mind that some important components of household consumption are not adequately reflected in any official statistics. Most notably, housing rents, utility prices, health care and education are still heavily subsidized. Therefore, aggregate indicators tend to understate their true role in consumption. Since housing services represent a large share of consumer welfare and their level has been relatively stable, the official consumption data overstate fluctuations in welfare of Russian consumers. Also, official data do not reflect a significant portion of the underground economy and household production, both of which play an important role in Russia.

Naturally, declining output in most branches of the economy was accompanied by declining employment in these branches and in the economy overall. But employment reductions have proceeded much slower than output cutbacks. By the end of the first half of 1994 total employment in the economy stood at 70.2 million people or only 0.8 million less than at the beginning of the year and about 2 million less than in 1992. The general reduction of employment was accompanied by a continuing shift of labor from industry and science to consumer services, the share of which in employment reached 40 percent as compared to 35 percent in 1992. Industrial employment fell by almost 10 percent during the first half of 1994, with the greatest reductions taking place in machine building and metal working, wood processing, and light industries.[50]

Growth of unemployment that was rather slow until mid-1994 accelerated dramatically by the end of the year, with the number of officially unemployed reaching 5.3 million people or 7.1 percent of the labor force.[51] Underemployment and hidden unemployment also continued to grow. By late 1994, about 8 million people or over 10 percent of the labor force were reportedly either underemployed or effectively unemployed.[52] One should keep in mind, however, that a substantial part of the Russian labor force is occupied in the informal sector including household production and the underground economy. Moreover, many of the underemployed at one enterprise are gainfully employed in a second job. In fact, the same source estimates the number of people holding two or more jobs at 8 to 9 million.

As in Poland, the initial spurt of inflation coupled with the government's decision to perform only infrequent adjustments of depreciation allowances helped many enterprises to show deceptively high profits. As time went on, the profitability picture began to deteriorate. The worsening financial situation of the industrial enterprises is reflected in the significant growth of the share of loss-makers. While less than 10 percent of industrial enterprises incurred losses in 1992 and 1993, this share increased to almost 20 percent in the first quarter of 1994. In part, this increase might have been due to the reevaluation of fixed assets in the end of 1993.[53] It is unclear, of course, what proportion of these enterprises reported losses only to avoid (or evade) taxes. The suspicion that this proportion may be high stems in part from the same source's report that retail trade, public dining, marketing and wholesale trade are among the branches with the highest proportion of loss-making enterprises. Casual observation and indirect data (such as changes in employment) suggest that these sectors in reality are among the most profitable in the Russian economy.

In sum, despite the similarities between Russian and Polish reforms, the Russian economy seems to be performing considerably worse than the Polish economy did at approximately the same stage in the reform process. Most important, while Poland began to recover three years into reforms, there are few signs of improvement in the Russian economic indicators. A partial explanation for this is that Russia is different from Poland. In order to provide more specific answers, one needs to examine the reactions of SOEs to reform policies in greater detail, as it was the behavior of SOEs and RPEs that determined many of the outcomes of these policies. Before discussing the SOE behavior, however, it is useful to describe the governance structure of the Russian SOEs, an issue taken up in the next section.

Internal Governance Structure of SOEs

Main Types of Enterprise Ownership

There are a multitude of distinct types of enterprise ownership in the Russian economy: state enterprises and organizations (SOEs), leaseholds,[54] joint stock companies, associations, proprietorships, partnerships, joint ventures, cooperatives, kolkhozes, private farms, collective enterprises, and various forms of mixed ownership. At the end of 1992, SOEs still dominated the non-agricultural sector, employing almost 50 million people, leaving fewer than 14 million in all other forms of ownership combined. The other major types of non-agricultural enterprise ownership, in descending order of importance were: leaseholds (4.9 million employees), joint stock companies (2.1 million), and proprietorships (1.1 million).[55] Moreover, leaseholds could be considered as a form of state ownership, and joint stock companies may have a significant share of the stock owned by the state.[56] By the end of voucher privatization program in June 1994 the role of the SOEs had been significantly reduced, but state enterprise ownership in general remains very important.[57]

Forms of ownership are supposed to be regulated by the law "On Ownership in the Russian Federation," which took effect on January 1, 1991, as well as other laws. The legal ownership arrangements, however, are often misleading as one of the most important features of the current economic environment in Russia is an almost complete disregard for the law on the part of economic agents, including the government officials themselves. The state has virtually no power over the day-to-day operations of SOEs or any other types of enterprises. For all practical purposes, most SOEs are run by their employees.[58] The only interesting issue with respect to most aspects of SOE performance is the balance of power between workers and management.[59]

What follows describes the main aspects of an SOE's legal and informal environment, and provides an analysis of the incentives generated by such an environment. The effect of these incentives on the outcomes of Russian reform policies will be outlined later in the chapter.

Enterprise Directors

The directors of all SOEs face essentially the same legal framework, with some variations being due to regional regulations and to the differentiated treatment under federal law of certain branches such as fuels and energy.[60] Nonetheless, the differences in the situation of enterprises may be quite significant due to the differences in informal relationships between managers and workers, the enterprise and the local authorities, and the enterprise and the banks. In addition, enterprises' responses to essentially the same system of incentives vary, depending on the enterprise's initial situation and the personalities of its managers and other employees.

Formally, the enterprise director works under a contract with the appropriate government agency.[61] This contract determines, among other things, the director's salary. In the first half of 1992, the government tried to hold down the directors' salaries, effectively imposing a cap on all salaries at the enterprise.[62] Some observers noted that this policy reduced the ability of the SOEs to retain skilled workers. In practice, however, the directors usually do not feel themselves restricted by the provisions of the government contract. Government agencies in charge of SOEs have been notoriously weak. Moreover, it appears that whatever formal power they do have with respect to the directors is limited by the need to solicit the cooperation of the enterprise "labor collective." Apparently, directors of SOEs are hardly ever fired by the state.

Even if directors do abide by the formal terms of the contract with respect to their salary, this has almost no effect on their real incomes. A director has plenty of opportunities to supplement his income substantially, within a certain range. This range is determined by the complicity (or lack of information) on the part of the rest of the management and workers. The complicity of the other members of the top management appears to be particularly important. Directors, together with the rest of the top management, have virtually complete discretion in disposing of output, obtaining inputs, and engaging in the other external activities of the enterprise.[63]

What follows from this? The main outcome is that a director's behavior is constrained mostly by informal mechanisms and customs. As long as the enterprise is able to pay its employees well, they are not going to mind the director's perks and bonuses. If the enterprise is not doing well relative to comparable SOEs, the director's opportunities to enrich himself may be limited. Note that it does not really matter if the enterprise pays its workers out of government-sponsored or other types of soft credits, or out of profits.

The current situation is quite beneficial to the SOE directors in that in most cases they have become *de facto* residual claimants on enterprise revenues.[64] Nonetheless, the director's objectives do not necessarily result in the (even approximate) maximization of the conventionally defined profits of the firm. For example, the ability to obtain government-subsidized credits may be a preferred alternative to generating profits in the marketplace. Also, the director may sacrifice some long-term profits in order to enhance his continuing hold on the enterprise.[65]

The director's *de facto* residual claimant status exists largely by default and, therefore, this arrangement is not stable. Under the law, many SOEs have to be privatized and the directors know that. Directors have incentives to formalize their ownership rights through privatization, as many of them did, even if the new formal arrangements would be somewhat less advantageous to them in the short term or to the enterprise in the long term. The goal of many directors is to assure that privatization takes place in a way most beneficial to them, and that their position is preserved and improved after privatization. Since many important aspects of privatization are determined by the entire work force of the SOE, managers in this regard also depend on the workers. In addition, the director and the rest of the top management depend on the workers' cooperation to improve the enterprise performance.

Whatever the incentives generated by the directors' status as residual claimants on revenues and their goals in privatization, many enterprise managers, at least in 1992, seemed to act out of inertia. The term "inertia" need not necessarily have a negative connotation. This type of behavior may be quite natural. Reforms brought about tremendous uncertainty concerning the outcomes of economic agents' actions. This uncertainty affects enterprise directors particularly strongly. Not only have the outcomes of actions become less predictable in general, but the predictive abilities of the agents brought up under the old system have decreased substantially, especially in the early stages of reforms. In other words, the gap between the agent's competence (C) and the difficulty of the decision (D) problems involved has increased dramatically (the C-D gap). Under these circumstances it is natural to expect economic agents to act according to a rather limited set of behavioral rules familiar to them: or in other words, to exhibit inertia.[66] The implications of the C-D gap for directors' behavior will be explored later in the chapter.

Although as time passes many of the managers do adapt to the new environment, this adjustment process has been slow. The refusal to adopt market-like forms of behavior might have been quite rational in the early stages of reforms because many directors did not believe that the government would let their enterprises (or most of their suppliers and customers) fail. As long as the government cannot credibly commit to refrain from bailing out unsuccessful enterprises, the incentives to become successful remain relatively weak.

Viewed from a somewhat different point, the immense economic and political uncertainty that has been characteristic of Russia over the last several years makes the long-term implications of various actions less relevant for risk-averse agents. Therefore, one can expect short-term oriented behavior from such agents, including enterprise directors. In particular, the directors would be unwilling to invest in projects with long-term payoffs, such as the major restructuring of an enterprise.

Relationships Among Enterprise Divisions

With respect to the internal structure of large enterprises, the prevalent tendency seems to be the desire of the functionally more or less independent and profitable divisions to split off and strike out on their own. Whether or not to allow this separation combined with privatization depends on which division of the State Committee on Property has jurisdiction over privatization of the main enterprise. Often, the federal State Committee on Property is reluctant to approve the separation of small units from SOEs under its supervision because then privatization of the separated unit would fall under the jurisdiction of the lower division of the Committee. Naturally, the lower division favors the separation of smaller units. The entire process often becomes a messy bureaucratic affair. The outcome in any particular case seems to depend mostly on the status of the main enterprise and the political influence of its management.[67] Sometimes, however, large enterprises want to get rid of less profitable divisions prior to privatization.

Often, some of the divisions of an SOE acquire partial independence and enter into a long-term contractual relationship with the main enterprise. The creation of the so-called "small (*malye*) enterprises" is particularly popular owing to their favorable tax treatment. Also, management sometimes tries to separate a particularly profitable part of an enterprise into an independent firm which can be privatized through a buyout usually benefitting the management.[68] In general, positioning for privatization appears to be an important factor in the relationships among the divisions of an SOE. As long as the separated division is not privatized, however, it usually remains under the control of the main enterprise. Defense-related enterprises, many of which are not allowed to privatize at this time, appear to hold on to their divisions particularly firmly.[69]

Workers

According to some observers, workers have a great deal of power in the SOEs and RPEs. In fact, there have been claims that most Russian enterprises should be viewed as a form of labor-managed firms.[70] While the laws do give workers certain powers, they fall far short of providing for "labor management." Moreover, a study of layoffs at the Russian SOEs conducted in 1991[71] and some more recent anecdotal evidence suggest that workers lack the power to affect the behavior of their enterprise in the market. It appears that, from the legal point of view, it is relatively easy to fire a worker if management so decides. On the other hand, since the beginning of the 1992 reforms most SOEs have refrained from mass layoffs even in the face of sharply lower demand for output. It will be argued later in the chapter that this fact has alternative explanations that do not rely on the purported labor-managed nature of Russian SOEs.

The power of workers at SOEs is limited by the relative weakness of trade unions. The old trade unions have compromised themselves by their subservience to the management and the Party under the old system. The workers' distrust seems to extend to the unofficial, so-called independent, unions as well. At the end of 1992 the total membership in the unofficial trade unions in the entire CIS was on the order of 500,000.[72] It has to be noted, however, that so far the Russian unions have often joined ranks with management in their fight against various government policies. In these cases the unions probably did represent the interests of many workers.[73] In general, at the early stage of Russia's economic transformation, the interests of management and of workers often coincided.

The weakness of the workers is partly due to the lack of good employment alternatives and to the looming threat of mass unemployment. The situation is exacerbated by the poor geographical mobility due to the system of residence permits and the housing shortage. The combination of some commonality of interests with management and of poor alternatives explain the passivity of the workers despite the decline in real wages for a significant share of the labor force. The work time lost to strikes in 1992 was several times smaller than that in 1991.

A very important aspect of the relationship between large enterprises and their workers in Russia has been enterprise ownership and management of various social assets such as housing, kindergartens, and hospitals. These assets were originally created for use of the enterprise employees but are usually used by outsiders as well. Often enterprises continue to own and subsidize the use of these assets even after privatization. In addition to these subsidies, large enterprises often administer some other parts of social safety net. For example, an enterprise may effectively pay workers unemployment compensation if it chooses to send them on paid leave instead of laying them off. Many enterprises also supply subsidized food and other consumer goods and services to their employees. All this provides for a considerable degree of paternalism in enterprise-worker relationship and reduces labor mobility. In addition, enterprise ownership of social assets and provision of welfare services creates obstacles for enterprise restructuring and scares off potential outside investors.

External Relationships of SOEs

Links with Other Enterprises

The old Soviet system of supply has been eliminated. Some of its old elements have reemerged in the form of trade associations or concerns or trade houses, but these are now operating as commercial entities charging fees for their services. The situation was greatly exacerbated by the collapse of the CMEA trading bloc and the disintegration of the USSR into independent republics, with their own currencies and customs. Nowadays most SOEs in Russia rely on direct links with other enterprises and on the new commercial structures, such as the aforementioned trade associations and commodity exchanges.

The underdevelopment of wholesale trade in Russia and the fact that legal remedies for breach of delivery contracts are virtually unenforceable result in the high importance of reputation and other informal mechanisms, including personal contacts and reliance on organized crime, for enforcing contracts and obtaining supplies.[74] In several surveys, enterprise managers explained various aspects of their behavior by appealing to the need to preserve their reputation among the workers and with the managers of other enterprises. To a large extent, reputational considerations as well as the need to support and preserve long-term customers served as the explanation for shipping output to nonpaying enterprises, for price differentiating among customers, and for certain other features of enterprise behavior. Note that according to manager surveys, reputation is associated with managers and not with their enterprises.[75] No wonder that many managers consider establishment of good personal contacts with managers of other enterprises as the best way to succeed in the Russian marketplace.[76]

Reputational considerations play a large role in pricing policy, which obviously constitutes one of the most important aspects of inter-enterprise relationships. In 1992 many SOEs had a multi-tiered system of pricing. Traditional long-term customers were charged relatively low prices that were sometimes differentiated according to the financial situation of the customer, and usually based on cost plus a small profit margin. The new large customers, which were either state-owned or represented some form of collective ownership (either a joint stock company or a leasehold) were charged higher prices. (The difference often reached 200-250 percent.) Even higher prices were charged to privately owned firms. All prices agreed upon in direct negotiation between the supplier and customer were generally lower than prices on the commodity exchanges. When firms belonged to vertically organized trade associations they could have separate agreements for trade with other association members. When SOE managers were asked to explain such price differentiation, they often appealed to their reputation among other SOE managers. If they tried to raise prices too much, they expected to lose privileged treatment by other SOEs.

Note that considerable tension exists between short-term orientation due to a highly uncertain environment, and reliance on reputation. After all, most of the benefits of a "good" reputation accrue over a long-term. Short-term orientation reduces the value of a good reputation. As a result, SOEs appear to remain loyal only to the most important traditional customers, charging them relatively low prices, forgiving delays in payments, etc. Other customers may be dropped altogether rather than simply deprived of privileged treatment. This is especially likely to happen if the customer is located in another republic of the FSU because a remote location can serve as a good pretext for breaking ties.[77]

An important phenomenon in inter-enterprise relationships during 1992 was the widespread use of barter. Barter has always been an important feature of the Soviet/Russian economy but in the wake of the 1992 reforms its role has been enhanced by the poor performance of the banking system in a highly inflationary environment (slow transfer of payments), cash shortage, crisis of nonpayments, high taxes, and the high variability of the inflation rate (which makes it difficult to adjust for future inflation).

Relationship with Local Authorities

The process of devolution of power from Moscow to the regions started long before 1992. Market-oriented reforms promoting decentralization of the economy naturally accelerated this process. The general weakness of the federal government and continual infighting within it have further increased the power of the local authorities. Beginning in 1992, if not earlier, the power of the local authorities on many issues concerning the SOEs had arguably become more significant than that of the federal government.

The relationship between local authorities and the SOEs has been somewhat ambivalent. On the one hand, they need each other. Enterprises need the local government to provide and maintain the infrastructure, including roads and utilities; reduce red tape; help with obtaining supplies, especially from other local enterprises; provide basic services to enterprise workers; and protect the enterprise from criminals. Local governments rely on the SOEs, particularly on the large ones, for their tax base, for providing a significant share of services such as housing and medical care to the SOE workers, and as a source of graft.

On the other hand, the interests of the local authorities and enterprises diverge on many issues, such as the optimal level of taxation or the allocation of responsibility for maintenance of workers housing and various social service facilities (e.g., day care, schools, hospitals). Both formally and especially informally, the local authorities have a great deal of discretion in issuing licenses, introducing fees and taxes, and in adopting and enforcing health, safety, environmental and other regulations. Also, the local authorities often control the utilities serving the enterprise. In addition, the local authorities play an important role in the process of privatization.

A major asset of local governments is their ownership of much of commercial real estate in the cities, particularly their formal control over most land and many buildings managed by privatized enterprises. Local authorities' control of commercial real estate keeps many large and small privatized enterprises dependent on politicians, thereby producing unclear property rights and preventing further depoliticization of economic decisions. Privatization of commercial real estate has been significantly lagging privatization of other assets. While the sale of commercial real estate or leasing it at market-determined rates would be highly beneficial to local budgets, it would undermine one of the most important sources of graft for local bureaucrats and their control over private enterprise. Therefore, it is often in the interest of local politicians to prevent privatization of urban land and commercial buildings. The hope is that eventually the need for revenues and political pressures from both potential sellers and buyers of commercial real estate will force the local authorities to cooperate in speeding up its privatization.[78]

Enterprises can also exert pressure on the authorities through bribes, withholding of taxes, or threats to dump their responsibility for social services and infrastructure on the local government.[79]

Often the local authorities and SOEs develop a mutually advantageous cooperative relationship. There have been instances of adversarial behavior as well. In any case, however, one of the main problems in the relationship between the local governments and enterprises has been the absence of a well-developed and enforceable legal framework for it.

The Role of Banks

The woefully inefficient banking system is often cited as a serious obstacle to the development of a market economy in Russia.[80] Russian banks are slow to process inter-enterprise payments—a particularly serious problem in times of high inflation.[81] More importantly, from their inception. Russian commercial banks have not been well capitalized, and the negative real interest rates effectively dictated by the CBR precluded real growth of the population's deposits. Therefore, banks could not adequately perform one of their most important functions in a market economy, namely, to provide investment resources for worthy projects. The average registered charter capital of a Russian commercial bank at the end of 1992 was around R60 million, or less than $150,000 at the exchange rate at the time.[82]

In addition, the Russian banks often lack skilled personnel and appropriate procedures to evaluate projects. The personnel problems, however, might not be overly important. In a reforming Russian economy adequate project evaluation has been usually impossible due to the overall economic and political uncertainty and the persistence of large amount of overdue inter-enterprise debt. The latter factor in particular makes it extremely difficult to ascertain the financial health of an enterprise carrying significant receivables on its books. Under such circumstances, the best policy for a profit-maximizing, risk-averse bank may be to restrict its lending to relatively small short-term loans or to require ample collateral.[83]

Difficulties with obtaining credit pushed many enterprises to pool their resources and organize their own banks to receive preferential treatment in obtaining loans.[84] The main reason for enterprises to found banks, however, has been the ability of these banks to serve as conduits for centrally allocated credits, mainly from the CBR. At the end of 1992 the outstanding credit issued by the CBR to the commercial banks was over R2.6 trillion (an increase of slightly less than 2,000 percent since the end of 1991). Almost all of this was earmarked for the enterprises. This amounted to about one half of the total enterprise ruble credit outstanding.[85] Also, CBR credits financed the settlements of inter-enterprise arrears in the second half of 1992.

Enterprises also wanted to become founding members of banks because banking has been one of the most profitable sectors of the economy. Prior to late 1993 real interest rates of CBR credits had been highly negative. Thus, when a commercial bank holds a CBR loan for some time before disbursing it to an enterprise, it can make a substantial profit. Banks could also delay disbursements on various extra-budgetary funds, such as unemployment funds collected from an enterprise, earning high returns in an inflationary environment. In addition, banks reportedly earn 3 percent on almost every fund transfer transaction.[86]

Banks do advance credit, albeit less readily, to other customers besides their founding members, differentiating among them. The larger enterprises appear to receive preferential treatment. Large customers are easier to deal with because the size of the transactions is large. More importantly, it is still believed that the government would not let the largest enterprises, particularly SOEs, go bankrupt. For this reason they often have been considered to be safer borrowers.

Role of the Federal Government and Central Bank

Since early 1992, the federal government has almost completely stopped direct interference in the affairs of most SOEs. It does retain, of course, indirect means of influencing their behavior. One of the most important such instruments is the tax policy. The two main taxes paid by the enterprises are the VAT and the tax on profits. A particularly important feature of the tax on profits is that "excessive wages" are taxed as profits. In 1992 the excess was defined as the portion of the wage fund which exceeds the product of the number of employees and the minimum wage multiplied by four (six in 1994). Additional penalties were imposed on enterprises with average wage exceeding eight times the minimum wage. The excess wage tax encourages enterprises to keep minimum wage employees, real and "dead souls" (nonexistent employees), on their payroll. This factor probably significantly biases Russian employment statistics. The high combined rates of the VAT, the excise taxes, and the profit tax push enterprises to shift at least part of their activities underground and to engage in barter.

The most common tool used by the central government in 1992 for supporting SOEs was the system of credits at negative real interest rates. Starting in mid-1992 and at least until late 1993 these credits, both in rubles and in foreign exchange, were generously issued by the CBR either via the commercial banks or through the Ministry of Finance to provide relief for many SOEs. At the end of 1992, the total outstanding credit to enterprises amounted to R5,102 billion or almost 33 percent of the Russian GDP.[87] The credits were commonly justified by the belief that without them the enterprises would stop paying each other completely, causing a collapse of the economy. While this might have been true, the opportunity to obtain credits at below market rates weakened enterprise incentives to restructure and to respond better to market signals. The executive branch often accused the CBR of issuing too many credits. The CBR, however, claimed that 90 percent of the credits it provided were given in order to implement direct requests by the executive branch for the support of SOEs.

The government has continued to finance significant investments even though its role in this area has declined drastically relative to the Soviet times. Some "centralized" investments are allocated to restructure and to expand existing SOEs, especially in the framework of conversion of defense-related enterprises. As in the case of government allocation of subsidized credit, centralized investments serve to politicize capital allocation in the economy, encouraging enterprises to direct their efforts at obtaining subsidies rather than at competing in a conventional marketplace. Enterprises receiving capital from the government are vulnerable to politicians' demands to sustain politically beneficial (in the short term) levels of employment, to distort output prices, and so on. Moreover, government influence over subsidized enterprises confuses property rights, thereby discouraging private investments.

The central government also affects enterprise environment through a multitude of regulations, although many of these regulations lack adequate enforcement mechanisms. Finally, the state conducts an anti-monopoly policy which has not been particularly effective, with the possible exception of the demonopolization procedures taking place during privatization. In 1992-1993 all enterprises accounting for more than 30 percent of the market share in any one of their outputs were deemed monopolists and were subject to regulation (consisting mainly of limits on profitability) for all of their output. This type of regulation was subject to abuse (e.g., in deciding on the relevant market definition), and provided disincentives for the most successful firms to raise their output above the 30 percent threshold. In 1994 these regulations were discontinued. Instead, the anti-monopoly regulators are supposed to watch for evidence of monopoly pricing and other types of anti-competitive behavior. The new policy appears to be difficult to implement.[88]

Foreign Trade

Largely due to the large size of the country and its remoteness from other major world markets, foreign trade has been less important for Russia than for East European economies. For this reason, the foreign trade regulations are discussed very briefly.

An important feature of foreign trade regulations in Russia is their instability and diversity. For example, after the introduction of export tariffs in January 1992, they were lowered in February (twice), in March, and again in May. The list of goods subject to export tariffs was also changed several times as were the rules for disposition of export revenues earned by enterprises. In addition, the government has granted a large number of various privileges to particular regions and enterprises significantly reducing the potential tariff revenues.

Currently, the foreign trade environment is characterized by export and import tariffs, regular VAT and excise taxation of imports, reimbursement (zero-rating) of VAT and excises on exports, extensive export licensing requirements, quotas for some export (mostly for fuels), and the almost complete cessation of centralized imports.

The import tariffs are set in the 5-150 percent range for the Most Favored Nations (MFN, a status granted to most countries). The lowest rates are for raw materials. Goods imported under barter arrangements are subject to the highest tariffs. Tariffs are doubled for countries which do not have MFN status. Developing countries face tariffs 50 percent below the MFN rates and the least developed countries are charged no tariffs. No tariffs are imposed on foodstuffs, medicines, children's clothes, printed materials, and goods for the disabled.

Export tariffs are collected in rubles at the CBR exchange rate on the date of payment. Since early 1993 export tariffs have been generally applied to goods exported to the CIS countries as well.

The most important tool of export regulation is the system of quotas and licenses. As of August 1993, about 700 organizations had the right to export "strategically important" raw materials. Only the Ministry of External Economic Relations is allowed to issue most types of export licenses. At the end of 1993, the Ministry stopped issuing new licenses for the export of oil, oil products, and chemical fertilizer. The intention was to reduce the number of licensed exporters for "strategic" raw materials, especially fuels.

Licensing is required for most of Russia's exports. On certain goods such as fuels, non-ferrous metals, timber, mineral fertilizer, and fish, licenses are issued only within quotas established by the government. A necessary (but not sufficient) condition for obtaining a quota is the existence of a signed contract. Certain enterprises are issued licenses to export on behalf of the state under contracts entered into by the state. Other enterprises may acquire an export quota by auction. It is widely expected that the government would eliminate export quotas on oil and refined petroleum products in the first half of 1995. The quotas would be replaced by an export tax which would decline over time. This arrangement would increase government's revenues and benefit oil producers by eliminating the implicit subsidy to the domestic consumers of artificially underpriced energy.[89]

Enterprise Behavior and Economic Reforms

Initial Reactions of Enterprises

The 1992-94 economic trends described above were largely determined by the initial reform policies and the reactions of SOEs, which largely determined the outcomes of these policies. For this reason, it is useful to inquire into 1992 developments in some detail. The SOE governance structure and their external environment described in the sections above will be particularly helpful in understanding SOE behavior.

The basic thinking behind the government's reform package of 1992 was as follows. Liberalization of prices, together with tight credit policy, would impose a hard budget constraint on enterprises forcing them to behave according to the conventional laws of supply and demand. Given limited consumer demand as well as reductions in government-financed investments and defense procurement, enterprises would not be able to raise prices too much. At the same time, they would gradually change their mix of output to better reflect the structure of final demand as producing unwanted goods became too costly.

Apparently, the government overestimated the readiness and ability of enterprises to adjust and to restructure.[90] Instead of adjusting to the new market situation, most SOEs continued to operate according to old concepts—trying to maintain output and disregarding real supply-demand relationships. The more than five-fold increase of regulated prices of fuels gave most of the SOEs the cue (or a focal point) to raise their prices accordingly (Table 7.3). Prior to 1992, energy was particularly greatly underpriced. To reach a market economy equilibrium, energy prices would have had to rise by a substantially greater percentage from their pre-1992 controlled levels than the prices of most other goods. In this sense, prices of non-fuels went up too much in January 1992. Russia was not a market economy, however. Following old habits, the SOEs did not mind paying virtually any prices for inputs, and were not afraid of lower sales due to the high prices of their output. From this point of view, it is somewhat surprising that prices of decontrolled goods did not rise even faster. Presumably, this did not happen because of the prevalence of cost plus pricing with respect to the SOEs' traditional customers.

Business as usual (or inertia) at the SOEs in the first three to four months of 1992 resulted in little change in anything except the price scale. Output remained relatively stable (Tables 7.9 and 7.10) despite a steep decline in consumer and investment demand, and a drastic reduction in government military expenditures.[91] Consumer demand went down in part due to significant real price increases, and in part due to the population's money illusion (i.e. failure by the population to adjust the nominal price increases for the increases in incomes). Also, one must keep in mind that by the end of 1991, consumers had accumulated significant inventories of consumer goods. Price liberalization increased the availability of consumer goods and made keeping these inventories less necessary, inducing many consumers to draw them down. The volume of investments was lower mostly due to a sharp contraction of investments financed directly out of the state budget. Also very important was the reluctance of enterprises to invest due to a high level of overall uncertainty brought about by reforms.

Stable output and falling final demand led to a high accumulation of inventories of intermediate and final goods. In a March 1992 survey of 112 Russian enterprises 37 percent had "above norm" inventories of finished products while only 18 percent had "below norm" inventories.[92] Note, however, that some intermediate goods inventory accumulation, particularly in the first quarter, could have been a natural hedge against supply disruptions and price uncertainties.

Inter-enterprise Debt in Arrears

Enterprises managed to raise prices and maintain production and employment in the face of the government's tight monetary policy by accepting IOUs instead of actual payments, particularly from their traditional trading partners. In effect, enterprises were issuing to each other interest-free credits. As of January 1992, inter-enterprise debt in arrears (IDA) amounted to R34 billion. By April 1 it had reached R780 billion.[93] Obviously, the rate of growth of IDA far exceeded that of wholesale prices.

TABLE 7.9 Seasonally Adjusted Output Indices by Major Categories, 1992 *(1989=100%)*

	Jan	*Feb*	*Mar*	*Apr*	*May*	*Jun*	*July*	*Aug*	*Sep*	*Oct*	*Nov*	*Dec*
Raw materials	79.5	85.4	82.5	81.9	75.7	73.1	70.7	66.2	67.4	71.8	70.8	73.0
Machines and equipment	77.1	74.9	76.8	78.8	70.2	67.8	66.6	60.9	68.0	67.0	69.3	63.0
Consumer goods	73.5	79.0	79.3	82.3	75.8	75.1	76.2	71.5	75.4	75.5	73.6	66.7
Incl. Durables	96.7	98.9	102.0	100.8	88.7	90.6	89.5	81.7	87.7	94.1	88.2	90.1
Foodstuffs	66.0	72.7	72.8	78.7	75.1	74.3	76.1	73.0	75.7	74.2	73.2	62.0

Source: Rossiiskaia (1993), pp. 79 and 81.

TABLE 7.10 Output Indices and Retail Trade Turnover in 1992

	Jan	*Feb*	*Mar*	*Apr*	*May*	*Jun*	*Jul*	*Aug*	*Sep*	*Oct*	*Nov*	*Dec*
All Industrial Output *(1989=100%)*												
Unadjusted	80.7	81.3	86.4	81.3	72.4	70.8	67.2	64.5	68.3	75.1	72.0	75.9
Seasonally adjusted	78.2	83.3	81.3	81.3	75.3	73.1	71.5	66.9	69.4	72.4	71.4	70.9
All Industrial Output *(% of prev. month)*												
Unadjusted	93.2	100.7	106.3	94.1	89.1	97.8	94.9	96.0	105.9	110.0	95.9	105.1
Seasonally adjusted	96.4	106.5	97.6	100.0	92.6	97.1	97.8	93.6	103.7	104.3	98.6	99.3
Retail Trade Turnover - unadj. *(% reduction to same month in 1991)*	63	41	50	18	33	34	33	34	26	31	37	41

Source: Rossiiskaia (1993), pp. 44 and 79.

While enterprises advance credit to each other in any market economy, such credit normally does not skyrocket because if an enterprise cannot (or does not wish to) pay its bills on time out of its own resources, it can usually borrow from the bank. And if the enterprise can neither borrow from the bank nor pay its bills, the creditors would normally force the debtor into bankruptcy.[94] At the very least, the supplier would stop further deliveries to a delinquent customer. In Russia, however, as well as in other economies in transition,[95] the creditors continued shipments to their traditional partners even after debts became overdue.

Why would an enterprise continue deliveries in this case? At least in the beginning this was partly the consequence of the "business as usual" approach on the part of many SOEs where the tradition of "mutual amnesty" remained strong.[96] Soviet enterprises used to be notoriously reluctant to seek damages for breach of contract through formal arbitration. In most cases it used to be more efficient to resolve matters informally. The SOEs assumed, as it turned out correctly, that things would be worked out eventually. The informal network of enterprise directors also fostered cooperation and exerted pressure on enterprises to be patient with other participants of the network. Another reason for continuing deliveries was that the woefully inefficient banking system often took months to transfer funds from one enterprise to another. Therefore, tardiness in payments was not always the customer's fault.

One of the important factors that contributed to development of the IDA crisis was the requirement that the enterprises pay into the state budget 50 percent of the windfall increase in their working capital which resulted from the January 2, 1992 price hikes. This immediately created a shortage of liquidity. The rapid accumulation of IDA and the tight monetary policy exacerbated this shortage. The tightness of monetary policy revealed itself in severely restricted bank credit even though real interest rates on whatever loans were available were negative. The SOEs had serious difficulties obtaining cash from the banks even for wage payments unless they could demonstrate their solvency. Establishing solvency, however, did not require any adjustment for the quality of their accounts receivable. Naturally, this gave the SOEs incentives to make deliveries even to enterprises with poor credit standing.

By the beginning of the second quarter the situation had worsened. The cash shortage exacerbated, and enterprises began to introduce a shortened work day or send employees on unpaid vacations. Also, payment in-kind and barter trade were becoming more widespread.

By May the appeals to the government for softening its credit policy had become almost universal, although some changes in SOE behavior began to take place too. In particular, output began to fall. Ironically, this exacerbated the government budget deficit, which was already widening because of a low level of VAT collections caused by the IDA accumulation. (Basically, enterprises did not have any cash to pay taxes.) In addition, starting around April, the ruble was being undermined by the credit emission on behalf of the other ruble zone republics of the FSU. All this, combined with the necessity to take into account seasonal demand for credits such as demand by agricultural enterprises and the Far North, forced the Gaidar government to soften its tight budget policy.

Nonetheless, the IDA kept growing, albeit at a slower pace. By then the crisis had acquired a momentum of its own. No enterprise wanted to use its financial resources to pay its debts unless it received what others owed to it. This was reinforced by the fact that inter-enterprise debt was essentially interest-free while inflation continued at double digit monthly rates. By July 1, the IDA had reached R3,000 billion, rising much faster than output prices.

As the IDA kept accumulating, many SOE directors were becoming more and more convinced that the government did not have any choice but to bail them out somehow. The softening of the credit policy, which might have been unavoidable at the time, only strengthened their conviction.[97] Such an attitude exacerbated the crisis because it lowered the incentives to reduce output, lay off workers, and lower prices. The final defeat of the government's stabilization policy came in late July when the CBR promised the banks to issue large amounts of credit to facilitate mutual cancellation of IDA.[98]

If firms do not cut prices and output in the face of lower demand, the only two ways to avoid a continuing surge in IDA would be to put the offenders into bankruptcy or issue other types of credit. Since too many firms would have had to go bankrupt and the institution of bankruptcy had not yet been developed, the Russian government chose to issue credit.[99]

The CBR credits reduced the volume of IDA, but they did nothing to address the underlying causes of the crisis. Enterprises were given more time to adjust to the new economic environment but their incentives to undertake such an adjustment were reduced by the bailout.

Although the immediate crisis was resolved, it was at the expense of a large increase in the inflation rate and a deterioration of the budget deficit.[100] Perhaps more importantly, the credibility of the government was severely undermined. The government showed its inability to stick to a tight monetary policy and to resist helping enterprises in trouble.

The temporary nature of the 1992 solution to the IDA crisis is evident in that large enterprise debts in arrears have continued to be one of the main symptoms of difficulties of Russian reforms since then. Having stabilized and even declined in real terms during 1993, the volume of overdue debts of customers of industrial output has been rising steadily during 1994, almost reaching the level of the beginning of 1993 by July 1994. At the time of writing, the level of arrears (in real terms) remains somewhat lower than it was at the height of the IDA crisis in mid-1992, but nonetheless it is still very worrisome.[101]

As in 1992, the renewed growth in nonpayments resulted partly from the tightening of monetary policy. Starting in late 1993, and throughout most of 1994, it appeared as though Russia was gradually moving toward greater financial stability. Between February and November, monthly inflation generally remained in single digits, while the ruble continued to appreciate against the dollar. During the same period, official real interest rates came close to zero from being highly negative since the beginning of transition. This encouraged non-financial sector deposits to commercial banks and reduced enterprises' desire for bank credit. At the same time, this situation provides extra incentives for customers to postpone payments to suppliers.

In some important respects, however, the 1994 nonpayments situation is quite different from the one in 1992. Changes in the rules for inter-enterprise transactions since 1992, such as the prepayment requirement, resulted in greater exposure of the Russian commercial banks to enterprise debt. Banks were also seriously hurt by the slowdown in inflation and reduction in CBR credits to enterprises in 1994. The share of overdue bank loans rose from three percent in the beginning of 1993 to 15 percent in the first quarter of 1994, putting a number of banks in danger of bankruptcy.[102]

Another important distinction of the 1994 situation is that the state itself has become a major debtor of enterprises. As of the end of the first quarter of 1994, the government owed enterprises over R11 trillion. At that time the total overdue accounts of all Russian enterprises amounted to R35.2 trillion.[103] During the second quarter the federal government paid off much of its debt, particularly to the defense-related and to agricultural enterprises, slowing the rate of growth of nonpayments in real terms.[104]

It is likely that these payments contributed to the subsequent increase in inflation to almost 14-16 percent per month in the last quarter of 1994.[105] They also were at least partly responsible for the continuing (consolidated) state budget deficit which declined only slightly (from 9.8 to 9 percent of GDP) in the first half of 1994 relative to the same period in 1993.[106]

The current nonpayments situation serves as evidence of the lack of significant change in behavior of many SOEs and RPEs. Apparently, large number of enterprises continue to make deliveries to nonpaying customers and accumulate large debts themselves. The fuels and energy sector, which the government still largely controls, appears to be the worst in this respect. As of July 1, 1994, over one half of all past due accounts in industry represented nonpayments for electric energy and fuels. In mid-1993 this share was less than one third.[107]

Another critical factor responsible for the relative lack of adjustment by the large industrial enterprises, and the continuing nonpayments in particular, is the delay in the effective implementation of the bankruptcy law (the law itself and the early problems with its implementation are discussed below). During 1994 Russian arbitration courts handled only 102 insolvency cases. There are indications, however, that the situation has been changing, with hundreds of enterprises declared insolvent by the Federal Bankruptcy Administration. It is unclear, though, what the implications of such declarations are and how many of these enterprises will actually undergo bankruptcy proceedings (see below). Whatever the number of real bankruptcies, much will depend on how effectively the cases are handled. With respect to large enterprises, the crucial test will be if a significant number of them are allowed to fail completely and be liquidated.

There are three commonly used explanations for the IDA crisis.[109] First, the credit-crunch hypothesis: a rise in the price level led to a sharp drop in the real value of reserves held by commercial banks and an increase in enterprise demand for loans, necessitating increase in inter-enterprise lending as a substitute for bank financing. Second, the composition-of-demand hypothesis: enterprises at the beginning of the technological chains did not perceive a change in the composition of final demand until it was too late. Third, the aggregate-demand-shock hypothesis: the cash shortage created a drop in aggregate demand by consumers, while SOEs kept producing output due to relatively greater availability of credit and rubles in "non-cash" accounts.[110] The last two hypotheses rely on the "non-market" behavior of enterprises which continued to produce essentially the same products while refusing to cut prices despite lower demand.

These three hypotheses have different policy implications. For example, the first hypothesis suggests that greater credit availability would have solved the problem while the third one would call for greater cash emission and less credit. Which of them is correct? Clearly, many enterprises were experiencing shortages of cash. It is wrong, however, to assert that non-cash rubles and bank or state credits were relatively easily available. The credit crunch almost certainly contributed to the IDA, at least initially. However, the root of the problem was in the lack of reliable information about the financial viability of enterprises and in the enormous uncertainty facing the economy in general. Even if capital markets in Russia were well-developed, enterprises would have had difficulties obtaining loans at more or less reasonable interest rates. In this environment, a greater availability of credit would only convert overdue inter-enterprise debt into overdue bank debt without solving the underlying problems of restructuring the economy.

The premise of the second hypothesis was certainly correct: the composition of final demand did change significantly and it did contribute to the crisis. Again, however, the crux of the problem was not in the changing demand but in the peculiar reaction of most enterprises to it. (A similar statement can be made about the third hypothesis.) The IDA crisis serves as an excellent example of how a standard policy approach (such as tight credit in order to stabilize the economy) may not work well if it does not take into account the idiosyncracies of the economic system.

As was mentioned above, the difficulties with nonpayments by enterprises were experienced in other reforming economies including Poland, Hungary and the Czech Republic. The crisis in Russia, however, has been particularly severe and lengthy mainly for the following reasons. The Russian economy was in many ways more distorted and Russia's market institutions, particularly the commercial banking industry, were less developed than was the case in these three countries. Therefore, Russia experienced a greater shift in composition of aggregate demand and, at the same time, it's economy had less ability to adjust. Russia is also much larger and its technological chains are generally longer than in the three East European countries. This weakens and slows the transmission of feedback from final consumers to producers in Russia. And Russian managers' traditions and mindset are more "Soviet" than those of their East European counterparts. This factor was particularly important in the critical initial stages of the IDA crisis, but it continues to contribute to proliferation of non-payments in early 1995 as well. Also, Russian government and Parliament, arguably, were not as committed to market reforms as were the first post-Communist governments in the three East European countries. Lack of government commitment undermines credibility of tight monetary policy, making IDA accumulation more likely. A related factor—high overall economic and political uncertainty—also was more prominent in Russia than elsewhere.

To summarize, the debt in arrears phenomenon is largely a symptom of the deep underlying problems of the economy. The greater severity of these problems in Russia than in the East European countries has been largely responsible for the more serious nature of the Russian crisis. At the same time, reform policies, at least initially, also failed to account sufficiently for the idiosyncratic difficulties facing the Russian economy.

Adjusting to the New Economic Environment: Evidence from Management

Despite some significant changes in the behavior of large industrial enterprises, most of the adjustment so far has been of the "passive" variety, such as reductions in output of products in low demand. Nonetheless, some enterprises have undertaken active restructuring, exhibiting the ability and willingness to adopt behavioral patterns similar to those of firms in a market economy. What determines which enterprises are more likely to adapt to the changing circumstances and which exhibit greater inertia?

The pattern of behavior depends largely on the individual preferences and competence of the managers. Presumably, the greater the C-D gap (see above) for the enterprise director, the more likely he is to exhibit inertia. Often, however, behavior is determined by the particular circumstances of the enterprise and its immediate environment rather than the personal characteristics of its manager. Even a competent director may be forced to rely on state support to preserve the enterprise and his own position in it.

According to some enterprise surveys conducted in Russia in late 1992, the difficulties encountered by the enterprises in conducting business as usual tended to push them toward adapting a market model of behavior. At the same time, when the enterprise does not experience strong pressure for change, it is likely to continue behaving in a traditional Soviet way.[111] In other words, enterprises operating in a competitive environment—with other domestic enterprises or with imports—would be more likely to adjust to markets than enterprises that do not face strong competition. In Russia, where enterprises have traditionally formed both formal and informal networks with their suppliers and customers, the degree of mutual dependency of enterprises also appears to play a significant role. Preliminary empirical results show that the greater this mutual dependency, the less likely enterprises are to adjust.[112]

Some enterprise managers find it difficult to follow the market behavioral model simply because they do not seem to understand basic economic concepts. For example, in a November 1992 survey of enterprise directors only 22 percent complained about a lack of customers, while 92 percent complained about the inability of their customers to pay for the enterprise's output. These directors seemed to view the demand for their products as independent from the ability of their customers to pay.[113] Interestingly, a survey conducted a year later apparently produced similar results.[114]

The degree of market orientation of Russian enterprises can be partly inferred from their "main goals" as reported by their directors. In a November 1992 survey, most of the directors whose behavior was closest to the traditional Soviet enterprise behavior chose "preservation of the collective" as their main goal.[115] Directors who revealed greater adaptability to market conditions chose either "increase in profit" or "increase in sales" as their main goal. Among the directors of the first type a greater proportion complained about elimination of state orders, whereas a larger share of profit-oriented directors were concerned about the lack of marketing skills, set prices based on market demand, were willing to cut extra workers before cutting expenditures on research and development, and were more optimistic about the consequences of privatization. Enterprise directors' goals as reported in the survey probably reflect their mindset, which to an extent determines their behavior in the marketplace. In any case, their objectives appear to be consistent with their behavior and enterprise performance.

In this respect, it is disappointing that a more recent survey of SOEs and RPEs still reports that the preservation of the collective was the most often listed enterprise goal, cited by 58 percent of the directors. The "achievement of stable financial situation" came in a close second. This latter goal was so prominent probably because the survey was conducted in late 1993, during a worsening of the non-payments crisis and 30 percent monthly inflation. The same survey also revealed that when the first and second goals contradicted each other, the first usually held precedence. All other goals were much less significant.[116]

Another recent survey performed by the Russian Economic Barometer group also reported that preservation of the collective was the main objective of 47 percent of managers.[117] In this survey, however, the desire to maintain volume of output was the most frequently cited goal (57 percent). Among the managers of the largest enterprises, preservation of the collective was listed by 55 percent of the respondents. The data also indicated that the managers for whom preservation of the collective was among the main goals had the lowest utilization rates of enterprise equipment and labor, were most dependent on the state in their decisions, and considered incentives for increasing output more important than fighting inflation.

One of the most important questions in evaluating the behavior of SOEs is to what extent it is determined by state ownership *per se*. It is, of course, too early to draw any definite conclusions, but one of the mentioned above surveys conducted in late 1993 did not find any significant differences between the functioning of the SOEs and their recently privatized counterparts. In fact, almost 50 percent of the managers of RPEs indicated that privatization had made no difference whatsoever. About 25 percent characterized the effect of privatization by a rather nebulous "increased freedom and independence." Only somewhat more than 10 percent of the privatized enterprise directors reported restructuring their enterprises and laying off superfluous work force. Less than 5 percent of the respondents noted that privatization improved personnel's attitudes toward work or prospects for restructuring.

There appeared to be little difference between the SOEs and the RPEs in their managers' evaluation of the main problems facing them, in their pricing policies, in establishing business contacts, and in the directions of investments. Only the enterprises that were privatized as closed-type corporations appeared to be more willing to lay off workers even though they experienced smaller decline in output. The closed-type corporations are different from other RPEs because they take their origin from the SOEs that chose to become leaseholds early in the reform process, before most of the privatization program became law. Naturally, their directors were more reform oriented to begin with, resulting in a self-selection bias.[118]

Particularly interesting is the survey result that the hardness of the budget constraint is about the same for both types of enterprises, even though the authors did not specify precisely how they measured this. Perhaps the greatest difference between a truly private firm and a SOE is that it would be more difficult for the state to bail out the former, should it become insolvent.[119] Therefore, the hardness of the budget constraint can ultimately be ascertained only when the enterprise is about to fail. The only way for the government to increase significantly the hardness of the budget constraint for RPEs is to let some of them fail. As of early 1995, the government may not be willing to allow that yet, particularly for the largest enterprises. Ironically, it might be easier for the state to make the SOE managers act as though their enterprises face a hard budget constraint by firing the directors of the failing SOEs. After all, if a manager is interested mainly in his own welfare it should not make any difference to him whether or not the enterprise has been rescued as long as he is out of work himself. The state does not have this option in dealing with privatized enterprises.

Some Theoretical Issues in Transitional Enterprise Behavior

Some of the recent literature on the economics of transition suggests that strategies of Russian enterprises are different enough from the usual firm behavior to require new theoretical constructs for their analysis. In particular, several authors emphasize the objective of enterprise survival as the main determinant of their behavior.[120] Another view is that Russian enterprises are essentially employee-owned (and managed), and they operate mainly for the benefit of their employees.[121]

Do we need these new theoretical concepts or can the behavioral features implied by them be explained within a more traditional framework? Consider first the concept of a survival-oriented enterprise. What are the main implications of a survival strategy? Some scholars argue that the survival-oriented enterprise would rather be owed rubles by another enterprise than cut production even if the repayment of this credit is highly uncertain. The survival-oriented enterprise is willing to undertake actions that have the effect of improving its cash flow even to the detriment of their long-term viability.[122] In general, such an enterprise concentrates almost exclusively on the short run. In fact, this concept of survival orientation is derived from the short-term planning horizon of the enterprise due to a highly uncertain environment. If all implications of survival orientation can be obtained simply out of the shortness of the planning horizon, the concept of survival appears to be unnecessary. Moreover, to the extent that this survival-oriented strategy is not caused by shortness of horizon, it simply reflects the desire of the SOE director to survive in his position.

One of the most puzzling features of the behavior of Russian industrial enterprises is their reluctance to lay off employees or significantly cut real wages, despite sizeable declines in demand and output. Thus, an almost 50 percent decline in industrial output during 1992-1994 was accompanied by a less than 20 percent decline in industrial employment.

These and other considerations, such as the similarity of positions of trade unions and management associations on many issues, may suggest that Russian firms, both state-owned and recently privatized, are acting as if labor-managed. As was argued earlier, the mutual dependency of management and workers at Russian SOEs probably exceeds that at a firm in, for example, the U.S. economy. The director of an SOE needs workers' complicity in exercising his residual claim on enterprise resources. The workers need the director's skills and informal connections to assure the enterprise's ability to stay open and pay wages. This mutual dependency puts certain limits on enterprise management, and they may elicit behavior, some aspects of which are similar to that of labor-managed firms. The relevant issue, however, is what will happen when changes in the external environment lessen this dependency. Only the future events will resolve this question. Until then, however, it is probably more reasonable to treat this mutual dependency of managers and workers as a short-term phenomenon rather than an intrinsic feature of Russia's corporate culture.[123]

Others argue that industrial enterprises hold on to apparently superfluous workers mainly because of the historically paternalistic relationship between management and workers in Soviet enterprises, and their mutual dependency. These researchers point out, however, that there is a clear tendency to move away from this model of behavior. They also note that the maintenance of a relatively large work force does not cost enterprises much due to the extremely low real wages of most workers.[124]

What remains largely unexplained is the rather high rate of hiring by many Russian enterprises. In the 1993 surveys performed by the Russian Economic Barometer, enterprises annually lost an average of 25 percent of all workers and hired 16-18 percent. Moreover, most of the departing workers did so voluntarily, apparently not fearing unemployment. This high turnover is particularly surprising since there are few signs of genuine restructuring, which would require hiring new workers with skills different from those of the old workers. Perhaps much of the turnover is accounted for by highly skilled workers who have little difficulty finding jobs even in the current economic situation.[125] At the same time, the excess wage tax continues to provide incentives for enterprises to keep the lowest paid workers on the payroll. Given the low minimum wages, it may be more advantageous for a profitable firm to keep a minimum wage worker than to fire him even if he contributes zero to output. The excess wage tax explains at least in part the reluctance of many enterprises to lay off workers.[126]

Large-Scale Privatization and Other Changes in Enterprise Environment in 1994

The Effect of Large-Scale Privatization

Many aspects of Russia's economic climate such as high uncertainty, overly burdensome taxation, and excessive regulation by a corrupt bureaucracy, to name a few, have changed little since 1992. Nonetheless, some momentous changes in enterprise governance and institutional environment have taken place. Arguably, the most important such change has been privatization of a large number of SOEs.

Privatization is often considered one of the greatest successes of the Russian economic reforms to date. Indeed, the numbers look impressive. Out of about 250,000 SOEs existing in Russia in the beginning of 1992,[127] about 104,000 had been privatized as of July 1, 1994.[128] More than 70 percent of these were retail trade, public dining, and consumer services enterprises. By the end of the voucher stage of privatization on July 1, 1994, more than 15,000 industrial enterprises had been privatized. They accounted for the bulk of civilian industrial capacity and employed over 60 percent of the industrial labor force.[129] More than 30,000 medium and large SOEs were scheduled to be privatized through the creation of joint-stock companies and the subsequent sale of their shares in the market. By July 1994, 21,300 of them had already registered as joint-stock companies.[130] As mentioned above, the employees of large and medium SOEs have overwhelmingly opted for acquiring a majority stake in their privatizing enterprises. Most of the revenues obtained from the sale of SOEs were channelled into local budgets (63 percent), leaving 25 percent for the federal budget and 12 percent for the state agencies administering privatization.[131]

Voucher privatization funds (VPFs) have emerged as important players in the privatization process. As of early 1995, there are over 600 such funds, most of them small. The ten largest funds, eight of which are located in Moscow, control about 65 percent of all assets held by the 200 biggest funds.[132] There are significant restrictions on the activities of the VPFs. They are not allowed to own more than 25 percent of the shares of any single enterprise (until recently this figure had been 10 percent); they cannot invest more than 5 percent of their assets into any one firm; and they are not supposed to guarantee fixed dividends. Also, there are restrictions on compensation to their management, and they have to report the results of their activities in the central press.[133] These restrictions can be circumvented, particularly in the environment where it is not clear how to value the funds' net assets because secondary securities markets are so thin. Nonetheless, the 10 percent restriction on ownership was counterproductive. Given a relatively small number of liquid shares in the market, this restriction can easily limit the liquidity of the fund's portfolio.[134] There are also serious concerns about wide possibilities for fraud, particularly in the smaller VPFs. Some observers suggest that banks should be encouraged to organize such funds. Apparently, the Russian banks have not been particularly active in this area. According to one survey, banks and other financial institutions served as founding members of about one-third of the VPFs.[135]

Unfortunately, as was pointed out in the previous section, privatization has been slow to change the behavior of large industrial enterprises. To some extent this is because RPEs face the same economic and political environment, including high uncertainty and the nonpayments crisis, as do SOEs. Another reason is that SOEs were essentially independent of the state even before the formal change of ownership. And, partly due to the lack of investment resources, privatization has not been accompanied by significant restructuring and the RPEs continue to use the same stock of physical capital.

It is also important to realize that many of the formally privatized enterprises are still partly owned by the state. Whereas by the beginning of 1994 the assets of state-owned enterprises constituted only 41 percent of Russian industrial assets, the assets of privately owned enterprises reached only 12 percent of the total. Most of the remaining 47 percent of the assets were under mixed state and private ownership. The respective shares for all capital assets were 43, 26, and 31 percent. In fact, of the major branches, only agriculture, trade and public catering, and "commercial activity facilitating the functioning of markets" had the majority of their capital in purely private ownership.[136] By early 1995, the share of SOEs in total assets has declined further with the mixed forms of ownership benefiting the most.

One of the main reasons for lack of change in RPE behavior might have been the insider-controlled nature of privatization. Given the political power of enterprise insiders and the stiff resistance of the former ministries, any successful large-scale privatization effort had to be supported by the SOE's workers and managers. At the very least, they had to acquiesce to the program. The Russian reformers hoped that the secondary trades of shares in the privatized corporations would eliminate management entrenchment and *de facto* employee-ownership relatively soon after privatization. While according to several recent analyses of the issue there are early signs of this trend, the picture remains mixed.[137] Based on the data from a survey of mostly large industrial and service enterprises from 32 provinces conducted in December 1993, Blasi reports that 91 percent had majority employee ownership and in 9 percent the employees held minority stakes. The average and median percentages of insider ownership were, respectively, 65 and 60, with top management holding on average about 9 percent of all shares (median holdings were five percent). Among the outsiders, slightly more than half of the shares belonged to the state. The insiders, particularly management, also held a majority of the board membership in most RPEs.[138]

It appears that during the second half of 1994 things began to change: "[A]s the market values of shares of privatized firms began to rise, workers sharply accelerated the pace of selling their shares. Outside (and sometimes inside) the gates of many companies, it is common to see a bus which serves as buying point of workers' shares."[139] Blasi, however, reports a considerably lower pace of sales by workers. According to him, only about

4 percent of the RPE shares were sold during 1994 by their employees, with outsiders purchasing three quarters of these shares and insiders (evenly split between top managers and workers) acquiring the remaining quarter.

The data on the distribution of enterprise ownership between insiders and outsiders must be interpreted with caution. There is considerable casual evidence that what appears to be an outside investor is often an entity controlled by the top management of the enterprise itself.[140] In other words, the data presented above probably significantly underestimates the true stake of top management in RPEs. Moreover, the most important outside shareholder, the state, usually sides with the management. The workers, on the other hand, are often passive on the issues of corporate governance. When they are not, top management is sometimes able to effectively manipulate workers' votes, either using threats of dismissal of the activists, or appealing to the commonality of the interests of the workers and management.[141]

Despite the apparent strength of top management in the newly privatized corporations, the available data indicate that around 15 percent of the general directors have been removed from the RPEs since July 1992.[142] Is this turnover rate high or low? Most observers would probably argue that this rate is too low and that Russia needs more "fresh blood" and less managerial entrenchment in the top management of its industrial enterprises.

What is wrong with managerial entrenchment? On the surface, a high degree of managerial ownership provides greater incentives for management to maximize profits. This may not always be the case, however, particularly for large corporations. If a manager controls a large firm, he is presumably already very rich and increasing his monetary wealth may not be as attractive as other forms of satisfaction that could be obtained from his position. For example, the owner-manager may be interested in increasing the firm's size or market share, philanthropy, greater visibility in the political arena, and so on.[143] While these goals may indeed maximize the manager's welfare, the other shareholders would view such behavior as dysfunctional. Another problem associated with high degree of ownership by the top manager is that changes in the corporation's profits greatly affect his wealth. If the manager is risk averse this would make him more cautious than the well-diversified shareholders would want him to be.[144] So far, the empirical evidence on the optimal share of management ownership (mainly in large U.S. corporations) has been inconclusive.[145]

Whatever the optimum for the U.S. corporations, however, the same relationship between management ownership and performance does not have to exist in a transitional economy, such as Russia's. Russian shareholders might have good reasons, of course, to be apprehensive of the entrenchment of the former Soviet managers whose skills and personal goals appear particularly ill-suited to profit maximization. At the same time, Russia presumably does not have an easily identifiable large pool of modern skilled managers ready to assume corporate leadership. Moreover, as was mentioned earlier, personal connections of top managers with suppliers, customers, local authorities, and so on, play a key role in their firm's performance. In this environment, replacing a manager is particularly risky. Finally, management ownership in Russia usually means ownership by several top managers. Therefore, even at enterprises with entrenched management it may be relatively easy to replace the general director with another insider, e.g. his deputy.[146] This possibility should keep the director reasonably conscientious. All these factors may raise the desired degree of management ownership in Russian corporations.

To let markets determine the appropriate degree of management ownership, Russia certainly needs to protect the rights of minority shareholders. According to a presidential decree issued at the beginning of 1994, no more than one third of the board of directors could be employed at the enterprise. It also prescribed the cumulative voting procedure for choosing the board. Under the old rules used at many enterprises, shareholders controlling 51 percent of the votes could elect the entire slate. Unfortunately, this decree has been widely ignored. Very few corporations in a survey by Blasi have implemented it and equally few were planning on doing this in the next one or two years.[147] Nonetheless, the mere existence of this decree strengthens the hand of outside shareholders.

The sales of RPE shares held by the state and an active secondary securities market may eventually lead to a significant reduction in the effective control of enterprises by their management. In the near future, however, the most important weapon against management entrenchment is probably going to be the enterprises' need for outside capital to restructure. As Shleifer and Vasiliev put it, "Managers would in fact be willing to give up some of their control rights in exchange for sorely needed capital, since the alternative is to remain at the helm of a rapidly declining firm."

Problems with management entrenchment notwithstanding, privatization in Russia has succeeded in vastly expanding the realm of legal private entrepreneurship and private initiative. The true test of the separation between the state and enterprises, however, will come only when some of the large RPEs face the threat of liquidation. If the government refrains from bailing out most of the failing RPEs, then their budget constraints can be viewed as hard and most of the Russian economy as truly privately owned. But privatization also brings some more immediate benefits. Besides reducing, albeit slowly, the influence of politicians on large enterprise behavior,[148] privatization has expanded and solidified significant political constituencies for further reforms. These constituencies include managers and workers of more or less successful privatized enterprises, their shareholders, and financial market participants. Employees and shareholders of the less prosperous RPEs may be also strongly interested in further market-oriented reforms because such reforms could help these enterprises become profitable.[149]

More generally, privatization upsets the *status quo* and necessitates structural adjustments in the entire economy and forces the government to make some hard choices. For example, active privatization of commercial real estate might generate significant additional revenues for many RPEs, as real estate often constitutes the most valuable asset of many enterprises. In addition, clarification of ownership rights over real estate could provide RPEs with collateral necessary to obtain loans for restructuring. This would facilitate the development of capital market benefiting the entire economy.

Another example of reform that became more urgent with privatization is the rationalization of ownership of social assets such as enterprise-owned housing, hospitals, and kindergartens, and provision of social safety net. While in early 1995 most local governments may not be ready to assume control of these assets and full responsibility for administering welfare programs, privatization has strengthened incentives of RPEs to push for solving this problem. In this sense, privatization program has been an essential ingredient in generating political support for further reforms.[150]

The government itself can no longer operate according to the old routines. It needs to decide which enterprises to leave in state ownership and which to privatize, how to manage the remaining SOEs, what methods to use for privatization of various enterprises, what to do with failing enterprises, and so on.

The Post-Voucher (Cash) Privatization

The voucher program left privatization of a substantial part of the economy at the discretion of the State Property Commitee as well as regional and local governments. It is unclear what criteria these authorities used in selecting what to privatize quickly. Because in many cases the local governments were major recipients of privatization proceeds, they had incentives to postpone privatizating the most profitable enterprises. On the other hand, many failing enterprises probably did not want to be privatized because they feared the loss of state subsidies or because they sorely needed outside capital that could not be obtained by trading equity shares for vouchers. These enterprises could lobby the appropriate authorities to delay their privatization. In any case, as was mentioned above, at the end of the voucher stage of privatization, about one-third of industrial enterprises continued to be state-owned. In addition, the state still owned large minority stakes in many privatized enterprises and was waiting for the end of voucher privatization to sell some of the shares for cash. Also, the government wanted to sell minority stakes in some enterprises which it continued to own, most notably several giant oil companies.

Most of the large and medium-size SOEs remaining after July 1, 1994 were supposed to be converted to corporations of the open type by January 1, 1995, and privatized largely via sale for cash with certain privileges provided to their employees. Small SOEs, i.e. those with fixed assets of no more than R20 million in January 1, 1994 prices (about $16,000), will be sold at auctions and through tenders.[151]

There were, however, a number of exceptions. Large enterprises—the privatization of which is prohibited by the *Gosudarstvennaia programma* (1993)—will not be converted into corporations. The federally owned enterprises not subject to privatization include *inter alia* organizations which receive most of their operating funds from the federal budget; irrigation and water supply systems; railroads and their property; nuclear power stations; radio and TV transmitting stations. Many of these and some other enterprises are to be converted into federal government factories (*kazennye zavody*) financed directly from the central budget and run by government representatives.[153] Also, enterprises scheduled to be sold to partnerships and those with partial foreign ownership will not be affected.

State Property Committees as well as other government agencies continue to have some, albeit more limited than before, discretion in determining whether or not to privatize an enterprise. The government can also decide to retain partial state ownership (51 percent or 25.5 percent of its voting shares, or the "golden share") in certain enterprises. Partial state ownership can be retained for up to three years in enterprises involved in communications, electric energy, oil and gas, mining of precious metals and radioactive elements, armaments, nuclear machine building, hard liquor production, certain areas of transportation, research and design, foreign trade and some others. After three years the government can extend the term of its partial ownership.

As before, privatization procedures of large enterprises consist one of three options, reminiscent of the voucher privatization options but without the vouchers and with significantly smaller discounts for the insiders. According to the *first option*, employees receive preferred shares for up to 25 percent of the corporation's initial capital free of charge. The value of this transfer, however, cannot exceed 20 times the minimum wage per employee. Employees also are allowed to purchase common shares for up to 10 percent of the corporation's capital (not exceeding six times minimum wage per person) at a 30 percent discount of their face value.[154] In addition, enterprise management is authorized to purchase up to 5 percent of the corporation's shares. The per person purchase in this case is limited to 2,000 times the minimum wage amount.

In a much simpler *second option* all employees are allowed to purchase (presumably at face value) common shares for up to 51 percent of the firm's initial capital. No discounts to face value can be used in this option.

Under the *third option* a group of employees or other people can contract to privatize and manage the enterprise for up to a year. If they fulfill the requirements of the contract they obtain the rights to purchase up to 30 percent of the common shares of the enterprise at face value. All employees, including members of the group that contracted to run the enterprise, can purchase up to 20 percent of the common shares (but not exceeding 20 times the minimum wage per person) at a 30 percent discount.

The privatization option is chosen by a vote of all enterprise employees. If any of the options fail to receive at least two-thirds of the votes, the first option is used as a default. If a 51 percent block of shares is retained by the state, the employees receive non-transferable preferred shares for up to 25 percent of the corporation's capital or 20 times the minimum wage, whichever is smaller. If the state retains a smaller block of common shares, then the employee privileges are determined in accordance with the first option.

The shares not claimed by either employees or the state are to be sold to the investors either through the investment tender (*investitsionnyi konkurs*) or the commercial tender (*kommercheskii konkurs*), or at an auction. The investment tender takes place when the purchasers are required to make additional investments into the privatized enterprise. The commercial tender presupposes some other conditions on the purchaser's management of the enterprise. Privatization auctions are managed by the appropriate Committee on State Property.

The distribution of shares takes place according to the following sequence. First, the shares are distributed to employees in accordance with the chosen privatization option. Next, large blocks of shares representing at least 15-25 percent of the capital are sold through one of the procedures listed above. The remaining shares are sold at a special privatization auction where all shares are sold at the same price that clears the market. All shares are required to be sold within a year from approval of the privatization plan. The sale of large blocks of shares that allow the investor to obtain a majority vote are supposed to be monitored for violations of the antimonopoly law.

In view of the severe problems in the development of the commercial real estate market in Russia and the importance of this market for the growth of the private sector,[155] the rules for privatizing real estate belonging to enterprises take on added significance. Unlike the 1992 privatization program, the current regulations allow for privatization of most commercial real estate that is currently leased or *de facto* owned by enterprises undergoing privatization. Typically, a lessee of commercial space in buildings cannot be denied the right to purchase it at a price not exceeding two or three times the annual rent. While significant restrictions on the privatization of commercial real estate continue to exist, the new regulations may alleviate the current shortages, facilitating the growth of private enterprise in urban areas.

More than half of privatization proceeds (51 percent) are given back to the privatized enterprise, with the remainder being distributed to local, regional and federal budgets, and to certain state agencies. The enterprise, however, receives none of the proceeds from the sale of its commercial real estate. SOEs that went bankrupt are generally sold in accordance with the presidential decree concerning the sale of bankrupt SOEs.[156]

So far, cash privatization has been off to a slow start. First Deputy Prime Minister Chubais named the slow pace of privatization as one of the main reasons for the "catastrophic" financial results of January 1995.[157] (The other reason was the delay in obtaining the $6.8 billion IMF loan.) He noted that by the end of 1994 privatization came to a virtual halt. Out of the R9.1 trillion forecast to be generated by the sale of state property during 1995, only R13 billion were received in January.[158] The reasons for this are unclear. Most likely the insiders of enterprises scheduled for cash privatization have been sabotaging the process. Most enterprises whose insiders were eager to privatize probably did so during the voucher stage that provided greater privileges to insiders. Another reason might be the continuing uncertainty of economic environment and difficult economic conditions in general.

Bankruptcy Law

No market economy can function well without a set of bankruptcy procedures. Some of the problems Russian reforms have experienced with eliciting changes in enterprise behavior can be attributed to the late introduction of the bankruptcy law.[159] Although the law took effect on March 1, 1993, it did not start making a discernable impact on enterprise behavior until well into 1994. According to this law, the insolvent debtor enterprise of any form of ownership could be subject to one of the three procedures: restructuring, liquidation, or reconciliation agreement. Bankruptcy cases are under the jurisdiction of the special arbitration courts. These courts determine whether the enterprise is indeed insolvent and if so, decide between restructuring and liquidation. If the court chooses restructuring, two different procedures can be employed: receivership and *sanatsiia*.

Receivership is a restructuring procedure under which the arbitration court appoints an outside "arbitration manager" to oversee the enterprise. The goal of this procedure is to permit continuing operation of the debtor-enterprise. An enterprise can be put in receivership at the request of the debtor-enterprise, its owner, or the creditors.

Sanatsiia, on the other hand, does not necessarily involve a change in management. Under this restructuring procedure the debtor is provided with credits in order to prevent liquidation proceedings. These credits can come either from the owner of the bankrupt enterprise, or its creditors, or other sources. If restructuring results in restoration of enterprise solvency the bankruptcy proceedings are terminated. Otherwise, the proceedings are resumed and the enterprise is liquidated under the supervision of the legal representative of the creditors. If an enterprise is found bankrupt for the second time within 36 months, *sanatsiia* is not allowed.

In order to use one of the restructuring procedures, the court must be petitioned for the appropriate procedure by the debtor, or its owner, or the creditors. In addition, the court must determine that there exists "a real possibility" to restore the debtor's solvency. In the case of SOEs, the court must accept the guarantees of the appropriate state agencies as sufficient grounds for ordering restructuring. If the court opts for restructuring, it suspends bankruptcy proceedings against the enterprise. Otherwise, the court begins the liquidation process.

Bankruptcy proceedings can be initiated by either the debtor-enterprise, the creditor(s), or, in certain cases, the public prosecutor (*prokuror*). To initiate the proceedings, the amount of overdue debt must exceed 500 times the minimum wage. Federally owned enterprises and enterprises in which the federal government holds at least a 25 percent stake can be declared insolvent by the Federal Bankruptcy Administration (FBA). Control over an enterprise that has been declared insolvent is transferred to the FBA, which can sell the debtor enterprise. The FBA also must decide whether to fire the director. If enterprise insolvency is directly caused by the central or regional government's nonpayment for its orders, the enterprise may not be forced into bankruptcy. Note, however, that this caveat no longer applies when government nonpayment causes problems down the technological line.

At any stage of the bankruptcy proceedings they could be terminated by a reconciliation agreement between the creditors and the debtor. Such an agreement has to be approved by the Arbitration Court. It is also possible for the debtor to enter into an out-of-court agreement with the creditors about voluntary liquidation. In this case, formal bankruptcy proceedings never take place. If the proceedings do occur, it is estimated that they would often take a long time (on the order of two years) and for this reason the bankruptcy law is not likely to affect the economic situation in Russia until late 1995. It is conceivable, however, that the threat of future bankruptcy proceedings could modify the current behavior of some SOEs.[160] By early 1994, only a handful of bankruptcy cases had been filed,[161] although the filings apparently surged later in the year. On January 16, 1995 the number of enterprises declared insolvent by the FBA stood at 1,200.[162] These enterprises employed two million people.

As could be expected, the FBA's formal insolvency criteria have taken on a life of their own, with the affected enterprises often worrying more about maintaining the appropriate values of their liquidity coefficients than improving their long-term financial health.[163] It appears also that the criteria the FBA are supposed to use to determine insolvency are much too stringent. For example, during the three months ending on January 31, 1995, the

FBA surveyed more than 4,000 enterprises and classified 80 percent of them as insolvent. Only 10 percent of them, however, are reported to be in danger of bankruptcy proceedings. Most of these are smaller enterprises that decided to self-liquidate because of mounting losses and inability to keep employees.[164] In general, smaller enterprises seem to be more likely to end up in bankruptcy after being declared insolvent by the FBA because they lack the political pull and connections of the large enterprises.

A well-functioning bankruptcy law is extremely important for alleviating the widespread nonpayments besetting the Russian economy. The government wants creditors to use bankruptcy procedures rather than advance credit and hope that the government would bail out the debtor. At the same time, the government prefers to avoid liquidating most of the bankrupt enterprises. Instead, it favors using *sanatsiia* which often amounts simply to state subsidies to ailing enterprises. There are not enough data to assess the effectiveness of the bankruptcy law in Russia. Much will depend on the details of its implementation. The very existence and use of bankruptcy procedures, however, represent a significant step toward letting markets work properly.

An Assessment of Russian Reforms

It is, of course, too early to judge the overall success of Russian economic reforms, except that it is clear that they have not failed yet, and some, albeit slow, progress continues. At least another two or three years will be necessary to begin to sort things out. At this time only a few preliminary assessments of some aspects of reforms can be made.

The major accomplishment of reforms has been to start the process of turning Russia into a market-oriented economy. The achievements of reformers could not be fully appreciated without an understanding of how close to complete collapse the economy had come by the end of 1991. The collapse was averted and the process of building a market economy was initiated with only a brief period of preparation for such an incredibly complex undertaking. Even though many things did not go as planned, the outcome could have been much worse. Among the specific successes have been the resolute approach to price liberalization, achievement of partial convertibility of the ruble, substantial freeing up of foreign trade, and rapid privatization.

The reformers should be highly commended on the comprehensive nature of the initial reform package. Nonetheless, the package contained a number of important omissions. Although some were later corrected, their negative impact may last for quite some time.

One of the major specific and straightforward policy mistakes was the reformers' initial disregard of the importance of the seasonal factor in the

Russian economy. The government eventually realized this, and belatedly issued significant credits to agriculture and the Far North. These actions, however, seemed to be taken under pressure and partly undermined the credibility of the government's commitment to tight monetary policy.

Preservation of price controls on energy and fuels was another major policy mistake. Given the quantitative restrictions on export of these commodities, the initial jump in their prices if they were liberalized right away would probably have been no greater than the actual controlled increase. At the same time, if energy prices were allowed to keep up with inflation, major price distortions would have been avoided. Also, the oil industry would have been better positioned to alleviate a drop in its output.

A policy error that was probably more difficult to avoid was the late development of many of the specific implementation procedures for privatization, as well as frequent changes in the legislation itself through the summer of 1992. Admittedly, it would have been difficult to get many of the regulations through parliament, but their absence during the first half of the year significantly contributed to the overall uncertainty and the shortness of horizon of enterprise directors.

The government is often blamed for not developing a strict anti-monopoly policy early in the transition. The monopolized structure of Russian industry is sometimes blamed for high inflation, the slow adjustment of the SOEs, and other problems of transition. While some improvement in the anti-monopoly legislation and its implementation may be in order, it is unlikely that the government could have done much better. The major economy-wide monopolies have been regulated. Particular care has been taken in preventing monopolies from forming through mergers, and some breakups have been instituted during privatization. By and large, however, the monopolies in Russia exist on a regional basis mainly due to the poor communications and transportation infrastructure. Such monopolies are very difficult to define in legislation. Also, many of these monopolies consist of a single plant which would have been very difficult to break up.

An important "tactical" miscalculation was made in the process of the revaluation of the fixed and working capital of enterprises in 1992. Revaluation of the working capital of SOEs was accompanied by confiscating some of the windfall profit into the Fund for Social Protection, thereby reducing working capital resources at a crucial time. At the same time, insufficient revaluation of capital assets resulted in low depreciation allowances and artificially high profits that were taxed away leaving enterprises little money to invest in restructuring.

Some serious policy mistakes also occurred in the area of taxation. Various unorthodox modifications to VAT and other taxes to improve collections in an inflationary and partly barter environment were introduced throughout the post-1992 period. While many of these modifications did increase tax receipts, they also distorted incentives and raised the uncertainty of the tax environment. Even more harmful were the numerous exemptions and reduced rates for certain groups of products, regions, or even enterprises. In addition, the unwieldy tax system is difficult to administer. Its complexity, high rates, uncertainty, and unfairness have created strong incentives for tax evasion reducing the tax base and fueling inflation.

It is particularly difficult to evaluate Russia's early post-reform policy toward the republics of the FSU. In hindsight and from strictly economic point of view, it was a mistake to allow the 14 non-Russian central banks to issue ruble credit almost arbitrarily to their enterprises. This policy was allowed to continue till the middle of 1992. At the same time, the immediate separation of the Russian monetary system from those of the republics might have been even more destructive of interrepublican ties.[165] Also, such a move could have resulted in greater political instability in the FSU republics with potentially serious adverse consequences for Russia itself. Similar considerations could be used to justify Russian subsidies to the republics in the form of relatively cheap prices for natural resources.

Much more generally, one might question the government's insistence on overly tight credit and monetary policies. While these policies are standard in certain inflationary situations in developed or even developing market economies, they did not work well in Russia. Strict restrictions on government credit and money emission were intended to produce a hard budget constraint and to restrain inflation. In a distorted economy without a functioning capital market and in the highly uncertain economic and political environment, the lack of credit from the government meant that enterprises could not obtain conventional types of credit at all. Combined with strong behavioral inertia on the part of the management and the absence of bankruptcy procedures, this quickly resulted in an explosive growth of inter-enterprise debt in arrears. The widespread and interlocking overdue indebtedness of firms further clouded their financial situation, making it impossible to distinguish between viable and non-viable firms. Under such circumstances, a prolonged tight credit policy would have resulted either in a nearly complete barterization of the economy or in the failure of many more enterprises than the government was willing to accept. In other words, in 1992, macrostabilization seemed to contradict the microeconomic goals of reforms.[166]

The tight credit and monetary policies attempted in the early stages of reform proved unsustainable. The government had to reverse the policies, and because the financial picture of the enterprises was essentially undecipherable, credit was issued almost indiscriminately. As a result, the credibility of the government and its entire approach to reform were severely undermined. Moreover, credits were issued at highly negative real interest rates, meaning that virtually every enterprise wanted to obtain them. At the same time, the interest rate on deposits was even lower, discouraging savings. This was a serious inconsistency in monetary policy.

It would have been probably better to maintain a softer and more consistent monetary policy, accompanied by well-prepared bankruptcy procedures. Of course, as in Hungary, stringent bankruptcy laws introduced too early would have resulted in too many enterprises becoming bankrupt. A better approach would have been to devise relatively liberal but consistent bankruptcy procedures for the initial stage of reform, for example the first two years, with a clear commitment to making the procedures significantly more stringent afterwards. If under such a policy only 5-10 percent of the enterprises were declared bankrupt in each of the first two years, the government would probably be able to manage this process and maintain credibility at the same time. Of course, some of the enterprises would have failed "undeservedly" in any case. But the policy would have remained credible and its costs would have been manageable, while both information flows in the economy and capital markets would have had a chance to improve.

A related serious problem with the government's reform package was the absence of a deliberate industrial policy outside of the defense industry conversion area.[167] This gap was due to the government's hands-off attitude toward most of the economy. If this attitude could be maintained (also disregarding the informational problems and underdeveloped capital markets), an explicit industrial policy might not have been necessary. However, given the need for restructuring, enterprise disincentives to investment during transition (due to uncertainty, tax disincentives in the inflationary environment, etc.), and underdeveloped capital market, the government was forced to provide credit, investment, and import subsidies and tax breaks to industries and enterprises. This was a reactive policy conducted on an *ad hoc* basis. The reactive and indiscriminate nature of this policy has been extremely counterproductive, softening the budget constraint for potential recipients of subsidies, undermining the credibility of government policies, and creating strong incentives for rent-seeking.

A major accomplishment of the reformers has been the fast pace of privatization. According to Yeltsin's address to parliament on February 16, 1995, the private sector accounted for 62 percent of GDP in Russia in 1994.[168] However, the formal transfer of legal property rights from the state to private shareholders or, in particular, the creation of joint-stock companies by itself is not going to solve Russia's economic problems. It may be just as difficult for the government in the future to resist bailing out a large private enterprise, as has been the case with the SOEs. Nevertheless, formalizing the new property rights structure may lengthen the time horizon of enterprise directors and, under certain circumstances, improve their incentives even in the short run. Moreover, speedy privatization created political constituencies for furthering market-oriented reforms and forced the government to develop new policies with respect to both RPEs and the remaining SOEs.

One key issue is whether the prevalence of the second privatization option will result in widespread employee ownership or management entrenchment. Much depends on developments in the near future. Economic efficiency would probably be enhanced if privatized corporations remained genuinely public. The stakes acquired by current management and by the voucher funds may serve as a basis for relatively concentrated ownership. Currently it is important to protect minority shareholders and develop an active secondary market in securities to guard against abuses that could accompany a highly concentrated ownership. An active securities market also promotes the development of capital markets and facilitates implementation of effective reward schemes for corporate management.

To summarize, Russian reforms have succeeded in dismantling the old Soviet economic system and are well on the path to creating a framework for a market economy. The advance of reforms has been uneven, however, with some serious policy mistakes taking place along the way. Moreover, many profound problems remain unresolved. Russia continues to endure high political and economic uncertainty and its government lacks credibility both inside and outside the country. The economy suffers from excessive regulation and taxes, an overblown bureaucracy with extensive discretionary power, high crime rates and a growing underground economy. A large number of enterprises are in a precarious financial situation and the country's financial system remains unstable. Whatever the overall assessment of the success of Russian reforms, however, the path to improved economic performance lies in the further development and strengthening of the institutions of a market economy.

Notes*

1. The case in point is the interenterprise arrears crisis which restricted the ability of the Russian government to conduct tight monetary policy.

2. This point is made forcefully in Leitzel (1995).

3. The average length of service for Soviet fixed capital assets was around 47 years in the late 1980s compared to 17 years in the U.S. Also, only about 2 percent of industrial fixed assets were retired annually during 1980s. The corresponding figure for the U.S. was 4-5 percent (Shmelev and Popov 1989).

4. The structure of capital stock does not suit the market requirements of "wrong" official prices and because Soviet planners did not seem to put a significant emphasis on conventional market criteria for evaluating major investment projects. To the extent that these criteria were used, they often produced

Due to the particularly large number of publications cited on Russia, this chapter has a separate reference list located after the Notes.

"wrong" results because Soviet prices and investment criteria were significantly different from those used in the market economies.

5. *The Russian Economy* (1992), p. 79. We do not know the precise legal status of a collective enterprise but presumably it was similar to a labor-managed enterprise. These data also do not include illegal enterprises. In addition, it is not clear how complete the coverage was of military-related enterprises.

6. Kroll (1991).

7. World Bank (1992). Two recent studies (Brown et al., 1993, and Joskow et al., 1994) questioned the relevance of these data, arguing that by some standard measures of industrial concentration, Russian industry did not appear particularly highly monopolized. These studies admit, however, that standard concentration measures might misrepresent the degree of effective monopolization of Russian industry.

8. Koen and Phillips (1993) offer a comprehensive review of price liberalization in Russia. Unless indicated otherwise, the data in this section are from that source and from CIA (1992).

9. Besides energy prices, the state retained control over public transportation fees, housing rents, and the prices of public services and basic foods. Education and medicine were still provided free of charge by state institutions. In addition, the government at first controlled the retail trade markup in state-owned retail establishments. Later in 1992 this policy was abandoned. Various controls on pricing (mainly limits in the 20-50 percent range on profitability) by enterprises in monopoly position continued through 1993.

10. In the second quarter of 1992, the federal government stopped controlling prices of basic foods, even though in many cases local authorities continued price controls for some foodstuffs. Other regulated prices were raised several times during 1992 and 1993.

11. Roberts (1994).

12. See Osband (1992) and Boycko (1993).

13. This is because the poorer people value their time relatively low and can earn an additional "shortage rent" by queuing up. See Sah (1987), Alexeev (1991), and Polterovich (1993a) for a comprehensive discussion of these issues.

14. See Leitzel (1994). Of course, this statement disregards the serious informational and contract enforcement problems of transacting in unofficial markets.

15. Strictly speaking, a large deficit would not have caused an immediate problem for financial stability if the government could borrow. The sources of credit for the Russian government, however, were extremely limited.

16. For example, the Soviet turnover tax presupposes controlled prices and is incompatible with genuine markets. The highly differentiated and sometimes virtually arbitrary payments out of enterprise profits common in the Soviet system also would not work in a market economy.

17. Lipton and Sachs (1992).

18. It is conventional to translate foreign currency amounts into dollar figures. In the Russian case, however, this may confuse rather than help the reader because of the steep decline in the purchasing power of the dollar in Russia since 1992. For example, during 1993, the ruble-dollar exchange rate about tripled, while consumer prices rose almost by a factor of 9.

19. Lipton and Sachs (1992). The CBR essentially used the commercial banks as its agents for allocating credits directed by the CBR to specific enterprises. The commercial banks were earning fees for processing these transfers.

20. The interenterprise arrears crisis will be discussed later in greater detail.

21. They were reinstated again in June of 1992.

22. The most important goods in terms of hard currency earnings such as energy products, remained under the quota system.

23. The First Deputy Prime Minister was Egor Gaidar who later became acting Prime Minister. He also held the finance portfolio. Here and below the administrative structure is presented as it existed in late February 1992. Prior to that time the precise structure was slightly different. For example, until February 1992 there was a single Ministry of Economy and Finance responsible, among other things, for the budget. It was later split into two separate ministries.

24. *Rossiia-1993.*

25. Lipton and Sachs (1992)

26. The issue of privatization of the defense-related enterprises has not been settled completely. The list of defense-related enterprises which are not subject to privatization is supposed to be issued only by the end of November (the "Vash Partner" supplement to *Ekonomicheskaia gazeta*, no. 37, September 1993, p. 18.)

27. It is not clear what happened if the enterprise could not find a buyer at any price. Perhaps in this case, the enterprise was liquidated.

28. The shares of a corporation of a closed type (*aktsionernoe obshchestvo zakrytogo tipa*) cannot be traded publicly. It is an entity similar to a privately held corporation or to a partnership. Creation of a closed-type corporation was allowed, however, in case of privatization of leaseholds through a buyout.

29. Relatively minor details of the options are omitted.

30. The face or nominal value was determined through an evaluation process described in a supplement to the Presidential decree on speeding up the privatization of state and municipal enterprises (*Rossiiskaia gazeta*, February 13, 1992.) In essence, the nominal prices of shares were calculated by dividing the book value of the enterprise, adjusted for depreciation, by the number of shares. While this book value had been adjusted more than once since the beginning of the 1992 reforms, it severely underestimated the true worth of most of the assets in Russia's inflationary environment.

31. During the initial period of privatization, share prices under this option were set at 1.7 times the July 1992 book value of the enterprise.

32. *Ekonomicheskaia gazeta*, No. 37, September 1993, p. 10. Local and regional authorities prefer selling property for cash because they usually receive at least a portion of the proceeds. The redeemed vouchers, on the other hand, had to be destroyed. Incidentally, this destruction did not always take place, and some vouchers were "recycled" back by the management of the property funds.

33. These auctions typically were conducted locally, with the bids accepted only in person and at particular locations. Note the difference between this arrangement and the computerized, national system in the Czech Republic.

34. Boycko et al. (1993).

35. The Russian Fund of Federal Property and local property funds were organized to conduct the actual sale of privatizing enterprises.

36. Goskomstat (1993).

37. See Whitlock (1993) and *Osnovnye polozheniia* (1994) for a complete list.

38. A classic work on the Soviet second economy is Grossman (1977). See also Treml and Alexeev (1994) for evidence of Russian underground economy growth, and Alexeev (1995) for its changing nature during transition.

39. Koen (1994).

40. See Atkinson and Micklewright (1992) for a discussion of this household budget survey.

41. Koen (1994) and Gavrilenkov and Koen (1994).

42. Recall, however, the caveats in the previous section. An alternative set of estimates designed to alleviate some of the problems, particularly undercounting of consumption by the official GDP data, is presented in Table 7.8. Even these alternative estimates, however, miss a large part of the underground economic activities.

43. The impact of underdevelopment of credit and capital markets was exacerbated by the difficulties in accumulating and maintaining own resources for investments in the inflationary environment with highly negative official real interest rates.

44. *Rossiiskaia* (1993), p. 78.

45. Keep in mind that the degree of underrecording in services has always been greater than in production of goods.

46. *Finansovye izvestiia*, no. 3 (132), January 19, 1995, pp. 1-2 and *OMRI Daily Digest*, Monday, January 16, 1995 and Tuesday, July 18, 1995.

47. See Table 7.5. Note, however, that no official sectoral decomposition of changes in real GDP has been published as of the end of 1994. The percentage changes in household consumption shown in the table represent rather crude estimates based on other Goskomstat data.

48. It appears that the revisions take into account the discrepancy between the low retail trade and paid services figures based on production statistics and the estimates implied by household budget surveys. See Gavrilenkov and Koen (1994).

49. According to *PlanEcon* (vol. XI. no. 7-8, April 7, 1995, p. 10), savings rate declined between 1992 and 1993, and remained stable in 1994.

50. *Rossiia-1994*. This shift of output and employment to services is probably seriously underestimated because the statistical coverage of the service sector in Russia remains considerably less adequate than that of the other sectors. In general, none of the data presented in this section take into account the apparently rapidly growing underground economy.

51. Goskomstat report in *Izvestia*, no. 9, January 18, 1995. *PlanEcon* XI(7-8), April 7, 1995 reports 5.5 million unemployed (7.4 percent unemployment rate) in February 1995.

52. These estimates are presented in *Rossiia-1994*. They include those who were shifted to part-time work, sent on unpaid or partly paid leave, and those whose salaries were reduced to the legal minimum. While this may be an unconventional definition of hidden unemployment, it does correspond well to the Russian conditions.

53. *Rossiiskaia* (1993) and *Statisticheskoe obozrenie*, October 1994, Goskomstat, p. 66.

54. In a leasehold, the employees lease the property from the government and pay rent for it. While the state formally retains ownership, the employees control the use of the property as long as they do not try to sell it. Many of the leasing arrangements allow the lessee to buy out the property.

55. *Rossiia - 1993* (1), p. 211.

56. In a leasehold all output, income, and property acquired out of the lessee's own resources is owned by the lessee after a deduction is made for rental payments and other charges.

57. See Pistor and Turkewitz (1994).

58. Often even at private enterprises and in joint stock companies the power of the managers and the workers is significant if not always dominant.

59. Of course, managers and workers are not homogenous groups. One may wish to distinguish between the director and other managers, upper management and lower management, workers and workers' councils, etc. For the time being, however, we will disregard these finer classifications.

60. The main legal document determining the status of enterprise directors is the Law on Enterprises and Entrepreneurship which took effect on January 1, 1991.

61. In 1992 this agency was the Ministry of Industry. That ministry no longer exists and the contracts are made with various relevant departments of the federal government such as the Committee on Industrial Policy.

62. Since then this policy has been changed and the directors' salaries tied to the average wage at the enterprise.

63. Their power on the shop floor, however, often seems to be somewhat limited (Burawoy and Krotov, 1992). In order to change things there the workers' agreement is usually needed.

64. The directors used to wield a great deal of power at their enterprises under the traditional Soviet system as well. Then, however, the appropriate ministry and the Communist party could occasionally interfere in the internal affairs of the enterprise and even fire the director. Also, the director's power was somewhat limited by the plan. Nowadays, however, one could argue that his power is limited by the market forces.

65. From this point of view, the concept of the survival-oriented enterprise discussed later in the chapter reflects the survival-oriented behavior of their directors.

66. This approach to analyzing behavior under uncertainty was developed by Heiner (1983). He argued that a large C-D gap results in a less complex behavior governed mainly by traditional rules. For example, suppose a manager has to decide whether to introduce a new product. If the product is "successful", the manager will benefit. Introducing an unsuccessful product, however, is costly. Suppose that the manager is unfamiliar with the new environment to the extent that he cannot even evaluate the odds of coming up with a successful product. Then it may be rational for the manager to refrain from introducing *any* new products. Moreover, he might want to ignore information which could induce him to change this behavioral rule because he has limited capacity to interpret this information.

67. Suhomlinova (1995) provides a detailed theoretical and empirical investigation of the separation process of enterprise units in the Russian construction industry.

68. Boeva et al. (1992) and Dolgopiatova et al. (1994).

69. O'Prey (1994).

70. See, for example, Burawoy and Krotov (1992) and Polterovich (1993b).

71. Hendley (1992).

72. Teague (1993).

73. One of the notable victories of the management-unions alliance was the decision to add what is now known as the second privatization option to the government's privatization program.

74. In fact, according to Boeva et al. (1992), a large share of the deliveries in the early stages of reforms was made without any formal contracts. One of the directors in the survey reported that his enterprise had formal contracts only for two out of twenty main types of inputs and with only three out of twenty of its main customers. Apparently, this situation was rather typical.

75. Boeva et al. (1992). Incidentally, this fact, combined with the virtual absence of a market for managers in Russia, explains how directors managed to become residual claimants at SOEs. A concerted action of workers could probably force out the enterprise director. The replacement, however, would likely be much worse for the enterprise in the short-term. Since high uncertainty makes long-term considerations largely irrelevant, replacement of a director rarely would benefit the enterprise. As a result, the director becomes irreplaceable and acquires great power.

76. According to a recent survey of 159 managers in St. Petersburg, "connections and personal contacts" came out as the most frequently mentioned management quality needed for success in the Russian market (see Longenecker and Popovski, 1994). In the survey this quality seemed to be more important than problem-solving skills, marketing and sales skills, leadership, and so on.

77. Boeva et al. (1992) and Boeva and Dolgopiatova (1993).

78. Boycko (1995). See Bertaud and Renaud (1994) for a detailed discussion of real estate situation in Russian cities.

79. Much depends, of course, on the relative size of the enterprise and the locality. Presumably, SOEs in company towns are relatively more powerful while in big cities the government has an advantage.

80. Russia has a two-tiered banking system consisting of the central bank and of commercial banks many of which were based on the branches of the old Gosbank, the single bank in the traditional Soviet system.

81. Reportedly, bank transfers often take as long as two (or even "several") months. Enterprise managers often accuse the banks of deliberately slowing down transfers of payment to make use of the funds for their own purposes (Dolgopiatova et al., 1994). At the same time, according to a CBR official, significant delays in payments (given that the funds for payment are available) can happen only when the transactions take place between banks served by different Accounting Centers. Otherwise, the accounts are settled in 1-2 days (*Finansovye izvestiia*, no. 42, August 20-26, 1993, p. 3.)

82. Calculated from Ivanter et al. (1994). The exchange rate is from Russian Economic Trends, Table A21.

83. The use of collateral may be somewhat limited by the still uncertain system of property rights, particularly on commercial real estate.

84. Some Russian economists call these the "pocket" banks (Ivanter et al., 1994).

85. *Russian Economic Trends* (1993). The CBR funneled the bulk of the remaining enterprise credit via the Ministry of Finance. See the next section for more information on CBR lending to enterprises.

86. See O'Prey (1994).

87. *Russian Economic Trends* (1993). Almost half of these credits were channeled through the Ministry of Finance which "directed" them to specific enterprises. The other half was allocated by the CBR to commercial banks for lending to enterprises.

88. Joskow et al. (1994) discuss Russian anti-monopoly policy and related issues.

89. *PlanEcon Report*, January 11, 1995 supplement.

90. For example, in an interview with *Delovoi mir* (February 11, 1993, p. 6) former acting prime-minister Gaidar said that "the system of regulations initially was built on the assumption that the financial discipline and responsibility of enterprises was relatively high, and that payments would be made sufficiently quickly."

91. In January 1992 retail trade turnover was 63 percent below the January 1991 level (Table 7.10). A drop in retail trade most likely overestimated the drop in consumer demand due to the existence of the second economy and compensation in-kind. The volume of investments in the first quarter of 1992 was 44 percent lower than it was during the corresponding period of 1991 (*Rossiiskaia*, 1993, p 90).

92. *Russian Economy* (1992), p. 111. See also *Rossiia-1994* (2).

93. These numbers may include other types of enterprise debt in arrears besides IDA. See discussion of this issue in Whitlock (1992). For a detailed analysis of the IDA crisis in Russia see also Ickes and Ryterman (1992, 1993).

94. This was not an option in Russia in 1992 as the Law on Bankruptcy was not put in force until 1993. Until the end of 1994 its implementation was slow.

95. See Slay (1992) for the Hungarian, Czechoslovak, and Polish cases.

96. Leitzel (1987).

97. Credits were necessary first of all to the agro-industrial complex, which could not possibly function properly without credits in light of the more than five-fold jump in wholesale prices in January 1992. Obviously, an enterprise that gets most of its revenues in late summer and fall and incurs most of the expenditures in the spring, would have great difficulties operating without government credits in an economy with only rudimentary capital markets. Seasonal factors are also prominent in the economy of the Far North. Gaidar called the initial disregard of the seasonality problem in Russia a "professional sin" of his government (*Delovoi mir*, February 11, 1993, p. 6).

98. The events of the IDA crisis of 1992 and their analysis are presented in Ickes and Ryterman (1993).

99. As was noted below, SOEs were beginning to cut output in the second quarter of 1992. Eventually, many of them would have done so in response to a reduced demand for their products. In the environment of large and growing IDA, however, the size of output cuts was unpredictable. It could have easily been much larger than acceptable for the government.

100. The initial effect of the CBR credits was to improve tax collections in September-October due to the renewed ability of many enterprises to pay taxes after mutual cancellation of IDA. The deficit worsened significantly by December, however (see Table 7.4).

101. *Rossiia-1994* (3). According to the same source, as of July 1, 1994, total customer debt in arrears reached R40 trillion or about 17 percent of the GDP.

102. Ivanter et al. (1994).

103. This information is from Ivanter et al. (1994) who concluded that the state was the main culprit in generating nonpayments. They argued that given the "minimum estimate" of the "debt multiplier" of 2.5, the Ministry of Finance nonpayments accounted for at least three quarters of all debt in arrears.

104. *Rossiia–1994*.

105. *Finansovye izvestiia*, No. 3 (132), January 19, 1995, pp. 1-2.

106. *Rossiia–1994* (3).

107. *Rossiia–1994*, p. 39.

109. This and the following two paragraphs draw heavily on Ickes and Ryterman (1992).

110. Non-cash (*beznalichnye*) rubles represented the SOE bank balances which could be transferred as payment to other enterprises but could not be readily withdrawn to pay wages. The non-cash rubles were in part a holdover from the traditional Soviet system, and in part a consequence of the cash shortage.

111. See Nabiullina (1993).

112. This empirical work was performed by Ickes et al. (1995), who also argued that this view does not contradict the conventional view of the role of competition. Suppliers and customers of an enterprise that faces competition for its output are less likely to be greatly dependent on it. Therefore, the network connections between the enterprise and its suppliers and customers is unlikely to be strong.

113. Boeva and Dolgopiatova (1993). Of course, these respondents might have been indirectly blaming the IDA crisis which prevented even solvent enterprises from paying their suppliers. The survey included 109 enterprise managers. SOEs comprised 42 percent of all enterprises and 28 percent were joint-stock companies. The rest were collective enterprises, leaseholds, and private enterprises.

114. After indicating that only 17 percent of the respondents reported a drop in demand for their output, Dolgopiatova et al. (1994) notes that the surveyed managers often blamed difficulties with selling their products on the poor financial situation of the potential customers without connecting this to reduced demand.

115. Nabiullina (1993). Preservation of the collective essentially stands for unwillingness to lay off existing workers. Almost half of SOE managers chose "preservation of the enterprise collective" as the main goal of their enterprise activity. For comparison, none of the managers of private enterprises chose "preservation of the collective" as their main goal.

116. Dolgopiatova et al. (1994)

117. Kapeliushnikov and Aukutsionek (1994). Russian Economic Barometer is a non-governmental research institution which has been conducting monthly industrial enterprise surveys since December 1991. Each survey includes 150–200 enterprise managers from various regions. About one third of the sample is replaced with different enterprises every month.

118. Dolgopiatova et al. (1994) and Dolgopiatova (1994).

119. See, for example, Stiglitz (1994).

120. These views are most forcefully expressed in Ickes and Ryterman (1994) and in Boeva and Dolgopiatova (1993). Dolgopiatova et al. (1994) also reports that most

enterprise managers they surveyed characterized the functioning mode of their enterprises as survival.

121. See Polterovich (1993b) and occasional similar statements in other sources. The concept of an employee-owned enterprise is not new, of course. However, Polterovich and others argue that employee ownership exists even in the absence of any formal arrangement to that effect.

122. Ickes and Ryterman (1994). For example, enterprises continued deliveries to insolvent customers. While this worsened the overall financial position of the enterprise, at least until mid-1993 it made it easier to obtain cash credits from a bank to pay wages.

123. Of course, as a result of the overwhelming popularity of the second privatization option, most medium and large former SOEs have become formally employee-owned. This situation is unlikely to continue for long, however, after the owners of shares begin to trade them in the open market. In fact, Shleifer and Vasiliev (1994) report a massive sale of shares by the workers of privatized enterprises in late 1994. The purchasers seemed to be mainly the investment funds and enterprise management. Even prior to this transfer of shares the management seemed to be generally in control at the enterprises which privatized according to the second option.

124. Kapeliushnikov and Aukutsionek (1994).

125. *Ibid*.

126. Consider a profitable enterprise with two workers, one being paid minimum wage W, the other earning 11W. If the low paid worker is fired, the enterprise ends up paying the excess wage tax (essentially, profit tax) of over 30 percent on the additional $11 - 6 = 5$ times W of its revenues. The tax loss is more than 50 percent greater than the saved minimum wage of the fired worker. This is true even without taking into account the extra penalties for average wages exceeding 8 times W.

127. *Rossiiskaia* (1993), p. 127.

128. *Rossiia-1994*. The total number of remaining state-owned enterprises at that time stood at over 138,000. Note, however, that enterprises could be split up in the process of privatization. Also, it is unclear how many state-owned enterprises were shut down during this period of time. Also, a disproportionate number of privatized enterprises were small. For these reasons, the initial number of enterprises and the number of privatized enterprises are not directly comparable.

129. *PlanEcon Report*, nos. 33-34, vol. X, October 4, 1994 and *Rossiia-1994*.

130. *Rossiia-1994*. Note, however, that the process of actually selling shares in the newly created joint-stock companies often takes a long time.

131. Goskomstat (1993) and *Rossiia-1994*.

132. *PlanEcon Report*, nos. 33-34, vol. X, October 4, 1994.

133. *Finansovye izvestiia*, no. 42, August 20-26, 1993, p. 7, and *Rossiiskaia* (1993), p. 137.

134. *Finansovye izvestiia*, no. 41, August 13-19, 1993. The VPFs' complaints and the fear of long-term management entrenchment at the insider-controlled enterprises pushed the government to raise the limit of VPF ownership of a firm to 25 percent.

135. Frydman et al. (1994).

136. These data are based on the results of reevaluation of capital assets as of

January 1, 1994, presented in *Statisticheskoe obozrenie*, October 1994, Goskomstat, p. 66. See also Pistor and Turewitz (1994) on the extent of state ownership of privatized enterprises in Russia, Hungary and the Czech Republic.

137. See Shleifer and Vasiliev (1994), Frydman et al. (1994), Blasi (1994).

138. Blasi (1994).

139. Shleifer and Vasiliev (1994), pp. 19-20. They add that by some estimates, the workers had already disposed of a quarter of the shares they acquired in the initial stage of the privatization process.

140. This phenomenon is richly described by Zubakin (1994) who manages "a group of voucher investment funds", and who claims that 10 to 50 percent of the shares of privatized enterprises have been acquired by the "pocket" firms created by the SOE management for "self-privatization." Shleifer and Vasiliev (1994) also mention this phenomenon.

141. Frydman et al. (1994), p. 4-6.

142. Blasi (1994), p. 36. Shleifer and Vasiliev (1994) report that in Vladimir, Yaroslavl, and Rostov, 10 percent of the general directors of RPEs were replaced at the first shareholder meeting.

143. As Shleifer and Vasiliev (1994) put it "[t]ycoons do strange things just because they are tycoons."

144. See, for example, Holmstrom (1982).

145. Looking at the *Fortune* 500 U.S. corporations, Demsetz and Lehn (1985) found no evidence that the degree of management ownership and corporation's performance were correlated. Morck et al. (1988) argued that this conclusion was an artifact of Demsetz and Lehn's linear specification of the relationship between management ownership and a company's performance. Under non-linear specification, performance seems to improve as the degree of management ownership rises from zero to about 5 percent and falls after that. (Unlike in a linear model, non-linear specification allows for the relationship between management ownership and corporate performance to vary with the level of management ownership.) In other words, the negative aspects of management ownership dominate at its higher levels. Jensen and Murphy (1990) found, in effect, that management ownership in large U.S. corporations is less than 1 percent. Shleifer and Vasiliev contend that this result is consistent with Morck et al.'s findings. If so, it would imply that the degree of management ownership in large U.S. corporations is far below the optimum for profit maximization.

146. In fact, Blasi (1994) states that most replacements of the general directors in Russia seemed to be with other insiders. Zubakin (1994) also reports that a "pocket" firm created by the general director to facilitate his control of the privatized enterprise sometimes turns on the director himself. As Zubakin puts it the "child" devours its "parent."

147. See Blasi (1994).

148. Note that even the RPEs with little or no state ownership may remain dependent of politicians as long as private capital markets continue to be under-developed and state credits serve as an important source of enterprise capital (see Boycko et al., 1993).

149. As of early 1995, 40-50 million Russians hold shares in RPEs (Boycko, 1995; *Ekonomika i zhizn'*, no. 6, February 1995, p. 2).

150. See Boycko (1995) for a fuller discussion of the political ("public choice") effects of privatization. See also McFaul and Perlmutter (1995) for a number of important papers on privatization and changes in corporate governance.

151. The outline of the cash stage of privatization is based on *Gosudarstvennaia programma* (1993) and *Osnovnye polozheniia* (1994).

153. See a presidential decree of May 24, 1993 "On Reform of State-Owned Enterprises" ("*O reforme gosudarstvennykh predpriiatii*"). In the process of creation of a federal government factory its work force cannot be reduced, it cannot fire the employees of the liquidated SOE, and it cannot transfer enterprise property to other legal entities or individuals. The newly created factory is supposed to be under strict government control. In particular, it needs an explicit permission of the appropriate government agency to sell, lease, or use as collateral its government property or to create subsidiary enterprises or serve as a founding member of other enterprises. In addition, it can receive credit only with government guarantees.

154. Face value of the shares is determined in accordance with the value of capital assets as of January 1, 1994. In the persistently high inflationary environment this implies that face value would usually be significantly lower than the market price of these shares.

155. Bertaud and Renaud (1994).

156. See below for details of the bankruptcy legislation.

157. *OMRI Daily Digest*, February 20, 1995.

158. In January 1995 the exchange rate was somewhat over R4,000 to a dollar.

159. The Russian Federation Law "O nesostoiatel'nosti (bankrotstve) predpriiatii," *Ekonomika i zhizn'*, No. 1, January 1993, pp. 18-20. Other important implementing legislation includes the government decree *O nekotorykh merakh po realizatsii* (1994) and the presidential decree *O prodazhe gosudarstvennykh* (1994).

160. *Izvestia* reported a case where the filing of a bankruptcy case resulted in the debtor enterprise paying off its debt.

161. Only one case was reported by late summer 1993 (*Izvestia*, no. 162, August 27, 1993). In February of 1994 the former finance minister Fedorov stated that 8 bankruptcy cases were being processed (*The New York Times*, April 26, 1994, p. C2).

162. *OMRI Daily Digest*, Tuesday, January 17, 1994. By the end of January this number was expected to reach 4,500. According to *The Economist* (February 18, 1995, p. 66), the Federal Bankruptcy Agency had placed 500 private companies in receivership and liquidated or sold 400 SOEs.

163. Ivanter et al. (1995).

164. *Izvestia* (January 31, 1995) as quoted in *Ekonomika i zhizn'* no. 13, April 1995, p. 6. The same article argues that more than half of U.S. corporations would be deemed insolvent according to the criteria used by the FBA.

165. In that case, however, Russia would have been better off by issuing credit to the republics for purchasing Russian goods. This way the CBR would have had a much better control over Russian monetary policy. Such a policy began only in mid-1992.

166. Rose (1993) provides more detailed arguments along these lines, particularly in the area of consumer behavior.

167. There were some other outlines of the industrial policy such as the Program for Deepening the Economic Reform, issued by the government in the summer of

1992, the creation of the State Committee for Industrial Policy, and some other steps. The Program, however, was to be implemented only after the economy stabilized, and the Committee has not yet accomplished much.

168. *OMRI Daily Digest*, February 17, 1995.

References

Alexeev, M. 1994. "Russian Underground Economy in Transition." Mimeo. Department of Economics, Indiana University. Bloomington, IN.

_____. 1991. "If Free Market Prices Are So Good Then Why Doesn't (Almost) Anybody Want Them?" *Journal of Comparative Economics* 15: 380-90.

Atkinson, A., and J. Micklewright. 1992. *Economic Transformation in Eastern Europe and the Distribution of Income*. Cambridge: Cambridge University Press.

Bertaud, A., and B. Renaud. 1994. "Cities witDolgopiatova. 1993. "Gosudarstvennye predpriiatiia v perekhodnyi period: formirovanie strategii vyzhivaniia." Mimeo (June). Institute of Economic Problems of Transition.

_____ and V. Shironin. 1992. *Gosudarstvennye predpriiatiia v 1991-1992 gg.: ekonomicheskiie problemy i povedeniie*. Institute of Economic Policy. Moscow.

Boycko, M. 1995. "Restructuring Russian Enterprises." A paper presented at the OECD conference *Performance of Privatized Enterprises: Corporate Governance, Restructuring, and Profitability*. (March 29-31). Moscow.

Boycko, M., A. Shleifer, and R. Vishny. 1993. "Privatizing Russia." *Brookings Papers on Economic Activity* 2: 139-181.

Brown, A., B. Ickes, and R. Ryterman. 1993. "The Myth of Monopoly: A New View of Industrial Structure in Russia." Mimeo.

Burawoy, M., and P. Krotov. 1992. "The Soviet Transition from Socialism to Capitalism: Worker Control and Economic Bargaining in the Wood Industry." *American Sociological Review* 57 (February): 16-38.

CIA. 1992. "The New Russian Revolution: The Transition to Markets in Russia and the Other Commonwealth States" Mimeo (June).

Demsetz, H., and K. Lehn. 1985. "The Structure of Corporate Ownership: Causes and Consequences," *Journal of Political Economy* 93: 1155-77.

Dolgopiatova, T. 1994. "Izmenenie otnoshenii sobstvennosti v Rossii: formy i posledstviia," *Problemy prognozirovaniia* 6: 24-31.

_____, Evseeva, I, and T. Edimenchenko. 1994. "Strategii vyzhivaniia gosudarstvennykh i privatizirovannykh predpriiatii promyshlennosti v perekhodnyi period," Materialy konsul'tativnogo ekspertnogo soveta po problemam ekonomicheskoi reformy (Proceedings of the Advisory Expert Council on Problems of Economic Reforms). no. 2. Moscow.

Frydman, R., Pistor, K., and A. Rapaczynski. 1994. "Investing in Insider-Dominated Firms: A Study of Russian Voucher Privatization Funds." Mimeo. Department of Economics, New York University.

Gavrilenkov, E., and V. Koen. 1994. "How Large Was the Output Collapse in Russia? Alternative Estimates and Welfare Implications." *IMF Working Paper* WP/94/154 (December). International Monetary Fund.

Goskomstat. 1993. *O razvitii ekonomicheskikh reform v Rossiiskoi Federatsii (ianvar'-mai 1993 goda)*. Moscow.

Gosudarstvennaia programma privatizatsii gosudarstvennykh i munitsepal'nykh predpriiatii v Rossiiskoi Federatsii. 1993. Presidential decree no. 2284 (December 24).

Grossman, G. 1977. "The 'Second Economy' in the USSR." *Problems of Communism* 26(5) (September-October): 25-40.

Hendeley, K. 1992. "The Ideals of the *Pravovoe Gosudarstvo* and the Soviet Workplace," in D. Barry, ed., *Toward the 'Rule of Law' in Russia?: Political and Legal Reform in the Transition Period.* New York: M. E. Sharpe.

Heiner, R. 1983. "The Origin of Predictable Behavior." *American Economic Review* 73(4) (September): 560-95.

Holmstrom, B. 1982. "Moral Hazard in Teams." *Bell Journal of Economics* 13(2) (Autumn): 324-40.

Ickes, B., and R. Ryterman. 1994. "From Enterprise to Firm: Notes For a Theory of the Enterprise in Transition," in R. Campbell, ed., *The Postcommunist Economic Transformation.* Pp. 83-104. Boulder, Colo.: Westview Press.

_____. 1993. "Roadblock to Economic Reform: Inter-Enterprise Debt and the Transition to Markets." *Post-Soviet Affairs* 9(3) (July-September): 231-52.

_____. 1992. "The Interenterprise Arrears Crisis in Russia." *Post-Soviet Affairs* 8(4): 331-61.

Ickes, B., R. Ryterman, and S. Tenev. 1995. "On Your Marx, Get Set, Go: The Role of Competition in Enterprise Adjustment." Mimeo.

Ivanter, V., Govtan, O., and V. Panfilov. 1994. "Finansovaia stabilizatsiia v Rossii." *Problemy prognozirovaniia* 6: 3-23.

Ivanter, V., Govtan, O., V. Panfilov, and A. Medkov. 1995. "Bankrotstva predpriiatii v Rossiiskoi Federatsii." *Problemy prognozirovaniia* 2: 22-42.

Jensen, M., and K. Murphy. 1990. "Performance Pay and Top-Management Incentives." *Journal of Political Economy* 98(2) (April): 225-64.

Joskow, P., R. Schmalensee, and N. Tsukanova. 1994. "Competition Policy in Russia during and after Privatization." *Brookings Papers on Economic Activity: Microeconomics*: 301-74.

Kapeliushnikov, R., and S. Aukutsionek. 1994. "Nekotorye osobennosti povedeniia possiiskikh predpriiatii na rynke truda." Mimeo. Moscow.

Koen, V. 1994. "Measuring the Transition: A User's View of National Accounts in Russia." *IMF Working Paper* WP/94/6 (January). International Monetary Fund.

_____ and S. Phillips. 1993. "Price Liberalization in Russia: Behavior of Prices, Household Incomes and Consumption in the First Year." *IMF Occasional Paper* 104 (June). International Monetary Fund. June.

Kroll, H. 1991. "Monopoly and transition to the Market." *Soviet Economy* 7(2): 14-174.

Kwon, G. 1992. "Productivity, Specialization, and Coordination in the Former Soviet Sectors: Evidence and the Reasons for Failure." Ph.D. dissertation (March). Harvard University.

Leitzel, J. 1995. *Russian Economic Reform.* New York: Routledge.

_____. 1994. "Goods Diversion and Repressed Inflation: Notes on the Political Economy of Price Liberalization." Mimeo. Duke University.

_____. 1987. "Contract and Breach in the Soviet Union." Mimeo. Duke University.

Lipton, D., and J. Sachs. 1992. "Prospects for Russia's Economic Reforms," *Brookings Papers on Economic Activity* 2: 213-65.

Longenecker, C., and S. Popovski. 1994. "Managerial Trials of Privatization: Retooling Russian Managers." *Business Horizons* (November-December). Pp. 35-43.

McFaul, M. and T. Perlmutter, eds. 1995. *Privatization, Conversion, and Enterprise Reform in Russia.* Boulder, CO: Westview Press.

Morck, R., A. Shleifer, and R. Vishny. 1988. "Management Ownership and Market Valuation: An Empirical Analysis." *Journal of Financial Economics* 20: 293-315.

Nabiullina, E. 1993. "Predpriiatie delaet vybor," working paper of the Expert Institute RSPP. No. 7 (February). Moscow.

O nekotorykh merakh po realizatsii zakonodatel'stva o nesostoiatel'nosti (bankrotstve) predpriiatii. 1994. A Decree of the Government of Russian Federation. No. 498 (May 24).

O produzhe gosudarstvenykh predpriiatii-dolzhnikov. 1994. A Decree of the president of Russian Federation. No. 1114 (June 2).

O'Prey, K. 1994. "Observations on Adaptation, Restructuring, and Conversion in Russian Defense Enterprises and Regional Government." Mimeo.

Osband, K. 1991. "Index Number Biases During Price Liberalization." *IMF Working Paper* (August). Washington, DC.

"Osnovnye polozheniia gosudarstvennoi programmy privatizatsii gosudarstvennykh i munitsepal'nykh predpriiatii v Rossiiskoi Federatsii posle 1 iiulia 1994 goda." 1994. In *Sobraniie zakonodatel'stva Rossiiskoi Federatsii* 1(13): 1976-2001.

Pistor, K., and J. Turkewitz. 1994. "Coping with Hydra-State Ownership after Privatization: A Comparative Study of Hungary, Russia, and the Czech Republic." A paper presented at a conference *Corporate Governance in Central Europe and Russia.* (December). Washington, DC.

Popov, V. 1995. "Obshchie tendentsii." *EKO* 2(248): 3-14.

_____. 1993. *The Russian Economy in 1993: Forecasts and Annual Survey of 1992.* Middlebury, VT:Geonomics Institute.

Polterovich, V. 1993(a). "Rationing, Queues, and Black Markets." *Econometrica* 61(1) (January): 1-28.

_____. 1993(b). "Ekonomicheskaia reforma 1992 g.: bitva pravitel'stva s trudovymi kollektivami." Mimeo. (May). TsEMI RAN. Moscow.

Roberts, B. 1995. "Welfare Change During Economic Transition: The Effects of Ending Shortages in Russia." Mimeo (January). University of Miami.

Rose, R. 1993. "Contradictions Between Micro- and Macro-Economic Goals in Post-Communist Societies." *Europe-Asia Studies* 45(3): 419-44.

Rossiia-1995: ekonomicheskaia kon'iuktura. 1995. No. 1 (March). Moscow: Center for Market Conditions and Forecasting.

Rossiia-1994: ekonomicheskaia kon'iuktura. 1994. No. 3 (November). Moscow: Center for Market Conditions and Forecasting.

Rossiia-1993: ekonomicheskaia kon'iuktura. 1993. No. 1 (February). Moscow: Center for Market Conditions and Forecasting.

Rossiiskaia ekonomika v 1994 godu: tendentsii i perspektivy. 1995 (April). Moscow: Institute of Economic Problems of Transition.

Rossiiskaia ekonomika v 1992 godu: tendentsii i perspektivy. 1993. Moscow: Institute of Economic Problems of Transition.

Sah, R. 1987. "Queues, Rations, and Market: Comparison of Outcomes for the Poor and the Rich." *American Economic Review* 77(1) (March): 69-77.

Shmelev, N., and V. Popov. 1989. *Na perelome: ekonomicheskaia perestroika v SSSR.* Moscow: Novosti.

Sheifer, A., and D. Vasiliev. 1994. "Management Ownership and the Russian Privatization." Mimeo (December). Harvard University.

Stiglitz, J. 1994. *Whither Socialism?* Cambridge, Mass.: The MIT Press.

Suhomlinova, O. 1995. "Constructive Destruction: Organizational Fission in the Russian Construction Industry." Mimeo. Department of Sociology, Duke University.

Teague, E. 1993. "Organized Labor in Russia in 1992." *RFE/RL Research Report* 2(5) (January): 38-41.

The Russian Economy: Spring 1992. 1992. Moscow: Institute of Economic Policy.

Treml, V. and M. Alexeev. 1994. "The Growth of the Second Economy in the Soviet Union and Its Impact on the System," in R. Campbell, ed., *The Postcommunist Economic Transformation.* Pp. 221-48. Boulder, Colo.: Westview Press.

Whitlock, E. 1993. "Industrial Policy in Russia." *RFE/RL Research Report* 2(9) (February): 44-48.

_____. 1992. "A Borrower and a Lender Be: Interenterprise Debt in Russia." *RFE/RL Research Report* 1(40) (August): 33-38.

World Bank. 1992. *Russian Economic Reform: Crossing the Threshold of Structural Change.* Washington, DC.

Zubakin, V. 1994. "Vtoraia ekonomika." *Voprosy ekonomiki* 11: 156-60.

8

Conclusions, Lessons, Prospects

Legacies and Initial Conditions

This study has investigated one of the most difficult common problems of economic transformation, that of "sensibly" restructuring state-owned industrial firms in the European centrally planned economies. Although there were many differences between Russia and the three Central European (CE-3) countries when fundamental systemic transformation began—differences rooted in their cultures, levels of development, historical experiences, as well as in varied other initial conditions—state enterprises in all these countries have been facing many similar problems.

One general common legacy of a centrally planned system is that of a *misdeveloped* economy. Misdevelopment is shown, for example, by the economy's sectoral structure, which is overdeveloped in heavy industries and underdeveloped in infrastructure; by the allocation of output, with a relatively small share to personal consumption and large shares to investment and defense; and by the fact that most industrial products are not competitive internationally. The basic cause of misdevelopment at the macro-, mezzo-, and micro-levels is that economic development strategies and enterprise decisions were largely driven not by market forces but by historical, ideological, political, and military considerations, as well as by the practices of central planning. (The term "misdeveloped" is not meant to suggest that central planning had only undesirable outcomes. Educational attainments, certain aspects of health care, and full employment were, from the point of view of welfare, some of the more positive features.) The main historical factor was the centuries-old desire of not only the Central and East European countries, but also of Russia and China, to catch up with the more developed countries. This was coupled with the transitory belief, or hope, of their rulers that Communism and central planning were the way to reach that goal.

State-owned industrial enterprises embodied certain basic features of misdevelopment. They typically had an inappropriately large size, wrong production profile and managerial incentives, excessive vertical integration (to reduce reliance on outside suppliers), skewed technological development and labor force skills, inadequate market orientation, and "soft" financing. Under the dramatically changed political and economic circumstances in which the Central and East European countries and the Newly Independent States (NIS) found themselves, restructuring their misdeveloped economies and enterprises could not be avoided. The only question was—and largely still is—when and how restructuring would take place.

This book has focused on the CE-3 countries and Russia. However, occasional references have also been made to China, given its importance and the fact that in many ways this Asian giant has also been transforming its economy from a centrally directed to a more market-driven system. Is its experience the same? If not, how does it differ from the European TREs?

Restructuring policies are a function of country-specific initial economic, political and social conditions, which in turn shape the transformation strategies that the countries pursue. Generally, an economy will be more constrained and its transition more difficult, the more severe its misdevelopment, the less developed its market mechanism, and the greater its macroeconomic imbalance. Not surprisingly, we found that among the countries investigated, Russia was the most ill-prepared in the early 1990s with regard to each of these factors, while China was relatively the best off in the late 1970s, when its transformation began (see Charts 2.1 and 2.2 on p. 9). Among the CE-3 countries, Hungary and Poland were in a relatively good position, although the Czech Republic also had certain advantages. Political-social conditions in a country can moderate or reinforce its "readiness" (or "unreadiness") to reform. For example, the almost complete discrediting of all aspects of communism and central planning made the Czech Republic more "ready" to transform than, say, Hungary, where economic and political reforms since the mid-1960s had created a degree of legitimacy for the "liberal" Communist political system. Although we seem to be saying that "good" legacies are "bad" for transformation and vice versa, the conclusion to be drawn is that the country best able to harness its legacies—whatever they are—to support the politics and economics of transformation will succeed most quickly in that difficult task.

Transformation Strategies and Progress

The "Pure" Models

The basic strategy of restructuring state industrial enterprises is partly determined by, and partly influences, the broad strategy of economic transformation that the authorities in each country pursue, purposefully or as the unplanned or unforeseen outcome of forces over which they have little control. Our approach in this study was not to begin with some preconceived notion of what *the* appropriate general model of transformation and restructuring might be, but to proceed empirically, to observe what each country has done, and then try to draw some broadly generalizable conclusions and lessons. Nevertheless, it is useful to sketch three greatly simplified transformation models, to serve as benchmark: *shock therapy* (broadly defined), the *order will emerge out of chaos* approach, and *gradualism*.

Shock Therapy. This model assigns a key role to the post-Communist governments in transforming the economy quickly and decisively. The authorities have a dual responsibility. One is to implement rapid economic liberalization by freeing most factor and product prices, including imports, and making the currency convertible. The other is to quickly put in place the new rules and institutions of a market economy, including effective bankruptcy procedures. This model typically includes macroeconomic stabilization via responsible monetary and fiscal policies, as well as the rapid but orderly privatization of the means of production. The advocates of shock therapy see a tradeoff between concentrating the pain over a short period to cure the patient quickly, which they prefer, versus lesser immediate pain, which will last much longer, with the eventual cure being less certain.

Order Will Emerge Out of Chaos. The advocates of this approach have a fundamental distrust of governments, especially those that are likely to emerge in the immediate post-Communist era. For radically transforming a centrally planned economy, "chaos is not all that bad," argues, for example, Nobel-prize-winning University of Chicago economist, Gary Becker.[1]

In this view, unbridled market forces will do a better job than politicians in shaping the norms of a newly capitalist society. Under particularly onerous governments, even corruption and organized crime may be providing a valuable service of facilitating market development by disregarding state rules that often hamper what should be routine market activities, such as importing and exporting. The best chance for successful transformation is for governments to stand back and let market institutions evolve from the ground up. Such a process cannot be forced onto a society by insisting that it try quickly to duplicate the institutional arrangements of developed market economies. At the same time, this approach shares with the shock therapy model the basic prescription of speedy price liberalization and macro-stabilization.

Proceed Gradually. This model is advocated by those who believe that it takes a long time to learn and practice the principles of a market economy because "knowledge travels with great difficulty."[2] The market mechanisms we find today in the developed countries have taken a long time to evolve. The advocates of the gradual approach cite with approval the example of China. That country first allowed the build-up of millions of family- and village-based ventures before tackling the more complex problems of creating modern financial institutions and reforming the governance and operation of state-owned enterprises (SOEs). Many advocates of the gradual model do not believe that a quick and radical political transformation to democracy can always be successful or that it would promote a market-oriented economic transformation. The quick attainment of sustainable democracy and an efficient market system is especially problematic in less developed, predominantly agricultural societies with no strong pre-Communist tradition of democracy and markets. Some proponents of this model also hold the view that—in poor countries, with no democratic tradition—gradual marketization should occur first, political transformation later.[3] The rapid economic growth of South Korea, initially under a single-party and highly authoritarian system, is an oft-mentioned example.

Observed Strategies

It is our view, shared by other observers, that there is no single best transformation strategy for *all* transforming economies. The best strategy will depend on each country's legacies, initial conditions, and current circumstances. And no country can be expected to follow any of the pure models. The actual strategy of transformation is likely to combine elements from each, although circumstances in a given country may make it more receptive to one of the approaches than to another. For example, China is, in many ways, sui generis because of its low level of development, population size and density, and cultural traditions, as well as because the Communist political system did not collapse, its economy was never fully centralized, and much of its output is highly labor-intensive.

Whatever one might think about the virtues of the Chinese model—namely, of letting the non-state sector gradually "grow around" and overtake the centrally planned core—the fact is that it was not a feasible approach in the Soviet Union and in CEE. The reason is the rather sudden and unexpected collapse of the Communist political system, owing to a combination of domestic and external circumstances. The collapse of the absolute rule of a single political party had also swept with it just enough (but not all) of the greatly discredited system features of central planning. Thus, a gradual reform of central planning was not a feasible option, although the scope and the speed with which central planning's legacies should be eliminated can be debated.

The CE-3 countries had to combine elements from each of the three models and there are many possible combinations. One example is the Czech approach, most closely associated with Finance Minister turned Prime Minister, Vaclav Klaus. He summed up his country's experiences by the end of 1994 as "a mixture of intentions and spontaneity." In his view, neither democracy nor price liberalization or privatization could wait. Furthermore, once an "institutional vacuum" was created by the collapse of the Communist system, "the government had to react and implement a coherent set of system-changing measures" as well as responsible monetary and fiscal policies.[4] In these respects, the Czechs followed *shock therapy*. At the same time, in Klaus' view, the government should not try to over-regulate how the market should function, but let certain institutions, such as who will control enterprises after voucher privatization, emerge from the bottom up. This aspect of the Czech strategy is consistent with the *order will emerge out of chaos* model. Coincidentally, political prudence has justified that certain painful steps—such as allowing bankruptcies to be widespread or large layoffs to occur before new jobs can be created—be managed by the government cautiously and gradually, so as not to tear apart the social fabric and thereby run the danger of losing political support for otherwise rapid economic transformation. In these areas, the Czech approach has been much more *gradual* than either Hungary's or Poland's.

Poland and Hungary have employed a different mix of approaches. Poland's first post-Communist government applied shock therapy success-fully by quickly freeing prices and bringing hyperinflation under control. But successive governments had only limited success, over five years, in privatizing and restructuring the large SOEs. The fact that the private sector has grown rapidly—in spite of several policy failures or inaction by the governments—while the state sector has eroded steadily indicates that market forces have become strong enough to shape the economy.

If shock therapy is defined, more narrowly, as rapid price liberalization and quickly bringing inflationary pressures under control (this is how economists usually define the term), then Hungary did not need such medicine because earlier reforms had already freed most of its prices, without high inflation. To be sure, given Hungary's large foreign debt-service obligations and the low share of investment in GDP, the level of consumption had to be kept in check by tight monetary and fiscal policies, not unlike those under shock therapy in the other two countries. The authorities did just that until about mid-1992, when the monetary and fiscal reins were loosened (too early, as it turned out). At the same time, in many other areas, including the restructuring of SOEs, Hungary repeatedly followed stop-and-go policies that yielded impressive achievements but also spawned many inconsistencies and problems. Thus, although Hungary had an early lead over Poland and (especially) the Czech Republic in the early phases of the transformation, its lead has narrowed and might even have disappeared by the mid-1990s.

Comparative Assessment of Progress

It is difficult to be precise in defining and measuring transformation's progress. Nevertheless, the question is often asked: "how much progress has a particular country made, as compared to others, to create institutions and policies resembling those of a well-functioning market economy? Most would agree that well-functioning market economies have common basic features, such as ownership that is predominantly private; factor and product prices that are mostly free from administrative control; adequate competition; and an efficient and well-supervised banking system.[5]

At the end of 1994, the European Bank for Reconstruction and Development (EBRD) prepared a comparative progress report on 25 TREs, not including China, focusing on five aspects: changes in ownership, price determination, extent of competition, banking reform, and enterprise restructuring. This is how the Bank ranked the five countries that in its view had made the most progress by 1994, as well as how it ranked Russia in this group of 25 countries. (The maximum point score in this computation is 24. Countries with identical scores are presented here in alphabetical order.[6])

Rank	Country	Point Score
1	Czech Republic	21
2-5	Estonia	20
2-5	Hungary	20
2-5	Poland	20
12-13	Russia	16

Let us comment briefly on these rankings and on the developments and perceptions they reflect.

We agree that Russia should be ranked approximately in the middle of the group of 25 TREs (tied with Romania). Our interpretation of Russia's transformation strategy and status as of early 1995 is the following. Russia (where transformation began a year or two after those in the countries of CEE) initially seemed to model its transformation on Poland's approach, combining extensive price liberalization with macro-stabilization policies. In addition, Russia undertook an ambitious privatization program, basically similar to that of the Czech Republic, on which it has made impressive progress in just a few years. However, the government quickly abandoned its stabilization efforts, mostly under pressure from enterprises. The decentralization of political as well as economic power to the regions has also complicated the ability of the center to implement its economic policies. For these and other reasons, after the initial push, economic liberalization has proceeded slowly in most regions. Low credibility of the government and persisting distortions in the economy stimulated rent-seeking efforts by various interest groups. To a large extent, the "order out of chaos" approach has characterized reforms in Russia ever since. (Unfortunately, the presence of rent-creating distortions, combined with government's inability so far to put in place an effective legal framework for a market economy, or often even to enforce order and contracts under existing laws, has contributed to a rise in organized crime.) At the same time, the implementation of bankruptcy procedures, the privatization of land and commercial real estate, and the rise of unemployment have been permitted to occur only gradually.

We are not fully certain that, as of 1994, the Czech Republic was clearly in the lead over Poland, and especially Hungary, in transforming its economy, impressive as the Czechs' progress had been over five years. Two of the Czech Republic's great advantages over the other two countries has been a decisive and articulate government pursuing a steady course in economic policy and the apparently greater degree of domestic political consensus behind those policies. These features contrast sharply with frequent governmental changes in Poland. They contrast also with the stop and go policies and the sharp *public* disagreements over economic policy in Hungary, both within the ranks of two successive governments as well as among the political parties. Nevertheless, in Poland, successive governments have followed quite similar economic policies (while that was so and why it is likely to remain so are discussed in the concluding section). And the output of Poland's "true" private sector has grown at least as rapidly as in the Czech Republic. The nub of the issue of how much comparative progress has been made in systemic transformation is the pace of privatization. If one interprets the Czech Republic's voucher distribution of state assets as completed privatization, then the country has indeed made impressive progress. But if one assesses voucher disribution as quasi-privatization and sale for cash as real privatization—an interpretation that we prefer (see below)—then it is not so clear that the Czech Republic clearly leads the other two countries in economic transformation. During *each* of the first five years (1990-1994), foreign investors had clearly shown their greatest confidence in Hungary's progress. To be sure, Hungary's large initial advantages over the other two countries have been eroding, as was noted.

Restructuring Enterprises

Definitions

Restructuring is a process that enables firms—originally created to serve the goals of a planned economic system—to operate successfully in a market economy. Restructuring includes processes that redeploy more efficiently the assets initially controlled by SOEs. Comprehensive restructuring of the inherited production units, especially the large ones (the main focus of this study) is necessary because most firms are not well prepared to compete in a market-driven economic system. (While the need to restructure firms also occurs with some frequency in a market economy, the scope, the extent, and the difficulty of restructuring are much less than in a TRE.) Although, in a broad sense, the entire transformation process in a TRE may be regarded as restructuring, here we are focusing on those actions by the authorities, and by the owners and managers of SOEs and of privatized firms, where the cause and effect relationships can be traced quite clearly, making restructuring outcomes more predictable.

Enterprise restructuring involves significant changes in one or more such aspects as basic strategy; products, markets, and marketing; production technology; finance; substantial reductions in unit costs; and organization and management. Restructuring tasks are quite different in large SOEs in, say, the energy sector than in modern electronics or in a large service organization, such as a financial institution. Even within a given industry, individual firms may require quite different restructuring programs, depending on the nature of their technology, markets, and management, to mention just some of the factors.

The results of restructuring can be observed at the macro level, from changes in the sectoral composition of GDP (but price effects should be separated from output effects); at the mezzo level, through changes in the branch and product composition of an industry; and at the micro level, through enterprise case studies. At the enterprise level, four kinds of restructuring may be distinguished, none mutually exclusive.[7]

Strategic restructuring takes place when an enterprise develops and implements a comprehensive, long-term business strategy in response to a profound necessity or opportunity. Strategic restructuring may involve the introduction of new product lines, new processes, new technologies, the development of new markets, and substantial downsizing. If successful, restructuring will significantly enhance the enterprise's net present value.

Defensive restructuring involves measures whose primary goal is the enterprise's survival. The measures taken, such as neglecting investment to pay wages, or selling real estate and other assets for the same purpose, often decreases the firm's value, in the long run. The key point is that the motive is short-term survival, not the enhancing of the enterprise's value.

Passive restructuring takes place when an enterprise's assets (which could include real estate, buildings, machinery, tools, employees, suppliers, markets, and receivables) erode—whether legally or illegally, by design or by happenstance, for personal gain. Enterprise insiders often have excellent and low-risk opportunities for "asset stripping." Restructuring is passive in the sense that its benefits do not, as a rule, accrue to the enterprise itself, as a going concern, but to its managers or workers and their "networks" in the private sector. The passive restructuring process is typically not visible to the public eye. Its contributions are embedded in statistics showing that a rapidly growing share of GDP originates in the private sector.

Restructuring through liquidation is one typical outcome of bankruptcy procedures. It usually occurs when the assets of an enterprise are not worth more as a going concern than if the assets are sold separately. It may also happen if the creditors cannot agree on a reorganization plan.

Key Findings

Our key finding is that considerable restructuring has taken place during the first five years of transformation, 1990-1994, in all of the countries. But, contrary to what was expected, *strategic restructuring* of SOEs has not taken place on any substantial scale, except in the Eastern part of Germany (a special case, where restructuring has occurred both before and after privatization) and, elsewhere, in those industry pockets where the SOEs were acquired by foreign investors (mainly in Hungary and mainly after privatization). Strategic restructuring has been under way for only a year or so in Poland, is just beginning in the Czech Republic, and has barely started in Russia. So far, much more common has been *defensive restructuring* and *passive restructuring*, which have occurred rather widely in all of the countries. Thus, over time, "autonomous" forces, not government programs, tend to accomplish a great deal of restructuring, though not as efficiently, perhaps, as it might be done under different circumstances.

We find that the scope, speed, and efficiency of the restructuring that remains to be done depend mainly on the following four sets of interdependent policy variables (each discussed under a separate subhead): (1) a country's privatization strategy; (2) the nature of the budget constraint facing enterprises, policies concerning enterprise bad debts, and the efficiency of financial intermediation (all three aspects are closely interrelated); (3) corporate governance arrangements; and (4) other aspects of a country's macroeconomic policies and institutional framework. Our policy-oriented findings are summarized for each aspect.

Privatization and Restructuring

There is a very large literature already on privatization in TREs.[8] Our focus here is to summarize the impacts of alternative privatization strategies on restructuring.

Criteria for Assessing Privatization. From the point of view of restructuring, the privatization strategy a country pursues should be assessed by the extent to which it results in (1) harder budget constraints for the privatized firms and (2) the acquisition of shares by new owners who are interested in, and capable of, maximizing the long-term market value of the businesses they acquire, and (3) achieving one or both of these key objectives speedily or slowly.

The two main alternative privatization methods are to sell assets or give them away through a voucher program. (Also important, but less pervasive, is the privatization of assets through liquidation or via leasing.) With either sales or distribution, preference may be given to inside stakeholders: labor or management.

Voucher Privatization. Giving away assets is apt to hasten the onset of a hard budget constraint for most privatized firms, which exerts pressure for restructuring. The budget constraint is likely to become harder because privatization tends to reduce the control of labor unions and like bodies, as well as that of the state bureaucracy that exercises ownership functions over the enterprises to be privatized. This reduces the pressure on the authorities to bail out enterprises the state no longer owns or controls. To be sure, if the creditor banks remain state-owned and control, directly or indirectly, the distributed enterprise shares—as is the case in the Czech Republic—then the budget constraint may not harden immediately.

Privatization by distribution is advantageous because of its speed. It does not require large amounts of capital at a time when accumulated domestic savings are tiny relative to the market value of the assets being privatized. Furthermore, distribution is perceived by the public to be the more equitable of the two approaches. Distribution also forces decisions by both the government and the new owners that might otherwise have been delayed or avoided. For example, the government must decide on the mode of distribution. And the new owners must choose whether, and to whom and under what terms, they are willing to sell their shares.

Distribution's main drawback is that most of the initial new owners are likely to be "passive." This means that they are not able or interested in effectively exercising such key ownership functions as deciding on the property's best use, selecting managers and holding them accountable for performance, and providing capital to restructure the enterprise, if needed. Thus, by itself, the distribution of shares in large enterprises should be considered semi-privatization. It is an interim step, as is emphasized, for example, by the Czech authorities. The initial owners—whether the enterprise's workers, other individuals, or small investment funds—are generally passive investors. Over time, however, they tend to sell their shares to *active investors*, who are more likely to have the interest and the capital to restructure the firms. Voucher privatization thus sets in motion a process of ownership change that will continue for years. In the meantime, however, the business value of the "semi-privatized" property may continue to decline. And whether the ultimate owners will be those who would want to, and would be able to, restructure the enterprises they control is an open question.

Conclusion: Voucher privatization may facilitate restructuring by hardening the budget constraint of enterprises, which may or not happen immediately. It also promotes restructuring by improving corporate governance arrangements, although only some time in the future.

Privatization by Sale. This approach is recommended mainly from a market point of view: those who put up money to acquire state property are the most likely to know, and care about, the best use and operation of the property, including its quick restructuring. These same buyers are also the most likely to be able to afford, or borrow, the investment funds necessary for this purpose. The approach also provides revenue to the government.

The main drawback of privatization by sale is its slowness, due to the difficulties of valuing the property and selecting the right buyer (if there is an interest, which is not uniformly the case). The latter is especially problematic and politically sensitive because price should not be (and generally is not) the only consideration. But this means giving discretionary power to the privatizers, which is likely to tempt political interference and corruption, or at least give the appearance of such, which politically damages the government. In any case, the government has to stand ready to justify the specifics of each transaction to an often suspicious, and envious, public.

The slowness of privatization has further serious drawbacks. One is that the business value of much of the property to be privatized tends to decline, often substantially, with each passing day. (To the extent that this happens owing to *passive restructuring*, that may be bad for the enterprise, and for generating privatization revenues for the government, but it may be good for the economy.) The other drawback is that since *any* type of privatization is politically always controversial, the longer the procedure drags on and the more protracted is the domestic political debate about it, the more that undermines political support for privatization, leaving less time, attention and support for the authorities to address other vital transformation issues.

Sale to insiders, generally involving leases, can be quite efficient for restructuring in small or medium-sized firms whose output is labor-intensive and thus require little capital for restructuring. Even in a large enterprise, leasing out certain units or activities to those insiders who make good business proposals and have the know-how and the commitment to implement it can be a good approach to privatization. Otherwise, insider control is likely to be counterproductive for large enterprises because the main concern of the insiders is likely to be the preservation of jobs and the enhancement of current incomes, and because they are not likely to have access to the capital needed for restructuring.

Conclusion: Privatization by sale hardens the budget constraint *and* improves corporate governance arrangements. Its disadvantage is its likely slow pace—more so in larger countries than in small ones. Small countries, such as the Baltic states, that have only a few hundred SOEs will find it easier to mobilize the expertise and the capital needed.

The Budget Constraint, Financial Intermediation, and Restructuring[9]

Another set of variables that influences the scope, speed, and efficiency of restructuring is the nature of the budget constraint facing enterprises, together with the quality of financial intermediation. One of the most acute problems in all TREs is the bad financial condition of a large number of SOEs. Many were heavily indebted to begin with, often because the authorities established firms with relatively little equity. The mode of enterprise finance was not important because the enterprises as well as the banks were state-owned and the authorities did not, as a rule, permit enterprises to go bankrupt. When market pricing and competition were introduced and markets in the former CMEA countries were lost, many firms began to sustain large losses and thus could not service their debts.

Initially, the "new" commercial banks (that had remained mostly state-owned) continued to supply unsecured credits. When a degree of financial discipline was imposed on the banks through tighter monetary and bank supervision policies, and they transmitted these pressures to enterprises by hardening their budget constraints, many businesses responded by accumulating large inter-enterprise debts.

Thus, in every TRE the early period of transformation coincided with a banking and financing crisis. (The main difference between these crises and those that market economies have also been experiencing is that, in the TREs, most of the bad loans had been made to public firms, not private borrowers, although this changes as transformation proceeds.) The overhang of large debts greatly complicates privatization and restructuring.

To deal with the bad debt problem, four policy tools are available, none mutually exclusive: (1) the restructuring of debtor enterprise *and* creditor balance sheets, more or less at the same time, and tying the financial restructuring to privatization; (2) the systematic governmental takeover or refinancing of the bad debts held by the creditors (mostly the banks); (3) insolvency procedures; and (4) reducing the debt to insignificant levels in real terms through high inflation.

Restructuring Debtor and Creditor Balance Sheets Simultaneously. Financial restructuring, which is designed to deal with a large volume of non-performing loans, involves two main tasks. One is to recapitalize the creditor financial institutions because otherwise they could not function well. The other task is deciding whether, and how, to provide debt relief to the debtor enterprise and to liquidate those judged to be inviable as business entities even after debt relief is granted. Such procedures, focusing on the debtor, are called "workouts."

For several reasons, it is advisable to link the bank recapitalization and enterprise workout procedures and, if possible, to also tie the workout to privatization. To be sure, although the recapitalization of the banks is the responsibility of the state, the restructuring (workout) of the bad debts of individual enterprises is best done by private interests, in order to depoliticize (as much as possible) such procedures. But some kind of linkage between bank recapitalization and enterprise debt restructuring is important because a bank's recapitalization needs are largely a function of the kind of debt relief that its debtors are granted. Furthermore, the creditor bank should have knowledge about the debtor's operations and management that would be useful to bring to bear during the workout negotiations.

The creditor bank should also have a stake in the terms of the workout. Without coupling bank recapitalization and the painful workout process, the banks are more likely to get used to the idea of being bailed out. It is also useful to link workout to privatization. How a potential buyer proposes to handle the target acquisition's outstanding financial obligations should be part of the negotiations over the terms of the privatization.

Although scattered examples of such a simultaneous approach can be found in each CE-3 country (much less so in Russia or China), only Germany could afford to implement this approach economy wide, and relatively quickly. This was because the German government was in a position to mobilize, on the one hand, the large required number of credible experts to manage the workouts and, on the other, the immense financing needed to foot the bank recapitalization *and* initial enterprise restructuring bills. Hence, history is likely to judge the German approach to be quite successful. In any country, ultimately the public purse pays, either directly, by paying off the creditors, or indirectly, through lower (in some cases, negative) revenues from privatization, as well as through an initial decline in average living standards.

Comprehensive Restructuring of the Creditors' Balance Sheets. This approach has been relied upon primarily by the CE-3 countries. The essence is that banks are recapitalized by the government. The central budget makes available, in some form, the estimated difference between the desired (and affordable by the government) level of capitalization and each bank's actual level of capitalization (which may even be negative, owing to the large bad loans in its portfolio and other factors). The banks are then either instructed to write off the bad loans or are given some incentive to try to collect what they can (in some cases by swapping debt for equity). An autonomous public or government-supported private entity receives the large portfolio of bad loans. The entity is given the task to restructure the finances of the enterprises whose debts it holds. How that is to be done is often vaguely defined. And case-by-case governmental interference concerning whether and how to restructure particular enterprises has been more the rule than the exception.

One problem with this approach is that it achieves restructuring mainly on the creditor side, not the debtor side, in effect "de-coupling" the two. Bank management is unlikely to change its previous behavior much vis-à-vis (old and new) debtor enterprises *unless* all of the following conditions are met: (1) a line is drawn firmly for the banks between their existing and future bad debts, and government statements that further bank bailouts will not be made are *credible;* (2) bank supervision becomes largely independent of politics and remains prudent and tough; (3) the informational-legal-regulatory framework required for efficient credit operations (such as the laws on collateral and their enforcement) is in place; and (4) bank management has the proper incentives to behave as prudently profit-maximizing commercial bankers should, which almost certainly requires that banks be privately owned or controlled. In the absence of these conditions, the moral hazard problem will continue to loom large. To date, several of these conditions have not been met in any of the five countries investigated.

The most important problem is the continued full or partial state ownership and control of most of the large banks. That, in turn, can be traced to two sets of issues. One is the reluctance of the authorities to sell controlling interests in the large banks to foreign strategic investors. The other issue is the business problems at the banks and the economic and political uncertainties in the prospective host country that may make large banks unattractive to strategic investors.

Our conclusion: until many of the large banks are privatized, competition among them is enhanced, prudential supervision is strengthened, and the legal-regulatory system becomes more "creditor-friendly," bank recapitalization, *by itself*, is not likely to be strongly conducive to the efficient restructuring of enterprises or to improved financial intermediation.

Insolvency (Bankruptcy) Procedures. This is an institution of key importance for hardening the budget constraints of enterprises, dealing with their bad debts, and privatizing state assets. As a general proposition, any hardening of the budget constraint, that forces non-paying debtors to go through insolvency proceedings, tends to promote restructuring because management and the work force usually find restructuring preferable to liquidation. But if the budget constraint becomes too severe, and persists for too long, then a large segment of enterprise managers may become discouraged, believing it to be improbable that their efforts would succeed in making their operations viable. If so, then there is a danger that the incentive for managers to work hard to restructure might be dulled.[10]

So far, Hungary has relied on insolvency procedures much more than any other TRE. While this has yielded a number of positive outcomes, the severity of its bankruptcy laws, and the institutional unreadiness for its implementation, have also caused considerable, though temporary, damage (Chapter 6). Poland has made somewhat better use of this tool (Chapter 4). So far, the Czech Republic and Russia have relied on it very sparingly (Chapters 5 and 7).

High Inflation. With the collapse of monetary and fiscal discipline in Russia, a high rate of inflation ensued, and SOEs' pre-transformation debts to the commercial banks were practically wiped out in real terms. (By the same token, since 1991, inter-enterprise debts have risen substantially and the real rate of interest enterprises pay to the banks has been generally negative)[11] Because of this virtual debt elimination, which reduced the SOEs' dependence on the old banks, the often private *new* banks are in a good position to compete with existing state-controlled banks by offering high-quality financial services. To conclude: Russia's high inflation can be said to offset some of inflation's many negative economic, social, and political consequences. But because high inflation causes so much collateral damage, it cannot be recommended as a solution to the bad debt problem.

Corporate Governance

"Corporate governance" refers to a wide range of issues that concern the power of, and the relationships between, different stakeholders in a firm—namely, its owners, managers, employees, creditors, customers, suppliers, and the authorities—who jointly determine a firm's goals and operations. An efficient corporate governance structure is a prerequisite of effective restructuring. Apart from the financial discipline issues discussed in the previous section, the most important set of incentives relevant for restructuring is related to the governance of firms.[12]

In most cases, the owners are the most important stakeholder group. Creative destruction is an inevitable part of a changing, growing, improving economy; its purpose is to quickly transfer resources into the hands of those who have a better idea of how to use them more effectively. But for this to take place, the institutions and procedures of bankruptcy, and financial intermediation generally, must function well. Governments have a key role in establishing and monitoring their functioning. In all TREs, a great deal remains to be done by the authorities to help private owners exercise their ownership functions well.

In principle, there are five main types of institutions that can perform, alone or jointly, such essential ownership functions as setting strategic objectives for the enterprises they control (fully or partly); appointing, rewarding, holding accountable, and dismissing managers; and establishing the structure and helping to secure finance for the firms. The five institutions are: the state, "real" private owners, public equity markets, investment funds, and banks. First we sketch how each institution works, in the abstract, then discuss their relevance for the TREs.

The *state* and its bureaucracy are generally not well placed to effectively perform the functions of ownership because politics and bureaucratic considerations are apt to interfere too much. However, this blanket statement must be qualified because state ownership is no impediment to efficiency if managerial incentives are set appropriately. Politics aside, the feasibility of setting appropriate incentives for managers is much greater if SOEs are islands in a sea of private firms (because only then can the market mechanism function well) than if private firms are islands in a sea of SOEs. This is why comprehensive and speedy privatization is a *sine qua non* of effective corporate governance.

"*Real*" *private owners* have the best prospects for doing the job well, provided the "environment" in which they find themselves is conducive to long-term planning and business operations generally. (The concept of "real" owners, and the likelihood that they are found through privatization, were discussed.) To be sure, many privately owned businesses fail because entrepreneurs or managers have made poor decisions or could not adapt to changes in the business environment. Although business failures may hurt the stakeholders of a particular business, "creative destruction" (to use Schumpeter's phrase) is essential if an economy is to function well. That process ensures that productive resources will, in most cases, be controlled by those who can make good use of them. Business failures allow well-functioning enterprises to prosper. From the point of view of economic efficiency and growth, permitting no business failures—as was the case under central planning—clearly hurts a nation's long-term economic interest. Even in a market economy, private firms whose ownership is diffuse are more likely to fail than those that have concentrated ownership. This is because managerial incentives tend to be poorer in the former than in the latter. In the TREs, the unusually large proportion of private ventures that fail mirror not a fundamental flaw of the capitalist system but weaknesses in the institutional and policy environments, especially in the early stages of transformation.

Public equity markets are of significant importance in a well-functioning modern economy because the institution facilitates the creation of "real" owners, by placing individuals and groups of investors in a position to acquire controlling equity in firms. Public equity markets also help to "control" the managers of listed companies because the (absolute or relative) rise or fall of the value of the shares is a vote of confidence (or no confidence) in the company's management. A well-functioning equity market facilitates the take-over of companies by new owners (presumably, in order to improve management). Both the threat of take-over and actual take-over are essential tools of corporate governance. Furthermore, by making equity liquid, stock markets promote saving, investing, entrepreneurship, and thus restructuring. Each of the five target countries has (re)established a functioning stock market, but they are as yet in infant stages of development.

Investment funds are of considerable importance in countries that have implemented voucher privatization. The problem with investment funds exercising effective corporate governance is that they face a fundamental conflict of interest:[13] On the one hand, they are holding companies that are expected to be involved in helping to restructure enterprises. On the other hand, they are mutual investment institutions, with responsibility to the "small investors" (who have entrusted them with what may be a large part of their savings) not to take imprudent risks with their savings. Furthermore, if the shares in such funds can be redeemed by the investors on demand, then the funds have to maintain at all time a highly liquid asset structure, which may not be conducive to financing enterprise restructuring. This potential conflict of interest can be mitigated if investments funds are owned or controlled by healthy commercial banks. To be sure, in such cases the potential conflict appears at the bank, whose commercial banking and investment banking functions must be well separated and supervised by the authorities, to protect the general public.

Investment funds are beginning to play significant roles in the Czech Republic and Russia, and are slated for a major role in Poland as well. Foreign venture funds, which have begun to be established to invest in the TREs (as "emerging markets"), are perhaps under fewer constraints than domestic investment funds to assist with restructuring. If these economies do well, the expansion potential of foreign and domestic venture capital funds is vast, and they could play an active role in corporate governance.

Macroeconomic Policies and Institution Building

The fourth set of variables influencing restructuring procedures and outcomes is macroeconomic policies and institutions. The main policy lessons we draw with regard to macro policies and institution building that would facilitate the restructuring of large firms are the following:

- Price liberalization and economic decontrol should be prompt, and the building of market institutions as rapid as possible. The more efficient the markets, the more rapid and efficient enterprise restructuring is likely to be. In the absence of reasonably free markets, it is impossible to determine which firms should be restructured, and how.

- Governments do have vital direct as well as indirect roles in restructuring. The most important direct role of the authorities is to establish clear strategies and procedures for privatization and to eliminate such obstacles to privatization as lack of clear titles to assets (in this respect, corporatization is helpful). The authorities should also work closely with the private sector to help relieve potentially viable enterprises of their non-performing debts to banks and other government agencies. The indirect but no less important role of the government includes macro-stabilization, banking reform, and establishing a stable and enforceable tax and legal-regulatory framework.

- For large, important firms, government has little choice but to remain involved, probably for several years. This is justified especially in the case of firms that have faced the collapse of the major markets for their products. Continued involvement is often politically necessary, in part because for some of them there will be no buyers or "takers," or because keeping them in temporary or permanent state ownership will be considered politically or economically prudent—as is also often the case in market economies. Although central governments might play a useful role in restructuring such firms to prepare them for eventual privatization, it is desirable for the restructuring process to be implemented in as decentralized a way as possible, without political interference beyond preparing, and monitoring the implementation of, broad restructuring guidelines.

- Our single main conclusion with regard to the economic policies of governments is the overriding importance of *policy credibility*. None of the key actors whose cooperation is vital for successful restructuring—the owners and managers of enterprises, the work force, the creditors, and prospective investors—are likely to respond to government policies as the authorities expect them to do if the actors do not believe that the government has sound economic and social policies and is willing to persevere in their implementation.

Transformation and Economic Growth Prospects

In the following paragraphs we project some plausible scenarios for political and economic developments in each of our subject countries by the early years of the twenty-first century. This is a medium-term projection since at the time of writing (mid-1995), the turn of the century is less than five years away. The projections focus on those aspects of their economies and societies that are especially important for establishing a base for effective corporate governance and restructuring.

The CE-3 Countries

An optimistic but plausible scenario for the Czech Republic, Hungary, and Poland to the year 2000 is shaped by the powerful drive of all three countries to be accepted into the European Union (EU) and, at least indirectly, into NATO. This drive severely constrains economic policy because it will be necessary for new members to meet certain economic criteria (e.g., the size of the budget deficit relative to GDP). Consequently, changes in government, even from one side to the other of the mainstream political spectrum, are unlikely to basically change the direction of policy. The essential continuity of economic, social, and foreign policies in Poland and Hungary under governments still dominated by former Communists supports this thesis. For example, financial and political pressure by the international community, in addition to domestic presures, had forced Hungary's socialist government in March 1995 to institute a drastic and domestically unpopular economic stabilization program.

We assume that around the year 2000, the CE-3 countries will all be on the verge of becoming members of the EU. To be sure, the EU will likely have become a multi-tier integration unit, in which some member countries will be given a longer period to achieve the strict economic conditions laid down by the Maastricht Treaty. Some of these conditions may be eased for some or all members. Thus, with the kind of economic policies necessary to strengthen this pending EU membership, it is reasonable to expect that:

- Inflation will probably be in the single digits;
- The share of the private sector in GDP will have increased from the current 50 to 60 percent to 80 to 90 percent, as a result of both private sector growth and the steady shrinking of the state sector;
- The institutional, legal, and regulatory frameworks of a well-functioning market economy will have developed considerably further;
- Financial constraints will have forced some real reforms in the government budget, especially in the large social expenditures component, such as pensions and health care;
- Labor costs will remain far below West European levels, with corresponding implications for comparative living standards, as well as production sharing (specialization);[14]
- Foreign direct and portfolio investment, mainly from Western Europe, will increase, driven both by better growth prospects than in the home countries and by the competitive pressures with North America and Japan (whose integration with low-cost Latin America and South-east Asia, respectively, will continue), as well as directly with the newly industrialized countries.

Under these circumstances, domestic investment can be expected to increase considerably as well, as a result of which a reasonable projection for economic growth would be on the order of 3 to 6 percent a year during the intervening five years. Accompanying this healthy growth will be a steady upgrading of production and exports, as all three countries expand their competitive niches in heavy industry, high-tech industries, food processing, and certain services. Indeed, this upgrading process must be viewed as part of continued "normalization," following the necessary but transitional concentration on labor-intensive production during the first few years of the transformation.

With regard to large industry, their size, as well as the share of state ownership, will shrink considerably, as a result partly of privatization but mostly of continued asset erosion. Private ownership will become more concentrated, with a much larger role for foreign investors and domestic capitalists and a smaller one for financial intermediaries, like domestic investment funds.

In the Czech Republic, investment funds may sell a considerable part of their shares to foreign and domestic investors, while concentrating the remainder on a smaller number of firms. The government's share will probably fall to about 10 percent and the foreign share will increase greatly, perhaps approaching the levels (about one-third of the total) found in most of the smaller West European countries, such as Austria, Belgium, and The Netherlands.

In all three countries, corporate governance will develop toward a mixed model, incorporating certain features from the German, the Anglo-American, and the Japanese models (which, however, themselves are changing). Each TRE has its own institutional legacies and preferences, so that no sweeping generalization can be made, even for the CE-3 countries.

The German model means a strong role for the banks. Whether the banks will be able to effectively exercise ownership functions over firms and also serve as reliable financial intermediaries—and thus help restructuring—will depend first and foremost on progress in privatizing the large banks, imposing hard budget constraints on them (also), increased competition in the financial sector, and an adequate legal framework, including banking supervision. At the same time, there will be a larger role than in Germany for foreign investors, as well as for various kinds of investment funds that will have mixed domestic and foreign ownerships (the American model). Banks, investment companies and firms that have business links will form cross-company networks for ownership as well as control, thus introducing elements of the Japanese model. There will be significant institutional variations in this "mix" in the three countries. Each is likely to borrow elements from several of the main market-economy models, reflecting the trend among the developed market economies toward a degree of convergence of corporate governance practices. Continued convergence is likely as each country realizes the shortcomings of its own traditional model and as global economic integration and competition hasten the transfer of the best features, and the elimination of the least desirable ones, of each of the traditional models.

Experience and trends in the West suggest that in large firms, the role of insiders in corporate governance will decline in the CE-3 also, as more and more of the new owners will learn that the effective exercise of ownership functions requires the professionalization of management. The market for managers will expand. Management/labor control will continue mainly in some small-to-medium-sized firms. Even in Poland, workers will have little direct role in management, except in the small private and the (generally large) state-owned firms. The new owners will direct and finance market restructuring of many firms.

Russia

Unlike the CE-3 countries, Russia is not pursuing a clear national objective, such as joining the EU, that drives and constrains its economic policies. And Russia is big enough to pursue inward-looking, protectionist, even isolationist policies without necessarily courting economic disaster. Consequently, there are several plausible political/economic scenarios for Russia, including a takeover by radical nationalists and continuing political instability, with an inability to sustain coherent, credible economic policies. For the purposes of this study, however, the only interesting scenario is one under which industrial restructuring can occur.

An optimistic scenario for Russia has a very good chance to be realized, provided three conditions are met. First, the Russian state is unable to revert to anything like central planning because of the dissolution of much of the control system, wide regional and local differences in their relationships with the central government, and a gradually growing vested interest in a market system. Second, any plausible Russian government will be severely constrained financially, which means that it could afford only selective subsidies to producers and consumers. Third, financing subsidies and other excessive government expenditures through the printing of money will be gradually halted because reducing inflation (along with crime) is likely to be the only platform on which politicians can be elected or re-elected; or the main justification for a possible military coup, followed by a period of authoritarian or totalitarian rule. This speculation, by the way, raises the troublesome issue: Is democracy absolutely essential for successfully transforming a country to a market-driven system? An argument can be made, we believe, that in countries with certain traditions, democracy is not absolutely essential *until* a relatively high level of economic development is reached. Japan, South Korea, and Taiwan are cases in point.

On the assumption that the three conditions noted in the preceding paragraph are met, it is reasonable to project the following economic trends by the early years of the next century and decade: inflation declining to annual rates of below 40 percent; industrial subsidies, including subsidized credit, increasingly limited to selectively targeted industries, such as parts of the military-industrial complex, coal mining, and other industries of "national interest"; and a further build-up of market infrastructure, such as commercial law and financial regulation. Economic policy is less stable, and markets remain more regulated and protected, than in the CE-3 countries. But, on the whole, the efficiency of both product and factor markets slowly improves. Although the opportunities for graft and corruption remain large, there will be a steady shift in rent-seeking business activity from illegal to legal channels, and some shifting from short-term to long-term perspectives in investment. The measured economy bottoms out during 1995-1996 and shows fairly rapid recovery in 1997-1999 (say, at about 5 to 7 percent annually).

With regard to large industrial firms, there will be a sorting out and concentration of ownership shares in favor mainly of individual domestic capitalists and financial institutions, as in the CE-3 countries. Workers, and at least the smaller investment funds, sell their shares to "real owners," most of whom have made money through legal or illegal rent seeking during the early transition years and are now trying to attain a long-term role as captains of industry, with a respectable status for themselves and for their descendants. The share of foreign ownership is much smaller than in the CE-3 countries (e.g., 10 to 15 percent), and is concentrated in a few industries, most prominently in the natural resource sectors. Banks acquire substantial interests in many firms and some of the larger investment companies become dominant owners, in part thanks to a broadening of the legal limits of ownership. The state retains a controlling stake, or a strong minority share, in many firms and industries (e.g., about a 30 percent share of all large industry). The Russian model of corporate governance will be built even more on closely-knit networks of firms than those in the CE-3 countries because of the smaller foreign role and the continued importance of long-established inter-firm contacts. Such networks will include banks, investment companies, large firms and their suppliers. Restructuring proceeds steadily, as access to capital improves, and out of sheer necessity for the great majority of firms that no longer have access to subsidized credit.

China

Although we did not investigate China in much depth, it is such an important poor and developing country, as well as a TRE, that we want to share a few thoughts about its likely economic future. Its economic performance between 1978 and 1995 has been most impressive. It has been able to make rapid economic progress because it advanced from a low initial level of productivity, has a highly labor-intensive economy, a very high rate of savings, and it did not destroy prematurely the state sector but allowed the private sector to "grow around it."

Although after Deng, the Communist party will remain the single political party and nominal Communists will be in charge of the central and local governments, Communism as an ideology—and the Party as an organization—will cease to be the kind of monolithic unifying force that it was under Mao and Deng. Increasingly, the military will become the main force that will keep the country unified.

The best guarantee that a post-Deng government will continue the market-oriented reform policy is also the main threat to the establishment of more efficient markets. China's political and military elites have gained hugely from market opportunities and are highly unlikely to kill the goose from which those gains come. On the other hand, many of the gains are feasible because of the continued controls imposed, formally or informally, by central and local governments over foreign trade, prices, land use, and many other business decisions, as was the case also in Japan after the 1880s and South Korea after the 1960s. Although markets are likely to expand and become more efficient as infrastructure and institutions develop, they will continue to be more segmented than in the former Communist countries of Europe, and more subject to arbitrary government authority.

According to a 1995 World Bank report, the state sector still accounts for 43 percent of China's *industrial* output. Another 38 percent is contributed by town and village enterprises (TVEs) whose ownership is not private, but incentives and thus business behavior are very close to those in the private sector. TVEs represent a source of competition for the SOEs as well as for the private sector, the latter accounting for about one-fifth of China's industrial output.[15] The need to continue to subsidize SOEs has become a major obstacle to reform of the financial system as well as to import liberalization, and thus to China's integration into the World Trade Organization. Because China's domestic politics is so unpredictable, it is difficult even to guess what is likely to happen in the future—to its economy generally and to the state sector specifically.

China might choose to deal with its SOEs just by letting the TVE and private sectors continue to grow faster. But then the chances are that the SOEs themselves would still grow larger. An alternative would be to follow the path of the European TREs by imposing a hard budget constraint and closing bankrupt SOEs. It is difficult to say whether any Chinese government would be prepared to take such measures.

The most likely alternative is a compromise.[16] The elements would include a progressive reduction of subsidies; a reallocation of the welfare burden from enterprises to the state; and institutional reform to provide greater managerial autonomy and more diversification of ownership. Under this—in our view, most probable—scenario, the SOE sector would shrink absolutely, even if slowly. In time, even comprehensive privatization may not be out of the question. Privatization's seeds had already been sown with the establishment of the Beijing and Shanghai stock exchanges.

Notes

1. As cited in the *Wall Street Journal* article (September 30, 1994), "Free-Market Group Is Divided on How to Bring Capitalism to Ex-Soviet Bloc."

2. Ronald Coase, another Nobel-prize economist, cited in the above *Wall Street Journal* article.

3. Lee Kuan Yew, the former Prime Minister of Singapore, is one strong advocate of this model, at least for China. See his interview in the *Economist*, June 29, 1991.

4. *Wall Street Journal*, op cit.

5. For essential similarities and differences among some of the main successful capitalist models, see Paul Marer, "Models of Successful Market Economies," in Paul Marer and Salvatore Zecchini (eds.), *The Transition to a Market Economy: Vol I– The Broad Issues* (Paris: OECD, 1991).

6. As cited in *Transition* (Newsletter of the Transition Economics Division of the World Bank), Vol. 6, No. 4 (April 1995), p. 3. There is less agreement on how important are other institutional and policy aspects, such as reform of the legal system. To be sure, everyone acknowledges that many supportive reform steps are needed if transformation is to be successful.

7. Two of the three distinctions are also made in Irena Grosfeld and Gerard Roland, "Defensive and Strategic Restructuring in Central European Enterprises." Discussion Paper No. 1135 of the Center for Economic Policy Research, London, March 1995.

8. For example, *Mass Privatization: An Initial Assessment* (Paris: OECD, 1995); John S. Earle, et al., *Small Privatization: The Transformation of Retail Trade and Consumer Services in the Czech Republic, Hungary and Poland* (Budapest: Central European University Press, 1994); *Privatization: The Lessons of Experience* (Washington D.C.: The World Bank, no date, circa 1992); Stilpon Nestor and Scott Thomas, "Systemic Privatization and Restructuring in East Central Europe," in *East Central European Economies in Transition* (Washington D.C., U.S. GPO, 1994); Compendium of Invited Papers by the Joint Economic Committee, U.S. Congress.

9. In preparing this section, we benefited greatly from the insights found in Nestor and Thomas, "Systemic Privatization ...", cited in the preceding note.

10. Economic Commission for Europe, *Economic Survey of Europe in 1993-1994* (New York: UN, 1994), p. 160.

11. Discussed in greater detail in Chapter 7. See also Gerhard Pohl, "Banking and Enterprise Reforms in Transition Economies." Speech delivered at the European Banking and Finance Forum, Prague, March 21, 1995. (Reprint of the Banking and Enterprise Reforms in Transition Economies unit of the World Bank.)

12. Nestor and Thomas, "Systemic Privatization ... " cited in note 8.

13. Ibid, p. 19.

14. In certain countries, such as the Czech Republic, real labor costs may increase as a result of real currency appreciation, since the Czech crown was notably under-valued during 1991-1994.

15. World Bank, *Meeting the Challenge of Chinese Enterprise Reform* (Washington D.C., 1995).

16. *Financial Times*, May 18, 1995, based on the World Bank report cited in the preceding note.

Index

Adjustment
  by producers to reforms, 3, 5, 24-
    27, 94-99, 196-201, 229-231, 237-
    239, 251-257
  See also State-owned enterprises
Agriculture, 12, 79, 85, 87(fig.), 114,
    154, 155, 163-165, 168, 174, 201,
    202(fig.), 259, 268

Bankruptcy, 5, 19, 31, 44-48, 77, 104,
    109, 120-121, 143, 180-181, 186-
    190, 192-193, 194, 197, 199-201,
    250-252, 265-267, 269-270, 294,
    300, 301
  See also Liquidation.
Banks
  bad debt, 44-46. 116, 142, 184-189,
    251, 298-300
  functions and operations of, 38-40,
    101-102, 116, 141, 147, 222-223,
    232, 242-245
  restructuring of, 31, 38-40, 131, 150,
    160, 190, 298, 300, 306
  See also State-owned enterprises,
    restructuring of
Barter, 130, 241, 244, 245, 249, 268
Black market, 55, 219
Blue Ribbon Commission (BRC), 181
Budget deficit, 16, 18, 19, 23, 24, 40, 42,
    80, 83, 92, 128, 163, 166, 189, 206,
    213, 219, 220, 250, 251, 304

C-D gap, 237, 253, 275
Capital-Asset Ratio (CAR), 189
Central Bank of Russia (CBR), 220,
    222-223, 232, 242-245, 250-251
CIS, 239, 245
CMEA, 11, 14, 22, 23, 68-69, 84, 85, 90,
    94, 127, 148, 154, 155, 156, 161,
    162, 185, 197, 202, 203, 228, 240,
    298

CMR, 73
Commercial real estate, 34, 242, 262,
    264, 265, 293
Competition policies. *See* De-concen-
    tration
Corporate governance, 193-196, 199-
    201, 207, 301-303, 304-308
Corporatization, 58, 67, 70-72, 76, 159,
    196, 224-225, 303
Corruption, 36, 58, 65, 174, 176, 224,
    289, 297, 307
  See also Second economy, Under-
    ground economy
CPI, 168, 199

De-concentration, 36, 87, 131, 133-135,
    139, 156, 303
Debt
  bad (non-performing), 39, 44, 114-
    116, 142-143, 184-189, 298-299, 303
  inter-enterprise, 46, 47, 142, 147,
    190, 198-199, 220, 243, 247
  restructuring of, 18, 48, 115-117,
    190, 298-300
  See also Banks, State-owned enter-
    prises
Decontrol, 32, 303
Defense-related enterprises, 224, 238,
    244

EC, 17, 161, 198
Economic policies, 4, 18-21, 31-78, 85,
    128-131, 154-167, 288-293, 303
  See also Decontrol, Fiscal policy,
    Monetary policy, Privatization
Economic structure, 85, 127-128, 153-
    155
  See also Industry
Enterprise boards, 157, 196

About the Book and Authors

In considering the roadblocks facing transition economies, this text focuses on a vital but generally neglected sector—large state-owned industrial enterprises. Even though many of the formerly socialist countries have made significant strides in privatization, they have all found it immensely difficult, both politically and practically, to dismantle large enterprises, given the massive unemployment and economic dislocation that would result. Yet these enterprises constitute a heavy burden on fledgling economies by drawing scarce funds away from profitable investments, notably in the private sector.

Comparing four countries that are rarely juxtaposed—Russia, Poland, Hungary, and the Czech Republic (with frequent references made also to China)—the authors draw out the important similarities and differences among them and discuss implications for the future. The first systematic, genuinely comparative analysis of one of the biggest hurdles to the development of true market economies, this study, with its wealth of data and informed interpretation, will be essential reading for students, scholars, and policy makers alike.

Maurice Ernst is an adjunct professor emeritus in international business at Indiana University at Indianapolis. **Michael Alexeev** is an associate professor of economics at Indiana University at Bloomington, where **Paul Marer** is a professor of international business.